The Making of Law

The Making of Law
An Ethnography of the Conseil d'Etat

BRUNO LATOUR

Translated by Marina Brilman and Alain Pottage

Revised by the author

polity

First published in French as *La fabrique du droit* by Bruno Latour © La
Découverte, Paris, 2002

This translation copyright © Polity Press, 2010
Reprinted 2010

Polity Press
65 Bridge Street
Cambridge CB2 1UR, UK

Polity Press
350 Main Street
Malden, MA 02148, USA

ISBN-13: 978-0-7456-3984-0 (hardback)
ISBN-13: 978-0-7456-3985-7(paperback)

A catalogue record for this book is available from the British Library.

Typeset in 10.5 on 12 pt Sabon
by Toppan Best-set Premedia Limited
Printed and bound in Great Britain by MPG Books Limted, Bodmin,
Cornwall

The publisher has used its best endeavours to ensure that the URLs for
external websites referred to in this book are correct and active at the time of
going to press. However, the publisher has no responsibility for the websites
and can make no guarantee that a site will remain live or that the content is
or will remain appropriate.

Every effort has been made to trace all copyright holders, but if any have been
inadvertently overlooked the publisher will be pleased to include any
necessary credits in any subsequent reprint or edition.

For further information on Polity, visit our website: www.politybooks.com

All internal images author's own.

Contents

Preface to the English edition

It's not my fault if this book is a little hard to read: it's about *law*; it's about *French* law; it's about French *administrative* law! English-speaking readers will forgive an ethnographer for telling them about the rituals of New Guinea or the folklore of the Scottish Highlands; they will absorb without difficulty the many concepts often retained in native languages, but certainly not if they are asked to make the same effort with regard to the legal niceties of the French State. Exoticism has its limits. You might be willing to cross the Channel to hear charming stories about Provence or Burgundy wine, but not to sit, for 300 pages, inside the Palais-Royal in Paris to hear exceedingly boring people discuss exceedingly subtle points of law. But the same readers will accept, with a certain degree of open-mindedness, an ethnography of a scientific laboratory or of a technical project that might be just as difficult. Ah, yes, but science and technology are supposed to be universal and the arguments might ring a bell in Cambridge as well as in Toulouse or Houston. But law? Law is so provincial, so stubbornly local. How could anyone pretend to interest them in French administrative law?

The reasons I insisted on writing this study, and then on having it translated, is, first, that this branch of legal reasoning is not a Code-based law but a precedent-based legal corpus entirely fabricated, over two centuries, by the judges themselves (who are not judges, by the way, but members of the executive, a queer feature about which we will learn more in due course). So, my meek retort is that, of all the branches of Continental law, it is the one that most resembles Common Law in the way it is elaborated and arrayed in reasoning.

Okay, but not a good enough reason.

The second reason is that administrative law, and especially what happens in the Council of State which plays the role of Supreme Court for this branch of law (yes, this is complicated: in France, administrative law is a completely autonomous and separate system from the judiciary, which has its own Supreme Court, called the Cassation), is almost totally unknown by the French people themselves. In other words, in the book that follows, everything is just as exotic to most French-speaking readers as it is to English-speaking readers. If it is strange to the latter, it is just as strange to the eyes of the former.

This is why, instead of bombarding the reader with technical terms in the local tongue – which can be done without any qualms when reconstructing the cosmology of the Iroquois or the assembly of gods in a Brazilian *candomblé* – I have chosen, for each function, words that have no common meaning in English. But they have no meaning in French either, except for the lawyers who work directly in contact with the Council of State. '*Commissaires du gouvernement*' in italics and quotation marks would have meant nothing to the English reader, nor does 'commissioner of the law' (the term I have chosen); but in French, 'commissaires du gouvernement' means so little that every single time a decision of the Council of State is mentioned in the press, you need a long paraphrase to explain what it means. Especially because, in the same palace, there are other people, also named 'commissaires du gouvernement', who are really sent and commissioned by the government, whose function is utterly different from that of commissioners of the law (who are sent and commissioned by Law only, as it is interpreted by their own conscience – and that of their colleagues). Too complicated? Who has said that the central institutions on which contemporary civilization are based should be simple and fully opened to the gaze of the ordinary citizen? Anthropology of modern cultures is just as hard in Paris as it is in Beijing or Tierra del Fuego.

But here is the real reason why I think it is worth taking the trouble to read such an ethnography about French administrative law: forget that it's in France, forget that it is only about administrative law (in contrast to the judiciary that deals with private and criminal law), and just consider the chance I had: for about four years – not continuously – I had privileged access (it took a long time to sneak in) to the private conversations of about six or seven counsellors who had to come to a conclusion about the cases that were coming to them. I was sitting not only in the tribunal room where the public audiences were given (not much happened there anyway since the lawyers for the plaintiffs say nothing and only the commissioner of the law stands up and reads his 'conclusions' and then sits down and that's all . . . no drama whatsoever), but also behind the closed door where the cases were discussed, or, as they say, 'reviewed'. A unique site for a unique access to the collective interlocution where I could observe in great detail (okay, too many details, I agree, but isn't that what ethnography is about?) the close knitting of legal reasoning.

At which point you might object that I observed not 'legal reasoning' but the ways French administrative law judges (and they are not even judges but political appointees, former ministers, heads of public companies, journalists, etc.) think legally. That's where I somewhat disagree. Anthropology of law has this interesting feature in that – contrary to, let's say, anthropology of science, my original field – there was never any question that all cultures *have* law. It might differ in content; the conclusion might horrify the ethnographer – or the plaintiff; the circuitous route of reasoning might look incredibly far-fetched; there might be blood all along; but it is always recognizable as tracing the path of something – quite elusive I agree – that we all call 'legal'. So, yes, a case study will always be just a case study, and it should not be generalized too much, but the whole book that you, hopefully, are going to accept to read is based on the assumption that the English-speaker does not need to learn about 'French administrative law' (unless they wish to) but about the *passage* or the *transit* of law, a question that, naturally, can be highlighted only thanks to a detailed case study but that may become, in the end, rather independent from it.

The true reason why I invested so much energy in this field work (I found, on the whole, law much more technical and difficult to follow than science or technology) is that it was precisely to compare the passage of law with the other types of enunciation regimes I had studied up till then (or have studied since). I belong to a small group of social theorists who believe that we have been pretty wrong in providing a 'social' explanation of anything – science, religion, politics, technology, economics, law and so on. Far from being what should provide the *source* of explanation of those phenomena, what we loosely call 'the social' is rather the *result* of what has been produced by types of connection ('associations' in my terminology) that are established by scientific, religious, political, technological, economical or legal connectors. If this theory (now called 'Actor Network Theory' or 'ANT') is even vaguely right, there is a paramount interest in defining, as precisely as possible, what it means to connect some association, let's say, religiously, or scientifically, or politically, etc. The use of the adverbial form is crucial to the argument, since there may be a great gap between speaking *about* politics or religion and speaking politica*lly* or religious*ly*. It's much easier to understand, and it will become even clearer in what follows, that there is similarly an immense difference, very easy to grasp, between speaking *about* law and speaking *legally*.

In the last thirty years, I have done much field work to define the scientific way of establishing connections: what I called 'reference'. The book you are about to read is the *Laboratory Life*, not for the construction of facts, but for the construction of legal arguments ('moyens de droit'). In the same way that I had been able to extract, from one admittedly limited set of case studies, a plausible definition of what it was to speak scientifically of some state of affairs, I have tried here, through another carefully devised set of ethnographic devices, to extract, to educe, to highlight a plausible definition of what it is to speak legally of a tort. My overall point, my general contention, is that we can't possibly provide a positive anthropology of the Moderns (who, I remind you, have never been modern, but that is only a negative definition: what have they been, then?) as long as we don't have a clear comparative study of the various ways in which the central institutions of our cultures produce truth. And clearly there are several types of felicity conditions for the various kinds of truth production (scientific, legal, religious, etc.) that define the former Moderns. There exists an inner pluralism in the way truth production is defined among the Moderns – which does not mean that they are indifferent to truth, quite the opposite. It is actually what makes law so interesting.

I have to confess that, until I had carried out this field work, I was not too convinced that my overall project had any chance of succeeding. Having tried to compare scientific felicity conditions to, for instance, those of religion or politics, I knew it was feasible, but there was always the nagging feeling that it was a lost cause, so powerfully had the ideology of science squashed those other contrasts beyond recognition. Whatever I tried to do, religious and political enunciations seemed always to lament and repent for *not* being scientific enough. The immense advantage of law – talk to a lawyer or a legist for five minutes and you will understand what I mean – is that they never have any doubt (a) that their way of arguing is entirely specific; (b) that there is a clear distinction, inside this way of arguing, between what is true and what is false (the felicity and infelicity conditions are clearly recognized even though they might be agonizingly difficult to put on paper); and (c) that this difference between true and false is totally different from what might be taken to be scientifically true or false. In other words, only law has maintained, throughout the modernist parenthesis, a sturdy confidence in the validity of its own felicity conditions quite independently of what has happened to science (even though there have been many attempts, and just as many failures, at founding a 'science of law'). It is this unique feature that allowed me to have confidence in the project of systematically comparing the felicity and infelicity conditions of the different regimes of truth production that define the hard core of our cultures. And there cannot be much doubt that the rule of law is one of the ways in which Western societies have defined themselves. And yet it is extremely difficult for outsiders to characterize what is legal in a legal reasoning . . .

Although there is no clear description for what I am doing, the closest is that of an empirical (not an empiricist) philosopher. This book tries, through the device of ethnography, to capture a philosophical question (and in addition a social theory puzzle) that would be inaccessible philosophically (provided the adverb had a real meaning, which I doubt very much): *the essence of law.* Knowing that an essence does not lie in a definition but in a practice, a situated, material practice that ties a whole range of heterogeneous phenomena in a certain specific *way.* And it is on the search for this specific way that this book is entirely focused. Now, once again, what is marvellous in law is that, to designate this apparently abstract question, it has a very explicit term, at least in French: the word 'moyen', for which the translators and I had a lot of trouble trying to find an equivalent. It is uttered ten times a minute by lawyers and judges, and yet this key term has no definition in law dictionaries. That's what this book tries to redress: to provide a description, understandable from the outside, for the word '*moyen*' – legal argument, legal ground, legal reason, this little vehicle on which is transported the rule of law, this value that we cherish so much – and with good reason.

To assuage the difficulties of the chase, the book is constructed in such a way that the reader learns about the site, the precedent, the cases, the functions, morsel by morsel, just when it is needed. So don't expect a presentation of the French legal system, a description of the overall institution, a summary of the cases. This is a completely zoom-free, context-free ethnographic description, which means it is, or it should be, a good ANT's view of law. Context is doled out when necessary to give you just enough to move to the next step.

A word to finish, on anonymity: the counsellors I had the patience to study were at the outset very wary about my publishing a book about the practice they had let me observe for so long. First, because the discussions about the cases should not be available to the plaintiffs, and, second, because they did not want their decision to appear as the result of a complex and humble situation of interlocution. The first problem was easily solved by a complex montage of cases where the names of the judges and the number of the cases were reshuffled enough to erase all the traces without losing the argument (impossible naturally to record on tapes – I had to scribble fast and inevitably I lost a lot). To the second objection, I could not submit: it would have meant abandoning the project entirely. For the few who read my manuscript in detail before publication, Law, at least in France, seemed to have no possible individual or personalized site: it had to speak from nowhere as the Voice of the Law. 'Since Napoleon's foundation of the Council', one of the counsellors wrote to me, 'never has the Voice of Law been downgraded to the level of a mere interlocution among individual judges'.

For a moment I thought that I was going to enter into the same dispute with judges I had been forced to enter with some scientists in the past: a realistic description of their practice was seen by them as mere debunking. Fortunately, judges seemed to be more open-minded than scientists to the ethnographic gaze (or, in the case of the *Council of State*, more thoroughly indifferent to what the social sciences can say of the type of truth they generate). To my great surprise, the book was a small success in French, to the point of getting me a few reviews, and I am told it is a required reading for every apprentice in administrative law. If I was accused of something, it was this time by the social critics of law who found my portrait of the Council too favourable – not to say complacent. And it's quite true, not only is this book context-free, it is also critique-free. To stand any chance of grasping the elusive passage of law required, it seemed to me, this breach in the usual methods of inquiry. Each study demands a different writing strategy in order to reach that most elusive of all the goals I have pursued in my career, following Harold Garfinkel's dictate: the 'unique adequacy' of the text to the matter at hand.

I would have lost courage in bringing this book from French to English if Alain Pottage had not constantly pushed for it, translating a chapter, revising others and convincing the publisher that a book on French administrative law was of no less interest than any other more exotic and sexy topic . . . I have since revised the translation quite extensively. I was encouraged in translating the result of this field work by the warm welcome of several jurists, especially Noah Feldmann in the United States, and Frédéric Audren in France. In Belgium, Serge Gutwirth and Laurent de Sutter were kind enough to comment at length on the French version of the book and to make this enterprise part of their own research project on 'Les loyautés du savoir'.

I

In the shadow of Bonaparte

In which we introduce the readers into the bicentennial celebrations, in order to get them warmed up – In which larcenous pigeons allow us to meet the commissioner of the law, who is a main character in this story – In which we discover the importance of a missing signature to a decree, and in which we familiarize ourselves with the 'review meetings' of a 'sub-section', which are the main empirical sources of this work – In which an editorial in the newspaper *Le Monde* allows us to introduce the distinction between civil or criminal law and administrative law – In which the readers begin to experience the particular force of the law, thanks to two contrasting cases discussed in the 'Counsel Section' – In which we show the readers the workshops of the 'General Assembly' where legal texts are written – All of which does not leave the author completely unperturbed as he ascends the main staircase of the Council

Two rather unfortunately chosen symbols

To mark its second centenary, which was celebrated on 13 December 1999 in the main amphitheatre of the Sorbonne against the backdrop of Puvis de Chavanne's wonderfully kitsch frescos, the Conseil d'Etat (from now on, 'Council of State') chose to represent itself by means of a very peculiar symbol. An impressive Doric column emerged from

nowhere to support a piece of architrave upon which rested the
detached fragment of a majestic cornice, which jutted forward like
the prow of a ship about to part the seas.

This stylized blue sketch appeared very peculiar to the ethnographer: by depicting this beautiful and moving Greek ruin from below,
it suggested that the Council was somehow suspended in mid-air with
no support or foundation, as though the column drew from within
itself the power to support a monument which might have been a
temple, but whose purpose could not be discerned without a view
either of the whole edifice or of the landscape which it would have
surveyed. Sitting in the public gallery, on the fringe of this illustrious
gathering, the ignorant ethnographer could not help but ask himself
why such an image had been chosen to celebrate the anniversary of
the institution. What was the point of designating the foundations of
the State by means of this kind of unidentified flying object? What
was signified by this pillar with no roots and no support, which held
up a ruin? Why return to the ancient Dorians to locate the emblem
of an institution that wished to project itself forwards into the twenty-
first century?

Sous le haut patronage de
Monsieur Jacques Chirac
Président de la République

Figure 1.1

The ethnographer's astonishment did not diminish when he found out from his neighbour that this was not a ruin but a rendering by the painter Ernest Pignon-Ernest of a corner of the monument which enclosed the courtyard of the Palais-Royal, which is the seat of the 'Haute Assemblée', as it is often called somewhat pompously in the press. And, if anything, his surprise increased when he found that none of the counsellors, auditors[1] or civil servants with whom he raised the question during the interval shared his surprise: 'But really, why does that surprise you?' Apparently, this fragment of power suspended in mid-air and seen from below needed no particular explanation. Had the ethnographer conducted his research over the past four years so badly that he was still unable to predict what should surprise the members of the institution he had been studying?

The uncomfortable feeling that he had so completely misunderstood his field intensified when he received New Year's greetings from some of those who had put up with him so patiently and for so long. In order to celebrate both the beginning of the year 2000 and the beginning of its third centenary, the representatives of the Council had had the even more peculiar idea of illustrating their greetings card with a painting which depicted Bonaparte standing on a rostrum in the shiny uniform of the Premier Consul. Standing ahead of Cambacérès and Lebrun, who remain discreetly in the background, the author of the coup d'état receives the enthusiastic tributes of the newly appointed counsellors, who are themselves opulently dressed in uniforms designed by the revolutionary painter David, while behind, barely visible against the sunlight, arms raised in a collective solemn gesture, the whole of the Council pledges its loyalty to the new Constitution in a single voice.

Our observer asked himself whether this was not a rather clumsy choice of painting. At the very moment when Europe and European law were acquiring increasingly greater importance, the somewhat embarrassing founder of the Council of State is moved centre-stage. As far as we know, Napoleon is not seen overseas as the model of a democrat, but rather as a bloodthirsty tyrant! And whereas the very

---

[1] Because administrative law speaks its own language, the reader will find in the glossary a reference in French and in English to the pages where most of the technical terms are defined. The complete bibliographic references can be found at the end of the book. By convention, we will use the French term the first time we encounter it and then the English equivalent, whenever it is possible, for the remainder of the book. If some of these words seem odd, the English reader should be reminded that they are just as strange for French speakers, most of whom have never heard of the Conseil d'Etat and are totally unfamiliar with the jargon of administrative law.

Figure 1.2

notion of a specific body of administrative law as something distinct
and separate from civil and criminal jurisdiction still provokes unease,
irony or indignation in the press, among elected politicians and
among jurists, what was set before the eyes of the public here was a
gesture of submission to the personal power of a man who claimed
to incarnate a State which brooked no opposition. Even more remarkable is the fact that the very Council whose bicentennial was being
celebrated had, throughout France's troubled history, unwaveringly
pledged its complete and absolute fidelity to a succession of regimes
which each in their turn sought to suppress it, but which it had always
outlived – as had France itself – but only at the price of quite a
few palinodes.[2] Is it really so clever to put the finger on a gesture

[2] See the long chapter in Collectif, *Deuxième centenaire du Conseil d'Etat* (2001),
entitled 'Le Conseil d'Etat et les changements de régime politique', pp. 77–144,
for a useful synthesis. As Pierre Legendre says: 'The Council of State is not
admirable, it just is. Its development, the demultiplication of its function and especially
the paradox of its permanence are the effect of a mechanism which has nothing heroic
nor even thought out about it.' Legendre, 'Prestance du Conseil d'Etat' (1975), p. 633

of fidelity that could be pledged at one moment and will be abjured the next?

It need hardly be said that the ethnographer was again alone in his surprise. Those members of the Council who were kind enough to send him this card were not being in the least bit malicious, and that is exactly what he should have understood.

In order to create a portrait of the Council of State, we will have to redraw Pignon-Ernest's pencil sketch a little. Although it is true that the Council is a pillar of the State, it is still improbable, for reasons that have to do with simple mechanics and the resistance of materials, that it could anchor itself in the void in this way! So, unlike the painter, we will seek to multiply the ties which, despite their fragility and insignificance, form entanglements and multiply weak links in such a way as to explain the solidity of the edifice. As for this monument itself, rather than treating it as a fragment of neoclassical temple mysteriously hovering above an astounded citizenry, our objective is to restore to it its materiality, its colours, its textures and its opulence, but also its fragility and perhaps its relevance, and – why not? – its utility. The picture will lose some of its solemn splendour and majestic isolation, but it will gain the vascularization and numerous connections that allow an institution to breathe.

In distancing ourselves from this architrave and ruined pile of Doric columns, we are also distancing ourselves from Bonaparte and from the occasionally sensational history that, from the Restoration through to de Gaulle by way of Vichy, allowed the Council to believe itself to be unchanging, as immune to the passage of time as the Platonic Idea of the Republic. We are interested neither in the version of this history that is tirelessly reworked by members of the Council, nor in its scholarly revision by (the somewhat rare) historians of the institution.[3] We are not going to follow the path of the archives, but

---

[3] There is no equal balance between the number of works dedicated to the glory of the Council of State and works about the Council. Even after the publications relating to the second centenary, voluminous but purely celebratory (Collectif, *Deuxième centenaire du Conseil d'Etat* (2001)), we still find only one sociological work more than thirty years old (Kessler, *Le Conseil d'Etat* (1968)); another book, more recent (Costa, *Le Conseil d'Etat dans la société contemporaine* (1993)) only barely touches on sociology; some stimulating articles by Monnier (Collectif, *Deuxième centenaire du Conseil d'Etat*, vol. I, pp. 643–7); then some research on the evolution of the 'corps', for example Roquemaurel, *Les membres du Conseil d'Etat et les entreprises* (1997), and Bui-Xuan, *Les femmes au Conseil d'Etat* (2000). That is all where external views on the institution are concerned. We find, on the other hand, some works of administrative science – Chevalier, *Science administrative*, vol. I (1994) and Burdeau, *Histoire du droit administratif* (1995) – excellent presentations of the legal and administrative role of the Council, from the most efficient – Stirn,

rather that of patient observation by someone who was initially
entirely ignorant of legal method and who had not even the most
minor responsibility in the State. It so happens that the person whom
we shall call the ethnographer – for reasons that will be made clear
further on – was able for a period of fifteen months spread over four
years to enjoy privileged access to the work of the Council, like a sort
of internship carried out under the supervision of eminent members
of the establishment, as a result of which he found himself in the
position that newer methods in anthropology sometimes describe as
impossible, not to say indecent, that of being 'a fly on the wall', an
observer reduced to silence and invisibility, but equipped with a notebook and a laminated card giving him access to the Council library . . .

A small matter concerning pigeons

The voice resonates across the room whose wooden furnishings have
been polished by years of use:

> Although pigeons can be enchanting for the users of public squares, they are a
> plague on the cultivators of sunflowers. This is the case of Mr Delavallade, who has
> tried unsuccessfully to obtain compensation of 100,800 francs from the commune
> of La Rochefoucauld for the damage done to his crops by the town's pigeons.
>   Today, he asks you to overrule the decision of 3 December 1991 in which the
> commune was held not liable on the basis that it had committed no serious wrong.

As in a children's story, these 'cases' always begin by evoking some
more or less picturesque place, place-names that recall a history or
geography lesson, or the more or less painful or comical incidents of
a daily life that is far removed from the plush atmosphere of the place
du Palais-Royal, which is situated between the Louvre and the famous
theatre called La Comédie Française. We are now in the 'Section du

---

Le Conseil d'Etat (1991) – to the most luxurious – Massot, *Le Conseil d'Etat. De
l'An VIII à nos jours* (1999). All other works are, more than anything, about administrative law and where they do discuss the history of one concept or another (for
example Berre, *Les revirements de jurisprudence en droit administratif* (1999)) or
one function or another (Deguergue, 'Les commissaires du gouvernement
et la doctrine' (1994)), a historian would have some difficulty in finding points of
reference in them. But of course there is no lack of moving, amused or ironic accounts
– there is even an atrocious novel about the minor failures of the Council: Lebon,
Meurtre au Conseil d'Etat (1990). One typical trait is amusing: the work concerning
the second centenary includes photographs of armchairs, platforms, wood-panelling,
but not a single image of a human being – only plenty of portraits of famous dead
white men . . .

Contentieux' (from now on, 'Litigation Section'), one of the two roles of the Council, the other being composed of what are called 'les Sections administratives' (from now on, 'Counsel Sections'),[4] though nothing in the complicated layout of corridors, hidden doorways and formal or obscure staircases, or in the arrangement of contrasting carpets, really allows one to separate the building into these two functional sides, which are entangled in a hundred different ways, and whose subtle ecology we will describe further on.

The speaker is standing on a rostrum, reading aloud from a carefully drafted document that is called his 'conclusions' because it always ends with the following formula:

And for these reasons, we conclude:
- that the decision of the appellate administrative court of Bordeaux be annulled;
- that the appeal of Mr Delavallade, and the remainder of his conclusions of appeal, be rejected.

The speaker is called 'le commissaire du gouvernement', but we should not be misled by the term: the main characteristic of this character, with whom we are going to spend quite some time, is precisely that he is not the official representative of a government; rather, he is one of the twenty members of the Council to whom are entrusted the task of advising the judicial body as to the proper grounds for decision, according to his particular view of administrative law.[5] Because everything happens as if he was commissioned by the Law itself to speak to his colleagues, we will call him from now on 'the commissioner of the law' thus retaining the origin of the word and taking out some of the ambiguous connotation of the French.

Although he is the only person standing, his role is not that of a public prosecutor because he does not bring proceedings in the name of the State, nor does he control the procedure of review in any way. And although he stands to the left of the adjudicating body, his role is not that of a defence counsel either. In this assembly, lawyers never

---

[4] To avoid a misunderstanding that the word 'administration' could entail, we have chosen the word 'Counsel' to designate 'les Sections administratives' since their main role is not at all to 'administer' anything but to advise and counsel the various ministries about all the bills and decrees they wish to pass.

[5] See, on the history of this function, Rainaud, *Le commissaire du gouvernement près le Conseil d'Etat* (1996). The term can give rise to even more confusion since, on the other side of the corridor, the 'commissaires du gouvernement' are persons who fulfill a totally different function: they are members of the Cabinet or senior civil servants charged with the task of defending their bills or decrees before the Counsel Sections of the Council of State. We will call them 'government envoys'.

speak, or they do so only in the rarest of cases, and although a bench
facing the judges is reserved for them, they sit in silence, giving only
a terse nod when their file is announced, at which time they mumble
something like 'I refer to my written conclusions on this matter'.
The function of the commissioner of the law is more like that of an
independent academic. Some weeks ago, his colleagues of the 'sous-
section' (from now on, 'sub-section')[6] to which he belongs handed file
no. 133-880 to him, on which he is presenting his conclusions today,
25 October 1995.[7]

Figure 1.3

However, nothing compels his judicial colleagues, who listen to
him more or less attentively, depending on the importance of the case
and the prestige of the commissioner, to follow his conclusions. He
himself is free to publish them, as would a researcher, because they
remain valuable even if the deciding judges end up preferring a very
different solution. Case reporters, law professors, amateurs of litigation, and litigants themselves learn to scrutinize these conclusions for
the first signs of a 'reversal of precedent', rather like weekend sailors

[6] One of the divisions of the 'Litigation Section', to which we will return and which
allows for the work on files to be distributed. There are ten 'sub-sections'.
[7] The sources of this research are of two kinds: ones that are public and which everyone can consult – these are the sources of administrative law; and the ones which
are completely confidential – these are the 'review meetings' which were observed
by the researcher.

searching for a breeze on a becalmed sea. But let us not rush to present the reader with terms that are better introduced slowly. For now, what is essential is the point that, in this preserve of administrative law, no one but the commissioner of the law ever speaks publicly.[8] The rest of the procedure is conducted entirely in writing. Let us try to understand the content of the text that he is reading in his neutral voice, which is occasionally enlivened by a touch of humour that might bring a shadow of a smile to the faces of his interlocutors:

The battle against the nuisance caused by birds unquestionably falls within the powers of the municipal police, which, according to article L 131-2 of the Code of communes, are exercised so as 'to ensure order, safety, security, and public health', and, more especially, within heading 8 which refers to 'the task of preventing or remedying the mishaps caused by the straying of harmful and wild animals'. In these terms, although pigeons are not wild animals, they are certainly harmful ones.[9]

Between the paragraph on p. 16 and this one an important operation has been performed. The pigeons which so delighted people in public squares with their displays of aerial ballet have now become 'harmful animals' 'according to article L 131-2 of the Code of communes', which makes them the responsibility of the Mayor and which 'unquestionably' authorizes Mr Delavallade to bring a complaint in the form of an appeal. The 'requérant' (from now on, 'litigant') – a name which is given to plaintiffs in administrative law – could have taken his gun to the pigeons in the sunflower fields of La Rochefoucauld and served them up as roasts; he could have hated the Mayor in his heart of hearts, or insulted him in public, but as soon as he assumed

[8] We will come back to this often, but the reader who is not a jurist must always remember that administrative law, in France at least, is an entirely separate branch of law, which must therefore never be confused with what we curiously call, by contrast, the 'droit judiciaire' or 'le judiciaire' (criminal and civil, public and private).

[9] The importance of the act of writing in the procedures that we are going to study is so great that we will try hard to always respect the layout, the typography, the tables, the space between the lines, the paragraphs – in short, all that we call 'the paratext'. This allows us to make the materiality of the text perceivable to the eyes of the reader. Since we will need to attract attention to the passages that we wish to comment on, we will use bold type. All the underlined or italic terms in citations are the same in the original. Conventionally, in the transcripts, we put between brackets all that is implied in the situation and that we can add in the certainty that we are not mistaken. We put between square brackets the connecting link that we are obliged to make in order to understand the document, but on which we might be mistaken.

the dignity of the 'litigant' by posting the piece of stamped paper in which he made his complaint to the administrative tribunal of Bordeaux, we find ourselves on this cold autumn afternoon linked by a thread which allows his pigeons, his sunflowers, his resentments and his Mayor to 'produce law'. It will take us the whole of this book to grasp the nature of this very particular operation, which we must for now be careful not to consider as a simple and homogeneous operation.[10]

The commissioner of the law continues:

> The municipality did not do nothing. It preferred to use the 'gentler' method of sterilizing the pigeons, which did not have particularly convincing results.
> Curiously, the litigant does not attack the decision on the basis that it incorrectly interpreted the law, which led it not to find fault, but only for the legal error that led it to look only for the presence of a gross negligence.

Let us listen attentively to the commissioner of the law, because things are about to become very complicated very quickly. If the case had been trivial, a filter introduced at the stage of submission of appeals in order to avoid the proliferation of appeals to the highest tribunal would have summarily dismissed this litigious claimant on the basis that no serious 'moyen' existed.[11] Later on, we will study in detail what is meant by this strange ambiguous and ubiquitous word 'moyen', that has been translated by the words 'argument', 'reason', 'ground' or '*mean*'.[12] Although both at first instance and on appeal

---

[10] We then follow roughly the rules of method as defined in the magazine *Enquête*, dedicated to the 'objectives of the law'. To capture the law 'in action', see in particular Hermitte, 'Le droit est un autre monde' (1998).

[11] It is the Commission of admission of appeals in the final instance which allows appeals to be dismissed when they are deemed to be without ground. The reader who is used to civil jurisdictions should note that it is important to remember that the Council of State can judge cases in first instance (for example for law relating to elections or appeals against decrees), but also on appeal and, more and more, on final appeal. The same panels of judges can therefore see their jurisdictions vary according to the cases brought. In 1997, the Council judged 21 per cent of cases in first instance, 11 per cent on appeal, 30 per cent on final appeal, and more than 30 per cent on referrals of tribunals and courts on issues of jurisdiction (*Rapport public* of the Council of State, 1998, Paris, La Documentation française,). Since this date, to the regret of certain members, more and more time is spent just on cases in final appeal.

[12] Since the whole book is a commentary on this word '*moyen*', it would have been awkward to leave it in French, so we chose to call it *mean* to keep the metaphor of the *middle* (in both English and French) rather than that of a foundation (as in 'legal ground') or that of discussion (as in 'legal argument'). Since the word 'mean' has no use in legal English, we have added an asterisk to remind the readers of its technical use, and when we have used the English synonyms (ground, reason, argument), we have also added an asterisk to underline that there is in French only one word for all those usages.

the claim should be rejected, we have to assume that there is neverthe-less some 'serious legal mean*' because we are sitting here listening to the commissioner of the law. Technical terms are going to prolifer-ate rapidly, and the readings will soon become opaque to both the observer and the litigant, who for this stage of the final appeal is obliged to employ the services of a lawyer qualified to appear before the Council of State.[13]

Although the allusion to the Code of communes, which authorized the elevation of pigeons to the rank of a harmful-animal-for-which-the-Mayor-is reponsible, did not pose any problem, the same is not true of the references to 'legal qualification', 'legal error' and 'gross negligence'.[14] An abyss suddenly opens up before the eyes of the researcher. Codes, with their clarity and elegant certainty, are no more: the commissioner of the law, whose voice acquires greater subtlety, enters into the infinitely more intricate fabric of the inter-pretation of administrative law, which rests only on *precedents*. Despite the difficulty of what follows, let us continue to follow the thread of his reasoning:

Where police measures are concerned, the distinction has long been based on the distinction between 'legal' acts and 'conceptual' acts, which is found in the law relating to fault (*Assembly, 13 février 1942, Ville de Dole, p 48*), and 'substantial' or 'executory' acts, which are reviewable only in terms of gross negligence ['faute lourde'] (*Section, 3 avril 1936, Syndicat d'initiative de Nevers et Benjamin, p. 453, aux conclusions Detton*).

But although this distinction is seductive, it is, as President Odent observes in his lessons (p. 1401), 'only apparently easy'. As a result, it has gradually given way to a more substantial distinction that is based on the intrinsic difficulty of the measure to be taken.

You have therefore admitted that there might be 'legal' police measures that are so delicate to conceive that the liability can only be based on gross negligence (*Assembly, 20 octobre 1972, Ville de Paris c/Marabout p.664*, for traffic regulations in Paris). And symmetrically, that fault ['faute simple'] might be sufficient where an executory measure, even when taken in the 'heat of the action', presented no particu-lar difficulties (*Section, 28 avril 1967, Lafont, p.182* on the monitoring of ski runs). And we could find many examples on both sides of this distinction so that one might almost be tempted to say that the criterion based on the <u>nature</u> of the police act no longer holds and that we should restrict ourselves to a criterion based on the <u>content</u> of this act (see the commentary of the authors of the 'Grands Arrêts' under the deci-sion of *10 février 1905, Tomaso Grecco, p 139*).

[13] This particular order, which a *numerus clausus* limits to ninety members and whose history goes back to the 'Ancien Régime', also deals with all the appeals before the Cassation Court: Massot, 'Le Conseil d'Etat. De l'an VIII à nos jours' (1999), p. 148. We did not have time to continue our research into the offices of these lawyers, which is a great pity.
[14] A gross negligence is a fault which shows gross recklessness or gross carelessness.

We will try hard to avoid extended citations in what follows so as not to discourage the reader too quickly. However, they are indispensable at this stage in order to penetrate the *textual matter* that is so characteristic of the world that we have to describe. To prepare himself for this task, the reader might imagine himself as a young product of the ENA (the Ecole nationale d'administration, from now on, 'National School of Administration') who, having just graduated from the School at the top of his class, has been allowed to choose an assignment to the prestigious body of the Council of State. Or he might imagine himself as one of those members coming 'from the outside'[15] – a journalist, Member of Parliament, Minister, General or Doctor – who is called by favour of the sovereign to hold a seat at the Council. These persons represent one-third of its members. Whether young or old, an ENA graduate appointed to a position within the Council or a person coming in from the outside, all new arrivals at the Council with no previous knowledge of administrative law will inevitably, sooner or later, be confronted with such jargon. They will gradually learn to recognize the turns of phrase and will quite soon learn to speak the language by writing 'notes' and 'drafts' for themselves.

Let us begin with the particular play of references that we will later (in chapter 5) compare to the play of references in science. The long phrases of administrative law are punctuated by citations of judgments showing the date in italics, the name of the case, as well as the page of the indispensable *Lebon* volumes in which everyone is able to find the complete text of the judgment to which the commissioner of the law refers.[16] All legal arguments move from the proper noun of the case to the date and from the date to the proper noun, much as an underground train moves from one station to the next; so much so, that the *'Benjamin'* or *'Blanco decisions'*, always in italics, seem as familiar to those who use them daily as the 'Waterloo' or 'Covent Garden' stations in the Tube.

At the beginning of the reference between brackets, we also find the expression 'd'Assemblée' (from now on, 'Assembly') or 'de Section' ('Section') which indicates the level of the judgment. A judgment of

---

[15] The counsellors arriving through the 'tour extérieur' ('the outside way'), generally older, by opposition to those who are recruited by competitive exams from the National School of Administration – see chapter 3.

[16] The volumes of 'Le *Lebon*', the local equivalent of the Bible, of an *Encyclopaedia Britannica* and of a Code (which is nonexistent in administrative law anyway), are displayed in each of the rooms of the Council, even though, nowadays, information technology could very usefully replace it with computer searches. For its composition, see chapter 2.

the Assembly carries more weight than a judgment of the Section, and the latter more than a judgment of the 'sous-sections réunies' ('united sub-sections'), which in turn weighs more than a 'sous-section jugeant seule' ('sub-section judging by itself'). We will gradually learn the reasons for these terms, as well as the composition of all the panels of judges through which the same file can travel from month to month and even from year to year if it is a somewhat thorny case.

Occasionally, we also find in the references a brief note saying 'in the Detton conclusions', which allows the commissioner to cite not the judgment but the conclusions of another commissioner of the law – a great and prestigious forebear such as Léon Blum, whose conclusion will have been published on the basis that it was particularly enlightening.[17] And then, standing out like a lighthouse to the lost, there are 'the lessons of President Odent', which are to this day the only interpretation that allows one to ground reasoning on a more or less solid body of doctrine.[18] Finally, there is the collection of the *Grands arrêts* (from now on, *Major Precedents*). This is a volume that is incessantly being re-published and expanded, and to which the counsellors[19] always try to refer when the reasoning gets complicated. The names of *'Benjamin'*, *'Blanco'*, *'Tomaso Grecco'* and *'Canal'* usually elicit the support of the deciding judges as if they were indisputable theorems of some kind. While the legal productions of the civil and criminal system are fashioned by stringing texts and Codes together, the administrative law relies on the resonance of the often charming, outdated, provincial and antiquated names of these poor people who have argued with the State and whose complicated cases allow this Assembly to move the law forward.[20]

[17] Since judgments are preferably short – we will learn later to describe them – the litigants obviously find them obscure. It is therefore important that the conclusions are sometimes published, whether they are followed or not. Reports and commentaries are added to these conclusions and together they constitute the Doctrine (but counsellors rarely cite academics or Professors of administrative law, whose presence, from the point of view of the Council, seems purely explicative and even parasitical).

[18] We should note the humour in the citation 'only apparently easy' in a reasoning which will very quickly attain a totally Byzantine complexity . . . On the controversial usage of Doctrine by the commissioners of the law, see Deguergue, 'Les commissaires du gouvernement et la doctrine' (1994).

[19] We will use throughout the word 'counsellors' to designate any member of the Counsel of State, whatever their age and status, even though, in French, the word 'conseiller d'Etat' refers only to the last and most prestigious grade of the 'corps' (see chapter 3 for more niceties).

[20] In the book of major precedents you will find nice stories of this sort: 'A raging bull had escaped in Souk el Arbas (Tunisia), the crowd set out to pursue it; a shot

Very curiously, it is the same Bonaparte, the flamboyant Premier Consul that we encountered in figure 1.2 who had the perverse ingenuity to invent both the Civil Code that bears his name and the exact opposite of what is known as 'Napoleonic' law. He attributed to his Council of State the task of conjuring up, from start to finish and through the mere interplay of its previous decisions and in the absence of any written text, in the Anglo-Saxon manner, a *sui generis* form of law whose specific objective is to protect the citizen from the excesses of the administration. Since the Assemblée Constituante, during the French revolution, had prohibited the civil and criminal judge from considering acts of State (*actes de gouvernement*) under the penalty of abuse of authority,[21] the administrative law has had – slowly and painfully – to invent a body of doctrine to prevent the 'coldest of all cold monsters' from crushing its citizens under the yoke of its tyrannical power. That is the source of the expression 'contrôle' (from now on, 'review'), which defines the essence of the mission of the Council. The problem is that this power of review is bitterly contested – as we shall see – because it must not completely obstruct State action and because it is exercised by particular civil servants who seem to be both judges and parties. Now, one of the most delicate forms of this review concerns police powers, which are exercised in thousands of dangerous situations in 'the heat of the action'. Hence the distinction between the review of 'gross negligence' – the Council of State only intervenes when the authority exercised has been truly excessive – and of 'fault' – the Council of State can sternly reprimand acts, even if they appear to be excusable. The question raised by the commissioner of the law regarding this matter of the pigeons therefore concerns the following problem: with regard to the municipality of

---

was fired, injuring Mr Tomaso Grecco inside his home. The victim asks for reparation from the State alleging that the shot had been fired by a policeman and that, in any case, the police service had committed a mistake by not securing order in such a manner as to avoid such incidents.' The 'Observations' in *Major Precedents* begin like this, p. 80: Conseil d'Etat. 10 févr. 1905, TOMASO GRECCO Rec. 139, concl. Romieu (D 1906.301, concl. Romieu; S. 1905.3.113 note Hauriou). It is not an insignificant detail that the author of the note is Hauriou, who is respectfully described as a 'great commentator'.

[21] By law of 16–24 August 1790 and the decree of 16 fructidor year III. Its article 13 provides: 'The civil and criminal functions are distinct and will always remain separated from the administrative functions. The judges will not be able, under the penalty of abuse of authority, to interfere in any way with the operations of administrative bodies, nor summon administrators before them because of the latter's functions', cited in Stirn, *Le Conseil d'Etat* (1991), p. 14. The Constitutional Court has repeated these arrangements in its decisions of 22 and 23 January 1987, giving them constitutional value.

La Rochefoucauld, should the Council assume the role of a severe judge who reprimands even minor offences, or, having consideration for the difficulties of police action, that of a judge who only censures 'gross negligence'?

We shall see how the commissioner of the law, with his legendary subtlety, deals with the issue. But let us pause to notice one of the most fascinating figures of speech in the extract (p. 11), which is so characteristic of the administrative law: '*You* have therefore admitted', he says, 'that there might be "legal" police measures, etc . . .'. At first sight, this is a very strange formula, because it would have been physically impossible for members then present in 1995 to have also been making decisions in 1942, 1936, 1972, 1967 and, a fortiori, in 1905 at the time of the famous *Tomaso Grecco*. Nevertheless, the commissioner of the law stands on his rostrum as though he were addressing an immense, ever-present body composed of a large number of members who have long since disappeared, leaving only a few hallowed names, a body that is said to have 'thought', 'considered', 'wanted', 'decided' and 'judged' something. It would take us a great deal of time to measure the anthropological weight of this corporate body to whom the commissioners of the law so solemnly address themselves. Even more so since this 'you' has neither the unquestionable and eternal character of a Code, nor the quick pace of progressive accumulation that characterizes scientific progress (see chapter 5). Rather, it resembles more the opacity, variability, confusion and weightlessness of a feeble human brain in need of enlightenment. Isn't that precisely the point of President Odent's observation that 'this criterion, which is intellectually attractive, is only apparently easy, and it has progressively given way to another'? The sovereign body to whom commissioners address themselves is therefore composed of 200 years of phantom counsellors, aggregated by the sheer power of the address in one unique and majestic body of thought that is *ne varietur*, but which nevertheless is endowed with an obscure and stuttering voice which, like that of Pythia, has to be ceaselessly interpreted, assessed, clarified and even rectified. This crucial role of educating this collective body while pretending to do nothing but merely interpreting what it has always said, belongs to the commissioner of the law, who continues his presentation – which should not be confused with pleadings – by using terms that are less technical than those he used a short while ago, but which are nonetheless surprising:

Without entering into this doctrinal debate, it nevertheless seems to us that the old distinction [between conception and execution] retains some justification, or at

least a practical value, in situations in which it is possible to distinguish two successive police operations: the first having the character of conception and the second of
execution. It seems opportune to us to introduce a distinguo, a gradation in the
requirements applying to each of these two stages. Policing is an art of execution. It
is then fair to say that, where possible, the government is not exposed to the same
rigorous scrutiny in the phase of conception as it is in the phase of execution.

The commissioner of the law goes back to the old solution, despite
the fact that it was abandoned for reasons of 'practicality', 'opportunity' and 'fairness' – weighty terms whose traces we will need to
pursue – but he does so while clearly refusing to enter into questions
of 'doctrine' and 'justification'.[22] This is somewhat curious, given the
intellectual subtlety of his invention of a 'distinguo' and 'gradation'
between the conception of an act and its execution! And yet we shall
often encounter this contrast between, on the one hand, fundamental
questions in which the counsellors refuse to become embroiled so as
not to 'lapse into philosophy', and, on the other hand, the often stu-
pefying multiplication of distinctions which seem to the observer to
be utterly baroque. There are many ways of splitting a hair and the
philosophical way – what is an action? what is a conception? – would
simply be a waste of time at this point, whereas 'practical reasons'
mean that one should introduce other distinctions that are no less
subtle but which are controlled by quite different dictates. We might
say that the commissioner of the law is practising a form of subtlety
divorced from conceptual foundations – even doctrinal foundations
– that is characteristic of the law even though it never ceases to surprise the philosophically minded.[23]

To confine ourselves to the matter which concerns us, that is to say straying
animals, you have already distinguished between the liability of a commune for

[22] 'Doctrine' does not play a very clear role in the elaboration of law. It often designates the law professors, academics and jurists whose job is to comment on administrative law but who do not produce this law themselves because they are not judges.
They might add foundations to this body of law but their glosses are sometimes
considered as more ornamental than technical – the members of the Council usually
consider 'la doctrine' to be superfetatory.

[23] A typical phrase in the administrative law course excellently taught at Sciences Po
by Bernard Stirn: 'One must guard oneself against an abstract view of things and
not ask oneself which are the abstract systems of independence and partiality in all
countries and at all times; we at the Council of State', the Professor adds proudly,
'we have done it without text, empirically, progressively, efficiently' . . . Nothing is
less philosophical than this requirement to 'not wreck one's brain'. This distrust
towards the great problems of foundations is not unique to the Council of State: 'A
witty remark', writes Atias, 'provides an illustration; one must, it seems to him, leave
doctrinal anxieties aside which are too fundamental to be discussed seriously': Atias,
Science des légistes, savoir des juristes (1993), p. 333.

'fault', based on measures aimed at controlling stray dogs, and liability for 'gross negligence', based on the execution of these measures (*27 avril 1962 Sieur de La Bernardie, p. 281*). And that solution was recently upheld in a case with analogous facts in your decision of *16 octobre 1987, no. 58465 consorts Piallat c/Commune d'Uzès, aux conclusions de B. Stirn.*

It would serve no purpose for the commissioner of the law to give his personal opinion on a question, despite the 'it . . . seems to us' of the preceding paragraph, were it not able immediately to find support in what the virtual body of the Council itself has already decided. The corpus, the 'you' addressed by the commissioner, is now faced with the fact that it has rendered two different judgments: the first, which followed President Odent and abolished the difference between conception and execution, and a second, which is in any case only a return to an older decision, which the commissioner of the law finds it more expedient to reintroduce. In this way, affirms the commissioner, he sheds fresh light upon what 'you have already distinguished', and he proposes to do so by recalling that 'you' did so not only thirty-three years ago, but also less than eight years ago in an analogous situation, and in case of doubt one need only read the conclusions of Bernard Stirn, an eminent member of the Council of State, who held the commissioner's office at the time and shared his view, and who now sits among 'you'. All these meticulously woven threads now start to draw together towards a conviction that is expressed in the first outcome of our case:

We propose that you apply the same distinction to this particular case: there is the principle of 'depigeonization' itself and then the means* selected to implement it, on the basis of which the commune might be held liable for fault. And then we have the setting of traps, the use of poisons, or – as in this case – the use of contraceptive foodstuffs, which is more difficult and can therefore only attract liability in cases of gross negligence.

Consequently, by not distinguishing between these bases of liability and by looking only for gross negligence in respect of the overall process of conception and execution, the administrative court of appeal has, in our view, committed a legal error in its judgment.

So the commissioner of the law, applying the distinction made in the preceding paragraph, proposes to overrule the judgment of the court of appeal. The latter upheld the judgment of the administrative tribunal of first instance which was charged with reviewing the acts of the government by preventing it from harming its citizens by means of inappropriate police measures. Just as administrative law reviews the exercise of State powers, the Council of State, as the judge of final instance, reviews the exercise of that particular State power that is administrative law itself. In the same way that the Mayor of La Rochefoucauld might have been at fault in merely distributing contraceptives to pigeons which had become a nuisance, so the judges of the appeal court of Bordeaux might have been at fault in not punishing the Mayor for his error, which was either minor or serious depending on which of the two definitions one accepts.

At this point, both the lawyer and the farmer, who has waited a good many years to receive compensation for sunflower seeds that turned the pigeons into plump and chubby-cheeked birds, can breathe a sigh of relief. They were absolutely right to submit the case for final appeal. The court of appeal did indeed make a 'legal error'. Their claim was vindicated in the end . . . One should never lose faith in the law of the land.

But Mr Delavallade should not be too quick to rejoice, and he should certainly not bestow a large dowry on his daughter in the expectation that his costs will soon be fully repaid. It is one of the peculiarities of administrative law that the Council of State, as the court of final appeal, judges both the form and the substance of cases, so that instead of sending the case back to a lower court of appeal – as is the rule in the civil and criminal law systems – the Council can resolve the dispute there and then. This is what we call 'évoquer l'affaire' (from now on, 'de novo review'), a term which is itself evocative. Those claimants who are naive enough to believe that the overruling of a judgment of a lower court of itself proves them right are often disillusioned. As is so often the case, the commissioner of the law, after having argued relentlessly that the decision of the court of appeal should be overruled, unfortunately goes on to suggest that the claim of the farmer persecuted by pigeons be rejected:

Because this is a relatively old file (the facts go back to the Spring of 1985)[24] and because the arguments* of the appeal have, moreover, been formulated in such a way that they would be valid even before a judge of the Cassation Court, we will invite you to revive the case and to decide the merits of the case.

You will therefore recognize that the commune of La Rochefoucauld was not at fault in its conception of the measures to be taken. Pigeons are not so dangerous that the risk that was taken by using a less efficient measure could not be justified by a concern not to endanger the health of human beings, the health of other animals, or the peace of mind of environmental activists, who are very hostile to more violent measures.

You will also reject the somewhat unorthodox legal mean which relies on the notion of fault arising from the fact that the pigeons were the 'property' of the

[24] This is a typical example of the black humour of the Council of State: the term 'relatively old' – for ten years of procedure! – means that a lot of other cases take much longer.

commune of La Rochefoucauld. This will necessarily lead you to reject the appeal of Mr Delavallade, as well as his claim for costs.

And on these grounds we conclude[25] . . .

Although the decision of the court of appeal was overruled because it confined itself to an investigation of 'gross negligence' when it should also have scrutinized the act for 'fault' at the period it was conceived (this is a judgment going to the form of the decision, and, as a court of final appeal, the Council pronounces only on that mistake in the drafting that is called 'legal error'), it by no means follows that, when we get to the substance of the case, the commune was 'really' at fault. Abruptly, in this crucial paragraph, the commissioner of the law leaves the terrain of the law and moves to that of fact, and speaks only of commonplace facts, common sense and basic politics. Pigeons are not as harmful as all that; the health of people as well as that of other animals weighs more heavily than the eradication of pigeons; the peace of mind of ecologists is preferable to the rage of Mr Delavallade . . . The subtleties associated with a 'legal error' have disappeared, as have the sublime intricacies of President Odent, and the contradictions of this bicentenary body. We are in the realm of facts, speaking the language of plain truths, bordering on opinion, and almost pub talk, and we discover that in fact no error was committed. Were the lower courts then right to reject Mr Delavallade's claim? On the facts, yes, but in law, no; they rejected the claim for the wrong legal reasons. Much as doctors prefer the patient who dies after having been cured to the patient who survives for reasons that cannot be explained, the commissioner of the law does not wish to reject an accusation of error while making another error in the process. After ten years of litigation, the claim of Mr Delavallade is finally dismissed, but this time according to the rules. The case is clear, at least for the commissioner of the law; there is nothing more to add. The word 'conclusion' means exactly what it says. The discussion is over.

The commissioner of the law has only to resume his seat. Then, to the great surprise of the observer, nothing else happens. There is no debate, there are no shouts, no legal posturing, no cries from the public gallery, no one says, 'Silence, or I will clear the courtroom!' The president merely says, in a neutral voice, that 'the matter will be deliberated'. Admittedly, the first time one hears this phrase it sounds as though it means 'let's postpone this question of pigeons indefinitely'. The frail voice of a court clerk calls out another case, another

[25] Then the conclusions cited on p. 7 follow.

commissioner of the law – sometimes the same one – stands up, and starts all over again with the reading of another conclusion. For the moment, the deliberation escapes us. At the end of the morning, the judges discuss the case again, but only among themselves and in the silent presence of the commissioners of the law and the case reporters, in order to decide whether or not to follow their conclusions.[26] Two months later, on 5 December 1995, the judgment 'is read'. In an institution bathed in the culture of the written word, this means that a computer-printed list will be up on a notice board at the foot of the superb marble staircase on which Napoleon stood for his portrait:

> Given that it follows from the above that Mr DELAVALLADE has no grounds for claiming that the administrative tribunal of Poitiers was wrong to reject his claim that the commune should be held liable for the damage that he has described;
> Given that the commune of La Rochefoucauld, not being the losing party in an appeal case, cannot be ordered to pay to Mr DELAVALLADE the sum of 10,000F for costs incurred by him before the administrative court of appeal, which were not included in the costs of the proceedings:
> DECIDES
> Article 1: The decision of 3 December 1991 of the administrative court of appeal of Bordeaux is annulled.
> Article 2: The conclusions of Mr DELAVALLADE addressed to the judgment of the administrative tribunal of Poitiers dated 12 April 1989 together with his conclusions arguing that the commune of La Rochefoucauld should be ordered to pay 10,000F for costs are rejected.
> Article 3: The remainder of the conclusions of the aforementioned claim of Mr DELAVALLADE are rejected.
> Article 4: Notification of this decision shall be made to Mr Pierre DELAVALLADE, to the commune of La Rochefoucauld, to the Minister of Home Affairs and to the Minister of the Civil Service.

The deciding judges followed the conclusions of the commissioner of the law exactly, which, we should remember, they were not obliged to do. The case has now been resolved once and for all. No superior court can re-open the issue. There are no more means by which to prolong the movement of the files whose path we shall retrace in a later chapter. Mr Delavallade, if he is still alive, will receive a letter by registered post in which he will learn, ten years later and with great interest, that he was right to contest a 'legal error' made in the judgment of the administrative tribunal, which did not investigate a

---

[26] Since the ethnographer was neither a judge, nor a graduate from the National School of Administration, nor an intern, it has not been possible for him to attend the deliberations themselves but only, as we will see further on, the 'séances d'instruction' in which these deliberations are prepared.

'fault' in the behaviour of the Mayor of La Rochefoucauld, but that he was nevertheless wrong to believe that the Mayor was in some way at fault for having failed to prevent the pigeons from stuffing themselves with his precious sunflower seeds.

A controversial decree

We are in a beautiful room on the third floor, whose windows look out over the most beautiful garden of Paris, which has not been entirely ruined by the unfortunate columns of Buren, around which children are playing at tag.[27] The lawyer, the clerk and the audience have all gone; we are no longer in a hearing, but in a courtroom furnished with a large table, some armchairs, and bookshelves into which are pressed the indispensable *Lebon* reports, bound in fawn leather. Once again, we find the commissioner of the law, this time seated opposite the 'president' of the 'sub-section' who is flanked by his two 'assesseurs' (from now on, 'assessors'). To the left or right of the commissioner of the law, depending on the case, the 'rapporteurs' (from now on, 'reporters') are sitting before enormous files which they are reading in haste so as to refresh themselves before questioning begins. Seated at the same table there are a few other members of the 'sub-section' who are awaiting their turn: a young 'auditeur' (from now on, 'auditor') who has just left the National School of Administration and who is learning the trade by attending all the deliberations, an intern who has come from an administrative tribunal to drink from the wellspring of the law and, of course, the ethnographer who has long since become invisible; with his notebook, his suit and tie, and his middle-aged, well-brought-up air, he seems to blend right in with these people who, like him, are making notes in files – just as long as he keeps his mouth shut, because his very first words would reveal his incompetence! In a corner there is a small table and a chair on which the secretary of the sub-section (an indispensable character, to whom we shall return when we follow the logistics of files in chapter 2) is seated, entering and leaving the room according to the needs of the president.

We are attending a 'séance d'instruction' (from now on, a 'review meeting'), a session which is peculiar to administrative law, and in which the members of a sub-section collectively prepare the deliberations for the following weeks in an atmosphere that is much more

[27] See, on this matter, Heinich, 'Les colonnes de Buren au Palais-Royal' (1995).

informal than that of a judicial hearing.[28] The ethnographer will draw
most of his field-notes from these sessions which are of vital interest
because they bypass the written, formal and solemn procedures of
legal expression, and they will allow us to understand the ins and
outs of arguments that will later be set in lapidary form. Thanks to
them we are going to enter one of the kitchens of the law, not in
the manner of a health and safety inspector checking on hygiene
standards, but like a gourmet keen to understand the recipes of
the chefs.

To give a first impression of the work that goes on here, we shall
follow at some length one of these sessions. Today, by chance, the
session begins with the 'dissents' of the commissioner of the law,
which are the most enthralling of the debates that take place in the
review meetings. Normally, the commissioner remains silent, merely
writing a few notes about the file with which he will become acquainted
in the course of the session, which he will have to put 'on his case
calendar' in a few weeks' time, and in respect of which he will have
to write conclusions after a thorough analysis of its contents. However,
the commissioner sometimes informs the sub-section, on the eve of a
hearing, that, having studied the case in his independent capacity, he
disagrees with the solution proposed by his colleagues. In principle,
this should not be of any great importance because, as we have said,
the commissioner of the law – like a captain of a ship – is accountable
only to his conscience and to the law. However, as a matter of courtesy, to give advance notice of objections, to facilitate the debate and
so as not to take his colleagues by surprise, he sometimes informs the
sub-section in advance that he will reach a conclusion that differs
from theirs, and that, if the deciding judges follow his opinion rather
than that of the sub-section, they will need to prepare a second
'projet' (from now on, 'draft') of the judgment.[29]

Before analysing one of many extracts from the review meetings,
we should briefly explain the way in which we have decided to present
reconstructions of these dynamics. In order to retain the interesting
aspects of these observations, the extracts have to be long enough to
reveal both the dynamics of reasoning and the numerous hesitations
and changes of opinion. It would make little sense to provide extracts
that were too brief. Given that there was obviously no question of

---

[28] Rather than the awkward word 'instruction', we retained the word 'review' for the
preparation of the judgment properly speaking.
[29] 'Projet' is the name which is given to the draft of the judgment which is drawn up
beforehand and which usually serves as the basis for the final judgment (see the following chapter for a guided tour through the different written forms).

recording the review meetings, which are strictly confidential, the only resources available to us are the notes that were taken as we went along. The technicalities of the files are therefore complicated by uncertainties of transcription, by the usual obscurities of the spoken word, by allusions thrown in by people who have known each other for years, as well as, of course, by the incomprehension of the observer. To these we should add one final problem: in order to maintain strict confidentiality in this book we have had to encrypt the numbers of the cases, the names of the characters, the dates, and even the numbers of the observed sub-sections, all of which means that we have to interrupt the traceability of the files, as well as any presentation of context that would immediately give away the identity of the case in question. Of course, all of this is entirely contrary to the principles of clarity and proper explanation . . . As a result, most of these exchanges are not immediately comprehensible. We have therefore chosen two levels of commentary. The first, set in italics, accompanies the remarks of the different protagonists and provides some essential indications. Then, but always after some time, we resume a more thorough analysis. The readers are therefore free to choose their own way of reading, though we are aware that we have done no more than moderate the difficulty of an inquiry that is as austere as administrative law itself . . .

Perrouard (commissioner of the law): I have a serious problem with this file, reported by Mr Bruyère.

> *The reporter is the person who has been charged earlier with extracting from the file a 'note' summarizing the case, and who drew up a draft judgment that has been discussed at a previous session. He is the only person in the sub-section who has an in-depth knowledge of the file, but because some time has passed, he can no longer remember it precisely, while the commissioner of the law has recently read everything again in order to be able to write his conclusions.*

Bruyère (reporter) (explaining the situation): There is a signature missing on a decree of appointment. The lawyer has made this an argument*. The Council of State requested a supplementary process of review document. They asked for the signature of the Prime Minister. The general secretariat of the government (SGG)[30] has

[30] This 'Secrétariat général du gouvernement' is an essential institution of the government which is little-known among the general public. This secretariat is accountable to the Prime Minister and is charged with the coordination and mapping of all the work carried out by Parliament and government. It ensures that there is an

returned it, but the signature of the Minister is still missing and it is in any case the wrong Prime Minister – it is Balladur![31]

As soon as a lawyer turns an argument into a mean*, *it needs to be answered; in order to do this the secretary asked for a supplementary process of review document. That is to say, she forwarded the lawyer's argument* to the general secretariat of the government so that he could respond to it by producing the contested decree.[32] Unfortunately, this response did not satisfy the commissioner of the law. And obviously, after two electoral changes, both the Minister and the Prime Minister have changed. There is therefore no question of remedying the absence of the signature by morally unacceptable ways.*

Perrouard: The lawyer says 'there is no signature'. The original bears only the seal of the Prime Minister, and is lacking a signature. We have the file, the document did not leave the office of the general secretariat. They believe that they can make out the signature made by the Minister for the Environment, but not that of the Prime Minister. The second document is a certified copy. It is a certificate attesting the signature of the document. But we have not been provided with a copy of the document itself. The general secretariat asks us to take their word for it.

A certified copy of a document attesting that the decree was actually signed is not the same thing as the signature on the decree itself. The SGG seeks to break the chain of writing and its particular traceability, by means of an oral act and a request for trust. Must the commissioner of the law be satisfied with this position?

---

interface between the Ministers and the Council of State. The position of Secretary General, which is very prestigious and exceptionally stable – there have only been seven Secretaries since 1945! – is always taken up by a counsellor of State. The two last Vice-Presidents of the Council at the time of the study have also been Secretary General of the government.

[31] The transcription, through its skeletal character, gives the impression that the language of the counsellor is little refined, haphazard and interrupted. The contrary is the case. They speak like books and use their 'monsieurs le president' and 'madame le commissaire du gouvernement' at every opportunity. We will try, later on and by other means, to give an account of the urbane character and of the solemnity of the exchanges that are indispensable for the comprehension of the legal enunciation.

[32] The verb 'produce' is often used as an intransitive, like so many verbs at the Council. It means to send a statement of defence or rejoinder. 'Has he produced?' means 'Has he sent a document to contradict that of which he has been accused?'

I have called them informally. I do not have the right of examination. The General Secretariat has discussed it. They have decided not to send the minutes to the Council of State. They say that this is an established and unshakeable doctrine: 'we do not make photocopies of minutes'.

> *Given that a file is entrusted to a commissioner of the law in the course of a previous session only once the file is complete, he does not have the right to repeat the work of inquiry himself but must be satisfied with 'what is in the file'. Nevertheless, in addition to the formal circuit of 'process of review' (in which the argument of each party is communicated to the other, so that they might respond to it and so as to respect the absolute rule of the 'contradictoire'),[33] there is also the informal circuit of contacts which are obviously alluded to only in this kind of contact.*

Now, in law we must review the act in its **substance**. We have a right of **full review**. The Leduff decision refers to certified copies, but these are not the act itself. A certified copy has some authority, but **we also need the decree itself**.

> *The argument is based on the conjunction of two elements: (a) the notion of review, which we have already seen but this time it is 'full' review or control as opposed to a 'limited' review; (b) an absolute rule: the decrees must be signed by the Prime Minister and by all competent Ministers autographically; as a result, the counsellors must be able to review the substance or the materiality of the act; good faith, trust, informal relations and photocopies are not sufficient.*

Dorval (first assessor seated to the right of the president): This is disagreeable. The reporter can go and look at the document **himself**.

---

[33] The French administrative judge, contrary to the civil or criminal judge but similar to the situation in Anglo-American law, does not rely on an inquisitorial but on an adversarial procedure, so the judge strictly confines himself to listening to the objections of both parties and cannot of his own initiative, as a 'juge d'instruction' would do for example, open an inquiry or raise a legal mean that neither of the parties has raised – with the exception, however, of 'legal means' which are said to be of 'public order' (see examples on pp. 76, 93). It is often said 'le contradictoire' (the adversarial procedure) 'should be respected', to indicate that the Council of State has indeed sent all the arguments raised to all the parties involved in the proceedings. This is the equivalent of *procedural propriety* in common law, by respecting the principle of *audi altera partem* (see Stirn, Fairgrieve and Guyomar, *Droits et libertés* (2006), p. 67).

This is **troublesome**, but it is also **troublesome** to have to go to Matignon to consult the original when the Secretary General has attested that the decree has indeed been signed by the Prime Minister.

> *The assessor is not speaking in legal terms, as the commissioner of the law has just done, but remains within an evaluation of relations of protocol, trust and due administration between the two essential mechanisms that are the General Secretariat and the Council of State. At this stage, he refers only to a feeling of 'embarrassment'. His wish is that the reporter should no longer insist on obtaining the document itself, but that he should go there to observe it de visu. After which we will simply have to trust the reporter . . . This compromise would allow the whole chain to be verified, whilst giving way to the administration.*

Luchon (president of the sub-section): But it is for them to give us the document! Things are entirely the wrong way around!

> *The president counterbalances the argument of his assessor, who speaks of embarrassment and trust, with the argument of his commissioner of the law who speaks of law. His indignation combines two sources in a single reaction: the protocol according to which the Council of State has the power to review the administration – it is not for us to go to them – and the direction in which embarrassment has to circulate – it is they, not us, who should be embarrassed. We see therefore that the great struggle of the Council of State to exercise its power of review still continues.*

Perrouard: Is the decree protected as some kind of secret?
Luchon: Not at all, this is just banal, ultra-banal, why complicate things? We can imagine all kinds of things; perhaps in **reality it has not been signed**. Or it was signed by delegation, **which is impossible for a decree**. Or there are handwritten corrections on the decree, which is also forbidden. In any case, that does not exempt them from having to send it to us. It is bothersome to have to go over there, but only because it is for **them** to send it to us.

> *The commissioner of the law, who has not yet taken an active part in government, as we shall see in the heated exchange that follows, changes register by asking the president about the practical workings of the government. The president replies to the question by referring to his own, personal experience, which is still very recent, of the real life of government. The administration must have*

committed some kind of blunder: this is neither a secret that is hiding something else, nor is it a conspiracy. And then he reminds his colleagues of the obvious rule that it is impossible to delegate the signing of a decree and that it is strictly forbidden to write over it, which would mean that the version seen by the Council of State would be different from that which the Minister actually approved, from that which was published in the Journal Officiel.

Le Men (second assessor, who is seated to the left): **We cannot reject the argument***. They have sent us a ridiculous memoir. This is not the case of a secret memoir that has been sent to us and that we do not share with the parties. On the other hand, **it is difficult for us to annul** the decree given our ties to the General Secretariat.[34]

The second assessor reconstructs the dilemma with consummate elegance. One of the branches of the mean* is unquestionably right in law: every mean* that is raised has to be met with a response, and this particular mean* is iron-clad because it refers back to the practice of writing that lies at the foundation of the State itself (this kind of decree requires the autographed signature of the Prime Minister). The second branch is of an entirely different quality, even if it seems just as unquestionable as the other, because it rests on the interests of good administration and the powerful links between the Council of State and the Secretariat. Faced with such a contradiction, the prudent solution (and this assessor is prudence incarnate) consists in waiting for the moment.

President: I will call them **with a copy** of the Leduff judgment. I will point out that **this poses a real problem for us**. I will ask the advice of Boulanger.

Let us suspend the review meeting at this point and recapitulate the provisional solution given by the president as to the progress of the case. As is often the case, he adopts the formulation of his preferred assessor, Le Men. There is nothing to be done because we are caught between two factors that have equal value even though they are not equally legal. On one hand, the lawyer is right, and we cannot

---

[34] The reader must familiarize himself with these two great terms, 'annul' or 'reject' which are to the administrative law what the quart and tierce are to fencing. 'Do you annul or do you reject?' is a question which recurs constantly and which allows, like the north and south on a map, to know where the reasoning is going. If they reject, that means that they seal the fate of Mr Delavallade's appeal. If they annul, that means that they accept the appeal and that the act of the government is reprimanded.

shake off his argument*. On the other hand, this is a quite insignificant technicality, and hardly a sufficient reason for incurring the
displeasure of the Secretariat General with which 'we have so many
ties'. We can already see the extreme delicacy of administrative law,
which has to review the acts of the government without uselessly
interfering with its smooth operation by imposing constraints born
of an exaggerated 'formalism'. In this case, the Council's power of
review is total in the sense that it cannot rely on the word of a civil
servant, even if it is given in good faith. It must be able physically to
touch the very 'substance' of the autographed document, just as St
Thomas wished to touch the wounds of the resurrected Christ. The
virulent response of the president ('Things are entirely the wrong way
around'), the implacability of the questions of protocol ('it is for them
to send it to us'), the importance of trying to explain the law to the
administration ('with a copy of the Leduff judgment') show us very
clearly that the history initiated by Bonaparte still continues 200
years later, demanding the same energy and stirring up the same
contradictions: the members of the Council of State are both judges
and parties to the case, but they must nevertheless be good judges. If
they give an inch, the government will erode their powers. But if they
become too troublesome to the government, it will either ignore them
or find a way of getting round their decision. Throughout this work,
we shall try to understand the peculiar quality of a legal judgment
that is compelled to avoid formalism while at the same time addressing the most technical and procedural of legal arguments, and that
must prevent the administration from getting away with a disrespect
for rules while at the same time maintaining a relationship of trust
with the administration. Judgments of this sort are as subtle as judgments of taste, and we shall have, little by little, to become keen
connoisseurs of these subtleties.

We can already see that these assessments would be incomprehensible but for the way in which the review meetings continually supplement formal reasoning with a series of informal contacts based on
the intimate knowledge that the members of the Council have of
government. Far from being parasitic on the work of law, or diverting
it from its true path, this multiplicity of fragile links is what actually
enables the law to move forward. If Dorval is 'troubled' about asking
the Secretariat General to show him the decree while doubting its
word, it is because, in an earlier life, he was one of those who drafted
that kind of decree, and he would be breaching a necessary relation
of trust. If the president, responding to the commissioner of the law,
is able to imagine what 'really' happened, it is because he himself has

experienced the fever, the disorder, the confusion and the heat of the action in several Ministries and he can therefore easily reconstitute the reason for the blunder. And if Le Men cannot envisage the nullification of the decree 'given our ties to the General Secretariat', it is because he does not see the Council of State as a judge standing outside and apart from government, and because he sees that a relation of continuity between the smooth running of the State and its judges has to be maintained. This is a specific feature of the Council of State; as we shall see, all of those seated at the table have been, or will at some time become, eminent members of the active government. Rather than occupying the position of judge for life, as is the case in the civil and criminal system, they should instead be seen as practitioners who, in some periods, are subject to judicial review and, in others, *exercise* judicial review. We cannot say that they are both judges and parties, which would be to call their judgment into question, but rather that they have all been one or the other successively.

But why does the president, who has decided to ask the opinion of those whose acts he must nevertheless review ('this poses a real problem for us'), conclude the discussion with the remark: 'I will ask the advice of Boulanger'? Here is another peculiarity of the Council with which we should become familiar, because it is so amazing to foreigners, who regard the anthropologist just as uncomprehendingly as if he were explaining the Jivaro practice of head-shrinking.[35] In the same institution, the same building, the same corridors, the same corps, we find an activity that is quite different from that of the Litigation Section, namely that of the Counsel Sections, which are charged with advising the government on all legislative bills and also with helping to draft decrees, many of which have to be approved by

[35] Tocqueville already confessed to the difficulties he had in presenting the Council of State abroad: 'But, whenever I sought to convey to them that the council of state in France was not a judicial body in the ordinary sense of the term but an administrative body whose members depended on the king, so that the king, after regally commanding one of his servants, called the council of state, to prevent the former from being punished; and whenever I explained how the citizen, injured by the prince's order, was reduced to asking that very prince permission to seek for justice, they refused to believe such monstrosities and accused me of lies and ignorance': Tocqueville, *Democracy in America* (2003), pp. 123–4. However, we must not represent the Council as being too exotic. In the United States, for example, the circuit of appeal courts for the district of Columbia fulfils the same role as the Council, and the Office of Legal Counsel that of the Counsel Sections. It is the same thing with the English Law Lords and what they call 'judicial review', which is the equivalent of our appeal to abuse of power.

the Council.[36] Apart from the young auditors, the president and the commissioner of the law who are entirely occupied with their respective tasks, all the members who are present at this sub-section also sit in one of the Counsel Sections. So the decree that is being challenged today by our intrepid lawyer has been discussed some years before by colleagues sitting in one of the Counsel Sections that is called the Section of 'Public Works'.[37] Thus, the colleagues who are still present in the Council can now provide invaluable information concerning the problems they had encountered in the course of those earlier discussions. One of the many consequences of this strange ecology is that the Litigation Section can always return to the files of the Counsel Sections while, on the other hand, the discussions of the Counsel Sections can constantly anticipate the type of litigation to which an unfortunately drafted statute or decree might give rise.[38] For the president, it therefore seems quite natural that he should 'ask the advice of Boulanger' and get his opinion, not least because the latter had been Secretary General of the government some years before and possesses an intimate knowledge of the practical problems posed by the signing of decrees. Because this bizarre system, which actually does make the Council as a whole both judge and party, is a source of pride for its members, while at the same time horrifying observers, we shall try later on to grasp its justification.

Now that the essential issues in the situation have been sketched out, we can understand the brief moment of tension which follows because it nicely reveals the difference between form and substance, as well as the keen opposition between the State as judge and the State as government.

[36] It concerns decrees which are said to be taken 'at the Council of State'. This is often the case with decrees regarding the application of laws (if laws are voted by Parliament, decrees are the responsibility of Ministries).

[37] Since the names of the Sections date from Napoleon, it is not easy to remember them. Each serves as a mentor to a few Ministries, the list of which, moreover, changes with each new government, through a decree of redistribution.

[38] This connection between Counsel and Litigation has been the case since an important reform in 1963 which General de Gaulle demanded following the violent *Canal* case (C.E. Ass. 19 Oct. 1962), during which the Council of State very much displeased de Gaulle because it prevented him from punishing the leader of the OAS (Organisation de l'armée secrete) – an illegal military organization supporting French rule in Algeria – through a military process before a special tribunal, which did not entail a right to appeal. Far from considering the osmosis between acting as legal counsel and acting in litigation as abnormal, this reform has – on the contrary – only reinforced it, by obliging all the members to hold a double appointment: see Massot, *Le Conseil d'Etat. De l'an VIII à nos jours* (1999), p. 84.

Bruyère (re-opening the discussion in the form of a commentary to which he attaches no other importance): But machines for making signatures are very common. A text that is not signed is simply not valid, full stop. I don't understand their attitude. If I were in the Secretariat General, you would have had the signature.

Luchon: This should not be allowed to become a habit!

Perrouard (in a dry tone): We should not encourage these bad habits.

Bruyère (in an ironic tone and with a provincial accent): Monsieur le commissioner of the law, I really believe that you should take up a post that is somewhat more exposed, like that of the Prefect[39] of Guyana or the Prefect of Corsica.

Perrouard: The more I progress, the less I believe it.

Luchon (appeasing and changing the subject): Members of Parliament do not accept any signature other than that of the Minister, so either people spend their time signing or there is a machine.

Perrouard (unshakeable and always icy): But the [machine for signing] is not for decrees, it is not the same.

Bruyère (as an aside to the commissioner of the law and continuing his acidic comment): I recommend the South West of France to you, that too is not bad as an exposed post!

Perrouard (now more amused and playing along): Oh! I shall be more tenacious than you think . . .

The contrast between Bruyère and the commissioner of the law is striking. The former is an ex-Prefect who came in via the 'tour extérieur', a round, thickset and tough-skinned man who was around in the Gaullist era, and who bestows his ironic and detached wisdom on the sub-section; the latter is small, slim, ascetic, reminiscent of one of Ignatius of Loyola's first disciples, a tireless worker, and – of course – a graduate of the National School of Administration. And what the former is willing to do in the name of 'raison d'Etat' makes the latter indignant. Hence the advice, which would be quite out of place in any other institution: 'You, my young friend, who find my proposal of imitating the Minister's signature so scandalous, I would like to see you in a job plagued by strikes and natural disasters, with troublemakers of all species, and terrorists of the sort one finds in Corsica, nationalists of the sort one finds in Guyana, or irate

---

[39] The 'préfet' (Prefect) is the representative of the State in a department or a region and is in charge of coordinating all of the various branches of the government. There are innumerable movements between the Council and 'la préfectorale', that is, the body of Prefects.

winegrowers of the sort one finds in the South West region.' And
indeed, it is entirely possible that at some point in the future the commissioner of the law will in fact be Prefect, a Member of Parliament,
a Minister or a businessman.[40]

Nevertheless, this is not a simple tension between 'raison d'Etat'
and the dictates of law; what makes the anecdote interesting is precisely that Bruyère in no way denies the necessity of the formal rule
that his young colleague insists upon ('a text that is not signed is
simply not valid, full stop'). His reasoning, however, is based on a
quite different logic. By contrast with the sturdy and efficient
Secretariat General of yesteryear, the current Secretariat is honest
almost to the point of absurdity: 'Given that the Minister's signature
is required, they should obtain it by any means possible, as I myself
once did.' Somewhat debonair, he derives a small measure of satisfaction from scaring the young president, who accepts the latter's position while exclaiming 'This should not be allowed to become a habit!'
But it would take more than this to shake the Robespierrian virtue
of the young commissioner of the law, who sits upright in his chair,
sensing that the provocation is directed at him, but maintaining his
demands for integrity in this delicate situation imagined by his mentor
'in the heat of the action': 'Oh! I shall be more tenacious than you
think . . .'. And it is all too easy to believe him. The counsellors can
allow themselves to have this discussion because they are all convinced that the ground* chosen by the lawyer is both irrefutable and
entirely procedural. From their point of view, it is permissible to
discuss the question because they must maintain the formal norm
without being obstructed by minor technicalities.

We will often see this conflict resurface, and it is based not on an
opposition between form and substance, but on an opposition
between form and *formalism*.[41] Bruyère is not proposing forgery, nor
does he give up on law, he is simply astonished that the administration was not sufficiently adept to obtain the necessary respect for

[40] As we will see more extensively when studying the dynamic of the *corps*, the commissioners of the law are younger. Since they are the *crème de la crème*, they are
recruited from the 'maîtres de requête' (the intermediary grade between auditors and
counsellors) who are particularly brilliant, and they are later called to the highest
positions to occupy posts as assessors, presidents of sub-section, etc., when they
return to the Council after some comings and goings. Naturally, the president and
the two assessors of this story have all been commissioners of the law.
[41] Another particularly powerful example is the following intervention of Le Men in
another case: 'It is, all the same, not our habit to make everything depend on simple
legal editing; we are here to "*say the law [dire le droit]*". I am not too pleased with
this: before accepting the solution of the 'Cassation', I believe that we *must hesitate*.'
See chapter 4 for the fundamental role of this duty to hesitate.

forms. As for the commissioner of the law, he too is indignant about the failings of the government, but in his case because it broke the vital connection between the very body of the Minister and the page on which the decree is inscribed. Both are concerned with a respect for form, but each would impose a different requirement on Ministers. Bruyère, as an old veteran, would like to see a skilful administration well staffed (with people who are capable of showing real dedication of the sort he showed his Gaullist Minister).[42] Perrouard, as a 'priest of the law', would like the Minister to have a virtuous staff. As for the president, he situates the problem elsewhere, namely in the archaic views of Members of Parliament, who still require autographed signatures where it would be more expedient to use a signing machine, a strange hybrid that allows for mechanical delegation while at the same time maintaining the principle of the autograph, because the ink does indeed flow from the pen of the authorized person without being either photocopied or pre-printed.[43] The only way of preventing the lawyer from interrupting the efficiency of this decree that is contested by his clients is to ensure that the bond that physically attaches the constituted authorities of the Republic to the text is not broken. Further on, it will become necessary for us to understand the logic of these movements and attachments, as well as the specific form of continuity that it allows from one text to another.

'A decision of the Tribunal of Conflicts gives rise to a lively controversy'

The peculiar feature of the cafeteria at the Council is that one eats well and inexpensively, but one has to eat while standing. There are

[42] When he refused to be interviewed by the ethnographer – whom he, moreover, despite the denials of the latter, called an 'entomologist'! – he explained that if he had to recall what the State used to be like at the time of de Gaulle then 'that would only discourage young people, it is better if they don't know . . .'.

[43] On the history of this act of signing, see the fascinating historical inquiry of Fraenkel, *La signature* (1992). As Pierre Bourdieu suggests: 'Beyond the intuitive half-understanding that springs from our familiarity with the finished state, one must try to reconstruct a deep sense of the series of infinitesimal and yet all equally decisive inventions – the bureau, signature, stamp, decree of appointment, certificate, register, circular, etc. – that led to the establishment of a properly bureaucratic logic, an impersonal and interchangeable power that, in this sense, has all the appearances of "rationality" even as it is invested with the most mysterious properties of magical efficacy': Bourdieu, 'From the King's House to the Reason of State' (2005), pp. 29–54. We will consider in the last chapter what to think of this notion of 'magic', which is itself rather magical.

no plants, lavish tables or soft armchairs, only some simple side tables on which one has to put one's plate while remaining dignified and Spartan. Keeping his ears open, as his job dictates, the ethnographer suddenly hears a president of sub-section exclaim indignantly: 'This is an attack on administrative justice. We must hit back immediately, that is the only way when it comes to public relations questions.' So that explains the harsh article in the previous evening's *Le Monde*, which took up six columns: 'A decision of the Tribunal of Conflicts gives rise to a keen controversy'.

The judgment rendered on Monday 12 May by the Tribunal of Conflicts under the presidency of Jacques Toubon,[44] in a case concerning illegal Moroccan passengers discovered on-board a freighter, has prompted various reactions. The reporter of the file before the Cassation Court, Pierre Sargos, has decided to resign over the affair.[45] In a letter addressed to the first president of the Cassation Court, Pierre Truche, he explains that in order to put an end to what he calls 'the survival of a form of "reserved justice", the 'Tribunal of Conflicts' should be presided over by the president of the Constitutional Council. Jacques Toubon, in a letter to *Le Monde*, contested the interpretation of the decision by magistrates' unions and humanitarian associations. According to the Anafé [one of these associations] 'Jacques Toubon has abolished *habeas corpus* in France.' (*Le Monde*, Friday 16 May 1997)

In these few sentences, all three French supreme courts are gathered together in a debate that will go on for several days. The slight excitement of life at the Council of State lies in this continuous movement between refined discussions held in closed rooms on confidential subjects – such as the discussion we witnessed in the last section – and the immense echo chamber of the media which is capable of making the whole of France vibrate to questions that in some sense involve the entire history of the law, from *habeas corpus* in the form invented by the English, through to this singular question of 'reserved' or 'delegated justice'.

Reading through the press file of the Council, it is easy to appreciate the importance and variety of the issues it addresses.[46] On 16 January of the same year, the Council dismissed the claim of Bernard Tapie against a decree putting an end to his mandate as a European

[44] He was the Minister of Justice or 'Garde des sceaux' of Jacques Chirac, who was Prime Minister at the time of the second period of cohabitation under the second presidency of François Mitterrand.
[45] In the annals, no other known case exists of a public resignation of a judge who, moreover, breached the secrecy of the deliberation.
[46] Forty years before, in 1955, Marie Christine Kessler found only nine citations referring to the case-law of the Council of State in the *Le Monde* of that year! Kessler, *Le Conseil d'Etat* (1968), p. 71. We can from this measure the immense growth in public visibility of the decisions and opinions of the Council.

parliamentarian, an event that is now a topic of conversation in the provinces. On the 20th of the same month, the Council reprimanded the government for its abuse of the right of asylum, because it committed a legal error in repatriating a Liberian citizen; organizations for the support of refugees see this as a 'historic decision'. On 14 February, the Lagardère group sought review of the privatization of the Thomson corporation, making its own contribution to a matter of national importance. And when, on the 17th, the Council refused to indemnify a child for the wrong of being born with Down's syndrome, it intervened in an ethical question that was of greater interest: 'we do not think that a child can complain of being born in the way it was conceived by its parents', and it expressed the wish that doctors should not have imposed on them a ruinous obligation to secure certain results rather than implement particular means. When, on the 22nd, the artist Fred Forest took action against the National Museum of Modern Art, the issue was of interest to almost no one but himself, but when on 3 March the Council of State 'blocked the resumption of the Superphoenix project', by annulling a decree authorizing the transformation of this atomic energy monster into a research installation, the question was widely discussed. The same thing happened on 1 April, when, by annulling 35 kilometres of asphalt, the Council called into question the policy of motorway provision as a whole; and again on the 7th when, in an astonishing decision to overrule the decision of the lower court, the radio station 'Here and Now', which had been condemned to silence by the broadcasting regulator on the grounds that it was racist, abruptly found its voice again thanks to a decision of the Council. Just when the observer, faced with the esoteric nature of horribly technical matters, is tempted to doze off in his chair in the manner of a number of hoary counsellors, he is abruptly dragged from his torpor by a set of important issues, which come about because some obscure points of law have begun to cause a commotion across the whole of France.

In the eastern wing of the Palais-Royal there is a magnificent and richly decorated room, with incredibly bad acoustics, which, having once been the duchess of Orléans' ballroom, now hosts the rare sessions of the Tribunal of Conflicts.[47] What function is described by this admirable term? By definition, don't all tribunals have the task of settling 'conflicts'? But as we have said, France has had two entirely different legal systems since the time of Napoleon: the civil and crimi-

---

[47] We must confess that, apart from the grand staircase, the architecture of the Council rooms hardly corresponds to arguments on the greatness and beauty of the temples of law: Anonyme, *La justice en ses temples* (1992).

nal system and the administrative system. The former settles disputes between individuals – private law – as well as crimes or offences – criminal law. The latter deals with all disputes with the State.[48] Whereas the civil and criminal system is ultimately overseen by the Cassation Court (literally, the Court that can 'break' a judgment from a lower court), the administrative law is headed by the Council of State (in its role of settling litigations).[49] In France, there are therefore *two parallel and independent supreme courts*, without counting a third called the 'Conseil constitutionnel' (the Constitutional Council), which was established in 1958 to deal with the constitutionality of statutes, and whose offices are located in the west wing of the Palais-Royal, just behind the wings of the Comédie Française.[50] Given this multiplicity of 'supreme courts', inevitably there are some cases which cannot easily be assigned either to the civil and criminal system or to the administrative system. The danger is that the unfortunate litigant might not know which tribunal to address if each in turn declares that it does not have jurisdiction.[51] In order to avoid this double bind, a special tribunal was created in 1849 whose role is not to decide the substance of cases, but to decide which one of the two branches of law is competent to hear those cases.

But what was Mr Toubon doing here? We again encounter the physical body of a Minister, who on this occasion is charged, not with using his pen to place his signature at the foot of a decree, as he was a short while ago, but with embodying, by means of his very presence, the role of a tie-breaker. The two branches of law, being

[48] This equality obviously does not mean that they carry the same weight in society. We may roughly consider that the administrative law – in respect of the number of cases – weighs approximately a tenth of the civil and criminal system.

[49] For a sociological description of the Cassation Court, where the muffled atmosphere is rather similar to that of the Council but whose role is entirely different, and which is only composed, contrary to the Council, of full-time judges, see Bancaud, 'Une "constance mobile": la haute magistrature' (1989).

[50] The term 'supreme court' is strongly disputed by doctrine. In order to be complete, we must add the two European courts, the one in Strasbourg for human rights and the one in Luxembourg, the court of justice of the European Community. But since there does not exist, contrary to in the United States, a single supreme court which is capable of arbitrating between all these hierarchies of norms, a possible confusion ensues which Olivier Cayla, in a harsh article, has not hesitated to qualify as a 'legal coup d'Etat', since the Council of State, thanks to the famous *Nicolo* decision, succeeds in by-passing all other courts: see Cayla, 'Le coup d'etat de droit?' (1998b).

[51] To distinguish what belongs to the Constitutional Council and the Council of State, respectively, there is no need for a Tribunal of Conflicts. The distinction is made by the nature of the subjects of claims: laws before the Constitutional Council, decrees before the Council of State.

independent and parallel, must be equally represented in this tribunal, with four members coming from the Cassation (amicably abbreviated as 'la Cass'), and four more from the Council. If it were otherwise, one branch of law would effectively have precedence over the other, which would upset the difficult exercise that was conceived by Bonaparte as a means of continuing the revolutionary struggle against the Parliaments of the Ancien Régime: that there should be two laws and that they should be autonomous. The admirable mechanism of the Tribunal of Conflicts therefore demands absolute equality. But no judicial bench has ever been composed of an even number of judges, because it would be impossible to decide cases in the event of a draw. What would be the point of creating a Tribunal to arbitrate cases if it remained undecided, four against four, hesitating interminably like Buridan's ass? Although justice has initially to be balanced, indifferent and hesitant, it must in the end incline to one side or the other. Hence the invention, for all judicial benches, of a deciding vote, whose precise quality matters little, and is a kind of $n + 1$ which ensures that the number of judges is always uneven.[52] Who better to fulfil this function than the Minister of Justice, the French equivalent of the Lord Chancellor?[53] That is why, on 12 May 1997, having deliberated the question inconclusively on 13 January, the members of the Tribunal of Conflicts had to call on the real and corporeal presence of Mr Jacques Toubon in person for four hours, despite his many obligations.

What is the source of the apparently derogatory expression: 'the survival of a form of "reserved justice"' in the newspaper article above? From the long lineages of those kings who 'made France' and with whom the Council, when searching for its roots, is not afraid to associate itself, even returning, in texts with historical pretensions, to the Council of Augustus! We should recall that the revolutionary break with the Ancien Régime didn't have the same meaning for administrative law as it had for the civil or criminal law; in the

[52] In the sub-section there is a deciding vote as well when voting takes place, without which the president, the two assessors and the reporter would form an even number. The commissioner of the law, who is present but silent and therefore virtually absent, is obviously not able to vote. They therefore use the auditor or even an intern or a 'mobile' civil servant which will allow the balance to tilt one way or another.

[53] Strangely, the Minister of Justice is not the hierarchical superior of the Council of State, but only of the civil and criminal judges. The latter, moreover, depend as civil servants for all their internal conflicts (appointments, promotions, appraisals) on the Council of State because the Council is also the judge of administration. Moreover, the Council of State also has the function of managing the whole machinery of the administrative law. Although Montesquieu was French, the principle of the separation of power is not respected here, at least in theory . . .

absence of a Code, administrative law can go back to well before 1804, when the Civil Code was promulgated.[54] Just as the 'King never dies' (*dignitas non moritur*), the State does not perish. One can therefore find cases in which decisions of François I, Napoléon III or the last Minister for the Environment are cited as though they belonged to the same corpus. Even if kings entrusted the task of judging to their privy council, they did not *delegate* justice to these councils but *reserved* it for themselves, so that, in the exercise of their absolute power, they could overturn the decisions of their counsellors, which they treated as mere opinions. So, when Napoleon created the Council of State – as a descendant of the King's Council – he maintained the principle of reserved justice, which reduced counsellors to the rank of simple 'advisers' (the name 'counsellor' in French is a rather weak term meaning the one who gives advice only).[55] The Council of State had to suffer this humiliating limitation until 24 May 1872, when, with the advent of the Third Republic, it finally became a court with full and entire powers and was then immune from government interference. They had finally moved from a regime of reserved justice to one of *delegated* justice. But in the eyes of those journalists and publicists who were upset by the judgment of 12 May 1997, the role of the Minister of Justice as the deciding vote in a case affecting civil liberties reduced the Council of State to the indignity of its place in the old scheme of injustice that kings and tyrants reserved to themselves, not daring to delegate it to independent judges with the power to reprimand the excesses of the State.[56]

[54] In addition to the 'water laws' which can go back several centuries, we can still hear commissioners cite the *Villers-Cotteret* decision of 1539, the ruling of *Moulins* of 1566 or the *Edict of the Navy* of 1681 . . .

[55] In fact, as Elizabeth Claverie points out (personal communication), the distinction between delegated and reserved justice is particularly ambiguous during the Ancien Régime, especially where the role of Parliaments is concerned – 'Strictly speaking, none of these political practices (of making reprimands public) was compatible with the theory of royal absolutism which saw in the monarch the only public person, the source and principle of unity within a hierachical society organized through orders and estates': Baker, 'Politique et opinion publique sous l'Ancien régime' (1987), p. 42.

[56] Let us recall that the other judiciary branch, however, is not exempt from the same conflict: 'The French attitude is on the contrary to confuse the powers. We find this cultural trait throughout the French legal system. We find it in the statute of the Council of State which is so particular, since it is at once judge and counsel of the government and in which, moreover, politicians and senior civil servants move from one to the other in almost total silence from the statute. We find it in the fixed role of the president of a hearing who instructs 'to charge or discharge'. We find it in the statute of magistrates which includes the magistrates of the Public Prosecutor's department as well as the judges on the bench, who have moreover attended the same school': Garapon, *Bien juger. Essai sur le rituel judiciaire* (1997), p. 165.

The counsellors blanch at this insult. On 24 May, one of them – under the pseudonym of 'Solon' – replies sharply on the opinion page of *Le Monde* under a title that is curiously unrevealing: 'A commotion that misses the point'. According to the author, the indignation of the press was just an expression of the general public's abysmal ignorance of administrative law in general and of the role of the Council of State in particular. Reading Solon's prose, which has none of the Attic clarity suggested by his Greek eponym, one might well excuse the man in the street his failure to grasp all the complexities of an opinion of the Council:

1°) On 12 May, the Tribunal of Conflicts did not have to decide the **merits** of the case, but only the question whether it was for the civil law or administrative law to review the (effectively contestable) legality of the measure prohibiting landing [by illegal immigrants]. By deciding that it was for administrative law, the Tribunal of Conflicts has not in any way **withdrawn** the facts of this particular case from legal review. It has only **identified** the competent forum.

2°) The rules relating to the allocation of jurisdiction in cases of administrative regulation are **clear**: it is for the administrative law to intervene, **unless** there is a 'gross violation' ['**voie de fait**'], in other words, an administrative action **that cannot be subsumed** within any administrative power and **which poses a serious threat** to basic freedoms. The Tribunal of Conflicts considered that the first of these conditions was not fulfilled (which does not imply, if it needs repeating, that the disputed measure was in any way condoned).

A finding of gross violation was quite rightly refused in the circumstances: the indefinite extension of this notion would ultimately lead to the **transfer** of an **essential part of proceedings** concerning the legality of administrative acts to the civil or criminal judge in any case in which a question of freedom is at stake (which is more or less **always** the case). (*Le Monde*, Saturday 24 May 1997)

There is no doubt that Solon is a Counsellor of State: he speaks their language. The first paragraph raises no difficulty: against what he calls 'diabolical approximations and melodramatic outbursts', Solon – having acknowledged that the refusal to allow the passengers to land poses a grave problem of legality – emphasizes that the tribunal did no more than resolve some simple questions of jurisdiction. The proceedings have only just begun. According to him, even the most ignorant member of the public can distinguish between form and substance. But his text becomes more complicated in the second paragraph. It is not certain that the rule he recalls is so 'clear' for the reader of *Le Monde*, unless the reader knows the definition of a 'voie de fait' (gross violation) from his reading of the *Dictionary of Administrative Law*: 'a particuliarly serious violation by the government of a property right or a fundamental freedom'.[57] Instead of saying that what was in question was a blatantly illegal police action,

---

[57] Conseil d'Etat 18 Nov. 1949, *Carlier*, RDP 1950.172, concl. Gazier.

which would have been more direct, Solon draws on the pathos of a leading decision to conclude that in this particular case the Tribunal of Conflicts did not recognize the existence of a gross violation.

The reason he gives for this in the third paragraph is quite astonishing, and is explained by the indignation of the president of subsection whom we encountered earlier, and who wanted a direct counter-strike against this 'attack on administrative justice'. The argument that Solon uses to justify the finding that there was no gross violation is no longer based on law but on the dangers represented by a 'transfer of proceedings' from one branch of law to another. If the actions of the border police in refusing to allow the disembarkation of two Moroccan passengers who were illegally aboard the freighter *Felix* in August 1996, deliberately so as to prevent them claiming a right of asylum, were characterized as a gross violation, the result, according to Solon, would be to allow the civil or criminal courts to exploit this indefinite extension of the concept and to erode the whole edifice of administrative law.

'So what?' cried a chorus of judges and humanitarian organizations: 'what would be so dramatic about that?' Isn't the survival of two autonomous and parallel legal systems just an outdated relic that is found only in France and a few other countries? Must these illegal Moroccans be repatriated just so as to maintain the existence of this historical anomaly, which Napoleon inherited from the Ancien Régime under the pretext that, as the old adage says, 'the king can do no wrong', with the result that policemen, as minor delegates of the king, can be censured only by a special judge? The civil and criminal judges' union (the Syndicat de la magistrature), which is politically to the left, sees in this: 'a political desire to limit the power of judges in the civil and criminal system to fulfilling their constitutional duty as guarantors of individual freedoms'. As for the professional association of judges (l'Association professionnelle des magistrats), which is politically to the right, it asks that we consider 'the disappearance of these two forms of jurisdiction, which are a curiosity of the European legal landscape' (*Le Monde*, Friday 16 May 1997).[58]

In defending this 'curiosity', Solon, who was probably appointed to the task by his colleagues, transforms the question into another, which does indeed seem more reasonable:

---

[58] The union of the *administrative* legal branch, on the other side in this issue, perhaps outdoes them by replying sharply that it considers that the reactions aroused by the decision of the Tribunal of Conflicts 'once more, in a deceitful manner, discredit the independence of the administrative legal system', about which the magistrates 'need not be lectured by anyone' (*Le Monde* of 17 May).

The real question is whether the tools available to the administrative law are as powerful as those available to the civil law in coming to the urgent rescue of a freedom that has been illegally threatened by the administration. Much has been done to achieve this in the past few years but it is necessary to do more. A process of administrative emergency appeal exists, but with one exception – namely, the *référé liberté* [interlocutory appeal] in matters regarding the legality of acts of territorial entities – it does not have the force of the process of emergency appeal in civil law. This is the real issue. (. . .) On the one hand, an ethic of responsibility, on the other an ethic of conviction (or exhibition?) . . . This is not a new division, and it will determine the evolution of French democracy for years to come.

We see that public polemic does not only have disadvantages. Having stirred up the question of *habeas corpus* and the murky history of reserved justice, the point now is to promote 'the evolution of French democracy' by distinguishing between a group of agitators who exhibit themselves in the media, and those, like Solon and the Council of State, who are trying – by means of an ethic of responsibility – continually to enhance the means available to the law in protecting civil liberty. Our author recognizes with admirable honesty that, because it has no effective procedure of emergency appeal, administrative law remains indeed 'weaker' than the civil or criminal law, and that this situation will have to be remedied sooner or later.[59] In law, what does it mean to say that a tool is 'powerful' and a procedure 'weak'? We are going to need to understand the meaning of the set of more or less solid ties that link customs officers, illegal migrants, humanitarian associations, journalists, court reporters, law professors, judges and lawyers to each other; a mysterious set of ties that extend across the whole of France like a hidden network of lymphatic vessels which remain invisible so long as they are not brought to expression in a dispute, and which remain nonetheless mysteriously in constant operation even when no controversy arises to reveal their persistent process of translation.

Can we refine a bit what is meant here by the 'force of law'? What is the weight of the formula 'gross violation' which, from the moment it is uttered by a lawyer, fixes the policeman in his wrongful act (which 'manifestly cannot be seen as the exercise of any governmental power')? Is it a magical spell which transforms the enemy into a broken marionette? Or should we see it instead as a precious resource which lawyers once possessed, but which they lost as a result

[59] It is because the administrative procedure of emergency appeal remained weak compared to the civil and criminal one that a recent law of 30-6-2000, which was proposed by the Member of Parliament François Colcombet who was a former judge at Cassation, has recently sought to make up for the difference: Colcombet, 'Rapport . . . relatif au référé devant les juridictions administratives' (1999).

of the decisive judgment of 12 May 1997? The authors of the 1999 edition of the *Dictionnaire de droit administratif* remained faithful to the kind of intertextuality that is so specific to law and to which we will return later: they incorporated the turbulent event we have just studied by indicating in their commentary the modifications that have taken place in the relative strength given to those multiple weaker and stronger ties.[60] They refer to 'recent case-law, according to which an irregular forcible execution does not amount to a gross violation unless it expresses a manifest absence of legal justification':

> The decision *Préfet de police de Paris c/TGI Paris* (TC 12 May 1997, RFDA 1997. 514, concl. Arrighi de Casanova) **confirms this tendency**, at the same time as it adopts a restrictive definition of gross violation, and reviews the Eucat case (TC 9 June 1986, *Rec.* 301). The application of the **theory** of 'gross violation' leads to a significant **derogation** from the principle of the *separation of administrative and civil or criminal authorities:*[61] the civil or criminal judge does indeed have full jurisdiction to establish the irregularity of acts or dealings which would result in a gross violation (. . .). This attribution of jurisdiction to the civil or criminal courts is often justified by the notion of a 'denaturing': the **seriousness** of the wrong that affects the act in question immediately **deprives** it of its administrative nature. Moreover, it can be founded in the **principle** that the civil or criminal courts are the guardians of property rights and individual liberty. The theory has prompted certain **criticisms**, and it has even been suggested its **disappearance** (concl. Fournier on Council of State 19 juill. 1965, Voskresensky, AJDA 1965.605). However, it is not at present in decline, but has on the contrary found **renewed favour** with claimants, and the tendency to invoke it before the civil or criminal judge expresses to a certain **weakness of administrative litigation** where urgent procedures are concerned – particularly the *emergency appeal.*[62]

So the notion of force is aptly used to describe the way in which commentators register minor modifications in the tensions that give law its weight: the decision with which we are concerned 'confirms a tendency', this tendency 'adopts a restrictive definition', and weakens existing case-law. Since 1997, therefore, whenever a lawyer wishes to invoke the mean of 'gross violation', he will no longer be able to

[60] Van Lang, Gondouin et al., *Dictionnaire de droit administratif* (1999), 289–90.
[61] We should not confuse the separation between the administrative and civil and criminal authorities with the separation of powers, since the civil and criminal system is not really a power but an *authority* in France. This is a question which, as they say, 'always keeps doctrine occupied'. As for the administrative law, it is wholly on the side of the executive since it belongs to the government, even though in practice, as we shall see in chapter 3, it has all the characters of complete autonomy.
[62] Let us recall that we have put in bold the terms that we wish to emphasize in the commentary that follows the extract, while the italics and the underlined terms correspond to the original typography of the citations.

convince a civil or criminal judge as readily as before, because, at least in cases in which there is no 'manifest absence of legal justification', the latter will assert his lack of jurisdiction: the lawyer will be directed to the administrative tribunal across the road. Thus a specific ground* has lost some of its power. According to a 'criticized' theory, the civil or criminal courts, as guardians of freedom, should have been able to assume jurisdiction as soon as the illegality of an act was so glaring that it could no longer pass as an act of the State. Renewing the traditional expression of the English monarchy, that 'the king can do no wrong', there was logically a relation of mutual exclusion between these two phrases: 'it is an act of State / it is an illegal act'. However, this original principle of non-contradiction was challenged by the conclusions of president Fournier in 1965, who wished to weaken the theory to the point of causing it to disappear. . . . Nevertheless, given that the administrative law suffers from a 'certain weakness', this argument*, which should have been enfeebled by the decision in *Préfet de police de Paris contre TGI*, actually has now, on the contrary, gained new strength, and is even enjoying 'renewed favour'. We will have to understand the exact nature of this glittering tapestry, which is reset on the loom each day by some mysterious Penelope, who weaves and unpicks her work, obliging teams of commentators to darn the fabric of all these interlinked texts so as to maintain their coherence.

In any case, despite the gilded ornamentation of the palace, the self-confidence of the counsellors of State, their smooth manner, the assurance of their speech and the authority of their opinions, it is clear that the dangers that threaten them soon remain visible through the interstices of their files. Not only do they still have to demand that the government show them the respect that they acquired in a struggle that lasted two centuries, as we saw in the last section, but the very existence of this branch of law as distinct from the civil and criminal system, and as difficult for the uninitiated to understand, is thrown into question as soon as issues of civil liberties come to throw suspicion on the virtue of judges. And yet the threats of a stubborn government and those of the hegemonic civil and criminal system are as nothing compared to the threats posed by European law, whose particular obscurity, which is 'very Anglo-American' (as counsellors say), owes very little to the opacity of the Napoleonic tradition, which was capable of simultaneously inventing a codified law – the 'judiciaire' – and a non-codified law – the administrative law. And yet, rather than focus complacently on the marks of arrogance that he encounters so often in his field, the ethnographer decided to be more attentive to the signs of fragility that inevitably run through the institution whose portrait he attempts to draw. Might not the solitary majestic column suspended in the void, the symbol of the bicentenary with which we opened this chapter, symbolize a mute anxiety that is much more worthy of interest than the legendary self-righteousness of a body hovering above all contingencies? Later, we shall have to grasp not only the peculiar texture of the law but also the specific *bearing* of the Council of State.[63]

The law is flexible, but it is the law

In its layout, the room is quite unusual: despite its wood-panelling, its impressive size and its solemn paintings, it isn't really a hearing chamber. Despite the bookshelves in which the inevitable *Lebon* multiple volumes are enthroned, we are no longer in a review meeting room. The table, which is much bigger and rectangular in shape, occupies almost all of the space. At each place, there is a small leather box marked with the name of a counsellor. This is in fact the only office available in the Council to those who see piling up before them the voluminous files of projects on which they will have to write a report. The quality of the armchairs corresponds to the dignity of the members, who are seated according to a ranking that is strictly determined by the order on the promotion roster called 'le tableau', whose subtleties we will explain in chapter 3. The most majestic and the deepest of the armchairs, placed before the fireplace on the shorter side of the rectangle, belongs to the Section president, who is one of the seven truly important characters of the Council.[64] In the middle of the room, the immense table leaves at its centre a large rectangle filled with chairs, as if for an exam in which the candidates are to be grilled by an impressive jury of some thirty persons. And in a sense this really is an examination room, because it is here that the meticulously worked legislative bills and draft decrees that are proposed by the government – after a painful process of negotiation between unions, Ministries, offices and Members of Parliament – are going to be carefully weighed by a jury composed of members of the Counsel Section, who will more often than not subject them to revision, erasure and deletion; who will, in short, rip them to shreds.

We should recall at this point that the Council of State's unquestionable predilection for obscurity means that the same term – 'com-

[63] According to the beautiful expression of Pierre Legendre, 'Prestance du Conseil d'Etat' (1975).
[64] Not to be confused with the president of sub-section who is only worth, if we dare say, one-tenth of the president of the Counsel Section. In fact the whole Litigation Section only forms one single section divided into ten sub-sections.

missaire du gouvernement' – is used to describe both those unfortunates whose texts are going to be so mercilessly rewritten, and those individuals in the Litigation Section who are charged, as independent minds, to 'say the law' so as to enlighten their colleagues. The difference between these two characters who have the same name lies in the fact that those who say the law – and we have already met – are not *at all* commissaries sent by the government, while the second species, also called 'commissaires du gouvernement' are really sent by the various ministries to do the 'commissions' of the government! The Minister sends them to the Council of State with their texts so that they can go through the process of quality control and record any amendments before returning with their documents, which will be submitted to the Members of Parliament in the case of a statute, or published in the *Journal Officiel* in the case of a decree. The fact that, four metres apart, hundreds of people use the same term twenty times a day to indicate two totally different offices, having been unable in the course of 200 years to invent distinct words, shows how little we know about socio-linguistics . . . In each case, however, the context quite unambiguously clarifies the meaning of the term, according to the room where we find ourselves. Since we are not able to transport this context into a book, we will call the true commissioners 'government envoys' to distinguish them from the commissioner of the law in charge of litigation.

The ordeal is indeed tough for the Minister's envoys, who wait in the corridor, uncomfortably seated in a tiny room with no attractive feature other than an indirect view of the pyramid of the Louvre, sighing intermittently because of the delay, and periodically checking the timetable pinned to a cork board. They have to wait to undergo their examination until a bailiff authorizes them to enter the room, and seats them right in the middle of the counsellors, by whom they are completely surrounded, and by whom they are assailed with more or less acerbic questions. Fortunately, like Daniel in the lions' den, the government envoys have some support in their ordeal, namely, the reporter of the Counsel Sections, who will have met them several times before, and will have ensured that the different ministries interested in the text have come to an agreement between themselves by means of a small document called 'le bleu de Matignon', which sums up the laborious process of negotiation through which the various *membra disjecta* of the State are made to act as a single person and speak in one single voice.[65] The reporter has drafted his own text, called 'the reporter's draft', which is placed before each member of

[65] Matignon, the palace of the Prime Minister, is the equivalent of 10 Downing Street.

the Section in a folder, alongside the 'draft of the government' (which is often very different) and together with the supporting documentation (see the following chapter on the path of the files). The session opens with a reading of the reporter's note, which is often very detailed and which he keeps to himself afterwards. Then, the president opens the discussion. At this point we enter what can only be called a 'writing workshop', because the text is collectively read and corrected, line by line, following alternately either the text of the reporter or, when the envoys of the Ministries complain too loudly, the text of the government. Throughout, the reporter juggles the various drafts and deletions in an attempt to keep track of the amendments.[66]

On that particular day, the case at hand is the classification of a forest. Once the reporter, Mr Bienaimé, who specializes in this kind of decree, has read his Ciceronian prose and concluded that, apart from some minor points attributable to the difficulties of conducting an inquiry into public benefit and to the number of owners of this woodland, the decree should be favourably received, the president, who has reread the whole file before the meeting, expresses his disagreement.[67]

So far, none of the members present has heard of this case, with the exception of the government envoy who is seated a little anxiously in the middle of the arena. In a few sentences, the counsellors are going to have to forge an opinion for themselves with no guidance other than that offered by the 'note' and the discussion (we shall be concerned later on, and in great detail, with the strange procedures that allow them to obtain a very peculiar sort of objectivity and disinterestedness). The envoys are right to be slightly scared: this distinguished assembly that examines their work has accumulated 560 person-years of experience of the Council of State (six of the members

---

[66] As with the review meetings, we only have notes taken in the course of the meetings, which have to be supplemented by a commentary of the kind used above. In order to capture the dynamic of the examination, which is essential to our work of interpretation, we shall try this time not to interrupt the continuity of these quite extensive extracts. Let us recall once more that the transcription necessarily cuts phrases into pieces and takes away the smoothness, the politeness, the apparent urbanity of the members of the Council, which are impossible to reconstitute without a tape recorder.

[67] The role of counsel of the 'Sections' is not the same when they give their opinion on the quality of a bill of law – when the government can basically do what it wants afterwards – as when they discuss the text of decrees, about which the law specifies that they must be 'approved in the Council of State', since in the first case the Section simply plays its role of legal counsel of the State, whereas in the second the finally promulgated text must be exactly the one which leaves the hands of the Council.

have been at the Council for more than forty years!), to which must be added the 300 or so person-years of experience of administrative law and high government held by those who came in via the outside – Ministers, Prefects, judges, Members of Parliament, political activists, directors of public or private companies, etc, without taking into account the fact that twenty members still sit for the rest of the week in the sub-sections of the Litigation Section where they sometimes, but as rarely as possible, have to annul the decrees that they might have seen in the Counsel Sections.[68] This strange system, in which an immense capital of experience is brought to bear on a text which was drawn up by administrations that many of those present directed or reformed, in part explains the speed with which the members can form a judgment. Let us recall that, unlike the Litigation Section, which can allow itself to move forwards with a considered hesitation and only after a plaintiff has sued, but with the last word, each of the Counsel Sections must simply give advice and, so as not to obstruct the immense machine of government, they must do so under time pressure – in real time, so to speak.

President Lebrun: There is a legal problem here. We have to consider Article L 411-5 of the 'Forest Code'. We are referred to the definition of the process of review file in L 411-3, but there we also have the land register, and the map of individual plots, etc. But Mr Bienaimé has just told us that there is an **error** in the map of individual plots. Seventy-seven hectares were counted as 67 acres. Anyone would have corrected this, but we cannot confuse the two measures. Fine, but there is something more troublesome; there are 24 hectares on the cadastral map which are **not** on the map of individual plots, and there are also some plots that are not in the right colour.

> The practical difficulty of these operations is such that they can forgive a certain number of errors, which is what the reporter proposes to do, but the president wants to discuss the question of at which point a number of small errors begins to amount to a big error that might later give rise to a problem of legality.

Our view is that we should leave the government with only the **minimum risk of litigation**, but if there is some illegality here, **we should say so**. Anyone could invoke the argument*, even if the risk

---

[68] These are numbers for 1999 which were compiled from the 'tableau' (the 'roster') for one of the arbitrarily chosen Counsel Sections.

of litigation is infinitesimal; but this **does not change** the fact that there is legal uncertainty.

> *The process of quality control foresees that, in a couple of months, the Litigation Section, on the other side of the corridor, might find itself faced with a claimant who has had the idea of challenging the decree by 'invoking the mean' revealed by the reporter.*[69] *Twenty-four hectares are not on the map of subdivisions. The duty of the Section is therefore to clarify the situation for the government so that it only takes risks that it chooses to take. Although, in this case, there is an infinitesimally small risk, if the government disregards this risk, then it must do so with its eyes fully open.*

   Government envoy: This was an enormous job for the administration, there are 20,000 plots. The data were computerized, and the software used by the surveyor and the State services were incompatible.

> *Although the government's envoy does not want to take a legal risk, his reasoning is not legal since he is weighing the hair-splitting of the president, which uses a thought experiment to anticipate the potential hair-splitting of a virtual claimant, against the enormous work that the Ministry has had to do to convince thousands of land owners to join together, to have their plots of woodland surveyed, and to accept the classification uncomplainingly. Must everything be brought to a halt just because of a simple technical error caused by a surveyor's incompetent use of computer software?*

   President Lebrun: Our job is not to say whether or not you have done the **right** thing, this is not a **value judgment**.

> *The president corrects the interjection of the government envoy who weighed the enormous work carried out by his administration against some minor slip-ups, but who has confused two types of evaluation. If you ask us for a legal opinion we will give it to you, regardless of the quality of your work. Anyone could invoke the ground* in the Litigation Section. Therefore, the only question is whether you will change your text now in anticipation of our objections, or whether, having been exhausted by the work that was*

---

[69] Remember that the means* ('les moyens' in French) to which we will return in the fourth chapter, are equipped in legal language with a rich and picturesque life: they can be 'raised', they 'prosper', they have 'branches' and even 'sub-branches', they can be 'accepted', they may 'bear fruit', some are 'working' ('opérants') while others 'cannot prosper' and are 'dismissed' as a consequence ...

done, you will go right ahead, fingers crossed, hoping that nobody will notice this little mistake. In any case, don't count on us to make the task easier for you because we know that the plaintiffs' lawyers are not going to spare you just because you have all worked hard and done a good job!

Guénié: As far as the risk of litigation is concerned, this is somewhat dangerous. OK, things are fine now, but what might a private individual say? They might disagree.

President Lebrun: Should we say that although there are errors we will adopt the decree because there is **no risk**? I ask this especially because I had a visit from President Besançon, who showed me a Declaration of Public Benefit that was not very good and also some impact studies that were questionable, and the opinion of the Litigation Section was that 'it is not very good but **it will do**'. So now I think we must be **more cautious**.

This demonstrates the ecology of the Council of State quite wonderfully since the feedback between the two principal functions of the Council works very quickly: the president of sub-section who was recently obliged to annul a Declaration of Public Benefit in the Litigation came to pay a courtesy call on the president of the Counsel Section that had approved the decree. It is never very pleasant for a president of a Counsel Section to have his decree annulled and it is always a bit delicate for a president of sub-section to come trampling on the patch of one of the seven most important members of the Council,[70] the more so because Besançon, a fount of administrative science, sets before him the text of the opinion, which had been carefully preserved in the archives (to which only the sub-section has the right of access); the text indicated that, despite a number of minor errors, the Section had been willing to close its eyes, and that is precisely what the reporter is proposing to do today. Here again we see the peculiar relations of force that we encountered a short while ago. In the light of pressure from the Litigation, which was relayed to him by Besançon, President Lebrun is now taking more care, and he can no longer so easily advise the government to disregard errors on the basis that the real risk of litigation is 'infinitesimal'.

Guénié: That is not our job, we cannot exchange our offices. It is for the government to take the risk. We can say that it 'is not good', but it is for the government to decide, not for us.

[70] See other examples, p. 158.

The reporter Bienaimé: We automatically re-open the file in a case where the public is being misled, but that is **not** the case here. These landowners have pocket handkerchiefs, they **are not going** to protest. The economists are happy. Alright, the errors here may have crossed a certain **threshold**, but there have been **others**.

> *The reporter does not dispute the description of the 'office' of a counsellor of State that has just been given by the last speaker, but he is defending his draft, which, as the result of a process of hybridization, is also the government's draft. The long work of preliminary writing has brought him closer to the government position, and he is now inclined to set the technicalities of the law aside in favour of practice, with which he is quite familiar, and he has no hesitation in attributing a certain psychology to the typical claimant, who, as the owner of a pocket handkerchief, could of course protest but 'will not do so'. He also relies on precedents, drawn not from law but from practice: 'we have been lenient in other cases, so why not here?' At the same time, he emphasizes a fundamental point of law: in this particular case, the public is not being misled, and this point will be taken up in what follows.*

De Servetière: I agree with the reporter. What we must avoid is inaccuracy in the final decision.

Le Men: I do not believe that we should take account of the risk of litigation **in this way**. The question is to know whether there might be **substantial** irregularities, and the 'note' we have to write regarding **potential** litigation must be drawn up as follows: 'these small errors are not likely to lead to, etc.'.

> *This is the kind of note that President Besançon has just brought to the president. When a Section makes too many objections to a text, it sends along with the revised draft a note to the government setting out the problems, and this note remains in the file. It indicates that the Section has, as it said, 'seen the problem' and that it has done its job of quality control, even if the government is always free to assume responsibility for itself.*

Boulanger: What does a map of individual plots look like? (Bienaimé passes him the relevant document in the file.)

> *Here, as so often happens in cases of hesitation, the counsellors return to the basic information so as to deepen the question posed by a preceding speaker. Is the error a substantial one that has to be censured even if the risk is that the governement has to begin all*

over again, or is it a minor, and therefore forgivable, one, as the reporter argues?[71]

Guénié: To back up the reporter, I would say that the inquiry is not one that entails making use of the 'theory of balance', it is carried out simply to find out what is going to happen to one's plot of land. Given that there is no 'theory of balance', whether there has been a mistake or not, no **substantial** error arises.[72] This error does not affect the public benefit. This is not a Declaration of Public Benefit, so it is different.

With this intervention, the word 'substantial' changes its meaning. It no longer means serious or minor, as it does in everyday language, but acquires a precise legal meaning. Had we been dealing with a Declaration of Public Benefit, the 'theory of balance' could have led, as a matter of simple arithmetic, to a situation in which 24 hectares more or less could have tipped the balance since no authorization can be given unless there is some demonstrable public utility. But, since in the present case a precise calculation of this kind is not being made, Guénié's opinion follows that of the reporter and his colleague De Servetière. The public has not been misled, which seems to him to be the most important thing.

Lagouat (indignant): We are being too lenient here; I was once the Prefect of l'Allier in Auvergne, and I don't join with the reporter in congratulating the Agricultural Ministry on its excellent work [which he has indeed done at length in his 'note']. I would vote against.

This intervention comes from a member situated quite low down in the ranking of armchairs and thus in the pecking order; his opinions are always trenchant but do not always attract support, but

[71] During the sessions of this Section, the documents in the file, such as the map and the aerial photograph, circulate often so that counsellors can see them 'for themselves'. This is a quick referential moment, which is nevertheless essential for the formation of judgment. The important documents are pinned on a big board made of cork, to which the envoys and reporters often refer with a quick gesture of the index finger (see chapter 5 on the comparison between science and law).

[72] The theory of balance is a legal construction which is particular to the Council of State and of which it is very proud. It is a balance, through which the Council will check that the administration strikes a balance, between costs and benefits for example, before deciding an expropriation. Thanks to this original way of counting, simply changing a number in the final adding-up means that the outcome changes from positive to negative, making it impossible to declare a decree to be of public utility. See *Ville nouvelle Est* 28 May 1971, concl. Braibant: Long, Weil et al., *Les grands arrêts* (1999), p. 641.

*his reference to a vote reminds the president that the Section's inde-
cision will soon have to be resolved.*[73]

President Lebrun: Yes, we shall vote; this is never very **pleasant**
for the government.

*The president therefore senses that the balance is starting to tilt
towards a rejection of the text. At the same time, as a former administrator, he puts himself in the place of the unfortunate government
envoys who are turning pale; he is well aware that the distinction
he drew earlier, between a value judgment and a judgment of law
is not going to be sufficient to absorb the shock.*

Boulanger: A great many mistakes have been made here; we have
to draw the line somewhere.

*Since the Council of State is at once counsel and censor of the
administration, its members, by virtue of their alternation between
these two functions, also take on the additional role of educating
the government. Boulanger therefore takes over from Lagouat – 'we
are being too lenient here' – and counters the precedents invoked
by the reporter – 'we may have crossed a certain threshold, but there
have been others' – with a terse expression re-imposing limits, which
is after all, the always fluctuating role of law: 'we have to draw the
line somewhere'.*

Renault: I'm just imagining how I would try to address the
argument* if I were in the Litigation; this is after all an error of 25
per cent. During the inquiry no one knew where the error was – now
we know.

Le Men: That is also my **feeling**; we would **love** to **save** the government, but we have to think of all the other cases of public inquiry;
the **tendency** is to **reinforce** quality, in this case it is difficult to
ignore the problem, it would really not be very good for the notion
of public inquiry.

Reporter Bienaimé: But it was the government that noticed the
error! The IGN [the national geographical institute] is not reliable,
the land register is not reliable; if the administration hadn't **corrected**
the error, you wouldn't even have noticed it!

Government envoy (almost pleading): You are in danger of putting
the government in a **difficult** situation, and of **discrediting** the

---

[73] Because the government envoys are standing in front of the president, they get
terribly stiff necks when they respond to questions from counsellors who are of a
less elevated rank, adding to the cruelty of the exercise.

work done on other files [regarding classifications that are still under way].

Two entirely different definitions of 'tendency' are in play here. On the one hand, Le Men and Renault, putting themselves in the shoes of the sub-sections to which they belong, would like to improve the quality of future public inquiries by putting an end to the slippages of administrative offices. On the other hand, the reporter and the government envoy, for the same reasons, emphasize the very high quality of the administration and the need to protect its work. Each side wishes to guarantee the quality of State interventions, but according to opposing criteria.

President Lebrun: We are here to **say the law**. The government can act regardless, but it **takes the risks on itself**. It wouldn't be the first time. We are not **judging** the work of the administration, indeed in this case the administration has done its job very well.

This is a reminder of the difference between jobs, and of the two kinds of quality control. On the one hand, the administration has functioned excellently; but on the other there has been a serious dysfunction in law, which has to be brought to an end. The government takes responsibility for itself; at least it now knows what is at stake. The Council of State has also done its job.

Rallou: This opinion does not call the administration into question; I have quite a clear recollection, it was very difficult, on the contrary, the argument must be turned around and our opinion should reassure everyone in the Region that the work has been carried out properly.

These are the words of a politician, a former Minister who came in via the outside but who is very high up in the ranking of armchairs. Drawing on his own personal recollections, he sees how to 'turn the situation around', and to allow the local elected officials and administrators to congratulate themselves on a job that has been very well done, even though it is going to be censured by the Council of State . . . a difficult balancing act, which is entirely in keeping with a political approach in which questions of law are less interesting than work on the ground.

Lebrun: Shall we vote? Is there no majority for the draft? Mr Bienaimé, do you persist with your draft?

Reporter Bienaimé: Yes, with a note to say that we have **noted** the problem.

*Following the principle of strict individual autonomy in the Council,
the reporter is not at all required to vote in the same way as his
Section. It would be catastrophic for litigation to arise and for the
Section not to have 'noted' the problem, thereby proving that it had
not done its job of quality control. This is one of the famous checks
and balances whose efficacy is ensured by the note accompanying
the file.*

The government envoys leave with their heads held low, and the
reporter briskly emerges to rejoin them in the ante-chamber, consol-
ing them with some soothing explanation of his colleagues' votes,
adding advice on how to present the text next time around. Another
group of envoys, bearing their weighty files, slips into the room to
face the Caudine Forks.

By insisting on their 'job', on their function of 'saying the law', on
the 'right way of evaluating a risk of litigation', on the difference
between a 'value judgment' and 'legal uncertainty', on the marking
of 'thresholds' and the imposition of 'limits', the Section at once edu-
cates itself, calls the government to order, raises the standards for
classification procedures, increases the cost of implementing article
L-415 of the 'Forest Code', reinforces its weight in relation to the
presidents of sub-sections charged with litigation and, finally, judges
the quality of the work done by the reporter who is in the minority
here. This set of minor adjustments, of micro-tensions whose direction has just been reversed, will later allow us to define the work of
the law. But this should not lead us to imagine that the strict rigour
of the law is always in opposition to the work of the State. If the
principle of *dura lex sed lex* had always prevailed, the Council would
never have fulfilled the function that Bonaparte wanted it to fulfil.

For us, the interest of this episode will be made clearer by contrasting it with another, briefer, episode in which the same Section deploys
an entirely opposed process of reasoning which, on the contrary,
'rescues' the government by inventing a hair's-breadth legal fiction
that allows it to escape the horror of a 'legal vacuum'.[74] A short
report made to the Prime Minister by a civil servant in the Ministry
of Public Works notes, in a somewhat horrified tone, that a concession
granted in respect of an airfield in an overseas territory expired on
1 January 1994, and that we are now in May of the same year . . .

---

[74] This expression has become popular but it has no legal meaning since, by definition, the law knows no void. There can be maladjustments, illegalities, but no hole
in it. We will return to the particular nature of what should remain always a seamless fabric in the last chapter.

The government envoy immediately proposes a draft decree rectifying the situation, which they send urgently to the Council of State so that it can enter the writing workshop as soon as possible.

Various amendments will have to be made to the terms of the bid documents establishing the concession of 7 January 1964.

This work is in hand, but further significant updating will be needed before the new concession can be adopted by decree in the Council of State.

The lapse of the current concession has given rise to a **legal vacuum** which might be proven to be **prejudicial** in the event of litigation by third parties, or by the users or occupiers of the airfield.

The draft of the decree and the attached annex therefore seek, by means of a codicil to the original grant, to avoid such inconveniences by prolonging the existing regime for a further two years. (*Extract of the note to the Ministry*)

Clearly, the word 'inconveniences' should be taken as a euphemism: law, like nature, abhors a vacuum, and in the case of an airfield a legal vacuum means that all transactions made in the past six months – contracts, acquisitions, hiring – might be annulled by legal action. If some unfortunate accident were to occur, a persistent lawyer might get hold of the case, and, through some brilliant legal manoeuvre, show that in law the airfield has not existed for months: it has disappeared into the Bermuda triangle of an abeyance of law . . . But the government envoys are going to encounter another inconvenience. The president of the Section, perhaps because he was in something of a hurry, made the mistake of entrusting the file to a reporter who is high up in the pecking order but also somewhat cantankerous, and who instead of doing his best to get the administration out of this quagmire, drafted a note that was even more pessimistic:

The Council of State **has not been able to give** a favourable opinion in respect of this text. Indeed, the concession and the grant that established its terms, granted for a duration of thirty years from 1 January 1964, expired on 31 December 1995. Given that it is not possible to approve a codicil prolonging terms that have expired, the only thing the government can now do is to initiate the necessary procedures for a recovery of assets (. . .).

The government envoys are in a state of consternation – all the more so because the counsellor concludes his report by explaining coldly:

The shameful deeds of the past, which modern vocabulary describes as 'turpitude', should be censured. I refuse to give a favourable opinion. The concession has expired, and approval was not given before 1 January 1995, so there is **nothing to be done**.

A short while ago, in the preceding episode, there was talk of 'setting limits', of respecting the 'tendency' towards an improvement of the State, of whether or not 'thresholds' had been crossed, but the objective was precisely to make texts *progress* by preventing them from slipping from the Charybdis of leniency to the Scylla of formalism. It was necessary that the thing, this mysterious being whose nature we are trying to understand, this unicorn – justice, law, mean – should *pass* and circulate as well as possible. Although the reporter uses the same terms, he does so in order to reach a conclusion that is not very Napoleonic: 'there is nothing to be done'. It is revealing that his colleagues (who are entirely familiar with his foibles, right down to the infliction of words such as 'shameful' and 'turpitude', which are those used in the right-wing press . . .) waste no time discussing his position, by contrast with the preceding example, in which Bienaimé was an eminent reporter who lost none of their esteem even if he was in the minority. Without attaching any importance at all to the position of the reporter, which is wrong in its construction because it leads to impotence and maintains a legal vacuum, the discussion resumes with a view to finding a solution *at any cost*. After some procrastination, the solution is found through a close examination of a photocopy of the original decree, which provides in article 43 that: 'The duration of the award is fixed at thirty years dating from 1 January **following** the grant of the concession.'

President Lebrun (after a silence): We are in an embarrassing situation, I tried to see if we could **rescue** the situation by relying on 'dating from 1 January which follows the grant of the concession'. We could stretch this as far as possible, that would be one solution . . .

Renault: That would be to shift one legal vacuum into another legal vacuum!

Boulanger: Allow me to point out a small contradiction in the reporter's position.[75] There is an irregular year, but is it 1964 or 1994? I would say that in the **interest of good government** it is that which is already behind us!

Le Men (after a break followed by a short flash of inspiration): No, no, but there is **no** problem; from 1 January 1964, if we start from 1 January 1965, thirty years takes us to 1 January 1995!

---

[75] The two counsellors have been located side by side for years, in the armchairs as well as in the ranking of the 'roster' in which they inexorably ascend – see chapter 3 – but they are at opposite ends of the political spectrum. That is where the extreme and slightly sardonic politeness which they express towards each other comes from.

The reporter (without great conviction): I find that terribly shocking.

President Lebrun: We have rescued the government by the skin of its teeth.

The reporter: Especially given that the administration admitted that the award had expired, if it was wrong on that point, the report to the Prime Minister must be changed [see p. 55].

President Lebrun: The concession is for thirty years but, in fact, it is for a period between 30 and 31 years, a judge would tear his hair out. The argument is stretched very thin, it's a **neat trick**! (subtle smiles)

[addressing himself to the government envoy] What do you **want**? What do you **expect**? 1995 doesn't seem very far off to me, would you have enough time (to renew the concession)?

The reporter: They say that because at the Council of State things take a long time . . .

Lebrun: It's straightforward, they take six months where we take two weeks, the Council of State is just a scapegoat.[76]

Of course this is a 'neat trick', of course it is so stretched that 'a judge would tear his hair out', and the government does have to be 'rescued', but the 'embarrassment' has finally been resolved, from a situation of being bogged down, from the small 'there is nothing to be done' in which the reporter wanted to dead-end them, without proposing any other solution. The law must pass, even at the risk of 'shifting one legal vacuum into another legal vacuum'. Just as the president did his job earlier by identifying legal difficulties where his reporter proposed to turn a blind eye to the minor mistakes of practice, so the same president now invents a solution which he acknowledges to be shaky against the opinion of his reporter, who sees a simple legal difficulty as an insurmountable obstacle. In both cases, and in the 'interests of good government', something *other* than the strict application of a rule is moved forwards.

Everyone agrees, of course, that if the concession has expired, there is nothing to be done. But has it really expired? No, one need only read the original text somewhat creatively: the concession began only on 1 January 1965, and in May 1994 it has not yet expired, so the government envoys have only to draw up their corrective decree and

---

[76] One of the numerous critical remarks on the slowness of the Council. Let us recall that, by definition, the Counsel Sections work under time pressure because they must rewrite the texts before the deadlines of the legislative calendar, which are always tight – cabinet meetings, parliamentary sessions, etc. They cannot allow themselves to adopt the senatorial pace of the Litigation Section.

need only renew the concession within the time limit contemplated by the original grant. One need not even suppose that 1964 was the year of an unnoticed legal vacuum, which would be somewhat extravagant . . . The slender footbridge of a *fictio legis* has provided a way out of an embarrassing situation, and enabled an escape from deadlock.[77] Everything now takes place as it should. The vacuum has been replenished. Aeroplanes can now land at this tropical airfield in all legality, with no risk of disappearing into a black hole. *Mollis lex, sed lex*: the law is flexible, *but it is still law.*[78]

What a strange writing workshop

It is often said that a difficult text should not be written by several people, and that a camel is a horse drawn by a committee . . . So what takes place in this enormous room, with its ornate mouldings, this immense amphitheatre whose wings abut a sort of tribunal in which are sitting characters whose considerable importance seems to be conveyed by the size of their armchairs? Above the platform, as if to symbolize both the uncertainty of the counsellors who are mired in their discussion and the perplexity of the observer, there extends a fresco depicting an old man in *fin-de-siècle* costume, who is so lost in thought that he is tugging on his beard in the middle of a dark forest, rather like someone who has just inadvertently lost his keys.[79] The Council has a decidedly strange approach to its choice of emblems. This is a Thursday morning, and we are now in the General Assembly of the Council of State participating in some immense writing workshop for adults.[80]

A voice thunders: 'Here we make law!' The voice is that of the 'Vice-president' of the Council, a character who is every bit as

---

[77] The word 'fiction' does not imply either cynicism, or unreality, but the invention of a solution to make the law 'move forward'. To convince oneself of this, see the magnificent article by Thomas, *'Fictio Legis'* (1995).

[78] This is a hint to the classic book by Carbonnier, *Flexible droit* (1998). The *'sans rigueur'* of the sub-title unfortunately applies to the sociology of the author as much as it does to the law he describes.

[79] The series of frescoes attributed to Henri Martin (1860–1943) and entitled 'laborious France before the Conseil d'Etat' does not seem to have found the best way to represent 'intellectual work', after having represented labourers working on the pavement of the Place de la Concorde, harvests and the harbour of Marseille . . .

[80] Not to be confused with the 'Assemblée du Contentieux' (Litigation Assembly) which represents the highest panel of *judgment* on the Litigation side. Here, it is the highest body able to provide *legal advice* sitting as counsel of the government.

Figure 1.4

impressive as the platform from which he is speaking or the monumental seat in which he is enthroned:[81]

> The government envoy (somewhat beseechingly): Monsieur le Vicepresident, the government is **particularly attached** to the term 'contract', which has been the subject of much **negotiation**. It enables the responsibilization of actors in the Hospital. That may not be its **pure legal meaning**, but an agreement between parties is not **very legal**, it is a general rule; these words have a strong value.
>
> The Vice-president (firm and banging on the table): This is the tyranny of words! Here **we make law**. We let 'accreditation' pass, but 'contract' **has** a legal meaning.
>
> Lebrun: Yes, here 'contract' has no meaning, the Hospital does not make a 'contract' with the Minister.
>
> Government envoys: The text of the government said, if I may say so, 'implementing contextualization'.
>
> The Vice-president: That is an even **uglier** use of the language!

[81] It is strange that the most important character of the Council, the principal character of the Administration in the order of protocol, who is surrounded by 'presidents' (of the Section and sub-section, former or practising ones) is the only one who carries the more modest title of 'Vice-President' – it is the Prime Minister who officially has the title of 'President of the Council of State'.

What are these peculiar phrases that have to have a 'strong value', to which the government is 'particularly attached', which have been the subject of 'much negotiation' and which nevertheless have no 'legal meaning' and constitute an 'ugly' use of French? Whereas the government envoys have one foot in active government, and still hear the voices of the unions, the difficulties of mayors, and are anticipating the objections of Members of Parliament and the sophistry of senators, they have to lend strong words the added force of the law.

We should notice the extreme discomfort of this writing workshop. On the platform, comfortably seated, we have in the centre the Vice-President, by rank the highest member of the whole French administration, flanked on each side by the presidents of the Counsel Sections, who are joined by the president of the Litigation Section. Before them stands the reporter, with his back turned towards them, which means that he has to twist his neck at each intervention; following discussion in a meeting of the Counsel Section resembling that which we have just followed, the reporter has drafted his own text, and is addressing himself to his colleagues, who are all eminent members of the Council ranked according to the strict order of the promotion roster. Behind them, randomly seated, we find the government envoys, a few interns, a number of younger members who do not have the right to vote but who come to sample the atmosphere when the case is sufficiently interesting and, of course, the irrepressible ethnographer, who had some difficulty gaining access to this most sacred of places, and who has been shoved as far back as possible in the uppermost benches. A blind bailiff adjusts the volume of the microphones according to who is taking the floor. He is a colourful character whose popular speech clashes somewhat with his solemn uniform. For important texts, passage through the General Assembly is the final test before a bill is submitted to the Council of Ministers, before being once again torn up and dismembered by the Members of Parliament and the Senate. Although the debates are recorded and transcribed in minutes that are kept on file, the discussion is strictly confidential, on the same basis as a discussion between a private client and his legal counsel. On this Thursday morning, we have penetrated into the privy counsel of Sovereigns: Ministers themselves have not yet read the texts that are discussed here.

As in a writing workshop, the collective task consists in improving the quality of the text by comparing two drafts, a pink text called the 'government text', which is defended by the government envoy, and a white text called the 'text of the Section', which is defended by the reporter and integrates most of the corrections that have been made, as we just saw, in the Section preliminary examination. As always at the Council, the explicit ordeal based on cases and texts is supplemented by another, that is more subtle, continuous and diffuse, but all the more merciless, and which is undergone by the counsellors themselves before their peers: have they done their job properly? Have they fully anticipated all the difficulties? Besides the reporters, the quality of the Counsel Section that prepared the Assembly a few days before is also being judged: did it see all the legal or practical contradictions? Is the reporter's draft a good one? If not, the Assembly might lose hours in the impossible task of drafting a horrendously complex text between so many people.

The reader should imagine this group of counsellors immersed in their files, comparing the not-very-synoptic versions of the different drafts, juggling with the documentation, annotating and deleting, recording versions that have just been approved, getting cricks in their neck from listening to the explanations thrown up behind them by the government envoys, all the while gesticulating to get the Vice-President, who resembles a thundering Jupiter, to give them the floor. This operation of transsubstantiating legally weak texts into legally strong texts is still mysterious to us. For now, we should observe only that it is the object of a constant fumbling in which the counsellors feel their way forward, as we see in this exchange, which occurred in the discussion of another important statute:

Vice-president: Why put '1.1.1998'? You are not going to recruit on New Year's Day, that is ridiculous!

A government envoy (very calm): Yes it is a **trick**. The unions have said 1998 and the government '1 January'. We have gained twelve months. They have fifteen days to take notice. It is a bit ridiculous [I admit].

Another government envoy: **Purely legally**, it is not necessary to say it again, to repeat it. But it is **the political heart** of the bill. It would be very embarrassing for us if the personnel did not **see** this provision [in the text]. It has to be explicit. We are quite insistent on this. This is not a useless clarification (. . .)

Robinet: I believe that **at the legal level** a heading must be given to article 12. There are reasons of **opportunity**.

Guénié: Each to his own profession. If the government wishes to do so, it can add one. **It is not for the Council of State** to do so. From a legal point of view, the position of the Section cannot be disputed.

Vice-president: Shall we vote? Each to his own profession. We're trying to make **decent** texts. It is for the government to take its responsibilities for reasons of political opportunity.

Once again, a confession emerging from the backstage of politics and a reference to the minor subterfuges of negotiations in no way alter the obligation to 'say the law', which the 'Vice-president' rather modestly calls 'trying to make decent texts'. Of course, the text changes shape under the pressure of unions and politicians, and in view of the necessity of being 'seen' by negotiators, but it does not fall apart. The government holds on to its risky formulations; the Council of State still has to produce solid legal texts. The final document will bear the traces of the different constraints that are recognized in the distinction between 'political appropriateness' and the 'sphere of law': 'each to his own profession'.

Sometimes the tension is much more vivid, as in a discussion which took place a few years earlier concerning a statute with significant political connotations.

The Vice-president (after having listened to the reading of the preamble): We are not in Rwanda! It is nonsensical to ask Parliament to approve a preamble in which it is said that the law is no longer being applied! That means that the Minister is incapable of appointing his own personnel. We have a Constitution! There is the separation of powers! If we allow this to be voted upon, everyone will feel unprotected and think that they have the right to take up arms to protect their property. This is scare-mongering!

A counsellor: [Yes] We live in a constitutional democracy, we have discussed this in the Section.

Another counsellor: This is a **political** declaration; it is part of a declaration to Parliament. This sort of thing is not to be **transposed** to the exposition of motives. If I were a Member of Parliament I could propose amendments. But **these are not normative texts**, this is **literature**! This would be too slack. [I propose] a straightforward rejection!

Reporter (approving): We should not go too far in this kind of exercise. A massive **deletion** must be carried out! (. . .)

Miss Répons: Things are generally becoming too slack. This is just a matter of programming, there are annexes for that. It is time that we put an end to all this by setting a limit. Parliament will be overburdened by texts that do not concern it. There will be normative parts and enormous annexes and they will end up forgetting what exactly is normative.

Third counsellor: It is not the custom of the Council of State to approve the exposition of motives.

Fourth counsellor (disagreeing): No, this is **important**. The fourteen-year-old daughter of someone in my block of flats has been raped; this is important, we have to **take care**. We must facilitate the passage of this annex. When things happen to other people, fine, but when they happen to those close to us, it is different! (. . .)

Miss Répons: None of us, not us, not the Parliament, not anyone, knows what we approve. Hence our **uncertainty**.

The Secretary General:[82] If the Council of State were to embark on the rewriting of annexes, we would be led **too far**. The government must simply take note [of the discussion or of the disagreement] of the Assembly.

In a few seconds the counsellors pass from weighty considerations of the 'constitutional democracy' or the 'separation of powers' to common-sense remarks about the rape of a young girl, by way of arguments on the difference between political ideology, 'normative texts' and 'literature', and ending with an argument about how to rewrite texts, about the customs of the Council of State, and on the best way of distributing arguments between annexes, preambles and general declarations. All these scattered elements have to merge into a text that still remains in the state of a draft. The Council must 'set a limit', 'take care', it must not allow itself to be 'led too far' – that is, it must write 'acceptable texts' that are not immediately dismantled by Parliament, contested by litigants or annulled by the Litigation Section: in short, texts that are capable of resisting any kind of ordeal.[83]

By now, the reader will have understood that the Council has two different but complementary roles: that of an administrative court in the Litigation Section and that of a legal adviser for drafting all legislative bills and governmental decrees. In the first of these roles, it takes account only of administrative law and intervenes only a posteriori, once a litigant has been moved, shocked, made indignant or injured, and has bestirred himself, usually with the help of a lawyer,

---

[82] The Secretary General of the Council of State is seated in these general assemblies to the left of the room, on a separate platform from where he follows the course of the whole procedure. He manages the whole institution as well.

[83] We do not pose the delicate question here of the usefulness of these rewriting practices . . . 'In reality', wrote Kessler in 1968, 'the domain of influence of the Council of State is very limited because it is situated in an intermediary zone between minor problems, on which the government consults it most willingly, and political problems on which its opinion is hardly heard': Kessler, *Le Conseil d'Etat* (1968), p. 302. It is difficult to appreciate whether, over a period of thirty years, the government's listening has improved or not. If we are to believe the rumours in the corridors about it, we will readily say that 'the level is getting lower'. Conversely, a counsellor does not hesitate to say: 'I have had much more power in the Counsel Section than as a Minister' (interview 24 June 1996) because of the absence of hierarchy, tension and self-censoring at the Council.

to find some flaw in a decision of the government, with a view to
having it annulled. The difficulty of the second role stems entirely
from the fact that the counsellors act a priori on the quality control
of decrees which not yet been contested and laws which have not yet
been scrutinized by Parliament. In this second capacity, far from
limiting themselves to administrative law, the counsellors have to
be familiar with *all* branches of law. Hence the vital distinction
between different 'Sections', each specializing in the legal output of
several Ministries. Whereas the arguments* raised by the litigants
guide – and contain – the reasoning of the Litigation Section,[84] the
Counsel Sections must exercise a mode of divination that is more
perilous: they have to anticipate through various thought experiments
all the problems, obstacles, ordeals and drawbacks that the draft of
the document might encounter. The Council works a bit like the
National Bureau of Standards, in which consumer products are
subjected to all sorts of appalling tribulations before being given a
label of quality authorizing their sale to the public. In order to give
mere words the strength to resist all these constraints, *everything
must be thought of in advance*: not only the law, but also the French
language, the feasibility of measures taken, labour practices, and
even the political timeliness of this or that bill.[85] However, the
solemnity of the occasion, the authoritative tone of the voices and
the grandeur of the room should not obscure the point that – by
contrast with the Litigation – this is only an advisory body, and that
the government can still choose, once its draft has been thoroughly
reworked, to present its own text.[86] In this particular domain, unlike
the rooms which we have visited on the other side of the palace, the

---

[84] Let us recall that, besides the means* which are said to be 'of public order', which
the Council can raise itself, the constraints of the principle that both parties shall
be heard obliges it to keep itself strictly to the arguments developed by the claimants.
Unless the members decide to 'make an "effort"', but that is always risky (see
p. 99).

[85] This process of quality control through anticipation can produce failures, as we
can see in the recent example of the reprimanding by the Constitutional Court of
the reduction of a new tax for low salaries as foreseen in the finance law of 2001.
As one of the senior civil servants in charge of the text said in an apologetic manner:
'We expected criticisms on certain points but not a pure and simple nullification.
Neither the Council of State, nor the Secretariat General of the Government *had
alerted us to this risk*' (my emphasis) *Le Monde*, Thursday 21 December 2000.

[86] The government can either maintain its initial text or adopt that of the Council,
but it cannot mix the two without it constituting another draft which would have
to be subject to a new passage through the Council. As the authors of a recent book
say, it is this which makes the question of the efficiency of the Council 'a delicate
subject': Massot et al., *Le Conseil d'Etat. De L'An VIII à nos jours* (1999), p. 77.

counsellors – as impressive as they might be – do not have the last word.

Before leaving Thursday's General Assembly, let us familiarize ourselves once again with the writing practices, and the very specific work of collectively improving texts of which we will need a good understanding for the next chapter.

Lebrun (president of the Section which presents the text to the Assembly): The text is monstrous, or at least complicated. But the Section could **see no legal objection** preventing the government from pursuing its bill.

A counsellor (rummaging through his file): Where is the impact study?[87]

The president of the Section of Public Works: It consisted of three carelessly drafted and useless pages; it was not distributed.

Vice-president (gruff and solemn): The Secretariat General of the Government and the Prime Minister have to see the full implications of this; there should be no clowning around. I am sceptical.

The reporter (in a placatory tone): We would need an impact study if we were colonizing Mars, but here I think we know what is involved (reading his text):[88]

'Article 1

Paragraph 3°) of article L 313 (. . .) is replaced by the following provisions:

'3°) elaborates, in the public interest, **recommendations** to partners for the purposes mentioned in 2°)'

Besançon (interrupting, having just read the other version): I have to say that the government's draft had the virtue of being **clear** [everyone refers to the draft in a ballet of rapidly turned salmon-coloured sheets] (reading):

'3°) elaborates in the public interest recommendations for the purposes mentioned in 2°). These recommendations cannot derogate either from the regulations or from the terms of the agreements provided for in 2°)'.

---

[87] In the same way as there are mandatory studies on the impact which some factory may have on the environment ('installations classées'), there is now a legal obligation for each new text of law to make a study of the impact that it can have on other texts of law – a bit as if the law were an overgrown forest, even a jungle, or in any case a second nature, whose transformations are difficult to foresee.

[88] The reporter does not present his own opinion any more as he did in the episodes studied in the preceding section. He now speaks in the name of the whole Counsel Section together, even if he does not in any way share its solution. This forms part of the subtle ordeals of objectivation that we will study in chapter 5.

Vice-president: 'Recommendation' – anyone can make a recommendation; this is not private law. Executive decisions are public law.

Another president of Section (addressing the room from the platform): If we use 'recommendation' in such a **banal** sense, it is hardly worth using it.

Third president of Section: If it is a recommendation then it must have a certain **force**, otherwise it has no purpose.

The reporter (turning his back to his colleagues): Yes, there is an article which refers to 'recommendations that must be respected', so there is a possibility of litigation.

Lebrun (speaking in the name of his Section): In our mind, 'recommendation' had the meaning that the Vice-president gives it, it has no mandatory force at all. The social economy might give it a certain legitimacy, just as CNIL [Commission nationale informatique et liberté] does for its members. But the reporter . . . (hesitating) that said, and **this hadn't occurred to me until now**, there is a **contradiction** here because the union has the right to enforce these recommendations. What did the government envoy have **in the back of his mind**?

Vice-president: Mr government envoy?

Government envoy: You are right, Mr Vice-president, that is the correct interpretation. In the case of a recommendation the State is not a party; it is a matter of private law, agreements are binding, recommendations are not. But we would still like to know what is going on. It's about gathering information, **there is no sanction**, it's a matter of being able to exercise control. Only serious failings are sanctioned, so as to set limits.

Vice-president: A certain **legal quality** is attached to recommendations; if there are serious and repeated breaches, they can lead to a sanction. This is no longer a simple recommendation. As a legal act, it is something of a **hybrid**. A single recommendation is nothing, but taken together, as a whole, they form . . .

Besançon: Careful, we are in the process of creating, *mutatis mutandis*, something like our *Orcibal* decision.

Vice-president (interrupting): Let's leave Mr Orcibal in peace! That is not our problem.

Besançon (obstinate): But we are intervening in private law. We should **go back** to the government's text!

A counsellor (a former president of Section): This is a private law text, which is subject to prevailing regulations; I'm not sure what point there is in saying so.

Vice-president: What is the view of the Section?

Lebrun: We **didn't** discuss it. I now see the problem, and I may be about to **change my mind**. The Section may not have been entirely **aware** of this problem.

A **fourth president of Section**: We are anticipating the interpretation of article 5, but I would maintain the very banal meaning of 'recommendation'. It would be a mistake **to give a legal value** to a simple recommendation.

Lebrun: We shall see then when we discuss article 5, which deals with sanctions. **We must be coherent**. So let's postpone. If we accept sanctions in respect of this article, then we have to change the meaning of article 2, in one direction or another.

In this way, every Thursday, those counsellors who are members of the General Assembly and who are highest in the order of the roster, the presidents of Section and the Vice-president, encounter each other and engage in a process of mutual testing. It is easy to imagine the courteous but nonetheless powerful pressure exercised on each by the objections of colleagues. This process of mutual surveillance is nicely revealed in the excuses which President Lebrun has to formulate for not having 'seen' the problem in his Section – 'We didn't discuss it.' The president of the Section has to acknowledge that he only 'became aware' of the difficulty under the pressure of the general Assembly and that he is in the process of 'changing his mind'.[89] It is here that one sees the justification for having a two-stage system – the Sections and then the General Assembly. Because of this system the life expectancy of drafts that have been thoroughly 'debugged', as programmers say of software, is increased. In this particular case, the error is minuscule, but as ever the enormous risk of litigation looms large in all uncertainty in a text. If the little word 'recommendation' takes on a 'legal value', then there might be 'sanctions', and therefore appeals. If the text of the law being discussed today is not clear, it might be thrown out by Parliament, struck down by the Constitutional Council; worse, it might give rise to a confusion between the norms of private law and those of administrative law, which is what Besançon, a living encyclopaedia

[89] This type of mild violence can be found in all of the work of the Sections. Renault excuses himself for not having 'seen' that it concerned a Declaration of Public Utility: 'I am sorry that I have not seen the problem before.' President Lebrun (paternal, but nevertheless driving the nail home) 'oh no, no . . .'. Or later, in the same case, Bienaimé suavely addresses a dear colleague: 'The reporter cites the "Guide of the reporter" which proposes dashes, but I would not have the cruelty to cite what it says: "the dash hides a deficit of thought!".' It is in this polite way that the counsellors mutually keep each other vigilant!

of the Council, suggests, despite the sharp reply of an impatient
Vice-president.

While climbing the main staircase

'How can this be? Is there really nothing more elevated going on in
this supposedly *supreme* court, beyond these infinitely small discussions on words and drafts?' the ethnographer asks himself while
adjusting his tie and straightening his posture at the foot of a grand
staircase. He is doing his best to walk with an air of gravity that
mimics, as well as he can manage, the style of a Counsellor of State.
He twists his tongue inside-out in the vain hope of learning to speak
like a counsellor. 'Is there really nothing above the law?' Is this the
way, in this skewed palace, by these hidden staircases, thanks to these
dozing bailiffs, on these worn carpets, in these piles of paper and
bound volumes, through these endless discussions, these candid confessions of prejudice and ignorance, and this archaic compilation
formed by cutting and pasting obscure texts, that the reign of the law
is established?

Naively, he looks at the ceiling and turns towards the beautiful
trompe-l'œil which adorns the main staircase (yet another curiously
chosen emblem of the grandeur of jurists . . .), as though he has missed
something, as though *above* the Palais-Royal there existed something
greater than these National School of Administration graduates, a
goddess of Justice (but no, he tells himself, even the frescoes have the
despairing banality of the dullest mythologies), perhaps another office
(but he has visited them all), or another body (impossible, because he
has drawn up a complete statistical map of all the members), a reservoir of knowledge (no, in the basement there are only archives, and
in the attics of other offices, only other archives), a source of absolute
certainty which had escaped him (perhaps the *Lebon* volumes? but
he has looked through them and they consists only of pages bound
to other pages), a president above the Vice-president (but that could
only be the Prime Minister, who never sits in the Council), a buried
hoard of authoritative commentaries (impossible, because here the
doctrinal glosses of faculty professors elicit only amused indifference). It has to be accepted: there exist no other means to 'say the
law', to put an end to disputes or to have the last word, other than
by way of these dense files, the slow work of rewriting, the incessant
reworking of documents, and by way of precedents retrieved from
the dust of the past, and opinions sought from colleagues in suits and
ties whose quiet and dull gatherings are more similar to an English

club of the nineteenth century. It seems that humanity has found no better way of having the last word, nothing firmer, more modern, more reasoned, more grandiose or more majestic. There is nothing superior to the supreme court. Above this somewhat derisory institution, there is nothing better, quicker, more efficient, more economical and, above all, nothing that would be more just.

Let us leave to others the sad task of bemoaning the arrogance of the Council – besides, the counsellors often make fun of themselves by mocking their own customs and foibles. All things considered, walking towards the site of his field work, the ethnographer feels rather emotional, gradually taking on, almost as though he were slipping into a toga, the physical habits of those he is studying, so as better to understand the place and to blend into the landscape. In fact, the analyst should admit to being quite moved by this hazardous configuration, this house of cards, palace of laws and mountain of paper, whose fragility by itself, without any other resources, warrants or reserves, secures the force of the law. 'Let no one enter herein if he believes in the transcendence of the law'; that is what should be inscribed above the overly solemn staircase. There are no angels, demons or supermen here, only ordinary National School of Administration graduates with no other instruments than texts and words. The quality of the work here consists entirely in bodies, mouths and voices, processes of writing and archiving, regularly maintained conversations, and the meticulous fattening of files in grey or yellow folders. We should not be surprised if the Romans would have been astonished by the grandeur of this sort of immanence, which has absolutely nothing in common with learned passion, religious or political enthusiasm, keen hatred or the devastating risks of strategy. Darning, knitting and a ceaseless, patient, stubborn and pedestrian piece-working: a grey-on-grey that is much more beautiful, and above all much more just, than the bright colours of passion.

2

How to make a file ripe for use

In which the readers, who are becoming more and more restless, try to follow the author who takes great interest in the fate of the files of the Council of State, as if it concerned the most important thing in the world – Where we discover the material, textual and graphic environment of the Council, fortunately assisted by some photographs – Where we immerse ourselves in the arrangement of quotations and folders in order to understand the legal work – Where we visit the 'workplace' of the counsellors and consider the difficult labour through which they produce writings from other writings

The trials and tribulations of a number

What is more grey, more dusty, more worthy of contempt than piles of files? Yet, the ethnographer has no choice. Since he does not know the law, he must – in order to follow its particular movement – discover something material belonging to it which is visible, and that can be located and traced. Now, there exists something that traces and organizes all the activity of the Council. It forms the object of all types of care, of all conversations, and it allows continuous movement – without missing a step – from the most inarticulate complaint to the most sublime points of doctrine and even to this ersatz of eternal life made possible by the *Lebon* volume: it is the *file*. Every case, at least in our countries of written law, is physically enveloped in a carton folder held together with elastic bands. Even though it is not attributed any place in legal theories, it is by moving through this palace while following this little animal that we are going to become acquainted with all the various functions of the Palais-Royal.[1] If the ethnographer wants to achieve this unstable mix of proximity (that only a field study can obtain) and detachment (which allows him to avoid immediately attaching himself to concepts which have been worn out by much prolonged usage), then it is sufficient for him to substitute the grand talk about Law, Justice and Norms with a meticulous inquiry about files – grey, beige or yellow, thin or thick, easy or complex, old or new – and to see where they lead him. Yes, let us begin law at the beginning, that is to say at the stamps, elastic bands, paperclips and other office paraphernalia which are the indispensable tools of cases. Jurists always speak of texts, but rarely of their materiality.[2] It is to this materiality that we must apply ourselves.

Figure 2.1

[1] The study of files, however, occupies an important place in the cognitive sciences as well as in the administrative sciences: Cambrosio, Limoges et al., 'Representing Biotechnology' (1990); Goody, *La logique de l'écriture* (1986); Roqueplo, 'Regards sur la complexité du pouvoir' (1990); Richards, *The Imperial Archive* (1993); and of course the pioneering work of Béatrice Fraenkel.

[2] Obviously, except in the works of Pierre Legendre: see, in particular, Legendre, *Leçons I* (1998); Legendre, *Sur la question dogmatique en Occident* (1999), but here

Files do not enter the Council through the solemn door which opens onto the grand staircase, but through the small door of the mail room and begin with a 'requête introductive d'instance' (introductory claim in proceedings) that can be written on a blank piece of paper. A simple letter posted to the address of the Palais-Royal, or even sent by fax, can suffice. Even though every lawyer introduces legal language into the claim, we can sometimes still recognize the smothered echo of the original complaint in it: rage, indignation, scandal, something which belongs to the psychological, anthropological and sociological subject matter and which has given rise to anger and sadness somewhere in France. However, it concerns an anger and a sadness which are not only expressed by violence and tears, screams and blows, but which – through a rather mysterious mutation – decide to transform into fraud and grievance: in short, in more or less well argued writing which is addressed to an administrative tribunal.[3]

There is quite a distance between groaning, growling or protest and the writing of a claim.[4] There are no statistics that would allow us to compare the small percentage of complaints which give rise to more or less violent conflict with the immense mass of administrative decisions which unfold without their particular history becoming known. Nor is it possible to measure, among this percentage, the infinitely small amount of rage or indignation which is going to be

---

it concerns a text transformed into the myth of a Book. We find in Bourcier and Mackay (eds.), *Lire le droit* (1992) and Bourcier and Thomasset (eds.), *L'Ecriture du droit* (1996), numerous articles on the legal text in which its textuality – in the semiotic sense – is well recognized. However, they have lost the oral element, which is indispensable for grasping texts, as well as the file in its very material sense, whose circulation alone allows us to qualify the legal trajectory. On the act of legal writing regarding environmental law, see Charvolin, *L'invention de l'environnement en France* (1993).

[3] A whole history of public space is of course needed in order for the confused complaint to become an articulated right. See, for example, on the exemplary case of blasphemy, the beautiful study by Claverie, 'Sainte indignation contre indignation éclairée' (1992), and, on the new tool allowed by Roman law, the unrivalled example of Boureau, *La loi du royaume* (2001), in particular chapter V on the monk Thomas of Marlborough at the papal court.

[4] One example among thousands in *Libération* of 12 July 2000: 'However, we have seen it, the statement of the jury deciding on the graduation for the bachelor's degree is not so clear. But the gracious appeal introduced in November by Daniel Escuirola, 20 years old, has been rejected by the chief education officer. Afterwards, *discouraged*, Daniel has *let* the matter *slip*, and has *not* submitted an appeal for litigation at the administrative tribunal. In any case, as was indicated to the local education authority, the administrative tribunal would not have given him the diploma. It would perhaps simply have increased his indemnity after four years of procedure' (emphasis added).

transformed into a claim in correct and due form. Daily 62 million French people complain of the State. Nevertheless, this only produces hardly more than 150,000 cases per year.[5] No statistic is sufficiently subtle to explain the reasons for this passage to action. It may have been an attorney who has put the idea forward to start proceedings: 'but we can plead that, dear Sir'. The claimant himself may have vast legal experience and not balk at a procedure which he knows will take a long time. It can concern an NGO – which has become familiar with the administrative law a long time ago and which hopes to obtain through it what other forms of public action or persuasion have not been able to give them – defending a certain site, environment or neighbourhood.[6] Perhaps it concerns a candidate MP who has been beaten by a couple of votes in a muddled election and who wishes to regain, through proper elections, the seat that he, according to him, has unjustly lost. A union for civil servants perhaps sets out to dispute a decree which disadvantages one of its members. Or a Prefect convinces himself that, if he does not appeal such or such decision of this or that administrative tribunal, his margin of appreciation will be reduced forever. In short, when the first appeal arrives at the Palais-Royal, it has already undergone a long history which for the most part escapes the ethnographer as well as the counsellors, but whose traces can be recognized at first sight from the type of letter-headed paper, from the presence and name of some famous and expensive lawyer's firm, from the manner of writing and from the greater or lesser display of legal knowledge, texts of laws and decrees and learned words taken from Molière.[7]

Whatever the degree of seriousness of its history – whether it concerns nuclear tests in the Pacific which are disputed by the organization Greenpeace or a sordid story of a tax adjustment – the mail is enveloped, from its arrival, in a carton *folder* with a grey colour and

[5] In 1997 the administrative tribunals received 101,590 cases, the administrative courts of appeal 14,477, and the Council 7,193. The tribunals dealt with 96,367 of them, the courts of appeal 7,461, and the Council 11,173. There were 188,653 cases pending before the tribunals, 24,016 before the courts, and 10,385 before the Council (*Rapport public* of the Council of State, 1998).

[6] See, for example, the Association TOS which has become familiar with the procedure, as studied by Christelle Gramaglia, 'La mise en cause environnementale' (2005).

[7] These are differences that are very visible in the attempt at generalizing the cause of all 'cases', as Luc Boltanski has shown well: 'La dénonciation' (1984). At the same time, the files of cases which he has studied nevertheless do not go on to produce 'legal means' of law, even if they gather together arguments, because they are not received by the networks which are capable of transforming complaints into an appeal.

is given a *number* drawn from the log book which is solemnly stamped by the Clerk's Office. This ordering number is going to serve as the indicator for the case until the end of its time. We find it in ARIANE, the information database SKIPPER, as well as in the *Lebon* volumes. The modest letter or voluminous mail which was sent by post, received and put in a folder will bear that number forever. It is this number that is going to put those in charge at the Council, who have their eyes fixed on the statutory time limits, in a cold sweat. This number enables them to measure the sometimes vertiginous delays that have accumulated: 'But in the end it is a 154,000 number, we cannot just send it back to the court of appeal!' a certain counsellor will say. The president will indignantly say, 'the 120,000 numbers are still pending', and everyone will understand that things must be speeded up and that the backlog must be gradually reduced. For the moment, this number is the only thing that the claimant receives in response to his letter: an acknowledgement of receipt and a place in a queue whose speed and, of course, eventual destination he is ignorant of.

Figure 2.2

However, we should not accuse the Clerk's Office of indifference or heartlessness. The tragic or petty, passionate or calculated history which triggered the complaint continues and, as we have seen in the previous chapter, constantly accompanies the progression of the file. However, it must now be presented in the form of accompanying documents which are called 'productions'.

To help the readers picture the material nature of a file, let us choose as one example a very sad file selected arbitrarily among many others. A young man has been killed while he was skiing in a part of the town of B. 'There is no need to insist on the pain of the claimant', writes the lawyer, 'who already was a widower and has been cruelly struck by destiny several times before, in order to understand the importance of the damage suffered by the loss of someone who, through the cruelty of fate, was his only descendant'. This file asks the administrative tribunal 'to be so disposed as to order the town of B. to pay [to the father] the sum of 306,492.19 francs as reparation for his moral and material damages with statutory interest counting from the day on which the contested judgment was rendered'.

Whatever pain a father may suffer when losing his son, he must now *prove* that the Mayor has committed an error by not closing the ski station during the heavy snowfall. He must seek to do this by using documents which at once refer to the state of affairs *exterior* to the file and *give confidence* – that is to say that they transport quasi-legal forms of trust. This is certainly the case with the numerous reports of policemen or bailiffs, attestations, certified copies, witness statements, certificates and other various documentary evidence, which all carry the mark of other institutions which are situated upstream and are already capable of producing law or, in any case, of putting pieces of empirical evidence into a legal format. Without these countless institutions, no file could support its claim with credible 'productions'. Even though our aim here is not to follow these institutions, let us not forget the role they play in the final judgment. When counsellors a few years later say 'the Council of State has decided', it has only pronounced itself on a file which is composed of documents that have already been profiled so as to be, so to speak, 'judgment-compatible'. The minute part of the work of the Council must merely be added to the immense labour of 'shaping' and 'formatting' evidence which alone allows for the Council to carry out its task efficiently. The whole of France, if we agree to see it that way, tirelessly 'produces' and in a way secretes innumerable documents through all its pores, which are able to transform themselves immediately, if circumstances require it, into useful pieces of evidence in a case.

In order to see this, let us flip through the pages of this particular folder. Among the productions, we find a report by a policeman which summarizes the witness statement of a passer-by who was asked to check the skis and clothes of the young victim. There is another report by a skier, who gives a witness statement about the fact that all ski-run markings prohibiting the use of the ski runs were

absent, despite the bad weather. There are several letters from different doctors at the hospital, who have examined and cared for the
body of the patient. There is a long disposition by the unfortunate
father, summarized by a police inspector at the request of the
'Procureur de la République'. There is a letter on a blank piece of
paper from the sports association that organized the trip, which
explains the whole event in its own words. There is a certificate from
the family doctor attesting to the good health of the victim throughout his whole life. There are several documents of preliminary inquiry
from the police, as well as a very thick file which they have prepared
and which gives an idea of the relevant locations, thanks to Ordnance
Survey maps and even photos of the ski run. There is a confirmation
from the national meteorological institute, which recalls the bulletin
for the fatal day (invoiced at 70F). There is a certificate of heredity
drawn up by the town council and signed by two witnesses, which
proves the relationship between father and son. There is a very modest
invoice from the parish priest for the funeral of the unfortunate boy.
There are invoices from the funeral director, which justify one of the
elements of the expenditure that has been put forward in the request
for damages and interests. There is the negative response from the
district insurer, saying that it has obtained enough information from
the file to prove that, according to the received witness statements,
the accident did not take place in the dangerous part but several
hundred metres lower: 'the ski-run markings and the fact that the ski
run was not closed off therefore bear no relation to the accident'. As
we can see, just the tireless control of inquirers and witnesses, forms
and maps, stamps, signatures and instruments, professionals and
persons in charge has allowed the file to be built with rather impressive pieces of evidence.

If, through some cruel thought experiment, we were eliminating all
these institutions and the services of the police, meteorological insti-
tutes, hospitals and insurance companies, the continuous vigilance of
passers-by, practitioners and elected officials, there is nothing, absolutely nothing with which the file could have been composed. We
would be left with nothing more than the pain of a father who was
absent at the death of his son and who, from the lofty words and
second-hand accounts, has shed tears in failing to understand who
killed his son. Even to prove that he is the only one who has a right
in relation to his son, he needs a certificate of heredity . . . We should
note that these documents are not all legal in nature, even if they
allow for a judgment to be rendered. In fact, if the death of this young
man had not been turned into an articulated complaint, then none of
these scattered papers, certificates, maps, meteorological bulletins

and invoices would have counted as pieces of evidence in the legal sense. Whether they would have been dispersed or archived, they would only have constituted useless pieces of information. It is therefore *because* they have been mobilized in the claim and because of the accident itself that these routine elements have taken on a legal form, but only *retroactively*. Still, if they have been able to slip into the file so easily it is because they had been preformed and pre-folded to respond to this type of contestation. But who is going to describe this pedestrian work of locating and controlling? Who will have the magnanimity to recognize in the solidity that is so often attributed to Law, the multitude of these tiny actions of surveillance and vigilance performed by humble brigadiers, researchers, town council secretaries, meteorologists and invoice clerks? These are the many obscure hands thanks to whom, in case of conflict, we find at our disposal the indisputable documents necessary to articulate our grievances. Before joining the three-piece suits, the impeccable pronunciation, the self-assured chin and the learned suavity of our counsellors of State again, let us salute in passing the multitude of these amanuenses, who are regarded with indifference but on whom claimants and judges alike depend for each page of their files.

Before it receives the unction of a counsellor, the file is nevertheless going to stay in the hands of another type of rank and file a bit longer. While there are approximately 200 members who are active at the Palais-Royal (see the following chapter), the Council depends on the groundwork carried out by more than 300 persons whose tasks are equally distributed according to the paths that the files take.[8] For the moment, the folder is still at the Clerk's Office. It is now passed on to the Analysis Service. This office examines the appeal and integrates it into ordering categories according to its general character (for example, degree of urgency: 'NORMAL'; nature of litigation: 'Ultra Vires'; submission to court: 'Cassation'). The office can also regroup on its own initiative appeals which have arrived randomly but which concern a similar subject, or send a badly assembled file back to a lower court. The Analysis Service also adds the list of relevant precedents to the file and starts to fill the folder by asking for the missing documents (such as confirmations of powers, communication of the file of first instance, etc.) by sending out various letters. After its

---

[8] To the members of the body (see the following chapter), we must add 56 high-level administrative personnel (said to be of category A, in particular the indispensable secretaries of the Section) and 57 of medium level (said to be of category B, operating the secretariat), to whom must be added 138 administrative personnel of category C, as well as 53 service personnel (all these numbers are valid for the year 1997, the year of reference for this work).

passage through the Analysis Service, the case possesses a number, a coloured folder,[9] and a computer-formatted form which classifies the file and specifies the stage of proceedings (if it is in first instance, appeal or 'cassation').[10] All this is summarized on a computer-formatted card for the claim, which is going to serve as the ID card for the case.

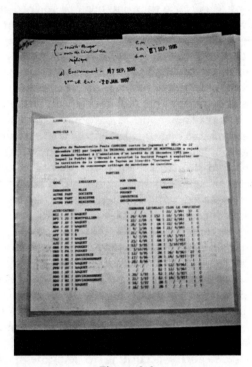

Figure 2.3

[9] Since the colours change according to the type of case – blue for tax, orange for cases concerning electoral issues – we can see the evolution of the Council at a glance. In 2001, for example, they say in the corridors that 'the Council was turning yellow at that time' as a result of the multiplication of referrals of suspension (*référés suspensions*) which are carefully wrapped in yellow folders.

[10] Contrary to the civil and criminal system, the Council of State in fact fulfils – as we have seen – three different roles according to the type of case. Therefore, each file itself must – at the hearing – specify the legal function of the assembly: 'You indeed have jurisdiction on appeal' or, on the contrary 'As judge in "cassation"', or 'You indeed have jurisdiction in first instance.' But the jurisdiction can vary in the course of the same session, just as the type of control exercised can vary: 'You exercise a limited control.' The commissioner of the law therefore affirms that he has indeed verified in which capacity counsellors 'are sitting': 'You indeed exercise full control, since Mr X is a citizen of the CEE', or 'Mr Tenager contests the Prime Minister, you are sitting as judge in first instance.'

Once the files have been passed on to the Analysis Service, they are gradually getting closer to the counsellors but also much weightier. The weight of a file is not a mental metaphor but a very practical one that requires carriers, wheel-carriages and a service lift to distribute the files between the different sub-sections according to their responsibilities and specialities. The distribution takes place through a meticulous operation which resembles the work carried out in a cargo terminal. The specialities of the sub-section, the state of the backlog and the obligation to avoid counsellors 'cutting corners' by becoming too specialized are all taken into account. Every activity is driven by the constant obsession with respecting the adversarial principle that both parties shall be heard, while at the same time moving as quickly as possible in order to diminish the backlog. It is at this point that the files fall into the hands of those essential and often remarkable characters: the secretaries of the sub-section, indispensable agents of the Council, nearly all of them women, who carry out the enormous work consisting of the logistical and legal tracking of files from their birth to their death. Or rather to the moment when they are archived, because the files, like the king, never die . . . Then begins the real legal work which is accompanied by a computer-formatted form which has been left empty up to that point, the 'plan d'instruction' (from now on, the 'schedule of review'), and which is first handwritten by the youngest auditor of the sub-section. It is this schedule which is going to allow the secretary to follow this movement which is so particular and so essential to the law: the principle that all parties shall be heard, called at the Council 'le contradictoire', which can be translated by 'due process'.

The documents which are added to the file are added by one of the parties, namely the party who initiates the appeal. First, the appeal must be communicated to the implicated party, whether that is the State – a Prefect, Minister, Mayor or even the Prime Minister – or, conversely, a private individual, an association, or a corporate body which the State involves in litigation because it wishes to contest a decision of an administrative tribunal which was disadvantageous to it. Then the documents of the file must be 'communicated' to this defendant, so that he 'can produce in reply' ('to produce' has been made an intransitive verb according to the custom of the Council). Except for this game of ping-pong, nothing is added and nothing *should* be added to the file. It is for the parties to respond to the reasons* which are being put forward against them. If the opposing party does not reply, replies in a wrong way, or replies after the statutory time limit has passed, then the judge can in principle do nothing about it.

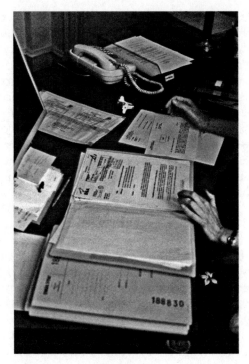

Figure 2.4

Date	Event	Quality	Actor	Time limit	Reply	NP
13/04/1999						

Despite the banal name, the type of files we are following do not resemble the many that we all have arranged on our desks in order to try to retrieve, in vain, some irretrievable order. Those files we can open, close, spoil and regroup, it matters little; no one will find any fault in that. Conversely, from the moment that it enters the Clerk's Office, every operation on the file we are discussing – which has now become legal – no matter how small, can give rise to 'legal effects' and constitute a grievance.[11] The files are therefore closely watched over, like milk that is put on to boil. If it was possible earlier to leave the Clerk's Office and the Analysis Service to work on them, prepare them and enrich them, it was precisely because none of their

[11] But to understand what the adjective 'legal' means here without begging the question will take the remainder of this book.

interventions could change anything regarding the respective positions of the arguments. Until now, the operations carried out were in some sense automatic, or in any case routine, and did not give rise to any discussion. It was sufficient that they were prepared adequately. From now on, these operations are going to involve the parties in the litigation. Each failed or successful operation could constitute a grievance, which would give rise to new litigation which will be added to the first. To lose a document, not to ask for the statement of defence, not to raise the means* of public order, or not to instruct the ministries to reply – all these small details which form part of the schedule of review are the responsibility of the secretary of the sub-section and of the auditor newly arrived in the Council. There exists a clear indication that the file has now penetrated deeper into the domain of the law: the passage between the automatic and the legal, between the indisputable and the disputable, between routine and initiative is revealed through the fact that, from now on, all post must be sent by registered mail and no longer by simple post. Every single pink slip from the post office is duly kept in the file, so that they are able to be shown in reply if ever issues concerning time limits are contested. No wonder that, through the statements, additional submissions, expert statements, diverse documents, notes and acknowledgements of receipt, the schedule of review is rapidly filling in and the folder starts to inflate substantially . . .

Figure 2.5

In the same way that our grandmothers slowly let their apples turn ripe – and sometimes go bad – during winter on wooden racks, the secretaries of the sub-section let the files turn ripe – and sometimes go sour! – on wooden shelves. Each row of these shelves corresponds to a stage in the complex activity which is about to start. As one of the secretaries says in a charming way: 'The file is like a fruit, in the beginning it is green, then it is "just right", and then we can work with them.' The shelves serve as a kind of visual memory, as an intellectual technology which provides a certain redundancy by allowing the members to locate at a simple glance the stages which they could also follow with the computer, but less easily.[12] Of all the different piles which are waiting for additional documents (the Ministers and their cabinets must have time to respond, litigants need time to reply, and designated experts need time to render their expert statements), one pile interests us in particular. That is the one with the files labelled 'ready for the reporter'. Figure 2.6 shows us precisely the stage in which a file that is ripe for use is 'harvested'. A counsellor comes to fetch the file which the president of sub-section has just designated to him according to his field of expertise, his own preferences, his lack of implication in the case concerned (failing which he is obliged to 'recuse himself'), his 'statistics' – that is to say the number of files that each must have dealt with in order to receive his productivity bonus – and the more or less urgent demands of the president of sub-section who has the duty of managing the backlog.[13] When there is too much specialization, the sub-sections – like the reporters – become worn-out by the repetitive tasks and start to no longer be able to judge and 'to cut corners' instead.[14] On the other hand, when there is too little specialization, the members are obliged to learn a new section of the administrative law each time. This slows down their pace and wastes the time of the litigants. The latter then become impatient and relentlessly call the secretariats of the sub-sections who now compensate for the tough discipline of

[12] We should not forget that, despite the archaic character of all these paper technologies, it is nevertheless possible for the 'president of Litigation' to track the progress of all the files thanks to the SKIPPER software.

[13] This productivity bonus is adjusted according to the effective productivity of the counsellor and can represent up to 30 per cent of his minimum wage. It is surprising to see such eminent characters being paid on a rate-per-piece basis, since the majority of specialized factory workers are no longer paid in this way. 'We are the last labourers who work on a rate-per-piece basis', says one counsellor (interview 19 April 1996), even though the sometimes boring and often repetitive tasks of factory workers cannot be compared to theirs . . .

[14] Routine is an enemy of judgment, as we shall see in chapter 4, because of the necessity of hesitating in order to judge well.

the written word by providing a bit of oral support. 'What is happening to my appeal?' Patience, it is now ripe for use: no longer by an employee, a technician, a clerk, a bailiff or a secretary, but by a judge, a real one.

Figure 2.6

Building a fragile bridge of texts

Why should we discuss all these sordid details, as if the ethnographer had the myopia of a paper-eating mouse or that of an ant? Because, even while we are following the slow fabrication of a file, we are not neglecting the intellectual and cognitive foundations of the law for one moment. If the observer is short-sighted, the law is procedural: it's an eye for an eye, a tooth for a tooth . . . It's precisely because the law follows a procedure that we might be able to discover the different professions at the Council by stubbornly following our cardboard folders and by noting how they grow and fatten, how they fold and unfold, as well as by noting the cupboards, offices, corridors, cellars, armchairs or desks on which they are put in order to let them turn ripe. Now, for the first time, the complaint is heard by a judge, or, rather, the documents from both parties are going to be read by a reporter in the silence of his own office before being discussed in the stuffy disorder of the rooms at the Council. Here, we have in fact arrived at the *work station* of the counsellors of State, the appearance of which will not fail to surprise us.

Figure 2.7

In order to understand the originality of this institution, it suffices to consider these big rooms where these characters, who are all equal before the law even though they are of different ages, collectively disappear behind immense piles of files in order to grapple with the innumerable difficulties of what literary critique calls 'intertextuality'. Very democratically, the members are all put in rooms without any partitions: old salons, dining rooms and ballrooms.[15] The Council is, through a mere shortage of offices, several decades ahead of the landscaped lay-outs of big firms who are trying to encourage 're-engineering', 'synergy' and the 'mobility' of their executives. The work, from now on, is at once totally solitary and totally collegial,

[15] Except for the presidents of Sections and sub-sections and for the commissioners of the law, who have bizarrely situated offices at their disposal – one behind a cupboard, another in an attic, a third below a hidden staircase.

without any sign of hierarchy. The youngest and the ones who have the most grey hairs are endowed with exactly the same resources. Twenty times a day, they can get up with a document in hand to ask the opinion of such and such a colleague, who is working next to them or who is smoking in the library (to the desperation of the librarian), on the manner in which to solve a certain difficulty or sharpen a certain formula.

At first sight, this workplace gives us the impression of being a rather miserable place, especially if we consider that the *crème de la crème* of the National School of Administration is assembled here. They have no personal secretary, no assistant and no intern; we might encounter famous former Ministers who are learning to type on the computer, important former Prefects who are discovering the joys of UHU glue, and old Members of Parliament who are making their photocopies before they cut them with a pair of scissors in order to proceed with a dangerous montage worthy of an palaeographer who tries to reconstruct the text of the Dead Sea scrolls. On the other hand, the working conditions are more luxurious than in the majority of laboratories or industries since the counsellors are able, every time they need to solve a certain question, to delve into this immense brain mass, these 5,000 person-years of experience of the administrative law and the exercise of authority which lives here, as if it concerned a sort of Academy or Lyceum.[16] We would not be surprised to see them dressed in togas while engaged in serious discussion, like in some neo-Greek fresco of nineteenth-century pompier art . . . Through some architectural and historical fantasy, these big landscaped rooms where this collective work is carried out, and which resemble more the sorting space of a post office, the social security office or the tax collector's office, are used here to organize the tasks of the primary institution of the State.[17]

It is in these places, on these desks, in these decorated rooms, that the pages of the file are going to be linked – through the intervention of the reporter – to the vast corpus of judgments of the Council and to the innumerable documents which record texts of laws, treaties, decrees, orders and regulations. Compiling all these documents occupies the entire library: the *Lebon* volumes, of course, but also all the Codes and the indispensable database ARIANE which gathers the collection of judgments of the Council. The reporter does not do anything else – but it is a dangerous exercise – but extract the means*

---

[16] See the statistics collected in chapter 5.
[17] On the sociology of administrative work, for a comparison, see Weller, *L'Etat au guichet* (1999).

from the confused pile which constitutes the file, in order to link these arguments* to other texts. From the point of view of the method which we use for this chapter, which consists in following graphical acts, the reporter establishes the connection, the coming-and-going between two types of writings: on the one hand, the ad hoc documents of both parties which are produced for and through the occasion, such as statements and various productions, and, on the other hand, the printed, authorized, voted upon and connected texts which are carefully arranged on the shelves of the library.

Figure 2.7 allows us to define this task in an even more material manner. On the table, we see the scattered, deleted and underlined documents which are all still full of complaints and raging oppositions. On the shelves, we see the filed, established, accepted, referenced and assured texts. The first are scattered and are put *flat* in a yellow folder, while the others are bound – and arranged *vertically* – with a cover of leather, imitation or real. The entire work consists of establishing the relation between these two collections of writings. The counsellor must decide (but what does it mean to say 'decide'?) by linking the first (but how?) to the second. Between these two corpuses lies a multitude of photocopies, drafts, attempts and copies of Codes which allow the reporter to visually superimpose (but through which operation of recognition?) the documents included in one pile onto those included in the other.

We could say that the reporter, in this way, draws up a tiny bridge of texts between these two types of documents. On the one hand, the documents which the parties have used in order to build the file and, on the other hand, the documents which are archived in the library and bound in volumes. It is a bridge which is as fragile as a footbridge of lianas thrown over an abyss. As we know, this little bridge is called a 'note'. The reporter adds the 'visas' (the citations taken into consideration) to this 'note', before he returns his file to the secretariat. The citations are an essential part of the file and form the object of incessant scrupulousness and vigilance, a vigilance all the greater because the austerity of the exercise is such a challenge that it requires the sharpest attention possible.[18] The citations concern – as their French name 'visas' indicates – on the one hand the totality of documents to which the claim quite literally clings, and on the other hand the documents which are used to include this claim in the network of legal

---

[18] Since it is possible to 'viser' (to cite, to take into consideration) 'a general principle of law' even though its definition is unwritten, as is done with a text (see Braibant, *Le Droit administratif français* (1992), p. 222), this proves that the expression 'viser' does not exactly follow the mere textual matter.

texts. When the reader of a note reads the citations, he therefore holds the two extremities of the footbridge – or its two points of anchorage – in his hands, as we can see in a judgment of the Litigation Section that we are going to follow for a while:

Taking into consideration the claim and the additional statements, registered at the secretariat of the Litigation Section of the Council of State on 24 March, 12 July 1993 and 25 June 1996, presented by Mrs Dominique PARREL remaining (. . .); Mrs PARREL asks the Council of State to annul:

1°) the judgment dated 19 January 1993 by which the administrative tribunal of Clermont-Ferrand rejected her request concerning the rectification of a material error in the judgment of that same tribunal dated 20 October 1992;

2°) said judgment dated 20 October 1992 rejecting her request concerning the annulment of the decision of the 'préfet' of the Haute-Loire refusing her the benefit of adding family allowance to her salary;

Taking into consideration the other documents in the file;

Taking into consideration the law n°63-809 of 6 August 1963 on the improvement of production and the proprietary structure of French forests;

Taking into consideration the Code of administrative tribunals and administrative courts of appeal;

Taking into consideration the ordinance no. 45-1708 of 31 July 1945, the decree no. 53-984 of 30 September 1953 and the law no. 87-1127 of 31 December 1987;

Law, Code and ordinance at one extremity; claim, statement, disputed judgments and documents in the file at the other extremity: between these two points of anchorage something must still be established. This is what is called in engineering 'the deck' of a bridge and what is designated here with the name 'dispositif', namely the proliferation of preliminary clauses which link with each other and which lead up to the dénouement, that is to say the decision properly called. We must take the term 'dispositif' very literally: two types of literature have been connected or arrayed through some weaving work, which we are going to follow in the next chapters. These two types of literature are like the weft and the chain; one supplies the elements which arise from the case – that is, everything which 'emerges from the file', including the few terms, arguments and writings which remain from the more or less unarticulated complaint of the claimant – the other supplies the elements of text, articles of law and Code, which allow in the end making a decision and disposing of the claim: rejection or annulment. The aim of the 'note' is to force the first and the second type of literature to interweave, one into the other, through a prose that becomes progressively more and more technical.[19] The *means**

[19] Let us recall that the 'note' is read orally in the review meeting, but that it disappears afterwards. In fact, it serves as an indispensable basis for the conclusions of the commissioners of the law. This sometimes does not go without some sour

occupy exactly the intermediary position that the name 'moyen' in French indicates: one half belongs to the case at issue, since they have triggered the claim, and the other half dons the robes of the law by using the same words as those used in published texts. The progressive articulation of the case, from the lawyer's office up to the display of the final judgment, consists of making the case speak more and more like the law just by having the arguments* or the grounds* at every stage better arrayed and regrouped.

We can clearly see this progression of the 'dispositif' if we continue to read the same draft judgment: the first preamble still recalls elements of the file, certainly cleaned and styled but nevertheless always present, while the second relates these purified facts to a text of Code which is cited *in extenso*.

Considering that Mrs PARREL has requested by letter to the president of the administrative tribunal of Clermont-Ferrand that, on the basis of article R-205 of the Code of administrative tribunals and administrative courts of appeal, the judgment of the administrative tribunal of Clermont-Ferrand dated 20 October 1992 be corrected. This judgment rejected her request which was directed against a decision of the Prefect of the Haute-Loire which refused her the benefit of family allowance to her salary on the ground that this financial allocation could not be received by a couple when both partners are public officials;

Considering that article R-205 of the Code of administrative courts of appeal provides that 'when the president of the administrative tribunal considers that a final judgment or an ordinance is tarnished by an error or a material omission, he can make the corrections to it that reason requires, by an ordinance rendered within the statutory time limit of two months counting from the day that the relevant judgment or ordinance was rendered. The notification of the rectifying ordinance re-starts the statutory time limit for appeal against the judgment or the ordinance thus corrected.'

What now remains is the sharp point of the 'dispositif' which is going to give rise to the decision and the dénouement. The bridge has now been established by fitting elements of the claim into the texts and by weaving the means* by bringing them closer and closer to laws and decrees. To draw out the metaphor of the bridge: *something* is now going to be able to *pass* from one side to the other. Either in one direction, and this is annulment, or in the other, and that is rejection. The task of the ethnographer consists in capturing what is passing in this way from one text to another, like a squirrel jumping

---

remarks from the reporters, who see their work being appropriated by others. In seeking to justify the hybrid existence of the commissioners of the law, Massot and Girardot write: 'In this respect, the commissioner appears as a functional splitting of the reporter' – Massot and Girardot, *Le Conseil d'Etat* (1999), p. 169.

from branch to branch. Either the claim will be given the power to follow its course and break one of these texts – orders, decisions, regulations or decrees – which together form the immense cloth of published texts: this is annulment. Or conversely, there is something in these published texts which has such force that it transports itself from one side to the other and blocks the progression of the claim definitively: that is rejection. Instead of, as they say, prospering, the grounds* are then said to be unfounded.[20] In our example, the Council strikes from two sides. It annuls the judgment of the administrative tribunal as the claimant asked, but it also confronts that claimant with an indisputable argument: 'tardiveté', that is non-compliance with the statutory limitation period.

Considering: that the effect of the aforesaid provisions is that they provide the president of the administrative tribunal with his own power to correct a judgment. That, when he is asked to make use of such a power, it is not for him to take a decision regarding jurisdiction to dismiss such a request, **which does not have the character of a claim.** That a consequence of this is that, on the one hand, by ruling to dismiss the request of Mrs PARREL in the disputed judgment the administrative tribunal of Clermont-Ferrand has exceeded the limits of its jurisdiction and that its judgment dated 19 January 1993 must, as a result, be annulled. That, on the other hand, the request presented by Mrs PARREL cannot prolong the time limit for appeal against the judgment of 20 October 1992;

Considering: that it **emerges from the documents in the file** that Mrs PARREL has received notification of the disputed judgment of the administrative tribunal of Clermont-Ferrand, dated 20 October 1992, on 10 November 1992. That her request has only been **registered** at the secretariat of the Council of State on 24 March 1993. That at that moment, her request was submitted late and is, as a result, not admissible;[21]

DECIDES:

Article 1: The judgment of the administrative tribunal of Clermont-Ferrand, dated 19 January, is annulled.

[20] Not to be confused with arguments* that are not 'working' ['inopérants'] which can be well-founded and true but without incidence on the claim.

[21] It does not suffice to establish 'non-compliance with the statutory time limits' by noting that there are more than two months between 20 October and 24 March. It must still be explained why the claim of Mrs PARREL has not 'halted the statutory time limit'. This was the case, precisely because it was not an appeal. The two decisions of annulment and rejection are therefore linked, a hair-splitting point which justified the passage of this case – which is apparently of little practical interest (except for the claimant) – to the Section. 'The effect of these provisions', we will read later in the analyses of case-law, 'is that a particular power of correction of a judgment is attributed to the president of the administrative tribunal. It is not for him, when he is asked to make use of such a power, to take a jurisdictional decision to dismiss such a request, which does not have the character of a claim.' The judge then has the right to use his power to rectify the mistake by making use of his reason, but he does not have the right to put the law in motion.

Article 2: The remainder of the conclusion of the request of Mrs PARREL is
rejected.
Article 3: This decision will be notified to Mrs Dominique PARREL and to the
Ministry of Home Affairs.

At this point, the reporter has done his job: he has connected the
claim to the texts and he has proposed a possible dénouement through
this connection. The power to tie and untie, which we often attribute
to the law, would not have any kind of meaning without this particular practice of linking, then weaving, subsequently merging and
finally erupting: the power of a legal mean which shatters a published
text, or, conversely, a text which has enough force to draw up an
insurmountable obstacle for the legal mean, as here, the 'non-
compliance with the statutory limitation period'. In the same way that
we do not understand anything of Science if we think that words are
distant from and opposite to things, in the same way we do not
understand anything of Law if we seek to pass directly from the norm
to the facts of the particular case without this modest accumulation
of papers of diverse origin.[22] Besides, the ethnographer merely recalls
here – through photography and the *slow motion* of external description – what we can find in every manual of administrative procedure:
to *proceed step by step*, that is what Law is, namely *procedure*! The
power of the Law, like that of a chain, is exactly as strong as its
weakest link and we can only detect this link by following the chain
link after link, without omitting a single one.

If it were true that legal work consists of qualifying an event
through a rule of law, then the task would be accomplished.[23] In fact,
that task only begins. Nothing in fact proves that the reporter is right.
His draft, called in French a 'projet', is precisely only a *project* and
not yet a judgment. When he sends the file to the secretariat of the
sub-section, enriched with the note and the 'dispositif', he knows full
well that the matter is not finished. According to the difficulty, the
file is now going to be put on its rack, for a longer or shorter time,
in order to become ripe for further review. The cases in the 'sub-
section judging by itself' obviously take less time than the cases
of the sub-sections judging together or of the Assembly, which are

---

[22] The reader who is familiar with James, *Pragmatism* (1907 [1975]) will have
perhaps understood that we are trying out, in this chapter, a type of step-by-step
following of mediations which uses the same manner of description as for scientific
reference: Latour and Woolgar, *Laboratory Life* (1979); Latour, *Pandora's Hope*
(1999b). See chapter 5.
[23] On the importance of this term of 'qualification' which is so problematic, see Cayla,
'La qualification' (1993).

carefully reviewed by the president of the Litigation Section. This important character, who is in continuous contact with the presidents of sub-sections, weaves an informal network of opinions and suggestions outside of the sessions, creating a network of pieces of advice and nudges in the right direction, which accelerate or slow a file down according to whether it is more or less thorny. From now, the reporter having only proposed a qualification, the essential operation still remains: to test this qualification by *collectively hesitating about it.* This can only be done by drawing on the different elements of the 'dispositif' in every possible way, in order to make other connections emerge between different aspects of the file and different texts. This is the role of the review meetings, with which we have already made acquaintance. It is time for us to immerse ourselves again in one of these sessions.[24] The readers will perhaps forgive us for imposing this chore on them, if they recall that this slowness, this heaviness and these continuous hesitations precisely form the primary material of justice, the material of that which will perhaps one day protect them or their loved ones when they are, alas, faced with fighting the coldest of cold monsters, the State.

Leafing through a file

Once the court schedule for his sessions has been confirmed, the president of sub-section is going to entrust the file to a 'reviser' a few days before the session. The reviser is going to summarize the entire file and test the weaving work done by the reporter. He will progressively increase the proportion of law in relation to fact by asking in particular to summarize the string of arguments* *orally*, so that these can be tested again by establishing as much as possible a connection between them and the regulatory texts. The commissioner of the law, as we know, discovers the file during the review meeting and, a few weeks later, after having written his conclusions, he will put the case on the court schedule for one of the public hearings. The collective manipulation of the file is essential for this complex alchemy through which elements of fact are incessantly kneaded, leafed through, summarized, forgotten, rediscovered and finally glued together, hooked

---

[24] The oral summary, in the civil and criminal system, of the collection of facts under the direction of a judge has no other aim. Garapon, *Bien juger. Essai sur le rituel judiciaire* (1997), p. 63.

up and juxtaposed to elements of text. In fact, the file possesses a fundamental property which is well known to ergonomists and anthropologists of cognition: everything in it is at once present and concealed.[25] Since each page of the file hides the others, each person can say very different things on the same subject, even though they all remain, as they say, 'within the limits of the file'. The right metaphor to understand this practice is no longer that of a footbridge, but rather that of the burners of great industrial furnaces where a violent and continuous agitation of combustible matter alone produces an almost complete oxygenation. The collective process of review – with its revision, discussion, conclusion and deliberation – ensures that there is no other way of dealing with, of kneading and of cracking a file. It also ensures, thanks to this continuous agitation and these violent ordeals, that the file has been brought into contact with all the texts of law which the counsellors who were successively charged with this case could think of. Qualification therefore does not signify anything if it has not been collectively tested.

To take account of the almost physical work of intertextuality that is necessary for the material fabrication of the judgment and for the physical engagement of judges with a case, let us follow a review meeting which concerns another case number. We are going to take particular interest in the act of consultation and of 'leafing through' a file, and in the collective consultation of pages. However, we will not try to follow all the mazes of this particular case, which concerns the contestation of a Declaration of Public Utility (DUP) which is, moreover, fairly obscure.

Bruyère[26] (reporter) (reading the 'note' concerning the district of Valjoli): It is a case concerning its main sewer. There is a problem with the Declaration of Public Utility (DUP) for the temporary works after the annulment of the DUP. The administrative tribunal of Versailles has annulled the Prefect's order *ultra petita*. The Ministry appeals.

---

[25] That is the entire problem of cognitive ergonomics: Hutchins, *Cognition in the Wild* (1995) and Suchman, *Plans and Situated Actions* (1987); for sociologists of action interested in the comprehension of familiarity, see Thévenot, 'Essai sur les objets usuels' (1993).

[26] I have maintained the same pseudonyms for characters who in fact correspond to several persons, in order to avoid the readers – who are being bombarded by too many names – getting the vertigo which is typically associated with reading Russian novels.

A tribunal can err by judging too widely (ultra petita) or too narrowly (infra petita). It has taken an annulled DUP as a pretext to annul, as a result, other orders which, according to the Ministry, were perfectly legal. That is why the Ministry submits a claim on appeal against the judgment of the administrative tribunal.

President (during the reading of the 'note'): **Pass me the file**, I am going to find the map. That way I will no longer disturb you, because that is not pleasant when one is reading a note.

The president rummages through the file and unfolds the map which is going to play an essential role in the discussion since the parcels of land are clearly visible on it while the claimants held that the precise list of parcels concerned was not annexed to the order of the Prefect. The question is therefore to know what it means 'to be or not to be annexed' to the file.

(playing the role of the reviser that day): Bruyère has done an excellent job. The administrative tribunal has annulled as a result. It felt **uncomfortable,** since there is case-law on the independence of different pieces of legislation. However, because it annulled the DUP, it believed that it had to establish a link and therefore also annul the provisional measures of access. We must first **make an effort** regarding the jurisdiction of the Council of State.[27]

'To do an excellent job' as a reporter, consists of extracting the grounds* from a confused file and in this way speeding up the work of the sub-section. The important expression 'to make an effort', which is constantly repeated in the sessions, marks the small nudge in the right direction that needs to be given in order for a mean* to be acceptable or not. That is to say, a convoluted element of the external world needs to come back into one of the possibilities offered by the texts. Here, the Council of State could have asserted a lack of jurisdiction.

(. . .) the **context** provided by the **case-law** is interesting. In 1892, there was a law on temporary occupation [during the time in which works were carried out], which was not a servitude but a prerogative of public power. What the case-law therefore looks into very closely

---

[27] Let us recall once more that we are not dealing with a transcription but minutes. Therefore, what is lacking is the impeccable French, the formulaic genre, and the urbane politeness under which a biting irony sometimes shows through. The readers unfortunately only see the skeleton of the exchanges.

is whether 'it concerns public works or not'. It does not consider whether there is a DUP or not. And mentioning article N. is mandatory and is subject to a sanction of nullity. **The case-law is enormous.** One must know **very specifically** which parcel it concerns. It is a kind of litigation where there is full jurisdiction (he cites a mass of judgments).[28] There is an abundant case-law about the independence of different pieces of legislation; the grounds* are not acceptable in many situations. All that is **in the note** and the **accompanying documents.**

> We should note that the word 'context' has its etymological meaning here of 'co-texts'; the president paints the intertextual landscape with broad brush strokes by materializing the abundance of caselaw and pointing to the documents accompanying the note that constitute the 'yellow parts' of the file that were obtained by the Documentation Service, which is charged with photocopying all the texts of laws or previous judgments of the Council of State at the request of the reviser. The photocopy plays an essential role in leafing through files, to the extent that it allows the establishment of an even better connection between the texts and the documents because they are all formatted in the same appropriate size so that their resemblances can be grasped synoptically.

Let us pass on to the arguments* on the merits which were submitted by the parties, because the administrative tribunal has made a mistake. The other day, during the previous review meetings, we annulled the judgments which annulled the DUP. As a result **the other orders** are **revived** and as a consequence the decision of the administrative tribunal which said 'I have annulled the DUP, I annul this order here' is no longer worth anything! So we have annulled the annulment. We can economize on arguments by using the formula '**in any case**'.

> It is often possible to measure the connection between the texts and the documents of the files, which becomes more and more important, through the oral multiplication of written formulas as if the members were already citing the preambles which they are in the process of drawing up mentally.[29] The formulaic language, like the

---

[28] We touch here upon property law, for which the Council then exercises an even more complete control than full control over the decisions of the State, since it verifies through the 'theory of balance' that there is indeed a balance between the general interest and the trouble imposed on the proprietors. On the notion of control, see chapter 1; on the 'theory of balance', see n. 11.

[29] We will be able to read in the final judgment: 'the appeal against the judgment annulling the order (. . .) is not valid *in any case*, since the legality of this order must be appreciated in relation to the date on which it was issued'.

photocopies and the citations, testifies to the progressive degree of fusion between the two types of writing. The counsellors end up speaking like books, or at least like the Lebon volumes.

We have revived the DUP. We must then examine the 'legal means' of the claimants. There is the argument which is drawn from the fact that article 3 of the law of 1892 was not taken into account: the parcels concerned are not mentioned. The reporter wishes to annul. **I hesitate**, I would not annul. **We can indeed refer** to the maps in article 1 of the order, the parcels are well defined.

The reviser points to the documents which are spread out on the table before them. The reporter has concluded that the parcels were not there and that the manifestly illegal order therefore had to be annulled with regard to article 3 of the law of 1892. From the same file, they can conclude on either the presence or the absence of parcels annexed to the order of the Prefect. The whole session is going to focus on this uncertainty. Without this hesitation which is commented on in real time and is experienced collectively, there could neither be judgment, nor justice.

I find that to annul on that basis is a little **formalistic**.

Bruyère (with a great gesture of the hand) [an air of saying 'ah all right, if you wish, **I have nothing to do with it**']:
President: Yes, yes, I know. I admit that **it is disputable**.

Here are three reactions which are fleeting as well as fascinating: the first recalls the difference between 'formal' and 'formalistic'. They indeed have to do with form, since this concerns knowing whether or not article 3 of the law applies to this case of the DUP, but they also must avoid 'formalism' which would lead to reprimanding the government for an insignificant mistake. Then, the reporter marks this complete state of indifference with a gesture which testifies to his disinterest, while his colleagues are contesting his note and his draft (see chapter 5). Finally, the president repeats, with a gesture of appeasement, the necessity, and even the obligation, of hesitation and discussion which allow them, according to him, to ensure the quality of the judgment.

On the access routes, I agree with the reporter. We **do not see them** on the maps; but **there is not a word on this argument* in the statements**. Are we going to invent a mean* even when it has not been presented?!

Here the adversarial principle that each party shall be heard is being recalled: the judge arbitrates between the reasons* presented by the parties. The reporter has seen the argument* (the map does not clearly indicate the ways of access concerning the parcels), but that argument* has not been raised by the parties. The reviser has verified this, by checking that the statements do not contain 'one word' about it. The last phrase is rhetorical because there is always the possibility, as we have just seen, of 'making an effort' and to make an argument* appear if that is truly important to avoid 'formalism'.

They have asked for annulment as a result. We **do not have to give it to them**, it is **disputable**. I am in favour of not annulling, there is no scandal. All right, then there is the mean* of Mr Dumoulin; he has no legal standing. All right, we can discuss it. It is above all the case, I believe, that he **says very little about it**. The case-law requires that the parcel be 'enclosed by a wall' and I **am not able to tell you** whether there is a wall or not. The issue is dealt with **in two lines**; we cannot accept such a mean*. I personally don't hesitate to reject the argument* . . .

Commissioner of the law: What does the government say, we have not made a supplementary **process of review**?
President: It has been communicated. The Ministry of the Environment has responded **in four pages**. The government has responded (consulting the file) no, basically, it has not responded. We could annul by saying that the government **did not respond**. The mean* is raised, we annul, but I do not agree. These arguments* do not carry **the same weight**.
Bruyère: I am wondering **whether there is no** document in the file in which they say 'it is enclosed by a wall' [rummages through the enormous pile].
President: Yes, that is possible, but there is **not enough** on it in the file. We can go and search in the cupboards, the photos, but I admit that **I haven't looked**.

At this moment, the reporter leafs through the file in order to find whether or not some proof exists that the parcel has been enclosed by a wall. We see that the argument* is explicitly raised here, but not with enough force or clarity ('in two lines'). There is nothing automatic in the expression of a legal reason*, even when it is accompanied by documents which they can either consider attentively or not. That is the whole problem of the file: its thickness itself makes it difficult to distinguish physically what is in it and *what is not. So much so that, in this case, the government has not produced in defence.*

Commissioner of the law: I understand your attitude, they are throwing arguments* at us and it is for them **to prove them**. Agreed. But this here can perhaps be a mean*, we can make a supplement to the process of review.

As always, if it is really a mean*, then the other party must be able to respond before the judge takes a position on it. Even in this session where they must normally put an end to the indecision, the file may very well be sent back to the secretariat where a supplement to the process of review can be added.

President: Ah no, no, I am not proposing that.

Commissioner of the law: But we cannot annul, we are in the middle of the ford, I do not feel like it . . .

President: If you request a supplement to the process of review, don't count on it before the session of 19 January! (he says with a little smile)

Commissioner of the law: Yes (in the same tone), that is exactly what makes me hesitate!

We suddenly edge over into humour and into the question (which is clearly designated as not legal) of the management of the backlog of files which needs to be gradually reduced and the internal organization of the flux of cases.[30] The treatment of the case therefore unfolds on two different levels: that of the backlog to be managed and that of the content of the claim. The commissioner of the law marks the ambiguity of the situation well by ironically using the verb 'hesitate' (which is charged with the scruples of law), to make it signify a simple concern about the management of his workload.

Dorval (assessor): It appears to be obvious that the judgment of the administrative tribunal is unorthodox, is that not what you are thinking?

President: No, that is an extra argument, but it was in fact a consequence. It (the administrative tribunal) was **embarrassed** by the case-law. It normally does not have the right to do that; it has **turned** things the other way.

[30] Even though recent decisions by the European Court have given a legal meaning to this question, since a procedure must not exceed reasonable time limits in order to be fair.

They now put themselves in the place of the judges of the first instance who wrote the judgment, by trying hard to understand their motivations. The intertextuality extends now to the psychology of the authors of judgments.

Dorval (reading the judgment of the administrative tribunal): We can interpret it **differently**!

Le Men (having listened to the reading of the judgment by Dorval): The administrative tribunal raises another 'moyen d'office', but it does not render its decision on that basis. It 'annuls as a consequence'.

They now spend a long time listening to the reading of the documents in the file; now it is time for the judgment of the administrative tribunal. In order to summarize the arguments, the review meeting precisely allows a mixture of the advantages of the oral practice with those of the written practice. The capacity to multiply interpretations is, at this stage, the effect that is sought after.

Bruyère: But you are annulling?

President: Yes, but on a different **ground**. We have annulled the annulment of the DUP.

Bruyère (ironically): The subtlety of reasoning of the Council of State never ceases to amaze me . . . I mean in a good sense!

Even though it concerns parcels of land and enclosures, the word 'ground' does not indicate the presence of an agricultural sphere here but that of another text, to which we can also relate the mean* . . . We see here exactly what the advantage of the revision and, afterwards, the collective discussion is. Not only are the arguments* present or not, according to the effort counsellors make, but they can be linked to such and such a text according to the grounds chosen. The subtle irony of the reporter marks the slight vertigo which overtakes this gentleman (and also sometimes the ethnographer) when faced with the flexibility of solutions which these two sources of uncertainty give rise to. Flexibility, hesitation, vertigo, the quality of the process of review – all this goes together.[31]

---

[31] This is all the more the case since there is a difference between asserting and proving. Asserting only consists of bringing something to light which is present, but still invisible. Proving renders this presence indisputable. For example, concerning a case regarding an escorting back to the border: 'Mr Z has *asserted* that he has two children and a lover, but he has not provided *proof* of this paternity, therefore rejection': Landowski, 'Vérité et vérédiction en droit' (1988).

Dorval: All right, I hesitate on the merits. What does the case-law say?

This is the magical formula which is pronounced in every difficult moment, after a shorter or longer silence. The Council, as we know, has constructed its own law; they must therefore, in order to resolve a difficulty, relate themselves to one of the judgments pronounced over 200 years by this collective body. There is no other solution than to consult the file of documentation annexed to the note, or to get up themselves to study the Lebon *which is standing in the cupboard.*

President: There is room for **hesitation**. If they do not specify the parcels, then it must be annulled. And afterwards, **as always**, there is case-law which can provide the nuances. If we nevertheless know where the parcels are, then that works. We are somewhere in the middle; is it **specific enough** in this particular case?

Bruyère (he reads the article of the law of 1882 concerning temporary occupation): Now, the disputed order does not announce anything. It refers to another order which has documents attached to it.[32] Does that mean that it has done its job, or not? I have **discovered** case-law [he reads] from 1967, all right, it is already a bit long ago.

President: Oh, the date does not matter at all, that is very good. The case-law is above all concerned with whether it is clear which parcels are concerned. Now, here **we have the parcels**!

Bruyère: Yes, but in a different document!!

President: Yes, we have to **make an effort** there. We **have** identified the parcels, **but in a different document. However,** the disputed order does name it.

We are still on the question of knowing whether the map of parcels is contained in the Prefect's order or not, even though physically it is not there. According to the pressure exercised by the case-law, the judges are going to test the entire gradation between indisputable presence and indisputable absence. The maps can, for example, be absent but named. Let us note the irony of the 'as always' of the president, which indicates the ambiguity of a very clear, but sometimes obscure and muddled, case-law. We should also note the

---

[32] Paragraphs 2 and 3 of article 3 of the law of 29 December 1892: 'This order indicates in a specific manner the works for which the occupation is ordered, the surfaces which it concerns, the nature and duration of the occupation and the access routes. A map of parcels, indicating with a **colour** the terrains to be occupied, is **annexed** to the order at least when the occupation does not have as its exclusive aim the collection of materials.'

*classification of the flood of case-law according to date. The judg-
ments can either wither away when they grow older, or – on the
contrary – improve like a good wine.*

Le Men: That is the **only delicate point**. There is the problem of
the access routes. It has not been raised; we cannot invent it. Then:
whether it is enclosed by a wall. The Prefect says 'it is not enclosed
by a wall' (he says while reading the file)
President: Have you **seen** that? where? well, yes, **in fact**.

*While the discussion continued, the second assessor stumbled on a
piece of evidence, while consulting the file, which ends the discussion on one of the previous points (the field of Mr Dumoulin is not
enclosed by a wall).*

Le Men: I agree to make an effort, **it must be decided**. The decision N must be specified. It has never been decided, **either in one
sense or another**.

*The second assessor suddenly makes the discussion edge over
towards another task of the Council: no longer that of applying the
law but of modifying it through a new decision. They are hesitating
today in deciding what the law of 1892 means by 'annexed to the
order', because the law – this administrative law which they themselves have secreted during the years – has never decided 'either in
one sense or another'. The question is then no longer that of qualifying a fact by making reference to a standard, but of modifying
the standard. The vertigo of the ethnographer increases even more.*

Dorval (while reading the order of the Prefect): I'm sorry but it is
less definite than Mr Bruyère says. Now, here in this particular case,
there is nothing.

*During the discussion, the assessor has re-read nearly all the impor-
tant documents in the file and has adjusted his opinion. He again
gives himself permission to disagree with the reporter.*

Commissioner of the law: The maps are in any case **enormous**.
They are at the office of the Prefect, we **cannot** transport them. So
that does not change anything with regard to access (which we
formulate in one way or another).

*This marks a return to the materiality of the file: it is no use at all
to complain that the order of the Prefect does not have the map of
parcels annexed to it, since these maps cannot be transported.*

President: It **must be decided**. The question to be judged is the question of knowing whether we can regard a map as being annexed **through connectivity**. That is the **only question**. On that, we can **vote**.

There we are, the discussion has arrived at its natural end. They now know the point of law which must be decided, and they can move on to the following case. The president has followed the second assessor. The discussion was fruitful, now they only speak the language of the law: a map can be present as an annex without really being present physically through a simple relation of 'connectivity', a legal fiction, an original intermediary between absence and presence, a new ontological category which allows the reconciliation of the physical weight of the actual maps with the law of 1892 and its requirements. The horrible complications of the case are now summarized in 'the only question'. It is a rather pertinent one which is subtly put in the language of the Council and which will form the subject of a vote in the framework of the review meeting and, more importantly, during the deliberation that is going to follow. They have fallen from the most extreme uncertainty into the relief of the decision. It is clear: this is being voted upon; this is being judged.

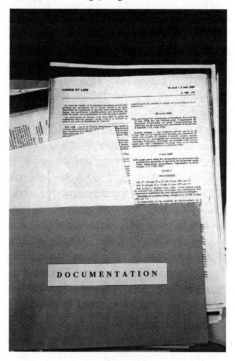

Figure 2.8

If we could understand through which alchemy they have managed
to move, during this session, from the multitude of details recalled in
the reporter's note – which are still present in the file, which the
assessors consult obsessively – to the question of law which in the end
concentrates their thoughts, arouses their interest and presents itself
to everyone as something that can be voted upon – that is to say,
something that can be decided – then we would have understood a
big part of the work of the Law and of its so particular form of truth-
telling. There is in this alchemy a subtle form of chemistry somewhat
akin to the chemistry which allows cellular receptors – through their
intricate make-up – to multiply their chances of interaction with their
catalysts. The discussion was fruitful, the collective work has paid
off, and the complete combustion has taken place. They now know
very precisely which arguments* have been raised, which are those
that are going to prosper, which grounds must be chosen to respond
to them and which new question they are going to be able to decide.
All thanks to this case, whose practical details have almost already
been forgotten (the reporter, moreover, says with a blasé gesture: 'we
work to generate case-law'!). The file can now be put on the court
schedule and be submitted to the trials of the conclusions of the commissioner of the law. It will then be subjected to the supplementary
scruples of another sub-section, which will be expressed during the
deliberation.

In order to prepare for this hearing, the other members do not receive
the entire file, which they only know about by listening to the conclusions of the commissioner of the law. They only receive, when the case
goes up to the 'Assembly of Litigation', a concise *green slip* from which
all the waste matter of the case has been cleared. These green slips are
like diamonds which have been extracted from the ore and whose
sharp cut in itself justifies all the work that has gone before it. It is the
only reason why the name of the file in the future will be recalled.

For instance, the Parrel case that we have followed above will be
summarized in one single line: 'in the case of article R-205 of the
Procedural Code, can a party refer the matter to the judge so that he
proceeds with the rectification of a material error or does the judge act
on his own initiative?' Because of the complaint, a point which had
not been decided on previously will now be decided. See here, for
another example, the green slip which is presented to the judges concerning a case regarding someone who is escorted back to the border.
An entire file of 100 pages is summarized in the following manner:

Article 8 of the European Convention on Human Rights relating to the protection
of family life can form an obstacle to the government's refusal to grant a stay to a
foreigner who maintains direct family ties with persons residing in France.

Does the mean*, drawn from the violation of the stipulations of this article, remain operative contrary to a refusal of a permit to stay when the permit in question is only accessible to foreigners who fulfil a specific condition (such as a student permit, a certificate of residence delivered to Algerian merchants, etc.) and the government refuses the permit because the applicant does not fulfil this condition?

[To which is added a thin file containing case-law, Section 10 April (. . .); texts of laws; photocopies of annexes; Article 8 of the European Convention on Human Rights; Article 5b of the Franco-Algerian convention; and ordinance of 1945.]

To judge at the Council – and we will return to this – is never merely to judge a case but always also *to judge the law* itself by using the particular case in order to specify and even modify the law in the case of an 'overturning of precedent'.

'We open the doors; the decisions are read.' Such is the magical formula which allows, at the beginning of a public hearing, the communication of the decisions of previous cases at the bottom of the grand staircase. The decisions are, despite the expression, never read aloud. From the moment when the deliberation ends, the file is going to undergo a radical transformation. The draft of the 'project' will become a 'minute', if it is accepted by the deciding judges and after the 'visas' have been added. It will be carefully re-read and interpreted by the secretary of the sub-section, the reporter and finally by the presiding judge. After this, the judgment will be passed to the clerk, and the file is transmitted to the Service of notifications, which carefully 'strips' it to its bare essentials. The SKIPPER software, which ensured the logistics of the file up to now, yields to another software with the equally significant name of SILLAGE ('in the wake of'), thereby announcing another significant stage in the proceedings. This software ensures that there is no risk of additional changes when the text is being typed out. Such changes could in themselves, as we have seen in the Parrel case, give rise to a grievance. After having swollen beyond every measure, the folder is now relieved of everything that is superfluous. Only the statements are now kept, while the annexed documents are sent back to the parties. The file is archived first upstairs for the next two years, then in the cellar of the Palais-Royal, and finally at Fontainebleau in the national archives. Up until recently, the reporter would recover his note, which was not archived. The commissioner of the law, however, retains his own conclusions which he is free to publish. The claimant receives notification of the judgment. The case is closed; and so is the file.[33]

[33] It is the end for the counsellor and judges in the last instance, but the matter continues for the parties who are subjected to the decision in the judgment and who must now pass over into action. They must reimburse unjustly received indemnities, rewrite a litigious order, republish new decrees, demolish buildings that were constructed under a plan of occupation of land which has become illegal, etc. Having

Figure 2.9

No, not entirely, since the claim now undergoes a transfiguration or even a resurrection of the flesh. If the case is not purely routine, if it has perturbed in one way or another the immense spider's web of the administrative law, then the *text* of the judgment is separated from the mortal body of the file and the notification, in order to become now an element of case-law which will enrich the corpus of decisions of the Council. In the same way as there are hell, purgatory and paradise for souls, for decisions there are return to total oblivion, access to category B – also called 'les tables' ('this decision will be *mentioned* in the volumes of the *Lebon*') – and finally the Empyrean or category A ('this decision will be *published* in the volumes of the *Lebon*').[34] The operators of this transmutation are three young, hand-picked persons, who are in charge of the Documentation Service and whose task it is, since 1953, to classify the judgments by order of

---

been indifferent to these small 'details of application' for a long time, the Council now follows the realization of the effects of the law more closely.

[34] All the judgments are in any case included in the database ARIANE. It is in this sense that a case never dies, thanks to computers. However, only the categories A and B form the subject of case-law analysis in this database. The young, who are used to computers, are criticized by their elders – who are used to the paper version of the *Lebon* – for failing to discern the different hierarchies of the case-law. They are said to put all of these elements on the same level, as if the cases were all flattened by the levelling-out of bytes.

importance after attending the deliberation as observers. This classification is effected by arranging the judgments through indexations on a classificatory chart. They are linked together through abbreviations, which allows strings of reference to be formed according to which judgments confirm, support, annull, contradict or interfere with each other (*Cf.* means 'confirm', *Rapp.* 'linked to', *Comp.* 'compare' and, the most rare: *Ab.jur* overturns previous case-law and *Inf.* means annulment on appeal or final appeal of a solution that was adopted until that time). Without the classificatory table of matters, which is tirelessly maintained by the case reporters, there is no doubt that the judgment would be lost forever. If the case of Mrs Parrel which reached the Section retains its share of eternity, it is because it is briefly reported in one of the categories of the table in the following form (as usual we strictly reproduce the paratext):

Section 1996-07-26
146448
To
Mrs Parrel
Mr Gentot, pdt
Mrs Touraine-Reveyrand, rapp.
Mr Sanson, c. du g.
   PROCEDURE
   POWERS AND DUTIES OF THE JUDGE
   GENERAL QUESTIONS (. . .)
54-07-01, 54-08-01-01-03
(. . .) Consequently, on the one hand, an administrative tribunal which rules by way of judgment on a request which concerns the correction of a jurisdictional decision on the basis of article R-205, exceeds the limits of its jurisdiction. And on the other hand, the submission of such a request cannot prolong the statutory time limit of appeal against the decision whose correction is requested.

The decision has become its own commentary. It is by virtue of the work of the case reporters that this virtual palace is established and drawn up, which must be added to the thick walls of the Palais-Royal, this corpus in which the body of counsellors of State resides, and which, on the other hand, has no other place of establishment, instantiation or presence than this body itself or these workplaces where, day after day, decisions are knitted together, warp and weft, threads of fact and of law, and where texts are incorporated which have been chewed on and digested by bodies, bodies which are dedicated to these texts. From now on, let us at least hope that no other case reporter will add an '*Ab.jur.*' to this commentary in 5, 10 or 100 years from now. Each lawyer, litigant, judge, law professor or student who is preparing her commentaries on the judgment will now be able to refer to the PARREL judgment and interpret it in the same way by drawing the same conclusions from this judgment which has turned into an analysis. Entirely involuntarily, Mrs Parrel has given – if not her body to science, then – at least her name and her sorrows, which now constitute a minute brick in the vast edifice of administrative law. It is a strange palace, a virtual ossuary, a gigantic columbarium, of which each rough patch, each niche, each lodge and each crevice carries the charming or outdated name, unused acronym or strange patronym of one of the parties in proceedings. It is as if all the troubles, all the misfortunes and disappointments, all the calculations and indignations of the persons involved in litigation have ended up, after a slow and difficult sedimentation, by becoming the text of the same law which serves now to give them justice. It is a surprising transubstantiation which ends, in the absence of any Code, by producing, from the material presented by cases demanding justice, the same rules thanks to which the counsellors are going to end up judging such cases!

3

A body in a palace

In which, after having followed the path of the files, we take a rest from law by doing a bit of sociology of high administration – Where we meet, in a very classic way, the members of this prestigious body – Where we measure the egalitarianism of this elite body, thanks to some statistics – In which we trace the different career profiles of these judges, who are also senior civil servants – Where the readers discover that the administrative law acquires its influence above all thanks to the different positions and professions which are occupied by the 'corps' outside the Palais-Royal

'Let's meet at the pigeonholes'

Several times a day, the members of the Council use a particular form of intellectual technology to retrieve their voluminous mail. A banal piece of furniture which at the same time serves as a disciplinary reminder, as a flow chart incarnated in the woodwork of a simple mailbox. This piece of wooden furniture is situated in a strategic position before the hall of the General Assembly, which they can access through a hidden door. It lies between the smoking room, where newspapers and magazines are spread out, and the library where texts and documents, laws and treatises are consulted, which form the subject matter of all decisions and opinions. It is close to the offices of the General Secretariat and, finally, a few steps away

Figure 3.1

from the telephones and the toilets. All the appointments take place in this room which is called 'La salle des casiers'. You would say that there is nothing surprising in the line-up of the wooden letter boxes on which the names of each of the members are inscribed, since every administration, every post office and every office make use of these sorting devices which the English language indicates with the poetic word 'pigeonholes'. Certainly, but none of these boxes that we can encounter everywhere has the particularity that it does not list the counsellors according to the banal alphabet, but according to the 'order of the promotion roster'. In the upper left-hand corner are the ones who are the most elevated in the rank of the 'corps' (except of course the Vice-President and the presidents of Section who have their own postal service).[1] In the lower right-hand corner are the youngest

---

[1] A peculiarity of the French administration is to have multiplied the 'corps', literally 'bodies', which are defined by a specific competitive exam, a specific status and a specific function: there is one 'corps' for inspecting mines (the famous 'corps des mines') and one for dealing with forests, another for roads and bridges, another for telecommunications, etc. The various 'corps' themselves are ranked according to prestige and it is the goal of all bright young men and women out of the French 'grandes écoles' to succeed in entering one as high as possible in the pecking order. Each of them functions not only like some sort of old-boy network, but also like a real administration since all moves in and out of it are carefully ruled by the managers of that 'corps'. To keep the organic metaphor, we have translated it by 'Body'.

persons who have just arrived, graduates fresh from the National School of Administration. As a result of the particular distribution of these pigeonholes, each of the members – whether he is stooped or standing upright, whether he directs himself to the right or to the centre of the rows – is literally 'reminded of his rank' when retrieving his mail. Each time, he necessarily records the position of those who are above and below him, from the upper row of pigeonholes (cruelly nicknamed 'cemetery lane' . . .) to the most recent promotion. When studying societies of primates, primatologists go to great lengths to record the ordering relationships which link individuals, families and clans according to more or less stable hierarchies. Here, at the Palais-Royal, a masterpiece of cabinet-making materializes the rank of all the members of the 'sages of the Palais-Royal', as they are often called by the press, without any possible contestation.

However, we should not believe that the order of the roster resembles the pecking order that we find in animal or human societies and which makes each junior into the master of the one who succeeds him and the servant of the one who precedes him. On the contrary, this piece of furniture, which arranges the Body of counsellors of State into an ordered relationship, also gives it its particular presence by guaranteeing the strict equality of its members. In fact, the word 'hierarchy' is not exactly right here, since, even if there indeed are auditors (the lowest rank), 'maîtres des requêtes' (the intermediary rank) and 'counsellors' (the highest), all the pigeonholes still are the same size and are made of the same wood. And even if they extend from the lower right-hand corner towards the upper left-hand corner, their owners move in the same direction with such a slow speed that nothing, absolutely nothing, could make them move from one position to another quicker – except the nomination to the senior functions of president of the Counsel Sections or of one of the sub-sections.[2] By having to find their position in the order of the pigeonholes again each day, the members are not verifying their state of grandeur or of relative unimportance – as if they gradually moved from sergeant to general, from the throne to domination, or from cherub to archangel. On the contrary, they verify that nobody has been able to steal a lead over them through privilege or has been able to modify, even if it were in infinitely small proportions, the strict parallelism of this slow movement of ascension. What this piece of furniture manifests in

[2] Apart from the quicker ascension to the functions of president, the only exception to the strict parallelism of careers comes from members who are on leave of absence and whose ascension in rank is suspended, which allows those who remain in activity at the Council, or who are on secondment, to by-pass them.

everyone's eyes is the irremovability of a body of judges whose careers escape everyone's influence and which no one can change, even if he is Vice-president or President of the Republic.[3] In the same way that the Code of Hammurabi has more allure once it is cut in black basalt, so the permanence of the Body of the counsellors of State is more forceful once it is manifested through the order of the pigeonholes. If he has a rudimentary knowledge of arithmetic, then the new arrival could calculate almost up to the precise year the time he would need in order to reach the top: almost fifty years![4] We easily understand that the perspective of a career that is so well structured and so slow considerably appeases any appetites for power. It is useless to outdo colleagues through lengthy conspiracies or to make them fall by cleverly pulling a fast one on them. The perpetrator will never advance more quickly than six pigeonholes per year in any case. . . . One should ask oneself what point there is in getting involved in the madness of competitive examinations and bending over backwards to pass as top of the class at the National School of Administration to enter into what is exactly the opposite of a rat-race.

However, the term 'irremovability' must not mislead us. The mortal boredom of those who gradually grow old together does not reign in this assembly. In fact, the pigeonholes constantly change place. Certainly, the respective rank cannot be modified, but retirement, a call to other functions, or resignations leave gaps that must be filled through a game of tag that is made even more complicated by the fact that old members return to the Council, after having left for a shorter or longer period of time, while others leave it for the time being. Let us add to these displacements the appointment of fresh counsellors who are designated by law by what is called the 'tour extérieur' ('the outside way') who come to squeeze themselves into this play of displacements, before they inexorably climb up in rank

[3] Curiously, since the members of the Council of State are not judges but civil servants of the executive, in principle they could be removed from office like any civil servant. The fact that they cannot be removed is therefore the fruit of tradition rather than of a text. Far from emphasizing the separation of powers, it – on the contary – emphasizes their intricacy, the intricacy which astounded Tocqueville. See p. 29.
[4] The calculation is easily made: between 1986 and 1996 it ranges from 2.2 ranks per year for those who have profited from long periods of leave of absence (the clock for moving up in rank then stops for them) to 12 for the Vice-president! Except for these slower or faster moves, the average career is 6.34 ranks per year . . . It therefore takes on average 50 years to move from the lower corner of the pigeonholes to the higher one. That a part of the Body is put on leave of absence, however, allows this distance to be covered in almost 45 years. We see that the term 'table of promotion' does not have the same meaning as it has, for example, in the army, since there it only orders members by age, without leaving any possible choice due to some heroic feats of arms.

like those whom they have just joined. If it is the role of the General Secretariat to manage the 'Roster', which each year forms the subject of a long-awaited and partly confidential publication, it is the role of the bailiffs to displace the wooden pigeonholes in order to constantly effect the materialization of that part of the Body said to be 'in activity at the Council of State'. That is to say, those on which the State can really count to perform the tasks of judge and counsel, approximately 200 of an effective total of 300. Since the entries and exits are incessant – according to the needs of governments, electoral changes in political power, the growing attraction of the private sector – the pigeonhole *qua* roster is constantly modified, and the bailiffs remain very occupied with the displacement of their wooden boxes. The effect of this is that it complicates the task of the ethnographer or of the new arrival even more. The disposal of a letter in the pigeonhole of a counsellor can take a long time, since each time one must integrate all the parameters of the Body: the age of the counsellor, if he attended the National School of Administration or not, if he comes 'from the outside way', if he has become in the meantime a president of sub-section, while remembering the position of the seat which he occupies in the Counsel Section . . . And in this way, by successively feeling our way forward, we end up finding the right box, which tomorrow perhaps will have moved towards the left-hand side or higher up.

A slightly restless body

Thanks to the previous chapters, the readers will already have understood the most important particularity of this Body: they are not judges, and are dying for people to cease to regard them as such. The counsellors come from politics or from government and often crave to go back to it, at least until they are exhausted by the ups and downs of public life, the toughness of the business world or the crushing hierarchy of government, when they wish to experience, once again, the muffled atmosphere, the absence of bosses and the less stressful workload of the Council. In France, the judges of the civil and criminal system are judges all their life. When they, as an exception, move from the judiciary to politics or to business, they rarely come back to their old function.[5] The counsellors of State, however, are judges and

[5] Another obvious difference: the age pyramid is much more pointed, naturally, at the Council than, for example, at the other supreme court for civil and criminal law, the Cour de cassation. All the interviews indicate the importance of this mixing, of this blend, between young auditors and counsellors who have aged on the battlefield.

counsellors *intermittently* and live at the Palais-Royal as if on the vast platform of an aircraft carrier for take-off and landing, heading for and coming from other functions. Those who have learned the austere profession of being a judge in administrative litigation, after years of hard labour, leave that position to occupy altogether different positions. Conversely, some who come through 'the outside way' as political officials, counsellors, military personnel or journalists, without any knowledge of administrative law, are going to be appointed to exercise the function of judge which they must usually learn from A to Z. Far from weakening the objectivity or the virtue of the judge and the counsellor, it is this movement of systole and diastole, this turn-over, which, according to the members of the Council, forms the most cherished (and also most peculiar) quality of their institution. In order to understand this dynamic, which is so important for the mission of the Council, and to evaluate in what way it matters for the construction of Law, we are going to make an X-ray of the Body. We will do this by making use of the last thirteen promotion rosters, to which we have added the data accessible to all in the *Who's Who* and the *Béquet*, an indispensable guide in the jungle of administrative functions. We have chosen to begin in 1996 – the year of the first government of cohabitation of Jacques Chirac who was Prime Minister when François Mitterrand was President – because it is at the time of big electoral changes of political power that the restlessness at the Council is most visible. The teams coming in, disrupting the tranquillity of the Palace, then cross the teams from the other political spectrum who are going out! The latter are going to take up their austere functions again, after a short interlude of well-deserved holidays (you can therefore easily recognize the losing parties by their tans).

Regarded in its entirety, the dynamic of the Body is very simple: it increases slowly, growing from 262 in 1986 to a little more than 300 in 1999. The members enter the Council either directly from the National School of Administration, as auditors, or through 'the outside way' which allows them to attain the rank of 'maître des requêtes' or that of counsellor, directly. In 1996, the year that we have chosen as a reference, there were 206 members of the Body, and 90 had been appointed through 'the outside' (half to the rank of 'maître' and half to that of counsellor).[6] However, the rule of one-

---

[6] To these must be added, for good measure, 11 'extraordinary members' who have been appointed at the end of their career. They take up a place on the Roster for two years, but are not really regarded as persons coming through 'the outside way'. They are already retired and can therefore not be included in the Body itself.

third of the members coming through 'the outside' for every two-thirds coming directly from the Body, minimizes the part that the National School of Administration plays. Of these people coming through 'the outside way', 33 have also attended the National School of Administration, without having been able, at the time, to integrate directly into the Council as 'the top of the class' (the majority have had to serve in administrative tribunals for a long time).[7] In fact, the true proportion of National School of Administration graduates is up to 80 per cent. Without any possible contestation, the Palais-Royal is a bulwark of the National School of Administration. While the weight of the years does not entirely efface the subtle distinctions between the two sub-types of that School's graduates (those who are 'of the Body' and those who have had to wait for a long time to finally join their old fellow students), nothing effaces the innumerable differences in career, dress, manners of speaking and humour between the gathering of National School of Administration graduates and the others, who have come through 'the outside way'.[8]

In principle, they join in order to bring in the competencies which the body lacks, from professional roles such as those of doctors, generals, academics and captains of industry. A certain number of civil servants who are said to be 'mobile' (15 in 1996) participate for a few years in the tasks of the Litigation and of the Counsel Sections. This allows them at once to relieve the counsellor of certain tasks and to perfect their knowledge of the administrative law. This will be very useful for them once they reintegrate into their judiciary function. Even though an extreme politeness governs the relations at the Council, the immense difference in rank between those who are 'mobile' and those who are true counsellors is openly expressed.

[7] There exist, in fact, two types of 'outside ways'. One is reserved for administrative tribunals – the ratio is one person through the exterior as 'maître des requêtes' compared to four persons from the Body, and one as counsellor compared to six from the Body. A second is said to come 'from government', but they can in fact come from any profession and are traditionally, more political. It is in this way that the members of cabinets, Ministers, and counsellors of the Presidency may end up holding a seat at the Palais-Royal.

[8] Even though this difference between ways of recruitment is constantly denied, it jumps out at the ethnographer. Witness, for instance, two schoolmates from the National School of Administration who were a few points apart in the competitive graduation examinations, one of whom is in an administrative tribunal while the other directly integrated into the Council. The first says, with a bitter and ironic smile, of the second: 'Yes, but you understand, he is so much more intelligent than me' . . . The distinction between recruits is moreover openly admitted in this sentence from Massot and Girardot: 'The professionalization is also manifested through the fact that the most important functions in the Council are almost entirely entrusted to members who have entered there as auditors' (*Le Conseil d'Etat* (1999), p. 37). We should therefore rest assured: the persons coming through 'the outside way' are not going to de-professionalize the Council . . .

Where do these 57 strangers, in a body of 306, come from? We cannot say that it exactly concerns people coming in from the *hoi polloi*. They come from the world of politics, law and State. There are 5 Ministers, 7 Prefects, 8 judges, 2 Members of Parliament, 7 military personnel, 4 university professors, a few high-ranking civil servants who have acted as aides to a Minister, and 2 lawyers. The ministerial cabinets are not a bad way to get into the Palais-Royal (7) and, particularly, the Presidency of the Republic, which has provided 8 counsellors, is a good route . . . We only find 1 engineer, 1 journalist and 1 businessman. The proportion of women is reasonable for France, since it is approximately a sixth (52 out of 306), even if they are still far from the famous equality. Ten years beforehand in 1986, they formed only 10 per cent (27 women out of 262 members).[9] Even though the world of judges and counsellors has participated closely in active government and even in politics, we cannot say that it provides a faithful image of the socio-professional categories of France. But then again, that is also not its aim.

However, it is not because of its modes of entry that the Body is interesting, but through the possibility given to its members to *leave* the Council for shorter or longer durations before returning to occupy the functions of judge and counsellor. In the same way that Rome is not actually in Rome, an important proportion (from 24 per cent in 1986 to 36 per cent in 1996) of the Council is not actually seated at the Palais-Royal but occupies other and sometimes very different functions. The Roster distinguishes three great rubrics, each corresponding to diverse degrees of separation from the Council. The first, which is entitled 'in function at the Council of State', allows the counsellors to fulfil some official roles which have been designated by law. That is the case of presidents of administrative tribunals, secretaries at the General Secretariat of government, and directors of ministerial cabinets. Then there are those who are on secondment (*en détachement*) (approximately 67 according to the calculation methods for our year of reference, 1996) in order to be able to occupy other functions, like those of Members of Parliament or senators (8 members), to serve in the great public offices and even in the competitive public sector.[10] Finally, there are those who have chosen to

[9] The women tend to be more stable at the Council than the men. For the women in 1996, the average term of office at the Council is 8.5 years, against 3 in the different types of secondment and 0.7 on leave of absence (the index of presence is 1.5 instead of 1.8). See Bui-Xuan, *Les femmes au Conseil d'Etat* (2000).
[10] In order to be complete, we would need to add the position of those who temporarily resign from office ('hors cadre'). This is a slightly less favourable position than

put themselves on leave of absence ('en disponibilité') (38) to occupy the most diverse jobs in high finance, legal council or, more rarely, for personal reasons. At the end of ten years' leave of absence, the members of the Body are struck off the Roster but until that time they can take up their place again when they wish, even if they will have stagnated in rank in the meantime.[11]

To the exterior renewal of the Body (through the arrival of young National School of Administration graduates and persons through 'the outside way', and through the exits due to retirement, death or resignation), one must then add the *interior* turn-over at the Body due to members who leave or return. It is in this way that, in 1996, 41 members changed function in relation to the previous year (they left or came back from secondment or leave of absence) and 15 were still going to change function the following year.[12] If it is true that the turn-over is more important in the years of electoral change of political power, it is still the case that by adding the two internal and

---

secondment, because it obliges one to wait to take up one's place and rank again at the Palais-Royal until a position becomes vacant. Since we do not seek to do administrative science here, we have usually regrouped these sometimes Byzantine subtleties in the calculations made below.

[11] It is very difficult to measure the real workload of the counsellor. The members who are novices and must therefore learn the profession must be distinguished from those who are presidents of sub-section, commissioners of the law, General Secretaries and case reporters. For the latter we are dealing with a full-time job, which does not prevent these naturally hard-working individuals from participating in a great number of other activities. It seems that the workload oscillates roughly between a large third of the time and a small half of the time. If we take ARIANE as 'snitch', we notice that the number of files per person and per year at the Litigation Section varies considerably: from 25 to 150 in one and the same arbitrarily chosen subsection. But the difficulty of files can explain the differences. It nevertheless remains to be the case – and this is one of the charms of the Council – that they can slightly adjust their workload by forsaking their productivity bonus, keeping just 30 files, or they can push Stakhanovism up to 70 difficult cases, even carrying 150 cases for which the arguments resemble one another a lot. It is the president of sub-section who, in his great wisdom, distributes the points and reprimands those who are exaggerating a little. Even if the workload is not overwhelming, it is wrong to say – as they did at the time of Stendhal – that the Council is a sinecure. As for the salary, that is not so unpleasant since a young 'maître de requête' after seven years of service (index 693) earns 53,000 euros (bonuses included) and a president of section, after almost forty years of service in the Body (scale F), earns 94,000 euros (these numbers were very gracefully provided by Massot and Girardot, *Le Conseil d'Etat* (1999), p. 39).

[12] For the year 1987, for example, the numbers are 38 and 11 out of a smaller total of 264 members. Of course, we do not count the numerous changes of function within the Council of State, like those of the 'commissioner of the law' or of the president, the assessor or the General Secretary, etc.

external sources of renewal, we can evaluate the ratio at approximately 17 per cent for 1996. Certainly, the restlessness is not frenzied, but in the end life at the Palace is also not entirely like that of a monastery. They can be assured that they will not find themselves fifty years from now always among the same faces, seated at the same table, in the same Sections and sub-sections. And the bailiffs have the certainty of having to move the mailboxes in the pigeonhole room often . . .

It is possible to reconstruct the *range of possibilities* from the Roster (see figure 3.2) with some precision.[13] This chart is obtained from all the careers of members who were present at the Council from 1980 to 1999, and from the whole of their respective careers. The direction of the arrows indicates the movements which are most usual from one position to another, while the junctions mark the career choices open to the members. The diagram shows nothing more or less than the condensed projection of the individual trajectories of counsellors, in the same way in which a myrmecologist could trace the displacements – accumulated over a long period of time – of ants through their nests. The chart is read from the lower right-hand corner. The trajectories begin either when they leave the National School of Administration (ENA) – as is the case for the majority – or, as we know, when they leave an exterior post, like the members coming from politics, government, administrative tribunals, ministerial cabinets or, more rarely, from the army or the private sector (the latter is particularly the case with members in extraordinary service).

In the middle of the chart, we find the 'nest' of the counsellors – that is to say, the basic service from where members can disperse towards a collection of diverse functions. In the upper right-hand corner are the positions of counsellors in the cabinets or as official representatives; above them are the positions of directors of high government services as well as the nerve centre that is the General Secretariat of the government. Always in the centre, high up, is the crucial function of the commissioner of the law which leads to many coveted positions, as we can see from the number of junctions. In the upper left-hand corner are the functions of director in big public companies, as well as important positions in what we can call the

---

[13] The charts in this chapter have been drawn up by Andrei Mogoutov, whom I thank very much for his patience and his indispensable insights. The method which he uses and has developed, Réseaux-Lu™, is explained in detail in Andrei Mogoutov, 'Données relationnelles en sciences sociales' (1998). This method has the incomparable advantage of allowing at one and the same time the elaboration of categories while conserving the variety of individual relations, because it is not based on statistical calculation but on a relative balancing of links between the very diverse entities.

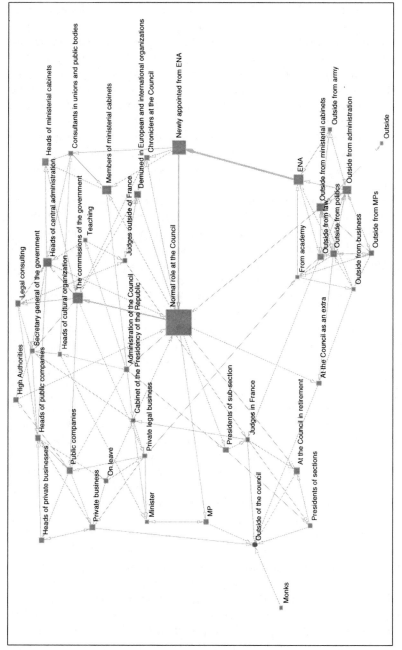

Figure 3.2

Higher Administrative Authorities, whose number and importance have multiplied with the course of time. Other choices, but certainly less numerous, possibly lead to private companies on the one hand, or elective functions on the other. Finally, in the lower left-hand quarter, are the counsellors who are the oldest, who are most passionately interested in law and government and who achieve great careers within the Council itself. They are the only ones, as we have seen, who break the rigorous equality of the members – presidents of Section, sub-section, or of the courts of appeal of the administrative tribunals. We can even see the unique case of a counsellor who has become a monk, which is nevertheless respectfully represented by the chart . . .

While it is sometimes difficult to understand why the top level of the National School of Administration graduates would fight to reach the Palais-Royal when we are faced with the overwhelming austerity of the matters dealt with, this range of possibilities easily explains the energy put into trying to enter the Body. The paths are wide open, the extreme diversity of positions and returns to the central, warm nest are always well accepted. The members can therefore at once benefit from the excitement of cabinets, the risks of business, the authority of high government, the heat of elections and, nevertheless, come back at almost any moment to take their place in the immutable work that ensures the continuity of the State and its missions.

No normal organization could cope with such an intense movement of entry and exit. But the tasks of litigation or counsel have the enormous advantage that they are *discontinuous*. All the work is in fact organized around numbered files which each constitute a small world; once these files are closed, this world passes away with it. Consequently, it is very easy to enter and leave a particular course of action, because the members arrive or leave while respecting the rhythm of the opening and closing of files. The only problems of coordination, which we have encountered several times, are posed when a commissioner of the law abandons his file before presenting his conclusions or when the reporter who wrote the note has left the Council a long time ago. Someone else must then immerse himself in those writings and recompose them or recompose the solutions they contain. But even then, the collective memory of the group (sub-section or Counsel Section) who discussed the case allows him to regain a foothold in the flux of files without great difficulty. Without this particular aspect of the Council – which also facilitates the work of the ethnographer who has been able to jump on and off the bandwagon easily without losing anything essential in the course of action – the Palais-Royal could never serve as a fall-back position like this for so many career plans without emptying the work of the law of its substance. The movement of this weaving, which we followed in the preceding chapter, this slow maceration which allows the connection of states of facts with the scattered pieces of texts, would be impossible without this coming and going that is so typical of the Council and which seems so curious when it is regarded from the outside.

Let us pause a few moments on this multiform experience, which explains a lot of the qualities which the counsellors attribute to themselves, and which allows them to sometimes look scornfully at the judges 'of the civil and criminal system' who are isolated for their whole life in functions of judgment, without ever experiencing the difficulties and tensions of political action, the military or the government. If we calculate, for the entire Body in 1996, the number of person-years during which the members have been a part of it – which we can easily do by consulting the Roster – we easily understand the journalistic cliché of the 'sages of the Palais-Royal': the Body benefits at every moment from an accumulated experience of approximately 5,000 person-years! When they are seated in the Assembly of Litigation or in the General Assembly, the members of the Body mobilize 5,000 person-years of accumulated experiences.[14] Certain members, like President Braibant, have held a seat at the Council for more than 38 years! Now, during almost 40 per cent of this time, the counsellors have exercised functions outside of the Palais (2,047 person-years), either on secondment or on leave of absence.[15] This is a considerable proportion which explains this inexhaustible reservoir of experiences which the members of the Body delve into, during the course of judgment as well as of counsel, to form an opinion, to convince their colleagues or to educate the government envoy on the duties of good government. It is not surprising that the arguments of political opportunity, good government, equity or feasibility are so often brought to bear on the knowledge of texts and the game of precedents. Even once they are integrated into the Body, the members have only passed 60 per cent of their time in the muffled atmosphere of the Palace. For

[14] For the National School of Administration graduates in the Body, 3,606 years; 520 for the people from 'the outside way' who have become 'maîtres de requête'; and 173 for the people from 'the outside way' who have become counsellors. If we were to count completely, we would have to add to this collective experience the long and often prestigious careers of the members who held exterior posts *before* entering the Body. Here, we only count the years when they rubbed shoulders with the administrative law.

[15] Respectively, 672 person-years for the first category, 1,079 on secondment, and merely 296 person-years on leave of absence.

them, Law does not only reside in the law, but equally in the context of application which they have seen with their own eyes and with which they have sometimes violently collided.

This capacity to come and go explains the diversity of careers that we are going to characterize, which is not easy since they are diverse. However, we can nevertheless regroup them into a few profiles.[16] At two extremes, we find, for example, Jean Marc Simon who, from twenty-six years of presence in the Body (always with 1996 as the year of reference), has only passed four years at the Council before spending some years on secondment in a Ministry. Then, after a short stay of one year at the Litigation Section, he has put himself on leave of absence in order to occupy high functions in a company, before finally being considered to have resigned.[17] For people like him, the Council has merely been a long 'grande école' which prepared him for other careers. Conversely, Nicole Questiaux has held a seat at the Council for forty-three years without interruption, except to occupy briefly the function of Minister of Health after the election of François Mitterrand in 1986.[18] She is representative of those whom we can call the 'virtuosos' of administrative law, like, for example, the amazing Bruno Genevois who is capable of citing hundreds of judgments from memory with the date, the page of the *Lebon* volume, and the name of the commissioner at the time, and who still only fulfilled strictly

---

[16] We find almost the same numbers in Kessler, *Le Conseil d'Etat* (1968). Let us note that, of the Body as she studied it in 1966, 45 members were still at the Council in 1996! We can quantify the different types of career thanks to an index of presence at the Palace (the total duration divided by the number of years effectively holding a position within its walls). Around 100 members, so one-third, corresponds to index 1 (all the time passed in the Body has been at the Palais-Royal, which is – let us recall – the case of persons coming through 'the outside way' and young auditors). Around 50 make up the ones who have a brief but brilliant career (the index goes up to 12.5! for Michel Dupuch who has completed his whole career, except for one short year, outside the Council of State). The rest (from 1.3 to 2.5) presents the typical profile with coming and going for a little more or less than half of the time (the total average of the index for the whole Body is 1.89).

[17] Since all the documents on the basis of which we establish these profiles are public, we have, for this chapter, suspended the rule of strict anonymity which would not have made any kind of sense.

[18] If we take the superior half of the Body (the 150 first ranks), the average career is roughly 15 years at the Council, 7.5 years on secondment, and 1 year on leave of absence (the average of the lower half is 5.7 years at the Conseil, only 2.3 outside, and 1 on leave of absence). But these averages remain not particularly informative. Let us recall that the young auditors cannot leave the Council before the end of their 'auditorat' (on average 4.7 years before becoming 'maître des requêtes') and that they will have to practise their patience for an average of 15.5 years before becoming a counsellor.

legal functions even when he was on secondment in active government.[19]

In the middle, we find the typical careers of great 'commis de l'Etat' like those of Jacques Fournier who, in forty-six years of presence in the Body, has held a seat at the Council for only fifteen years. He has been coming and going from posts as commissioner of the law to temporary resignation from office, then coming back to perform his functions at the Council, leaving again on secondment, and becoming commissioner of the law again for a few months. Then he was called in 1981 to the Presidency of the Republic, then to the General Secretariat of the government; subsequently he was on secondment at the SNCF (the French railway system) as director, before returning again to be seated in the Counsel Section of Public Works. Then he was in 'active retirement', only to leave the Council in 1999.[20] Equally typical is the career of Olivier Schramek, who was first commissioner of the law, then chief adviser at the Ministry of Higher Education. He subsequently became commissioner again for two years, before returning as director of the cabinet at the Ministry of Education with Lionel Jospin and finally came back for two years at the Litigation Section. Then, after five years of secondment at the Constitutional Court, he became director of the Prime Minister's office until the latter's fall in May 2002.

These careers of great servants of the State distinguish themselves from those of pure jurists as well as from those who have a quick and brilliant career but who are mostly looking for contacts (like, for example, Jacques Attali, who only held a seat at the Litigation Section for five years, between his political adventure with François Mitterrand and his adventure in consulting). But they equally

---

[19] However, the term 'pure jurists' should not mislead us. We only find, all in all, two law professors who have come from the University. The disdain for 'doctrine' is universal at the Council, except when it comes from old classics like the lecture of Chappus which we already cited. The almost total rupture with the university and the world of research in general – social sciences, political sciences, administrative sciences and cameral sciences – is a source of continuous surprise for the observer (see the last chapter on the role which this inquiry plays). Even if this disdain is vigorously denied by the counsellors, to convince oneself one has only to consider the number of doctorates obtained by counsellors or to count the number of memoirs and doctorates which study the Council – except for the ones dealing with strictly legal matters.

[20] So as not to deny themselves these treasures of erudition and experience which the old counsellors represent, and above all the old 'presidents de Section administrative', the Council calls on those who are retired to remain in function until they reach sixty-eight years of age. However, they are no longer able to occupy the roles of 'president'.

distinguish themselves from those rather remarkable careers of elected representatives who come back to the Council when they have been beaten and who leave again when they have found support or a majority again. That is the case for example of Cazin d'Honinctun who, after a few years on secondment, came back to occupy his place at the Litigation Section and then left it again to occupy a seat as an elected representative. He returned again for three years and left again to become a Member of Parliament. As soon as he was beaten in the elections, he put himself on leave of absence to become a lawyer, while nevertheless leaving open the possibility of coming back if things turned out for the worse, like they did during his delegation to Parliament. The Council then plays the role of a bus shelter or a fully comprehensive insurance. Fortunately, there are people who come through 'the outside way' and whose already accomplished careers mean that they provide much greater stability once they have reached the harbour of the Palais-Royal.[21]

However, we should not believe that these coming and goings are looked upon badly. On the contrary, from its foundation by Napoleon onwards, the Council had to serve as a nursery for diverse assignments within the State, as every reader of Stendhal knows. If you were to pass seven or eight years at the Council without moving, as auditor and then as 'maître des requêtes', people would be worried to see you staying on at the Palais-Royal without trying your chances elsewhere or without becoming the object of desire of Ministers, central governments, public companies, and even of business. The typical career of a National School of Administration graduate in the Body presupposes a rapid call to other functions quickly after the 'auditorat'.[22]

---

[21] There are famous exceptions, like that of Régis Debray who has recounted his setbacks in *Loués soient nos seigneurs* (1996), and the less famous one of Jean-Pierre Aubert who only spent one year at the Council before putting himself on leave of absence to become director of a bank (he nevertheless came back in 1999 to take up his place at the Litigation Section again, before the period granted for his leave of absence expired). The average career of people arriving through 'the outside way', still based on 1996, was 7 years at the Palais, 2 on secondment, and 0.1 on leave of absence. We see then that they are much more stable, which is logical since their career is partly behind them.

[22] For the body such as it was in 1996, only two members, after leaving the School, passed more than ten years without a break from the Palais. However, one of them also holds elective functions; some local mandates are compatible with a function at the Council.

An import–export profession

This movement of exportation of methods and principles of law and importation of problems and preoccupations, which we have just seen at the level of the Body, is perceived even more clearly by arbitrarily choosing a sub-section and looking with a stronger zoom lens at the movements of exchange which the restlessness of the members gives rise to. Let us take a sub-section which we will call 'the Tenth'. If it were to meet in its entirety to deal with a file, it would benefit from the experience accumulated by its members, who have been Prefects, at the General Secretariat of the government, at the headquarters of the air forces, at the 'Commissariat du Plan', at the cabinet of several Ministries, at the French railway company, in Parliament as Members of Parliament (and one subsequently as Minister of Home Affairs), at Foreign Affairs and even in particle physics! And, conversely, the temporary departure of its members to occupy other functions means that, in dealing with matters, several administrations, a constituency and the National Health Service will benefit from the experience of the sub-section.

A Counsel Section, like the one for Public Works, can give a good idea of this sort of breathing which is so particular to the Council. When it takes up a draft of a law or a decree, the collective experience of 800 person-years is going to be applied in the session: 38 person-years (p/y) of ministerial cabinets and 62 p/y as commissioner of the law, which is the most technical of the functions as we have seen; 88 p/y of the careers of members who were designated through 'the outside way' have unfolded in the position of judge in administrative tribunals; other persons who have held exterior posts have been Prefects, government officials in large cities, political activists, Ministers or persons in charge of important services. All the members of the Body have participated in the management of government (22 p/y), have held elective functions or have presided over administrative tribunals. The members who held a seat at the Council in 1999 have used their robes in this same Section for a total of 121 p/y, four among them were already there in 1989, and two have held a seat there for more than fourteen years.

Is it possible to make the extract from career profiles more precise in such a way that we can give the reader an idea, this time no longer of the range of possibilities but of the *choices* made by all the members at once? The statistics would then still not be very interesting, given the diversity of career choices and the importance of representing the atypical careers at the same time as the characteristic profiles. We have asked Réseaux-Lu™ to classify in five clusters the members who were part of the Body in 1980 as well as in 1989, and to shorten the list by not taking into account either entries or departures.[23] For all these members, we have reconstituted the totality of positions occupied since they left the School up to 1999, including for those who still were at the Council at this date. We have simply counted the number of full years which they spent in each of these positions. Afterwards, it was easy to extract automatically the most differentiated career profiles, while also showing, thanks to the procedure, the position of the individuals who belong to one or two clusters at once. The direction of the arrow goes from the grouping to which they belong most to the one to which they belong the least. The double arrows mark their exclusive belonging to a single cluster.

Figure 3.3 shows the entirety of the Body at once, thereby providing the complex but nevertheless readable geography of the paths of all the members who are present at any one time. For each cluster, the names in bold emphasize those of the members who are the most representative of their type. The circular envelopes regroup those who share the same atypical profile and who straddle two clusters.[24]

A few contrasted profiles appear clearly. First there is the one which we have called the 'basic service' at the Council, which occupies the whole right-hand side. Then there is the small group of 'elected representatives' in the upper right-hand corner and the one of so-called 'private enterprises' to the left. Then we find a well-characterized profile in the lower left-hand corner, which is the one of those who occupy the functions of the presidency within the Council after a longer or shorter time spent in high administration. Two more confused profiles – we can see this from the number of individuals who belong at the same time to other clusters – group, on the one hand, those who occupy important positions in public companies,[25] and, on the other, those who have been commissioners of the law and who

---

[23] For the purposes of this chart, we have left to one side the people coming 'from the outside' whose careers are often behind them – in any case the 'maître de requête' and the counsellor – in order to concentrate uniquely, and somewhat unjustly, on the National School of Administration graduates who have left the School at the top of their class.

[24] In order not to get lost in these charts, one must remember that only the lines and their relations carry information. Distances are not pertinent and are merely used for reasons of readability.

[25] Given the subtle swing of the pendulum for the last thirty years in France between nationalization and denationalization, one must not attribute too much importance to the distinction 'private companies' / 'public companies'. In case of doubt, we considered that leave of absence instead of secondment indicated a crossing of the blurred barrier between public and private. On all these points, see Roquemaurel, *Les membres du Conseil d'Etat et les entreprises* (1997).

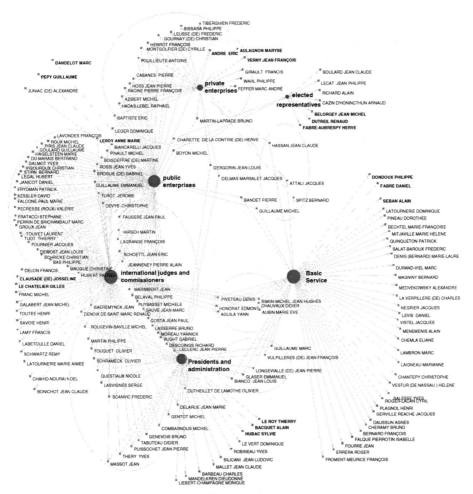

Figure 3.3

participate in numerous functions as judges – in particular outside France – or in diplomacy.

Let us remember that this shows relative positions and not a strict belonging to one category. This is the case, because each individual is linked to one or two clusters, depending on which clusters all the others belong to. In order to rearrange the clusters, it therefore suffices to move a few names. As a result of this, the general labels given to the regroupings are necessarily artificial. However, from the point of view of the sociology of professions, the chart represents a more exact overview of the distributions, since it is probably in this way – through blurred groupings – that the members position themselves, one in relation to another.

When we consider this chart, we easily understand that the Law represents merely one dimension of the Council, but to follow the other dimensions we would have needed to embark upon a study of the sociology of high administration, which has never been our goal. So, we will then leave the counsellors to their diverse and fascinating adventures in order to apply ourselves to the mere history of files and cases, which is infinitely more grey. The reason why we wanted to reconstruct the movement back and forth, in and out of law, was to point out one of the most interesting features of French administrative law, which otherwise seems so exotic: the career paths of counsellors prohibit law from being regarded *as a separate sphere*. Nothing is less autonomous than this law here; it must be accompanied by the most remote activities in order for it to maintain its efficiency; it must be incessantly confronted with practical problems, which have been brought back from these diverse activities in order to produce legal reasoning. It thus offers an ideal example for simultaneously following the fabric of law (more than the biographies of the jurists) and yet contesting the idea that law is apart from anything else. And yet *it is*, as we are now going to see.

4

The passage of law

In which things become terribly complicated for the readers, who have to
absorb much more law than they would wish – In which we pay close
attention to the minor dramas created by the turbulent career of the
means* invoked by litigants – In which a case concerning the expulsion of
a foreigner allows us to weigh the respective roles of prejudice and law
– In which a fussy litigant initiates an administrative action and shows us
the strange power of texts – In which the reversal of precedent allows us
to grasp the particular rhythm of the formation of judgments – In which
we summarize the transfer of value objects so as to get a better sense of
the lively movement of the law

A brutal shift of reason

Now that preceding chapters have enabled the reader to gain some
familiarity with the rather exotic domain of French administrative
law, and with the remarkable way in which it deals with files, we can
reach further into the heart of the matter, drawing on a careful
attending of review meetings in order to clarify what the members of
the Council mean when they assert that their job consists of 'saying
the law' ('dire le droit'). The ethnographer's only advantage is that,
unlike lawyers, judges, philosophers or sociologists of law, he does
not have to presume that the problem has been solved in order then

to explain it, comment on it, reshape it, enhance it or deepen it. He can therefore take all the precautions that are needed if one is to grasp what is going on while at the same time making the effort not to understand things too quickly. In other words, he can turn his awkwardness and incompetence to good use by not distinguishing too fast between that which is essential and that which is peripheral.

In the detailed episodes that follow, we shall seek to reconstitute the actors' *reasoning* step by step, without being overly concerned with its logical or rhetorical form.[1] Not being an orator, a psychologist or an expert in cognition, the observer has no means of penetrating the mental states or neural connections of those whose arguments he observes; no medical imagery, no scanner and no 3-D reconstruction of the sectors of the brain is available to him. Besides, were he to indulge in this kind of study, the likelihood is that the complexity of the legal issues would be a considerable obstacle in the attempt to extract reasoning in its pure state; in order to bring out modes of thought, it is better to attend to simpler things than the mysteries of administrative law, in which the psychologist would get lost much more quickly than those he observes![2] Besides, nothing says that judges – even though most of them are bright graduates of the National School of Administration . . . – display particularly brilliant styles of reflection. We should apply to lawyers the hypothesis that the anthropology of science once applied to scientists: that is, we should provisionally leave the specific *mental* dimension to one side in order to focus on the *subject matter* of their activity, on the basis that their particular way of being right is not explained by the form of their thinking but by its *content*.[3] As we will see in the following chapter, the only difference between law and science arises from the fact that the subject matter on which our counsellors work does not have the obviousness of the subject matter of laboratory work. For those readers who are not jurists, it takes a little bit more effort to point this out. Let's say that, in the anthropology of science, the subject

[1] For this, see the classic works by Perelman, *The Realm of Rhetoric* (1982) and McEvoy, *L'invention défensive* (1995).

[2] In his wonderful study, *Culture and Inference* (1980), Hutchins shows that it is a mistake to attribute cognitive capacities or incapacities to Trobrianders. Rather, their dreadfully complex laws led ignorant colonists (and the first anthropologists) to say that these 'poor savages' 'thought' in the 'wrong way'. Hutchins suggests that before speaking about their modes of thought, it would be better to examine their laws. In general, the content of reasoning is always worth infinitely more than the banal container of that reasoning.

[3] For a justification of this hypothesis, see Latour, *Science in Action* (1987), Hutchins, *Cognition in the Wild* (1995), Suchman, *Plans and Situated Actions* (1987).

matter is highly visible and texts much less so; in the anthropology of law, it is the other way around: texts are omnipresent, and the subject matter is invisible.

Let us begin with a banal case which will allow us to identify what the semiotic analysis of the dynamic of the novel calls the circulation or the transfer of 'value objects'.[4] Although mental reasoning is inaccessible to the observer equipped only with a notebook, the sentences uttered by the members of the Council nevertheless bear *explicit* signs of the changes of position they make with respect to the files that they are dealing with, and each of those signs indicates the transition, movement or metamorphosis of the particular force whose dynamic we are attempting to reconstitute. Such are the more or less recognizable traces that we will use as empirical findings, and that will enable us to ensure that the foundation of our commentary is not too fragile, and that the reader is always able to check for himself that we have not over-interpreted the documents. We will try to grasp what the counsellors make *pass* through their interactions which allow them to judge the quality of their action. To borrow an expression from the theory of speech acts, on the basis of which signs do they recognize the *conditions of felicity or infelicity* of legal statements?

Among the slight tensions which run through the Council, the first is the ongoing examination that each member has to go through at the hand of all of his peers during the review sessions and the deliberation, and by means of which he proves the quality of his work to his colleagues. On this particular warm day in June the examination begins badly for the reporter who suffers a slight loss of authority by allowing himself, quite unusually, to be interrupted in the middle of the reading of his note by the reviser, who addresses the sub-section in the following terms: 'There is an omission here, because there is an argument* that has not been cited.'[5] Let us take note of this omission, and take as our first value object the weight, or the *authority* of a member, her capacity to speak without being interrupted, and to gain her colleagues' support for her opinion. This particular 'value object', the members' authority with respect to their colleagues, changes from session to session, and throughout their entire career at the Council dealing with cases and files. It changes because of the

---

[4] 'Narrative discourse often presents itself in the form of a circulation of value objects: its organization can therefore be described as a series of transfers of values': Greimas and Courtès, *Semiotics and Language: an Analytical Dictionary* (1982), under 'value'.

[5] Remember that all the words with an asterisk (ground*, argument*, reason*) are English equivalents of the single French term '*moyen*', also translated by mean*. See note 12, p. 10.

continuous processing of case-loads, through the altering and crushing of opinions rubbing against each other, piled on top of one
another, polished as pebbles by people who see each other constantly,
who sit side by side for whole mornings or afternoons, and who end
up knowing each other with the mixture of respect, equality, indifference and autonomy that is characteristic of monks collaborating
in an intellectual task in a monastery, with no clear hierarchical
divisions.

Dorval (after having interrupted the reading of the reporter): To
save some time for the sub-section, I have to say that I **disagree**
with the reporter: there is a mean* that he has overlooked and which
seems to me to be well founded.

> *As we have already seen, these famous means* are not always
> entirely clear: we can regroup them, make them emerge or, as is the
> case here, overlook them, even where they are used as headings in
> the lawyer's statement of claim.*

(Dorval summarizes the case, taking up some of the time allo-
cated to the reporter's speech, instead of waiting until the reporter
has finished, as is usual.) The case concerns accountants; they have
made some unlawful advertisements in the telephone directory, see
the 14-1-1989 'decision by the Financial Services Authority', I note
that this decision **is not** in the file.

> *To be or not to be 'in the file', that is always the question, because
> it provides confirmation of whether, in the present case, what is at
> issue is a mistake made in the process of review (which means that
> the sub-section has not done its job well) or an ill-conceived reply
> made by a party which has not prepared its case very well.*

Mr Huntel appealed; Sofinomel was sentenced to a reprimand,
which was noted in his file; Sofinomel defers to you for a final appeal
within the statutory time limit, while the other party (the association
of accountants) asks you to **reject** the claim.

> *The Council of State serves as the court of final judgment for a
> multitude of professional organizations, medical associations,
> organizations of experts, accountants, etc.; the situation which is
> to be ruled upon is far from clearly decided since the two parties
> take exactly opposite positions: one asks that the decision of the
> professional regulatory body to punish him be declared null and
> void, while the professional regulatory body seeks to have this claim
> rejected; the expression 'within the statutory time limit' reminds us*

*of the fact that, in these matters, cases can only be instigated within
rigorous time limits, generally two months.*[6]

The successive reporters reject all arguments*, but without
responding to the **only** well-founded mean*; which says that there
is a **problem** with the interpretation of the claim. Although this is
explicitly raised, it is **less clear** in the additional memoir.

*Since this case has dragged on, there have been several successive
reporters, and, according to the reviser, none has been entirely
competent; the additional memoir is a new written document which
the claimant has submitted to supplement his statement of claim;
remember that the judge cannot raise any means* other than those
which have been explicitly raised by the parties; now, the whole
discussion will be concerned with the question of knowing whether
that mean*, visible in one document but obscure in the other, has
indeed been raised by the relevant party or not; such interpretation
requires what is called an 'effort' which is only admissible within
certain limits, which are always defined on the spot.*

The company asserts in its initial statement of claim of 8 April
1992 that the decision of the professional regulatory body to decide
on the issue **behind closed doors** was unusual.

*This tiny point of law makes all French professional regulatory
bodies tremble because an increasing number of their decisions do
not fulfil the conditions concerning 'due process' that are required
by European law.*[7]

This is **undisputed**.

*The expression does not mean that it is true, but that the opposing
party has not disputed it and that therefore the part of the file which,
according to the file, has not been contested by the opposing party
can be considered as an established fact.*[8]

[6] When a case is not instigated within the statutory time limits, this is called 'tardiveté' and the case is sent back to the lower court without even having been examined.
This rigour concerning time limitations unfortunately does not apply to the rendering of the judgment itself which can drag on for years ...

[7] See, for example, a more recent case in Section M. DIDIER, 19-11-1999, regarding
a decision of the disciplinary commission of the Financial Services Authority (the
COB in France), which was judged to have had little regard for due process (in that
case the judgment consisted of a rejection).

[8] In chapter 5, we return extensively to this extraordinary definition of 'fact', which
is related to the scientific meaning of 'fact' only as a homonym: whatever is not
contested, despite the opportunity given by the procedural fairness of the law, is
taken by the judge to be a fact.

I **consider** the argument* to have been raised in the memoir of
1994: we cannot say that the argument* has been abandoned, even
though Paridole (the lawyer) **drowns** the mean* in a series of arguments (Dorval reads the memoir).

> *It is always difficult for the reviser to make the argument* emerge
> in spite of its almost subliminal presence and the efforts of the
> lawyer to 'drown' it; in general, lawyers who argue in court have a
> rather bad reputation and are always accused of not doing their job
> properly – even though they are the ones who have extracted the
> means* in the first place and therefore have their own complaints
> about the work of the counsellors . . .*

In addition, in 1994, we had **not** yet decided the Maubleu case.[9]

> *A decision by the Assembly, thus carrying maximum weight,*[10]
> *rejected a similar appeal by a claimant who wished to establish that
> the 'Bar Association' (l'Ordre des avocats) was in breach of the
> European Convention of Human Rights. After publication of the
> judgment on 14 February 1996, it consequently became easier for
> lawyers to formulate a reason* whose evident logic was reinforced
> by this judgment. The reporter means to say that, even if the sub-
> section does not wish to make an 'effort' today to discern a legal
> mean* which is obscured by an untidy statement of claim (especially
> since the lawyer nowadays only has to 'do a Maubleu'), such indul-
> gence is justified for a case dating from 1994 in which the mean*
> existed in outline but had not yet been established through 'our
> Maubleu decision'.*

It is clarified by the initial formulation of the argument* (he reads
the first statement of claim) on the European Convention on Human
Rights **even though it has not been explicitly articulated.**
Following the line of Maubleu 14-2-96, you have previously declared
a decision to be null and void because it was taken behind closed
doors . . . (he cites a case of a dentist, then another, then a third).

> *The reviser, carried away by his enthusiasm, uses the Maubleu deci-
> sion retroactively in trying to make the judgment of 1996 consistent*

---

[9] Assembly 132269, 1996-2-14, M. Marchand rap. M. Sanson, c. du g.
[10] Let us recall that the Assembly of Litigation is constituted by presidents of the six
sections of the Council of State and the Vice-president. In order of decreasing importance, we then find the Section (only the 'Litigation' but with all the presidents of
the sub-section), subsequently the 'sub-sections united', then the 'sub-section judging
by itself', lastly the president of section judging by decree.

with the claim expressed in 1992, assuming that the latter includes a mean* which is not expressed but which is nevertheless present; this is less a matter of fitting the case into a certain type than one of changing the case after having modified the type.

President Luchon: Wait! You were saying? (he writes down the decisions).

The president has the delicate responsibility of checking the content of all the texts that leave his sub-section. Even though he is not a reviser in this case, it is important that he be able to check the precedents in order to prepare the final approval of the written judgment once the stage of deliberation has been completed, for which preparations are made today.

Dorval: We have, you have rendered decisions null and void in all these cases of professional discipline.

The cases are so to speak 'topical' since they concern professional regulatory bodies and are more or less similar to the present case.

The only **obstacle** is the text of the decree of 1945 on the association of expert accountants; it says (he reads) 'the sessions of the regulatory bodies are **not** public'.

This presents an 'obstacle' to his interpretation which consists in extracting the famous mean*, which has barely been mentioned in the statement of claim itself. This obstacle prevents him from progressing: it is a perfectly explicit text of 1945;[11] the claim of 1994 is stuck in the middle between a flood of texts originating from 1945 which conveniently point to the rejection of the claim, a set of precedents which equally conveniently suggest that the decision of the professional regulatory body be made null and void, and the retroactive weight of Maubleu in 1996, which weighs in favour of rendering the decision null and void even though it concerns a decision in which the claim was rejected;[12] the suspense lies in knowing

---

[11] The Ordinances (a particular form of laws which do not require the agreement of Parliament) of 1945 made by de Gaulle have considerable weight since they gave a new foundation to the French State after the collapse of the Vichy government.

[12] The important decisions ('arrêts') which make the case-law evolve are often decisions in which the claim has been rejected: 'In reality we endeavour to judge in fairness and subsequently we fashion a suitable solution; or conversely, the decision is of little importance, we are indifferent to the solution, and our only interest is in the law, which is why we love the great decisions in which claims are rejected, so there's a contradiction' (interview with commissioner). Let us not forget that the entire reasoning at the Council is organized, like right and left, by the two directions of either rejection of the claim or a judgment rendering the decision null and void.

*whether the reviser will succeed in weakening the decree of 1945,
which is an obstacle to his interpretation.*

But the arguments **you** made in respect of the association of
dental surgeons must be **dismissed**, because of (he cites several
decisions) it (the decree of 1945) must be dismissed because regulatory power is **bound** with respect to treaties; so **it is clear** to me;
I have **made a new** draft judgment.

> *This is a slightly massaged argument: a text of 1945 cannot presup-
> pose an illegality constituted by an international treaty which is of a
> later date;[13] so, the obstacle of the decree of 1945 has evaporated and
> the discussion has come to an end, at least for the reviser who, strid-
> ing onwards, has rewritten a draft judgment which is completely
> different from that of the reporter.[14]*

(He reads his 'dispositif') 'Article 6-1 of the European Convention
on Human Rights is not recognized by the relevant article of the
decree of the Council of State of 1945'; therefore we overrule the
judgment, send the case back to the lower court and order the
defendant to pay 10,000F.[15]

The discussion comes to an end at this point, the argument* having
been extracted, obstacles overcome, the 'dispositif' having been drawn
up to include the fact that the decision against which the litigant had
appealed is rendered null and void, and the precedents for this course
have been aligned one after the other, rather like the stones left in the
depths of the forest by Tom Thumb. We have just witnessed a minor
drama in which a second value object, the *fate of the claim*, which
had suffered the misfortune of being stifled by clumsy reporters and
incompetent lawyers, is luckily rescued, formulated and summarized

---

[13] Let us recall that since the famous 'arrêt' *Nicolo*, the Council of State has modified
the hierarchy of norms: international treaties take precedence over French laws, even
if they are of a later date, and of course take precedence over prior decrees. We shall
encounter this problem of hierarchy again in the case on p. 144.

[14] The considerations which form the basis for the judgment are contained in the
draft judgment and are called the 'dispositif' (see chapter 2). Let us recall that the
draft judgment is a draft of the decision as it will be delivered in the 'séance de juge-
ment' (deliberation) if the sub-section is followed.

[15] There is no difficulty whatsoever in rendering null and void a decision which relies
on a text of 1945 which is rendered ineffective by a text signed thirty years later;
jurists practise an art of anachronism that is impossible for historians to understand
and which we must investigate later. Time does not pass for them as it does for other
professions.

by the reviser; the text of the decree of 1945, which almost proved the death of the claim, has luckily been disposed of by 'our decision Maubleu', despite the fact that it is of a later date. The draft judgment of the reporter, which followed a different strategy, has now been substituted by that of the reviser, who in this case is quite aptly named as such: he has indeed revised the previous opinions. One last step remains: the draft judgment now only has to be approved by the sub-section and then accepted in the deliberation.[16]

And yet, in a couple of seconds, things are ruined for the reviser in much the same way as he ruined them for the reporter whose reading he so brutally interrupted. To understand the jujitsu move that comes next, we would have to be able to paint a portrait of the second reviser, who is seated to the left of the president. As in Patrick Suskind's *Perfume*, in which Grenouille extracted the eternal fragrance of Woman from the hair of all the girls he sacrificed, so in this case the reviser collects the specific tone of the Council of State in a single individual, a single tone of voice, a single body. To capture his countenance would be to paint a portrait of the whole institution. After the first reviser has finished speaking, Le Men takes the floor with a polite, thoughtful, smirking, distrustful, self-assured and yet modest tone, his chest pushed forward slightly, adopting an inquisitive, questioning, manner:

Le Men: The draft judgment conforms to the standard; . . . but shouldn't the act of the company be pardoned? The law of 1995 has been adopted, it concerns an exoneration (an exoneration must be granted).

Dorval (stopped dead in his tracks): I have asked myself the same question . . . (very bothered) but since we say that the claimants are right. . . .

Le Men (more firmly): Ah no, no, the exoneration **takes precedence**, it concerns a pardon here; a reprimand is **typically** something which is pardoned.

Within a quarter of a second, the terrain has completely changed: it is not worth the trouble of searching as far as the European Convention: a much closer law deals with all reprimands and minor offences which can be excused.

[16] Let us recall that, for simple cases, we will remain with the 'sub-section judging by itself'. It is exactly the same counsellors who instruct and deliberate; the only difference is that they will have to discuss the case again among themselves, after having listened to the conclusions of the commissioner of the law, who, during the review meeting, simply listened, merely taking notes in silence.

President Luchon: That's interesting.

Here we can detect a new and third value object. The interest lies not in the history of the claimant – whether the company was reprimanded justly or unjustly matters little since the claim will not have to be examined any more – but in the dynamic *of the reasoning itself which has made the subsection pass from one terrain to another in such a short time; the brief expression 'that's interesting' always brings a sparkle to the eye of those counsellors who are sensitive to the intellectual drama of the change of terrain: no longer are there obstacles to be overcome, omissions and reversals; it's even better than that: the two revisers can simultaneously, but for totally different reasons, say 'it is clear to me' – that's what awakens* interest here.

Let us take things in order. The exoneration? (mentally searching whilst turning towards the secretary who is seated in the corner) do you see what I mean, what file I have in mind?

Secretary of the section (with the speed of a double click): It is 'Commission bancaire'![17]

President: Ah thank you, we must indeed retrieve the case; can you find it? (the secretary leaves the room to look for it); it concerns a 'mean'* of public interest, we will draft it during this session.

The authority of the second reviser is such, in relation to that of the first, that the president, armed with weaponry and equipment, or rather with secretary and file, immediately proceeds to the solution suggested by the second reviser. Since a similar case was dealt with recently, the name of which is whispered to him by his secretary, the 'dispositif' of that case is directly copied to write the new one. It is 'not worth the trouble of being bothered too much, we will draft it immediately'; 'means* of public interest' are the only ones which the judge can raise himself *even when neither of the parties have raised them; instead of immersing themselves into the complicated work of bringing 1992 in accordance with 'Maubleu 1996', they go back to the routine of copying and pasting . . . the case which was in a muddled state will suddenly be able to progress more quickly.*

[17] When a case becomes known it is no longer necessary to cite the case number. Instead, these known precedents are amicably cited by their shorter name: as with 'Commission bancaire' or, a short while ago, 'Maubleu' or 'Chambre des vétérinaires'.

Le Men: All the same, it needs to not be 'contrary to honour and probity'; since it is a reprimand, it is not very serious; I **often** see that elsewhere;[18] reprimands for unlawful advertising are always pardoned; the claimant did not set up a fraudulent scheme? The idea of the pardon was invented for such a case.

No trace of triumph in the voice of the reviser who reflexively makes an opposing argument and, as always in the Council, mixes a legal definition ('it is the aim of the pardon'), a judgment on the importance of things (the 'reprimand' proves that the offence had been minor anyway and that the claimant had not engaged in serious fraud), and a testimony rooted in his own experience outside the Council ('I often see that elsewhere').

Dorval (reads the judgment against which the case has been brought):

We will get back to this in the following chapter, but nothing in his attitude indicates that he has suffered dearly from having been put so clearly in a position that has been contradicted; he has apparently shifted onto the terrain of his colleague without fighting back and only double-checks now that the offence is indeed excusable and thus covered by a pardon.

President: We will **stop here**, we will see if the 'Commission bancaire' file **works**; I do indeed want to draft a decree; we have plenty of cases in the 'sub-section judging by itself', it is not in our interest to **burden** it with more cases.

The decree permits the president of sub-section to decide alone on the less important cases; the term 'work' here means that the precedent is so similar that only the names of the litigants need to be changed for it to be used automatically.

What we have witnessed here, in the president's sudden concern that these sessions should not be 'burdened' by a case whose significance has altered completely by the second reviser's lightning-strike intervention, is a fourth value object with which presidents of sub-

---

[18] As we have seen in the previous chapter, the members hold an immense number of official positions (close to 400) in their capacity as members in addition to their activities at the Council. These positions must not be confused with all the activities which they pursue in a private capacity such as teaching, conferences, presidency of associations, etc. Here is a good example of the usefulness of life experiences ensuring an ever-tightening link between facts and the law.

sections and Counsel Sections have to deal with constantly: namely, flows of files that have to be dealt with as items of stock and which require similar managerial and organizational skills to those of any factory manager or other person who is responsible for 'just-in-time' production throughput. How should one keep control, share out work equally, minimize the scandalous delays of the system and achieve the objective of every organizer, namely a situation in which there are zero flaws, if not zero delays? Regular meetings between the presidents of sub-section and the president of the Litigation Section allow the problem of the overloading of sessions to be addressed, along with the role of each of the different commissioners of the law, or the 'statistics' relating to members which are used to determine the payment of bonuses. But these meetings have less to do with legal questions than with the effective administration of the flow of files. These are *logistical* questions. Obviously the president of sub-section has most to say about these matters because he is the person in charge of ensuring that the institution runs as smoothly as possible.

Let us follow the exchange through to the end of the episode to see how the paths of the different value objects that we have distinguished intersect:

President Luchon: Is it based on article 6-1 (of the European Convention)? Does the claimant raise it? We will reach agreement more easily on the first point (the pardon) than on the second.

The reporter: I myself did **not feel authorized** to accept the ground*; it is we who raise it; the claimants do speak of the Convention on Human Rights, but of the freedom of speech only.

> *The reporter, who is in a weakened position, lives up to his relative inferiority in relation to the second reviser, Dorval, who was ready to make the case-law progress by insisting on the force of the decision Maubleu; thus, the reporter does not 'feel authorized' which says as much about the relative power of the counsellor as about the power of the argument* 'raised' and subsequently 'drowned' by the lawyer; a strong counsellor is precisely one who 'feels authorized' to 'accept' an abandoned mean*; the grounds* are indeed value objects, in need of allies and of multiple supports in order to 'prosper' during the course of their long careers.*

Le Men: Yes but that was before Maubleu.
President: Yes, we have used it three times already, but if the mean* has not been raised, the sub-section will be **divided** (he looks at the claim as reinterpreted by Dorval); generally, the case-law of

the sub-section is that if a mean* is not included in the memoir, it has **not** been raised.

> *'Case-law' here is used metaphorically as it designates the varying idiosyncrasies of each sub-section, indicated by the use of 'generally'; the president relies on the particular tradition in his sub-section; the 'division' of the sub-section refers to the disagreements which seem to be inevitable between Dorval and the others about the question of whether the legal mean has been raised or not.*

Le Men: Particularly where there is a very competent law firm, like Paridole; there are usually ten arguments*; in my opinion they have **clearly** abandoned this; they understand that the case-law would never **fly** (before Maubleu).

> *Since competent lawyers also have their idiosyncrasies which are well known to the Council (such as presenting means* thirteen to the dozen), everything seems to lead to the conclusion that the argument* was not raised, since the lawyers felt that it 'would never fly' because it would not overcome the obstacle, and that the reviser made a mistake in suggesting that it had been raised for this second reason. Here, we mix the fate of the argument* with the respective authority of the lawyers and the revisers, both of which have undergone a slight modification during the ordeal.*

(. . .) **President** (after a pause in which he contemplates the file): We copy the case 'Commission Bancaire' (the file he previously requested from the secretary); I have drafted the mean* of public interest; I could not have drafted the decree alone; we talked about it during the review meeting, **that's good**.

> *The ceremonial tasks of closing the session include the auto-evaluation by the president of his own judgment, recognizing the fundamental role of the discussion between colleagues ('it was too delicate for me to do it alone'), even though in this case they end up with a decree signed by him alone. This sort of quality control, which the president exercises from the corner of his eye during the whole discussion, indicates the presence of another value object, the quality of the debate itself, which needs to be the object of great vigilance.*

We should acknowledge that these minor dramas, miniature farces or pocket operas have few spectators and would hold little fascination for the masses. Yet, these are still dramas: indeed, no element is missing, there are heroes, ordeals, allies, opponents, traitors and even, at the end of the day, triumphs. Let us draw up a somewhat provisional account of the value objects that we have seen making their way through the ordeals:

1) the variable *authority* of the members, which changes in relation to their success in making cases progress;
2) the *progress* of the case, in the course of which legal arguments* either prosper or are rejected as a function of the continuous action of lawyers, reporters, revisers and judges, in which some push and others pull;
3) the *organization* of the flow of files, which has to be quite rigorously managed by the presidents of sub-section;
4) the modifications of *interest* which allow the members to qualify the dynamic of their evolution in real time; 'uninteresting' cases being those which are purely routine, and the 'very interesting' ones being, as we shall see, those which compel a judgment to be made on some novel point;
5) the variable *weight* of case-law, which undergoes, from file to file, either a progressive relegation, or, on the contrary, an elevation and a reinforcement as for this case 'Maubleu', depending on whether or not a decision is taken up again or not;
6) and, finally, the ongoing process of *quality control* that is exercised by all members of the Council, but especially by the presidents, and which allows them to assess whether a discussion has been fairly conducted, justice rendered or a process of review closed.[19]

In this set of subtle transformations, it is evident that what is involved is not exactly a process of reasoning, in which a flow of homogeneous ideas are linked together more or less logically, nor is it an ordered body of texts, which it would be sufficient to stitch together in order to generate another document. Nor is it about the hesitant process of 'applying' a standard text to some fact, as if one were trying to identify the category 'duck' using an atlas of the birds of France to make sense of a fleeting vision of a feathered object skimming over a pond. The passage of law first manifests itself in the

[19] Greimas well understood this particularity of law which consists in the continuous explanation of its own process: 'The legal practice is at the same time a *recurrent procedure of verification* of the validity of the instituted legal language' (Greimas, *Analyse sémiotique d'un discours juridique* (1976), p. 91). This reflexivity is specific to law because despite its ubiquity and anxiety, it does not imply any anxious search into its foundations – indeed quite the opposite.

modification that all of our value objects undergo in the course of the ordeal, through which their circulation is either accelerated or slowed down. In each small episode, a whole series of tensions, vectors, currents, pressures is slightly rearranged. Subjects gain or lose interest; reputations are made or unmade; revisers, reporters, lawyers and presidents gain assurance and authority; they slip up, they overcome obstacles, they invoke legal means*, they do not make things fly, they glide over another terrain, they reinforce precedents, they revise interpretations. We should not hurry to distinguish which of these vehicles transports 'pure' law and which are mere accompaniments or parasites.

In legal reasoning, everything counts

Having examined the process by which an opinion is overruled, we shall now try to clarify the movement of those who 'say' the law by combining the dynamic of value objects with the movement of files that we followed in chapter 2. But in order to do so, we have to dispose of two counterweighing obstacles which might otherwise get in the way of our inquiry: first, there is the quite widespread idea that law is a sort of wrapping for power relations.[20] In order to gain access to the reality of what lawyers do, one should not look at what they do but one should reach behind formal appearances or the technical surface of things, to get at the solid reality of interests and passions. Behind the appearance of the judgment, one would find the irresistible force of prejudice, or at least of presuppositions. If this were the case, the members of the Council would be doing little more than repainting society's excessively violent play of colour in the dull tones of the law. The grey deadly tedium of technical issues would indeed have a function, namely, that of clouding the vision of the dominated while

---

[20] The canonical formulation has been proffered by Pierre Bourdieu: 'In making a legal decision reach the status of *verdict*, a process which undoubtedly owes more to ethical dispositions of the actors involved than to pure norms of law, rationalization confers to it the *symbolic efficacy* which every action exercises when it is recognized as legitimate rather than as arbitrary' (Bourdieu, 'La Force du droit' (1986), p. 8). The crudeness of the argument is only subtly veiled by the idea of an 'autonomous juridical field' which permits the sociologist to deflect cleverly the accusation of taking a typical sociologist's approach. At the end of the day, the law only possesses an arbitrary force of domination which it does no more than 'legitimate'. In spite of the denial of the sociologist, legal form does not add anything, other than the impossibility of criticizing the resources that it hides behind its pseudo-rationalizations.

developing an elaborate camouflage for precisely those power relations that we should be attempting to overthrow.[21]

The second obstacle lies in the idea that legal enunciation can be
reduced to the mere expression of a form, to the application of a rule
or to the classification of cases in general categories. This time, the
argument is that, to understand what lawyers do we should fasten
ourselves to the formal scheme while eliminating all the hesitations,
compromises and obscure negotiations which deflect judges from true
judicial reasoning. Much as scientists, feeling their way forward in
their laboratories, reveal weaknesses which must then be tidied up so
as to extract the pure process of reasoning that they need to follow
and which was, albeit unknown to them, their true guide, so too the
reality of law is to be found not in the hesitations of practice but in
the hidden structure of legal chains, which are the invisible guide of
all legal reasoning and which legal theorists are able to reveal by
means of a work of reconstruction.[22] These two visions – law construed as fancy dress and law construed as formalism[23] – would
compel us to leave the winding path of practice in order to focus on
another reality, one that is invisible to the actors themselves but which
is supposed to explain their behaviour: either the true reality of
society and social violence or the true reality of the rule and its
immanent logic. However, as we shall see in the last chapter, it is far

---

[21] This is what critical sociologists often do when they use the word 'legitimate'
(which, by the way, comes from law), as though they were expressing a profound
truth, whereas in fact they only restate the question posed by the enigma of the law.
To legitimate is to add much more than a simple legitimacy. For a critique of the
expression 'legitimate', which is related to 'co-ordinate', see Olivier Favereau's
remarkable analyses, which are of essential importance for the sociology of law:
'Instead of seeing the field of law in its entirety as anathema, it would be more
productive to exploit critical resources further, precisely because one can expect
neither an ideal dynamic of complete co-ordination nor a despairing dynamic of
complete reproduction from law. The law is not inevitably the "justified force" of
which Pierre Bourdieu speaks, that is to say justification in the service of force, rather
it is *force in service of justification*. It might be said that the difference here is slender,
but it is this slender difference that marks the division between those societies
that are constituted by the requirement of democracy . . . and others' ('L'économie
du sociologue' (2001), p. 298).

[22] We recognize that the epistemology of law always consists in an a posteriori reconstruction of the rational core of the discipline, rather like the epistemology of the
sciences, to which it is related.

[23] The notion of 'sticking to form', which does much more than merely dissimulate,
must be taken very seriously. 'The owl of the Law awakens after the owl of Minerva',
as G. de Geouffre de la Pradelle amusingly observes: 'However, he adds, this belated-
ness must not be underestimated: after all, this is what a civilized people expect
from the institution of a legal state' ('La réforme du droit de la nationalité' (1995),
p. 171).

from obvious that these perceptions of law are any more real than the law they claim to explain. And if we are led to question the notion of 'power' or of 'society', we will also call into question the notion of a 'legal rule'.

The whole point of frequent attendance in the review meetings lies in the new vision that it affords of problems both of power and of form *explicitly* posited by the members of the Council, who solve them on a case-by-case basis, by means of solutions which take us away from the first vision – that of concealment – as well as from the second, that of the application of a rule. Rather than follow the contradictory advice given to us, by sociologists on the one hand and epistemologists on the other, about how to grasp the hidden reality of Law, we are quite deliberately going to *remain on the surface of things*, stubbornly following the hesitant course of judgment, in which judges quite clearly admit their prejudices while asserting at the same time that they alone cannot determine the solution, or in which they attach themselves quite passionately to legal forms while constantly rejecting the dangers of what they call 'legalism' or 'formalism'. Neither by recognizing social violence nor by focusing on the presence of rules can one predict the movement of the law. At this point, there might be no need to go in search of some invisible layer of reality other than this *winding* of reasoning itself in order to explain how it forces its way through all these obstacles. Having avoided these two pitfalls – the theory of the fancy dress of power and that of the formal scaffolding of law – we will hopefully begin to understand what the group of slaves chained to heaps of files do in the golden prison of the Palais-Royal on beautiful summer days.

In no area is the brutality of power relations more clearly visible than in the question of the expulsion of illegal migrants, which the Council of State has to address. Here is the example of a case in which a man's life is at stake, and in which the review meeting quite clearly reveals the social interests and class feelings of the members who discuss it with such seriousness. And yet, as we shall see, the relation of law to force is not that of a clothing of naked violence. Something else is at work, which we shall try hard to define. Once prejudices have been admitted, the question of what it means to put something into law begins. Again, the relation here is not that between truth and its disguises, or between the contents and their wrapping, but rather between the transfer of force and the peculiar movement of law.

The readers no doubt having become increasingly familiar with administrative law as these pages progress, we can gradually reduce the number of incidental comments and present longer pieces of the

discussion so that they can also form their own judgment with no
untimely interruptions from us. Today, the reporter of this sub-
section has the tone of a provincial country squire and a very aristo-
cratic appearance, and he has, as one might imagine, little sympathy
for a plaintiff who has had a number of serious convictions for drug
trafficking, who is also an undocumented alien, and whom a Prefect
wants to repatriate by force. The reviser, as always, is responsible for
reviewing the file before the session and for discussing the note of the
reporter, and for doing so by focusing only on those points that are
worthy of discussion.

Le Men (reviser): Yes, here we have an **interesting** case, simple
but complicated.

De Servetière (reporter reading the 'note'): It's a case of expulsion;
Mr Farouk appeals; he asks that the judgment be overruled; he is
right; the lower court of the administrative tribunal indeed has jurisdiction, it did not need to declare itself incompetent; we overrule and
review de novo ('évoque')[24]; this Iraqi will be put to death in his own
country, he invokes article 3 of the European Convention; the ground*
is **working**;[25] there is the Pasqua law; you have overruled in your
judgment of sub-section 2/6; the Iraqi cites a newspaper of 1989
which does **not suffice to prove** that he will be attacked or killed
in his own country; he invokes article 8 of the Convention on Human
Rights; I reject it.

Le Men (reviser): This is not a problem of law but it is delicate **in
fact**; the administrative tribunal has made a mistake.

> *We recognize here the 'interesting' problem which reflects on the
> work of the members of the Section itself and on the intellectual
> obstacles which they must overcome; again, we also see the change
> in weight which must be attributed to a piece of case-law; the legal
> problem is settled, the tribunal made a mistake in declaring itself
> incompetent, a serious mistake, the claim is deemed admissible; the
> expression 'in fact' is not meant in the banal sense, but in the
> stronger sense of 'in reality,' as opposed to the legal question which,
> in itself, 'is not very difficult'; this little phrase indicates, as is the*

[24] Like in the case of the pigeons, p. 2, de novo review (or *évocation*) is a privilege
of the Council of State as final court of appeal; it can not only overrule and send
back to a lower court, it can also decide on the merits of a case itself.
[25] The working means* (*opérants*) are those with enough force to enable the judges
to move the case forward. The means* are called 'not-working' ('inopérants') when
the opposite is true. They can also be working but 'lacking factual basis'. The reader
should now begin to see the central complexity of this little word 'mean*'.

case in all immigration law cases, that resolving the legal problem is not sufficient to close the discussion; the file which circulates during the session, and which everyone can consult, contains a translated article from an Iraqi newspaper describing the penal situation of that country in very vague terms, as the only proof of the fatal risk run by the claimant.

Mr Farouk is a **very negative** individual. He has been involved in heavy drug trafficking for which he has been definitively prohibited from residing in French territory; no solid proof at all is provided by the lawyer to the Council of State of the fact that his life is at risk, but all the same Iraq is designated as the country of expulsion. We have taken account of what we currently know; we consider his fate with regard to article 3, even if it is not article 8; he is married to a French woman, he has a French child; it is different to the case of 10 May 1996 which concerned an Algerian fundamentalist who had abandoned fundamentalism, that case was **clear**; but here **I have doubts** and want to submit the case to the sub-section.

As has already been suggested by the misleading character of the expression 'in fact', they move to a factual definition of the claimant as a drug trafficker. In accordance with the Penal Code this definition entails a prohibition against residing in French territory and necessarily dictates a return to the border[26] 'due to operation of law'; the individual is not commendable, no outstanding effort will be made for him, his lawyer has not helped him much in building his file;[27] but at the same time there is a question of European law which gains increasing importance with each passing day (is French law in contradiction with article 3 or article 8?) and a geopolitical question on the human rights situation in Iraq; all this creates the 'doubts' which suspend judgment, and which cause the reviser to hesitate, requiring a discussion among colleagues.

Dorval: I have **doubts** but **proof** must be produced; why does his lawyer not produce anything? That is what convinces me (to harbour

---

[26] The principle of 'double jeopardy' lies at the origin of strong protest movements by humanitarian organizations and certain political parties.

[27] Here we see yet again the Council making scathing remarks about the poor work of lawyers, who assert for their part, of course, that the Council shamelessly appropriates their labour, in particular where it concerns the extraction of legal arguments* from the shapeless stew that most claimants present to their lawyers, poorly articulated accusations which the lawyers must subsequently transform into admissible claims.

doubts similar to Le Men's), because what **is happening** in Iraq is truly disturbing.

> *To 'produce' is, as we have seen, a technical term, an intransitive verb which means 'to respond or reply'; the second reviser does not hesitate to express a direct opinion on the political situation. Since he himself knows things about Iraq, in a sense, 'directly' through the media, why is the lawyer not capable of presenting proof in favour of his client?*

Perrouard (commissioner of the law): What bothers me is the existence of the death penalty for drug trafficking; that **goes against** the Convention on Human Right; is it safe in Iraq? That must be **verified**; that bothers me a little; it is a bit **more legal**; it is a country which applies the death penalty to drug traffickers and now we are going to send him back saying 'this is a drug trafficker'.

> *Normally, the commissioner of the law does not take the floor, but as he is already informally preparing himself to write his conclusions, he pushes in a 'more legal' direction the position of the last speaker who only used common sense.*

President Huchon: But beware, it was the civil judge who failed to respect the convention and article 3 by sending him back by force indefinitely; **can** the administrative judge apply a judgment which is contrary to article 3?[28]

Le Men: It **has been decided**; we can't say **anything**, *res judicata*; **we are bound**: the administrative tribunal **only** decides on the country of expulsion, the expulsion itself is dealt with by the civil court.

> *We again witness the distribution of tasks – very bizarre in a case like this – between the two branches of French law: the administrative law can only be concerned with the decision of the Prefect in choosing the country of expulsion; all the rest depends on the civil judge, and the judges of the Council of State, no matter how distinguished, are 'bound'; they cannot do anything; the case of Mr Farouk has already been judged and the civil law judges have already pronounced his expulsion (because of the authority of res judicata), the only margin of discussion for the sub-section lies in the question of whether the Prefect has acted ultra vires in sending Mr Farouk back to Iraq.*

[28] 'No one shall be subjected to torture or to inhuman or degrading treatment or punishment.'

President (indignant): Wait, we cannot allow such an **important** question to be left to the skill of a lawyer; **we see** horrible things on television.

Bruyère: It is a press extract, that is not **worth** anything.

Dorval (bothered, turning towards the reporter): But **is it true** that he risks the death penalty?

De Servetière: How could I know?! **The lawyer** needs to cite some cases for us . . . ; agreed that we cannot ask the lawyer to prove that he, Mr Farouk in particular, risks the death penalty, but there are after all human rights NGOs (capable of adding information to the file), etc. . . .

President: **Can** we be sure of this?

Bruyère: But how should we be able to know, if his lawyer doesn't? Let's ask the Foreign Affairs; in any case, whether he is mujahedeen or not does not present the least difficulty: (he makes a gesture as though he was cutting his own head off) 'snap'.

Le Men (a little shocked): We will not tread the **unofficial** path by 'making inquiries'; if we want this to appear in the file, a rejoinder must be submitted (by the Home Secretary).

The reviser is shocked both by Bruyère's brutal expression – Bruyère an old soldier from the days of de Gaulle's 'strong State' – and also by the idea of an informal transfer of information – or, perhaps, more shocked by the second point than by the first . . . ; in fact, what the president asks for amounts to a supplement of the process of review which, respecting the principle that both parties must be heard, must form the object of a rejoinder: we cannot add a fact that supports Mr Farouk 'informally' without giving the opposing party the opportunity to reply.

President: Is it **scandalous** to ask the office of the Ministry of Foreign Affairs? We **can do what we want**, we tend to consider ourselves too **bound**.

As on p. 26, we are again seeing here the question of who has precedence between the Council of State and the government; the president pleads for some leeway, in contrast to the last speakers who, according to him, are always too quick to say 'we cannot'.

Bruyère: Can we do this? (he says doubtfully)

President: We have the law on our side! After all this is **very important**, is this going to set a precedent?

We cannot say that this exchange is free of prejudices: the reporter quite clearly admits to his prejudice that this drug trafficker, although he is married to a French woman and is the father of a child, is the kind of person who 'does not matter' to him in the least;[29] by contrast, the president considers that something 'very important' is at issue here, something so important that the fate of this poor soul cannot be left in the hands of an unskilled lawyer who is incapable of building a file; moreover, he has no hesitation in invoking what he has seen on television like everyone else. Dorval, the other reviser, also finds the situation in Iraq 'truly disturbing', and the good Bruyère, who was not easily frightened during the Algerian war, does not hesitate to predict the fate of Mr Farouk, which he seals with a resounding 'snap' ... Even the commissioner of the law quite ingenuously acknowledges that 'everyday' mujahedeen are forcibly repatriated, sending them to a certain death. Although the personality of Mr Farouk obviously plays a role in the reasoning (the judges will not go to great lengths for this 'very negative' individual), the geopolitical situation of Iraq also plays a role and in a contrary sense.

Nor can we say that what is involved is a process of examination, in which, like the angels of the Last Judgment, we can weigh the intrinsic quality or the soul of the claimant. In fact, there are as many expressions recalling the presuppositions of each and the geopolitical context of Iraq as there are expressions recalling, indicating or emphasizing rules of law: Dorval asserts that he is ready to doubt but that he cannot do so if the file 'offers no proof'; the commissioner of the law himself says that his concerns are 'more legal' and that they have to do with the question of the death penalty for drug trafficking which 'would go against' the European Convention; the president, moved as he was by the fate of Iraqis, asks himself whether administrative law 'can apply a rule that is contrary to article 3', to which Le Men asserts in response that it is impossible, recalling the unquestionable persistence of the 'it has been decided': we, the Council of State, can say nothing, the division of labour between the civil and administrative law having been settled once and for all, and we cannot consult the Home Office discreetly without compromising the procedure at the Council.

Although the discussion is not confined to the terrain of evidence and presuppositions specific to the common-sense experience of each ('the horrible things on television'), nor does it hide from the real

---

[29] At the end, in an aside, de Servetière tells the ethnographer: 'This guy can go hang himself, I don't care.'

world by remaining within the simple logic of texts and rules. We cannot even say that the discussion alternates *between these poles*, or indeed that it tries to discover the result, average or line of least tension, between contradictory concerns that are brought together in a *single* bundle consisting of the situation in Iraq, prejudices of caste, class and possibly race, or of being for or against foreign drug traffickers, respect for *res judicata*, a willingness to respect international treaties, guilt at sending the father of a French child to his death when he has already served his sentence . . . The passage which we have had the unique chance of witnessing is much more subtle than a mere *synthesis* or *summation* of the incommensurable elements that produce a decision without us knowing how, much as a neural network solves problems by a simple balancing and repetition of electric potentials. The evolution of the discussion does indeed encompass incommensurable kinds of argument, but it is not for that reason a complete ragbag.

The exchange which follows the naive and exasperated question that Dorval addresses to the reviser – 'But is it true that he risks the death penalty?' – is especially revealing. The counsellors' difficulty is easy to see: at this point, they would love to be able to jump outside the file and rejoin reality instantaneously by means of one of the referential chains with which we will become acquainted in the next chapter. But the reporter impatiently refuses the role of being an expert on Iraq that the others wish to foist upon him ('How could I know?!') and he again translates the question of fact into a question of law: 'It is for the lawyer to put, under our eyes, something more than an old newspaper article dated seven years ago in the file!' The same movement is visible when the president asks the same question in a different form – 'Can we be sure of this?' – which leads to the old hand's proposition to get the information by activating his own parallel networks ('I can call my colleagues at Foreign Affairs to find out if there is the death penalty in Iraq for drug traffickers or not') and to the second translation proposed by Le Men's admirable response: 'No, we cannot make informal information circulate without creating an effect of law, that is to say entailing a rejoinder by the Ministry, the only way to make it *appear in the file* so that it can count in our reasoning.' Twice in succession the question of 'being able to know' is interrupted, shifted, re-centred and translated again into another procedure which replaces the quest for knowing more with the respect for a rule concerning the composition of a file, and it is precisely because of this that we can trace the passage of the particular movement of law. In qualifying that movement, we need something other than a transfer of information.

The dynamic of the judgment does not alternate between fact and law, nor does it seek to reconcile them by means of some unstable compromise. Instead, it does something completely different: it picks out the elements which will allow the file to be made to progress according to a particular thought process that we can only call 'legal'.[30] The markers of this remarkable movement are to be found throughout this whole episode in all of those expressions which indicate *hesitation*: 'it is complicated', 'it is delicate', 'I have doubts and want to submit the case to the sub-section', says Le Men; 'I have doubts', responds Dorval; Perrouard is 'a little bothered'; 'beware' says the president, who asks 'is it scandalous?'; to which Perrouard responds 'why not?' What is so revelatory here, is that these expressions are surrounded by terms which indicate exactly the opposite: 'This is not a problem of law'; 'the administrative tribunal has made a mistake'; 'we can't say anything; *res judicata*'; 'we are bound'; 'that is not worth anything'; 'that does not embarrass me psychologically'; 'that does not present the least difficulty'; 'we have the law on our side'. Quite distinct from the difference between facts of common sense and formalisms, another drama is played out, which makes the discussion progress from one hot issue to another, supported by cold issues, until the point at which the president makes this magnificent remark: 'We can do what we want, we tend to consider ourselves too *bound*.' By shaking up the habits of dependence vis-à-vis the administration which paralyse the formation of judgment by the sub-section, the president, by changing doubts into certainties and embarrassments into efforts, is pushing something else which is at work in the whole discussion, the progression of which he evaluates reflexively and continuously watches over closely.

What should we call this little 'je ne sais quoi'? Initially, we might say that it is to do with a kind of reserve of degrees of freedom in the definition of our capacity of judgment, an aptitude to *unbind* which permits us only to *bind again* without attaching ourselves in any durable manner either to the brilliantly coloured multitude of external events to which we have little access or to the strict application of rules and texts which are never sufficient to define our task. If they consider themselves to be 'too bound' they will never be able to exercise their faculty of judgment: they must then, through all this labour, effect some kind of 'unbinding'. Only then will they be able to stick to their position.[31] Let us then add a new, seventh, value object to

---

[30] We will try to deal with the apparent tautology later – and in the last chapter.
[31] It will not change anything for the claimant, since his lawyer will read the following short decision at the end of the 'dispositif':

those which we have already identified, and let us define it as a certain capacity to multiply the room for manoeuvre, a capacity that is marked by hesitation, doubt and the recognition of indisputable resistances defining what we can or cannot do. Again, we should not be too hasty to purify the nature of this movement. Let us profit until the end from the opportunity of not being a legist ourselves and hence of not understanding too hastily what in those movements is purely legal and what is not.

It is impossible, in any case, to define the expression 'to say the law' if we eliminate from it the hesitations, the winding path, the meanders of reflexivity: the reason why we represent justice as blind, and holding scales in her hands, is precisely because she hesitates, and proceeds feeling her way forward . . .[32] We must then follow her as she is pushed in one direction, or pulled in another, by the weight of prejudices which do not of themselves explain her zigzags; dragged in one direction or another by the presence of texts and precedents, she cannot find in the respect for some form the right way which will allow her to progress, since formalism and legalism rather lead her astray. Her progress is rather like that of the Hebrews in the desert, following a column of smoke that is right in front of them, and which enlightens them because it shows them the way, and blinds them because it conceals what is under its cloud, the difference being that, even in the Council of State, there is no all-powerful God or guardian angel to guide the judges' steps! In moving blindly from left to right in this way, justice uses only ordinary reasoning, the kind of inter-rupted syllogisms that we all use to organize our daily lives, the heterogeneous totality of which is rather like a taste, a sense of smell, a nose, a thing of habit, of culture, of experience and common sense. But what she feels, what she sniffs if we dare say it, is in the nature itself of the cases through the presence of embarrassments, bother-some things, troubles or 'shimmering' to which she must put an end through solutions whose aim seems precisely to be to appease, to close, to finish, to end this erring. Justice only writes law through

---

'DECIDES

Article 1: the judgment of – counsellor delegated by the 'president du tribunal administratif' of – is rendered null and void.

Article 2: The claim presented by Mr Farouk before the administrative tribunal of Bordeaux and the remainder of the conclusions of his claim are rejected.

Article 3: This decision shall be notified to Mr Farouk and to the Home Secretary.'

[32] It is bizarre that such striking features do not play any role, apparently, in the sources of classic iconography of the scales held by a blindfolded woman (and some-times with hands cut off!) such as have been reconstituted by Jacob, *Images de la justice* (1994).

winding paths. In other words, if she had refused to make mistakes, if she had applied a rule, if she had summed pieces of information, we could not identify her as being either just or indeed legal. *For her to speak justly, she must have hesitated.*

'We touch on the heart of the State'

Of all our value objects, that which we point to by means of the word 'moyen' (the eighth element in our provisional exercise in identification) seems to be the most common, and seems to offer the most original definition of the passage of law. What is more banal, or more polysemic, than this small word, which serves moral, technical, organizational and the most humble practices, and which yet has a meaning that is at once highly precise and utterly implicit when used by lawyers?[33] What is transported by those arguments* which are deemed admissible by the Council? We are going to try to clarify this in taking up a case in which the respective weights of prejudices and formalisms play exactly the opposite roles to in the preceding episode. Counsellors had to try hard to save this drug trafficker and use the full weight of the European Convention to support him in his struggle against the Prefect, and now they will be literally *forced* to censor the President of the Republic in the exercise of one of his essential powers, that of appointment, because the thrust of a point of law raised by a fussy claimant is stronger than all the contrary prejudices of the members of the sub-section. This time, everything must prevent the ground* from 'flourishing', and yet it does, despite the efforts of the Jacobin counsellors who do not want to deprive the State of the power to appoint its civil servants according to the dictates of the general interest. Let us start for once at the end and read the conclusion of the commissioner of the law: quite straightforwardly, he admits that what is at issue is a thrust, a force, a pressure: 'We think that this appointment is illegal. Our first intuition, if you allow us this confession, was the *opposite*. But the progressive, reasoned and also somewhat implacable advancement of the stages of the examination of this unique legal argument* has *reversed* our impression' (p.

[33] 'The "legal means" are the necessary support of the claim and the defence. They form the grounds of the case. In support of their claim, the parties can assert "legal means" of fact or of law, the divisions between them are called "branches"', we read in *Lexique Dalloz des termes juridiques* (10th edn) which warns us not to confuse them with *arguments*. *Le Robert* dedicates no more than one citation to the legal meaning (after 'means of transportation'!): '*Reason* of law or of fact invoked before a tribunal in support of a claim'.

5). In other words, there are means* that are capable of deflecting first intuitions as well as prejudices, arguments* of which we say that they progress in an 'implacable' manner. What makes the case even more interesting from our point of view is that the point of law raised will force the Council to apply a rule of law that had previously almost never been applied. We are therefore getting closer to the ethnographic study of the questions of rule and obligation which seem so important to legal theorists but of whose application there exist very few empirical descriptions. How can an unapplied law invoked by a tiny claimant make the State tremble? How to tackle the description of what we must indeed call the objectivity of the law which imposes itself on all, even though no one clearly senses the power of this reason* until the claimant has invoked it?

Let us begin by discussing the case as it appeared for the first time in the sub-section. A tiny company, ironically called Epsilon, brings a case against the decree of appointment, signed by the President of the Republic, of a civil servant who moved directly from a Ministry where he had the 'supervision' ['tutelle'] of a bank to the presidency of that same bank. The claimant accuses him of using a revolving door (*pantouflage*) invoking a breach of the Penal Code.[34]

Deldago (the reporter reads the note too quickly for the ethnographer to be able to write it down): there is **no discussion** on article 432-13 of the Penal Code; that goes back to Roman law. (She cites *Digeste*, St Louis 1254, Charles III on the governors!)

> *Remember that for all the other members of the sub-section the case is new: the judgment is formed through the comparison between the note which is read out rather fast and the oral summary of the whole case by the reviser who gives a more 'legal' account.*

Lebras (reviser): That can take us very **far**, its impact is **considerable**; I agree with the note; I will summarize the facts.

Legendre holds his position from 1-1-1995 onwards; the claimant is a **regular customer** of the Litigation Section, he has been a litigant in many different cases; Epsilon owns twelve shares in Crédit Urbain at 35F a piece!, it's a beautiful paradox; its legal standing follows from this ownership, even though it is symbolic, it has the right to bring a legal action **even if** it is a minimal right; even if,

---

[34] This is a term which in French literally refers to a slipper, but it concerns the situation where someone who is working in the civil service leaves to work in the private sector; English prefers a more technical metaphor for the same phenomenon.

perhaps, it has bought shares just to be able to bring this legal action. The 'means* of external legality' are inconsistent; an extract of the decree is cited but it does not have any importance as the countersignatures suffice.

> *The claimant is one of those regular pettifoggers versed in legal reasoning who are sometimes called, with a mixture of affection and irritation, 'occasional agents of public service' because they attend all cases and leave their mark everywhere. They know almost as much about the mysteries of administrative law as do the coun-sellors; nevertheless, their litigious spirit cannot be held against them and the fact that this claimant has only bought shares so as to put a spanner in the process of revolving doors does not justify us ignoring its claim – a legal action not being affected by its motive; 'legal standing' is a fundamental term clarifying who has the right to bring a case in law against an act of the administration; although its use was very restricted in the early stages of administrative law, it has spread since; in this case a shareholder of a bank unquestion-ably has the right to bring a case against the decree by which the director of that bank has been appointed; according to the usual procedure of the process of review we begin with the 'means* of external legality' – which are signatures, dates, visas – before passing on to the 'legal means of internal legality' which are aimed at the heart of the matter.*

What remains to be discussed is the 'mean* of internal legality' (she reads article 432-13 of the Penal Code again): 'It is punishable with two years of imprisonment and a 200,000F fine for a person who has been given the responsibility, as civil servant or official or employee of a "governmental institution", of assuming supervision or control of a private company or of expressing his opinion on the operations effected by a private company, to take or receive partici-pation through work, advice or capital in one of these companies before the expiration of a time period of five years following the termination of his governmental function'; you see that it is a very broad provision, only monopolies like railroad and utilities escape it, there are not many other companies that do; I mention the important points again; it is **applicable** and it has not been recognized in the case at hand, these are the two delicate points of law; no rule of civil service can **derogate** from a matter of penal law, **that is in** 27-1-1969, or in 24, I don't remember, p. 39, in any case it is of the Assembly,[35] and there is also the chronicle written by N, well the

---

[35] She cites here the precedent: 24-1-1969 *Ministre du Travail c/ Syndicat des cadres des organismes sociaux* (*Lebon*, p. 39) renders null and void a decree concerning the

case did not go **as far** at all as our case does, because that case concerned a civil servant who was temporarily working in a company while remaining employed by the government; **we have the answer** (it lies in the precedent); what we still need to consider is whether Paridole's statement of defence (the lawyer of the civil servant and of the Minister) makes valid arguments. Apparently, they feel that the situation is quite **desperate**. The law says that there should be a decree in Council of State, 17-1-1991, and that it provides for the consultation of the commission, then there is a second series of texts, 28-06-1994, with an obligation to consult the commission of deontology, but according to the decree 95–168 in Council of State of 17-2-1995[36] there is **no incidence at all** with our case since our case arises after the second series of texts and the first decree does not regard the contracting of a civil servant; and in any case the civil service cannot ignore the Penal Code.[37]

> *Again we observe our second value object, the claim which is pushed by the claimant on the one hand and pulled by the opposing party on the other, each making use of texts but one of them possessing the Penal Code, which is – because of the way it originates – stronger than the decrees of the government (these decrees cannot 'derogate' from it). The other party invokes, in a 'desperate' situation, texts 'without incidence' regarding the irresistible 'mean* of internal legality' (a juicy detail worth noting is that the claimant is managing without a lawyer while the Ministry has had to appeal to a law firm!). There is indeed a whole series of procedures of consultation to distinguish, from among the cases of revolving doors, those cases which are permissible and those which are prohibited. In this specific instance, the opinions of the various commissions have all been favourable towards the nomination of*

appointment of a civil servant in the capacity of director of a social security fund. The functions previously exercised by the official within the regional direction of the social security fund included direct control of the National Board. On the basis of this precedent, concerning a less important case, the commissioner of the law further constructs her 'straight-line' reasoning – see below.

[36] See *AJDA* chronicle, p. 155, n. 30: this decree, to which the reviser refers, established a special commission in the civil service that must be consulted so that it can assess whether a particular office is compatible with the previous functions of a civil servant who has left the administration.

[37] We touch here upon the hierarchy of norms that gives texts their respective importance: in the same way that an international treaty takes precedence over a French law even if it is of later date, a regulation of the administration cannot contravene a provision in the Penal Code. For the French version of the hierarchy of acts and authorities, rather than of norms *stricto sensu*, see Béchillon, 'Sur la conception française de la hiérarchie des normes' (1994). In any case, the invocation of the superior norm in this case puts the question beyond dispute.

*Legendre, but according to the reviser that does not change any-
thing because no commission can authorize an act that is contrary
to the Penal Code.*

   I **remember** the proceedings of 2-2-95, the case has refreshed
my memory, Our colleague Mrs N. asked 'why (do we) not permit
civil servants to work in the private sector?' Mr B. said 'why? **because**
of the Penal Code', so that was completely **foreseen**: and after all
in this case it **suffices** to read the administrative Bottin, which is
very enlightening, it reads 'Bureau BIII: "control of Crédit Urbain"'!,
it is not in accordance with regulations, but it is **enlightening**; I do
not see **how we can avoid holding the decree to be null and
void**; the administration has rather **lost sight** of the rules; that is a
pity since Mr Legendre is an **excellent** director;[38] I am not sure that
such a thing could **be judged** in 'sub-sections judging together'.

*In the same way that the 'very negative' character of the drug-
trafficking claimant in the preceding episode did not prevent the
point of law being raised, here the fact that the claimant is a notably
litigious party and that the civil servant against whom the case is
brought is an 'excellent' director does not prevent the acceptance
of the claim: psychology and common sense, however apparent, are
of no consequence from a legal point of view. An important advantage for the Council of State is that the reviser, who, as should be
remembered, also sits in the Counsel Section, can call on his recollections of the discussion of the decree on the commission against
the phenomenon of revolving doors. This way, he can verify whether
this issue has indeed been 'foreseen' by remembering the discussions
between his colleagues at the moment that the text was written,
which allows him to clarify its implicit meaning; the transcript of
the parliamentary debates can also serve this purpose. Moreover,
in using the administrative Bottin in the library, he is able to verify
that the civil servant had in his portfolio the bank of which he is
today a director. This is one of those informal pieces of information
which are enlightening without necessarily being decisive for the
case (*obiter dictum* in opposition to ratio decidendi*); the reviser
does not see how 'we can avoid holding the decree to be null and
void' in spite of all these drawbacks which will 'lead us very far';
the importance of the stakes must lead, in his view, to a change in*

---

[38] In this whole case, the Penal Code is not concerned with the particular individual
at all – who in any case could only be sentenced by a criminal judge – but with the
act of his appointment by the administration. As the commissioner forcefully concludes: 'We should fully understand that the personal integrity of Mr Legendre is
not at issue. (. . .) all comments which are made and which rely on your decision to
"censure" his behaviour would therefore be defamatory statements' (p. 18).

the process of formation of judgment, since the 'sub-sections judging together' is too low in the hierarchy to give such a slap in the face to the administration which has 'lost sight' of the rules and of the penal law.

President Oury: We can discuss that; the more it is raised (in the formation of judgment) the more **embarrassing** it is for the government, but the report and the draft judgment are **so decisive** that I do not see why we would go **higher up**, so, we must first discuss it in depth.

They may go higher up in the hierarchy of tribunals either because the case is important or because they are uncertain; in this case, they will end up going as high as possible, namely to the Assembly.[39]

Fléval (second reviser): It seems to me that the final word **has been said**, in any case at our level; it makes the whole state of affairs in the Treasury **fragile**.

President: Not only in the Treasury. At the time I asked about Huilier who has gone from the French Railway having come from the Ministry of Public Transport; this has been known for a long time in the administration; what **shimmers**[40] for me is that this article (of the Penal Code) has become partly **outdated**; the whole SNECMA (an engine company) is made up of chaps like that. Why have we **never applied** it? How has the Secretariat General of the government **let** all this **happen**? There is an **incredible gap** between what you are saying now and the fact that we never apply this article of the Penal Code.

Basically, in the end we couldn't even manage to have a legal discussion!

Perrouard (the commissioner of the law): **Except** if the legal standing of the claimant is based on bad faith: that would give rise to a procedural decision in the Assembly; all the same, it is a **pain** in the neck.

Fléval (continuing his reflection on the degree of indignation which the case should give rise to): I myself find this case to be very **healthy**.

---

[39] Remember that the 'Assembly of Litigation' must not be confused with the 'General Assembly of the Council of State' which is constituted of all counsellors and where they do not act as judges, but in their capacity as advisers, as we have seen in chapter 1, p. 58. When the reviser talked about going 'higher up' 'in any case the Assembly', he acknowledged the importance of the precedent.

[40] This is a very odd expression, even in French – 'il y a quelque chose qui miroite' – but very revealing that something is amiss and that it should be attended to.

Lebras (having looked at the file and responding to Perrouard): No, no, the file shows that Epsilon indeed owned its shares on 21-12 and the decree against which the case is brought is of 29-12! (so we cannot prove bad faith).

President: I will see, but it is **quite clear** that this will pass to the 'subsections judging united'. Its **impact** will be very significant, especially because the Vice-president was secretary at the General Secretariat of the government at the time, so he will be very troubled;

Lebras: I had a word with him about this; he told me that 'they have not been very observant'.

President: Let's not **dramatize** this; we are not going to ask him to recuse himself!

> *Because of the nature of the Council of State itself, in which members of the administration enter and leave again (see the preceding chapter), it often happens that members are confronted again, as a judge, with a case that they have had to decide upon as active civil servants or political representatives; in these cases they 'recuse themselves', which amounts to slightly shifting the angle of their armchair and not taking part in either the discussion or the vote! It goes without saying that to ask that of the Vice-president is not insignificant, especially for a simple president of sub-section; they are not going to 'dramatize' the conflict which the legal decision will create, but the members of the sub-section do not conceal the consequences, either because they find them dangerous for the administration, or because they regard them as 'healthy'; the essential point is that agreement is reached on the point of law: 'the final word has been said'.*

Fléval (ironically): Wait, the commissioner of the law will perhaps not agree, you are anticipating that she will!

> *At this point, we are only in the review meeting; the commissioner of the law who takes notes of the matter can very well come to a different conclusion from the sub-section and not find the case so clear-cut as the last speakers.*

Lebras (laughing): Ah ah, so the Bank Crédit Urbain is going to pay for Perrouard's new apartment?

Deldago: Moreover, there is a problem with the **context** in which this case arises, the Crédit Urbain is in the middle of insolvency.

President: We cannot leave this matter for three months, it is very **serious**, we are participating in the discrediting of the administration and it is very **troubling** for the party concerned.

Three different manners, one amused and teasing, the two others serious, in linking the future judgment to its practical consequences, consequences which are understood and assessed but which cannot change the solidity of the argument* which each agrees to find decisive.

'Basically, in the end we couldn't even manage to have a legal discussion!', exclaims the surprised president of sub-section. For once the law is moving in a straight line; the mean* that has been invoked, even though it might have been invoked in bad faith by a litigious claimant, is so powerful that it is able to 'go very far' – so far, indeed, as to limit the right of appointment of the highest individual in the State, to destabilize a major private bank, to force the Vice-president to 'recuse himself', and to put the lawyers in such a 'desperate' situation that they can only bring texts and arguments 'without incidence' to bear on the principal argument, which has to do with the hierarchy of norms. And yet everyone recognizes that the individual concerned is competent, that his virtue has not been impugned, that he is an excellent director and that there was no good reason for him to be put in this embarrassing situation. This embarrassment, or hesitation, does not arise from the law itself but from the 'extraordinary gap' which the administration has allowed to develop between the letter of the law, which 'has become outdated', and practice. The president of the consulted Section acknowledges that 'they have not been very observant' in an aside made in a corridor, one of the innumerable informal channels which give the Council its charm and the ethnographer a great interest in the rumours that run through its corridors. . . . For much the same reason, the second reviser observes that this is a 'very healthy' case because, thanks to a stubborn squabbler, they can remind the administration that it is unable to derogate from the Penal Code, and allow the litigant to 'put a stop' to a phenomenon of revolving doors that discredits the administration.[41] The peculiar expression 'something shimmers' is often used at the Council to describe the hot spots that force the reasoning to shift: here, the president uses the expression to refer to the gap between a rule that has always been part of the Penal Code and the negligence of the administration. This gap 'feeds' the irresistible force of the argu-

---

[41] The French word for a legal decision, 'arrêt', also means a 'stop'.

ment*, and at the same time raises questions as to why the rule has never been applied before: there might be good reasons why this law was never made to express the force that it holds ('it is a pain in the neck').

This 'shimmering' makes it clear that the relation between article 432-13 of the new Penal Code, the claim of the Epsilon corporation and the decree of the President of the Republic appointing the civil servant is not the relation between a rule and its application. Even in this case, in which they 'couldn't even manage to have a legal discussion', the transportation of the rule into the case was due not to a simple automatic reflex but to a host of evaluations which quite promptly forced them to reopen a legal discussion that they thought had been definitively closed. In legal practice we are never concerned with *rules* but with more or less powerful *texts*, on which the dynamic of reasoning can or cannot rely. Article 432-13 might well be in the Penal Code, but obviously it never had much force because it never hindered the acts of the State or forced commissions against revolving doors to render an unfavourable opinion: they quite casually carry on appointing civil servants to high positions in corporations which they previously were responsible for supervising. Admittedly, the members of the sub-section are now scandalized, but that is only because the claim made by the Epsilon corporation brought to life and revealed the gap between the highest norm, the Penal Code, and reality by giving a new prominence to the legal argument invoked. What scandalizes the sub-section, makes the lawyers for the defence desperate and worries the president of Litigation, is nothing like a causal *obligation* which would compel all those who come into contact with it to conform to it; rather, it is more like a *basis*, a *guarantee*, a *potential* whose efficacy needs to be constantly refreshed and which, were it not for the obstinacy of a litigious claimant, would have been lost in complete oblivion. This is the paradox of an obligation that is binding only where all the elements that are needed to transport it are in place.

How might this paradox be explained? By recognizing without remorse the weight of context, which today works in favour of the claimant more than it did yesterday. The commissioner of the law clearly admits this in his conclusions. Non-legal aspects are, dare we say, an integral part of the discussion. That is hardly surprising because, as we saw in the last chapter, the judges who attend the discussion have all occupied, or are all going on to occupy, more or less important positions in the administration, and the majority of them, sitting in the Counsel Sections, continue day to day to advise the government on the texts of laws and decrees.

So, obviously the question put before you is **not strictly** legal. The question of the movement of civil servants to the private sector is of interest to the sociology of administration and to the media. The use of the Penal Code against administrative actions is becoming banal. This case could uncover others.

What's more, because of the danger of delays in process of review, the process will probably continue after the formidable crash caused by the insolvency of the Crédit Urbain, and it will obviously have an effect on the **climate** surrounding the recovery of the institution. (Conclusions, p. 5)

And the commissioner of the law resumes the closing section of her oration:

This decision is undoubtedly bound up with a number of other issues, that cannot be **reduced to entirely legal elements.** (. . .) First, people have expressed concern about the **earthquake** that this might cause. (. . .) It is also claimed that you are in danger of **suffocating** the public sector. (. . .) Moreover, there are a number of signs suggesting that public attitudes are in the process of **changing.** Although they were once distant and not well known, these sorts of arrangement are increasingly present in the minds of civil servants and army officers who are seeking to leave the public sector. (p. 18)

This is frank enough: the entire socio-political context of the moment works towards restoring the vigour of a section of the Penal Code which, since 1919, has been progressively reinforced by successive drafts,[42] but which was only ever applied once, by the Council in 1969 in a much less important case.[43] That which binds or compels, which carries weight, goes far or has force is therefore a mixture of 'climate' and law. The argument* progresses with a force that is unstoppable, but it does so on its own two feet.

How can the unquestionable force of the mean* be prevented from transporting itself into the case at hand, forcing the Council to render the decree of appointment null and void, in the knowledge that, on the one hand, this will trigger an 'earthquake', and, on the other, the discredit of the State would force each civil servant to have 'present in his mind' something which up until this case had only a weak power of restraint? Obviously, the counsellors are going to try everything to wriggle out of this trap, which is built partly of law and partly of non-legal implications. First, they can try to say that this bank is not in fact a private company. Unluckily for them, however, a public advice of the Counsel Section for Finance clearly explains in black and white that this bank cannot receive money from the

[42] 'We are not unearthing a fossil today', exclaims the commissioner, 'because it was last amended barely four years ago': p. 2.
[43] 'The appointment of a governor of a bank is obviously not "superimposable" to that of a mere director of the lower social security bureau': p. 5

State.[44] They could also try to assert, by means of a 'praetorian construction',[45] that in this case, and in this case alone, the Penal Code cannot have been 'intended to deprive the President of the Republic of a power that is essential to the realization of his objectives'. But this objection is swept aside by the commissioner of the law:

> It is true that we could maintain, with a bit more subtlety, that the criminal law has never **reached** so far as to embrace the case of **discretionary** appointments, and that there is therefore no need to derogate from it so as to avoid it. The Penal Code itself might be said to have **anticipated** this exception in some way. (. . .) How could a civil servant be tempted to favour a firm which he knows is powerless to choose some of its employees? Doesn't an authoritarian appointment process by definition exclude all risk of interference? (. . .) (p. 11)

However, it is impossible to hold this position, asserts the commissioner to her colleagues in the Assembly:

> The only limit on suspicion is the imagination of those who spread it; it spreads like a rumour. The object of the criminal law was **to cut off all the heads of this Hydra**, which is why the prohibited action remains a material prohibition, and why it sanctions a purely factual situation (. . .) That means that the safeguard applies to everyone and to the simple act of appointment, however high up it is made, and however imperative it may be. The prohibition has an exemplary function. You do a disservice to the power of appointment by preserving it so well: paradoxically, the effect of giving a **minimalist interpretation** to this 'anti-suspicion' law would be to revive and foster suspicion.
>
> In short, Ladies, Gentlemen, **you cannot conclude** that the Penal Code was intended to preserve some forms of appointment. With the result that this small island of impunity, which has no basis in the legal texts and which a judge in a criminal court would refute without hesitation, would quite unfortunately come to be seen as a rod that was invented to punish only the weakest. (p. 12)[46]

[44] We see here once again the paradoxical advantage of the link between the function of an adviser and the function of a judge, which allows rapid alternation from one to the other even though the two roles seemingly collide.

[45] 'Praetorian' goes back to Roman law and to the capacities of administrative law freely to give judges scope for interpretation superior to texts, even though these texts may be explicit; here, for example they could act as if the Penal Code could not possibly have 'meant' to say that the President is limited in one of his essential powers; 'construction' indicates that this argument is an expedient legal fiction invoked in order to avoid a difficulty like the one observed on p. 54. Remember that those judges are part of the executive branch and are thus much less worried about breaching the division of powers than English judges.

[46] Let's note the noble transposition by the commissioner of the law of a more brutal observation that was made during one of the sessions: 'We hurt the weak person who is nominated for a small position, but we let the big fishes go, I can give you names, they were all in my school year.'

In other words, even they cannot make the President immune from the criminal law, not even in the case of a discretionary appointment. To do that would be to return to the long-disgraced principle that 'le roi le veut' ('the king can do no wrong'), against which the whole edifice of administrative law was built over the centuries as a defence.[47] Through the luxury of the precautions proposed by the commissioner, we can sense the excitement that everyone is beginning to feel. As one counsellor said in a corridor before the case was passed to the Assembly: 'This is the heart of the State, you can render the decrees null and void, but with the power of appointment you touch on everything.' We see that this case, which 'excites everyone', which takes up pages of political commentary in the newspapers, and which makes the corridors buzz with rumours, is neither entirely removed from social context nor entirely devoid of legal rules. The counsellors affirm that they are not going back to the kind of justice that kings dispensed without any form of justification, according to the principle that 'tel est mon bon plaisir', even if the Jacobins in the Council cannot see what is to be gained by depriving the State of a power that is essential to the pursuit of its objectives.

The law is obviously flexible; after all, it was completely forgotten, not only by the administration but even by the 'inattentive' General Secretary of the Government; so it might be plausible to use some praetorian interpretation to isolate this single instance of the application of the Penal Code by means of a legal fiction. And yet, we cannot deny that it possesses such a force that, for the past six months, both lawyers and counsellors, for once united, have been trying hard to find some way of escaping the jaws of the argument directed against the President of the Republic and his decree by an obscure stockholder of the Epsilon corporation, who has obtained twelve shares worth 35 francs each, and whose only objective is to stir things up and remind the State that there is a law against revolving doors. If we want to understand the quasi-objective pressure exercised by this legal ground*, we must trace both the 'implacable' logic of legal reasoning and all those elements of context which allow this reasoning to become unquestionable. In law even more than in science, *apodeixis* – demonstration – evolves with apodictic force only if the full weight of *epideixis* – the conviction of the totality – is behind it.[48]

---

[47] Here we are far from the superb response that Pope Innocent III made 'ex certa sciencia', so as to shut off Father Thomas's irrefutable arguments (see Boureau, *La loi du royaume* (2001), p. 180).

[48] On the difference between *apodeixis* and *epideixis*, see Cassin, *L'effet sophistique* (1995); these two words have the same etymology, the first serving to construct the demonstrations of logicians and the other the rhetorical flourishes of sophists, but

To the surprise of the commissioner of the law, to the satisfaction of the sub-section and the manager from the Epsilon corporation, to the consternation of the individual who was centrally concerned and, presumably, that of the General Secretariat and the President of the Republic, after the Litigation Assembly the following text was displayed in the great hall at the entrance of the Council for all to read:

Article 1: The decree dated – appointing Mr Legendre as under-governor of Crédit Urbain **has been rendered null and void.**
Article 2: The remainder of the grounds of the claim is rejected (. . .).
Article 4: This decision shall be notified to the company Epsilon, to Mr Legendre, to the President of the Republic, to the Prime Minister and to the Minister of the Treasury.

The commissioner of the law has been 'followed'; the General Secretariat of the Government will undoubtedly be 'more careful' when the next appointment comes to be made, and doubtless the commission that deals with revolving doors will become more strict. We can understand why the counsellor considered this to be a 'very healthy' case: it allowed a blow to be struck against the scandal of an unapplied Penal Code, and for preventing civil servants from participating in the discrediting of the State. However, this decision cannot be seen as the simple re-expression of a force which was already contained in the text of law and whose application was a mere 'logical consequence'. Admittedly, the praetorian construction proposed by the Jacobins in the Council did not go so far as to make revolving doors an 'act of State',[49] but it would have allowed the members of the Council to find an ad hoc way of saving at least this particular appointment in the interests of the State, the bank in question being in a state of collapse and therefore very much in need of an unimpeachable director. A few years ago, perhaps even a few

---

in practice they have never been separated. On their application to logical reasoning, see Rosental, *Weaving Self-Evidence* (2008).
[49] 'An organically administrative act, which benefits from total jurisdictional immunity: its legality is not liable to be reviewed by administrative or civil courts, and the State is not responsible for the potential consequences of compensatory damages': Van Lang, Gondouin et al., *Dictionnaire de droit administratif* (1999), p. 12. This notion of an 'acte de gouvernement' ('act of State'), which was common from the time of Napoleon onwards, has been progressively restricted. Consider the impassioned example of Greenpeace's action against President Chirac's order resuming nuclear tests in the Pacific. The doctrine of 'acts of State' would have allowed the claim to be rejected: administrative courts are forbidden to review this type of act, it is their ultimate limit.

months ago, that is precisely what would have happened. The choice of one solution rather than another, and hence of one way of linking the texts of the Penal Code to the case at hand, *depends* on the spirit of the time, on the image we have of the administration, on the shrewdness of lawyers, on the stubbornness of the claimant and on the multi-formed pressure of the press. And yet, the word 'depends' explains very little, because in their secret deliberations the judges have chosen, by means of a configuration of considerations and a selection of visas, *precisely* how they understand this 'dependence' – how, in other words, their decision should be *linked* to the vast body of law and argument on which they rely. They have followed the particular configuration which their commissioner of the law suggested to them, an arrangement that was all the more eloquently expressed for being only one among many others:

Of course, it is in the **general interest** that the State should not be hindered unnecessarily, and that it should be able to choose people who are best suited to its needs. But it is **just as much** in the **general interest** that the State should quite strictly observe certain legal limits, especially because today it is expected to be transparent and neutral. If there were good reasons to compromise on this rule in particular cases, this could deal a **mortal blow** to the exigency to maintain a firm line and to show that we maintain it. This is even more important in matters concerning **public morality**.

It is, Ladies, Gentlemen, as much about the impartiality of the State as it is about reputations: they are only gained in constancy. **It is open to you** today **to situate yourselves firmly in the direct continuation** of your decision of 1969. In the sceptical and bewildered **climate** of the time, that interest is undoubtedly worth **more** than that which attaches itself to a particular case.

On these grounds we conclude that the decree against which the case was brought should be rendered null and void. (pp. 18–19)

Is this prose not worthy of Brutus in Shakespeare's *Caesar*? Only in the Council of State, and only from the mouths of those commissioners of the law can we hear today, in Paris, and at the end of the twentieth century, these truly Roman words resonate! The paradox of the transition of a mean* is entirely contained in this extraordinary expression: 'it is open to you ... to situate yourselves *firmly* in the *direct* continuation of your decision of 1969'. This connection will only be 'direct' for those who are concerned with public morality, for those who put the general interest of a State which is exposed to a climate of suspicion before another general interest of an earlier State that was more regal or more Jacobin, and for those who choose constancy against arbitrariness in this 'sceptical and bewildered' time. Forget these high-minded considerations and you will sway, you will revoke your opinion, there will be no more direct connection and you will have dealt a 'mortal blow' to the general interest, understood as such, of the administration. The law is only law if the whole context is taken into account, according to a certain conception of public morality. It is essential for the quality of law that there is nothing but law in law.

Let us admire the beauty of this address to the second person plural: 'it is open to *you*'. The commissioner of the law consistently reminds this great virtual body of what, over the past two centuries, it meant to say and what it decided in an immense corpus of hundreds of thousands of decisions. It is almost as though he were addressing himself to a sphinx that no longer knew quite what it thought, and for whom administrative law was a sort of penumbra or unconscious in the midst of which the commissioner could trace well-defined paths and identify clear rights against this obscure background, reminding him of what law is, what the State is, what the general will is, and what the profound opinion – always to be recaptured, reinterpreted – of the Council of State is. That is the proper role of the commissioners: to remind this composite monster of what it meant to say and of the virtues to which it is still bound. There always is a certain measure of impertinence in the highly respectful addresses of the commissioners, because they act as though this sphinx with 100 heads really does not know what it wants, and as though it needs them constantly to refresh its memory; they trace its duties, remind it of its past behaviour, and solve its innumerable contradictions, putting an end to ambiguities, oversights and confusions. Sometimes, the commissioner seems to play the role of a father scolding a child, sometimes that of a haruspex examining the intestines of a sacrificial animal, and sometimes that of a trainer trying to make a lion jump through a flaming hoop . . .

In response to each address, the sphinx does no more than growl – if we dare to speak of such a prestigious body in such terms. In fact, the Council of State sitting 'in Litigation' never expresses a direct opinion on the conclusions of the commissioners, but does so only by means of the brief 'dispositif' of the decision, which is itself as enigmatic as any of Pythia's answers. That is why the commissioners who are responsible for 'saying the law' are joined by a group of 'chroniclers', whose role is rather like that of the interpreters at the Temple of Delphi, who explain to claimants the meaning of judgment fallen from the golden mouth. The chroniclers, a word that conceals the elitism of young auditors behind a modest title, are essential for the understanding of the commentators of administrative law because they attend the deliberation without participating in it. Their anonymous chronicle[50] appears in an independent journal, the *AJDA*,[51] and summarizes the judges' mode of reasoning without betraying anything of the deliberation; by itself, the text of the decision, which is as succinct as possible, would do nothing to clarify the judges' reasoning. In this case, the chroniclers have understood perfectly well the intention of the commissioner, who has been followed by the judges. Since in this case the unapplied rule of criminal law becomes powerful, both the image of the State and the definition of the general will have to be changed.

The specificity of this rule of criminal law, which until now was only **very rarely applied**, is that it prohibits and sanctions behaviour which is not in itself contrary to integrity. There are other laws that apply to cases of corruption. Article 432-13 has a different object: it prohibits a situation which could give rise to instances of corruption or at least **raise the suspicion** that such instances are produced. (. . .)

We must, however, ask whether the Litigation Assembly decision in 1969 [date of the decision cited in note 155] would have applied the solution it accepted in order to approve an appointment made by a social security fund, to an appointment made by the President of the Republic. The decision rendered **in 1996** on the claim of the company Epsilon **translates strengthened requirements** of transparency and neutrality into the relations, whether private or public, of administrative and economic actors. The negative presumption which is attached to the presence at the head of a company of a civil servant who was previously in charge of controlling that company **has prevailed** over the positive presumption attached to an appointment pronounced by the highest authority of the State. The principle of the separation between the controller and the controlled inscribed in the Penal Code **has not given way** to a discretionary power of appointment made by a public authority with specific economic objectives; it is thus **particularly forcefully asserted, in conformity** with the general evolution of the law and of public attitudes'. (*AJDA*, 20 February 1997, p. 156)

A few years earlier, the opposite solution would have been reached, the 'positive presumption' would have prevailed over the negative, and discretionary power would never have ceded before the second exigency of separation between controller and controlled. That which is 'forcefully' asserted by the chronicles is, rather bizarrely, 'the general evolution of the law *and of public attitudes*', combined in one package which would have remained unthinkable had Epsilon's claim not provided a quite unexpected opportunity.[52] But here, the relation-

---

[50] The whole mechanism of the Council is characterized by a subtle form of anonymity as the 'chronicles' are signed by two names without the reader ever knowing who has written what.

[51] *Revue d'actualité juridique du droit administratif*, published by Dalloz and the main source for understanding this branch of French law.

[52] As we see in comparing this 'slick text' with the hesitant remarks collected by the ethnographer, the chronicles express the essence of the tensions and discussions

ship between inside and outside is not like the relationship between
that which is made public and that which remains secret, or between
a wrapper and its contents, because the weight of history, of presuppositions, of mentalities and of morals is quite straightforwardly
admitted. And there is nothing awkward about this admission because
it does not lead to the inference that the solution reached is in any
way diminished, limited, contested or weakened by the deployment
of the multiple concerns and interests that are *attached* to it.[53] In fact,
the better the chronicler is at showing all the particulars of the decision, the more one has the impression that all the conditions of felicity
have been fulfilled and that it has been judged *well*. Therefore, the
quality of the judgment does not depend either on total independence
regarding the social and political context and relations of power, or
on the strict application of forms (since in this case the relevant provision of the Code had never been applied), but rather on the breadth
of the disjointed elements which they managed to retain after having
extensively and decently 'hesitated'. What is crucial is the mode of
attachment, the knot with which the judges tied together, on the one
hand, a President, a sceptical opinion, an efficient administration, a
powerful State, a free economy and, on the other, the immense body
of precedents of the Council, not forgetting the litigants, who can
make the Republic tremble, without the help of a lawyer, through the
simple mean of a letter on blank paper.

'Take advantage of this long dreamed-of opportunity to shake the case-law!'

As we have learned, French judges, even those of the Cassation Court,
do not have the power to change the law. This is expressed by the
famous article 5 of the Civil Code: 'it is forbidden for judges to reach
a decision on the cases which are submitted to them by way of general
and regulating disposition'. In theory, the same principle applies to

---

which the instruction meeting documents, albeit in an elegant and muted style. This,
moreover, reduces confidentiality issues a little. In a sense, the deliberations of the
Council of State are not truly secret since the young auditors keep a sufficiently
detailed record of them . . . As one of the chroniclers said: 'We are paid to betray the
secrets of the deliberations . . . '

[53] Only people involved in critical sociology are able to believe that they fully understand the law, when they reveal the relations of dominance which it merely legitimizes. The entire efficiency of law lies precisely in this little addition, the legitimacy,
which always deviates from the foreseeable path, transport and progress of relations
of dominance. See p. 142.

the Council of State as a court of final appeal. Yet, there is not a single line of text in the immense edifice of administrative law, the heap of precedent, or the body of doctrine that was not authored by the Council itself. No Member of Parliament has ever voted for 'the theory of detachable acts',[54] the Byzantine concept of 'privilèges du préalable'[55] or even for the 'sublime construction' of 'the public interest' or the 'theory of balance'.[56] General principles of law ('les principes généraux du droit') are said to be 'discovered' by the Council of State based on the *lack* of an explicit text.[57] 'Believing itself to be the servant of these principles, the Council of State has made itself the creator of them.'[58] Whereas, in every other case, the judges' reasoning must unfold as though it were just applying a rule to a particular kind of case, or, in the most problematic cases, as though it were just modifying the interpretation of a text which they can in no way touch, in the review sessions of the Council we have quite often been able to observe the fascinating situation in which judges become legislators.[59] *Filius et pater legis*, as the jurisconsults of the ancient world put it.

[54] See below, p. 171.

[55] According to this principle of French administrative law, public bodies are authorized to take certain decisions irrespective of any prior approval by the parties who will be affected by such decisions. It is also not required that a judge has previously decided that the public body is authorized to take such decisions.

[56] See p. 51.

[57] On this important point, see Jeanneau, 'La nature des principes généraux du droit' (1962); Ewald, 'Une expérience foucaldienne' (1986). One example in thousands: 'In the GISTI decision, the Council of State *seems* to have expressly admitted the existence of an autonomous body of superior rules, which is situated *above* the positivist written law, and from which the judge *extracts* in some way a general principle of a particular character': Long, Weil et al., *Les grands arrêts* (1999), p. 675 (emphasis added). We do not know what to admire most in that sentence, the existence of a law superior to the positivist law, *à la* Antigone, or this little verb 'seems' which amply indicates the indecision of the commentators who are, nonetheless, the most authorized – see below, p. 190, the same incertitude, with the chroniclers obliged to turn themselves into the ethnologists of the mute Council.

[58] Kessler, *Le Conseil d'Etat* (1968), p. 326.

[59] This difference between the two branches of law should not be exaggerated, since the interpretation of laws can play the same role in civil and criminal courts. It does remain the case that the administrative law bears more resemblance to the common law of the English-speaking world than to the law of the Civil Code. The difference between these two laws of precedents resides, however, in the odd fact that administrative law only cites in its decisions laws and decrees, and never its own decisions, which are only to be seen in the conclusions of the commissioner of the law and in the analyses of doctrine. The ethnographer has never encountered anyone who was baffled by what had always seemed to him a key difficulty in understanding this branch of law.

This enables us to take a decisive step forwards in our understanding of what we have called 'the passage of law', since the movement of hesitation which we have followed, until now while the law was stable, will come to shake the legal structure itself in showing us in real time what is called a 'reversal of precedent'. It will allow us to see how a premise of judicial reasoning is modified rather than being used to find a solution. The embarrassments – or 'shimmerings' – which have till now been so important to our understanding of legal enunciation can be resolved in two main fashions: one in which judges end up tracing a path between the texts and a type of case (it is this one which we have just seen), and the other in which, taking the type of case as a pretext, they modify a rule either wholly or partly. Either they judge a case according to the law, or they *judge the law itself* given the opportunity provided by the right sort of case. This shows just how badly formalism explains the transition of law, because we are going to observe how the judges, precisely so as to avoid a rule that has become 'purely formal' over time, allow themselves to modify the form that they were about to apply, and manage to extract enough meaning from the claim to alter the law itself and, through such an exercise, ensure the quality of the whole movement, or, in other words, that cases are reconciled with the body of precedents.

Nothing seems more strange to the observer than the incessant movements which run through the corpus of administrative law in a constant state of reshaping and which yet never cease to have a coherence which is invented step by step, and which each commissioner, each deliberation, each judgment kneads for better or for worse, throwing to one side that which other commissioners, other deliberations, other judgments, with the patience of Penelope, try hard to mend. We shall immerse ourselves in this fabric of discordant and concordant discourses, trying not to become entirely lost; nothing appears here that is not a 'logical development' of precedent, despite the fact that the cohesion of all these contradictory judgments has to be repeatedly adjusted by means of more or less bold interpretations, all of this being done with sufficient care to avoid tearing the fabric. These new conditions of felicity bear upon the very quality of the law. At this point, the judges exercise their skill upon the organization of the law itself, its coherence, its logic and its viability, and, as they do so, we will be able to detect the final value object in the list that this chapter is trying to compile.

Once again, in spite of the laborious nature of the case and the demands we are making on the readers, we are going to follow the discussion step by step, with the promise that in the next chapters we shall give up this difficult procedure. For the time being, however, this remains the only way of familiarizing ourselves with the hesitant path that we think characterizes the movement of law.

President Luchon: We will first take the case of the Assembly, it is a **difficult** case, there is case-law from 1905 where a third party cannot request that an act be rendered null and void because it is *ultra vires*; we wonder if we are **shaking** a case-law **already in trouble**; the sub-section did not want to shake this **pillar**; it was the president of the Litigation Section who said 'You are being quite timid, why don't you **take advantage** of this **long dreamed-of opportunity** to shake the case-law'; this case which has no lawyer, or an evanescent lawyer, is very **interesting**.

> *We again meet here the fourth of our value objects, the famous 'interest of a case' which grabs the attention of the judges; we understand that it is important here since the president of Litigation himself suggests they should not hesitate to shake the pillar of a case-law which the sub-section was too timid to pull down; but obviously the more vigorous the shaking, the more 'difficult' the case is, because a mass of diverging precedents has to be put in place again by means of some tectonic rearrangement; and this seriousness indicates the presence of a new value object which we want to follow: what else must be changed in order to modify that rule?*

Deldago (reporter) (reading the 'note'): (. . .) All this preceding case-law extends the right of users, all that **remains** is **to 'make the move'** to contest a contract directly; I believe that we need do no more than **simplify** a procedure that has become very **formal** and there will not be **serious disorder** so far as jurisdiction is concerned; but we **risk** seeing a multiplication of claims; a **criterion** for legal standing must be found: (a) if the act is 'detachable', (b) if the act is 'regulatory', (c) only if the act is opposable to the third party;[60] I have drawn up a draft annulling the contract: the argument* is **not working in the present case-law, but if we modify** the case-law then the claimant **is right!**

[60] Contracts between a private company and a public body often contain clauses which only affect the contracting parties, and clauses which are of a regulatory nature and which, even though they are not strictly directed at third parties, also affect third parties. A distinction is made between 'actes contractuels' and 'actes réglementaires' of the public body. Third parties cannot claim on the basis of the former (only the parties to the contract can do so), but they can claim on the basis of the latter (since third parties may be directly affected by certain acts, for example when a public body enters into a contract which contains clauses which impose obligations on third parties).

The reporter is a young, energetic woman, who, as is usual for a member of her age, will shortly leave the Council to seek election to Parliament; she conveys in very few words the atmosphere that usually surrounds the reversal of a precedent: it is time to revamp this piece of law.[61] The adjective 'formal' is used to describe the existing state of the case-law, which it is possible to 'simplify' provided only that judges decide to 'make the move', which the reporter carefully defines as 'very small' because it would not entail 'serious disorder', while recognizing at the same time that if that move is made there is a 'risk' of triggering plenty of claims which must then be limited by clear unambiguous new 'criteria'. So as to cross a minor threshold, one must build another threshold, located at a different point in the flow of claims. 'To simplify' does not therefore mean 'to alleviate'; rather, it means to change the allocations of risks. Her wonderful concluding sentence suddenly reveals to us the efficiency of the famous legal means* whose meaning we are trying to grasp: in the present legal framework, it is not 'working', we cannot accept it, it will not prosper, the transfer of the value object of the claim (in the eighth sense recognized above) will come to a complete halt; but *if we modify our case-law*, then 'the claimant will be right' and the mean* will become 'working'. The law itself will have changed. It is obvious that what is involved here is a novel value object, one that is quite different from the others.

This horribly complicated case turns on the difference between the law of contract, which is based exclusively on the agreement of particular individuals, irrespective of the wishes of third parties (an example being an agreement for a lease made between landlord and tenant, about which no other person can complain), and the administrative decisions which are by definition unilateral. This aspect of public law is often said to be excessive; it imposes obligations on third parties (because, even if they have not expressed any intention, the public interest justifies compelling them to do something) as well as giving them rights (they are able to challenge administrative decisions by taking their case to an administrative tribunal). The position seems entirely clear: civil law courts hear disputes concerning contracts, which by definition concern only the contracting parties, while administrative courts hear cases concerning 'unilateral' contracts that confer rights and obligations on all third parties. This would all be

---

[61] Her presentation is only atypical in one respect, namely her draft rendering the contract null and void. In fact, through a perversion peculiar to administrative law, those cases in which precedent is overturned are almost always those in which the claim is rejected. Only the considerations for the judgment introduce novelty by considering, for example, that a claim is admissible. That will be the case here, since the reporter will not be followed on this point.

quite straightforward but for one thing. Administrative bodies, in this particular case a consortium of towns, are able to enter into contracts, for example contracts with companies providing refuse collection services, which contain *some provisions* resembling those of a classic contract, and which cannot therefore be challenged by third parties, mixed in with others that *resemble regulatory decisions*, and which, rather like 'unilateral' contracts, can be challenged by third parties before an administrative tribunal! In such cases the claimant is *both* a third party in the second sense, that is to say a third party with legal standing *and* a third party in the first sense, that is, a third party *without* legal standing . . . In the case at hand, the question is whether such a claimant can bring an action against the Mayor of his town for having required him to contribute – by way of taxation – to what is a 'public service' (refuse collection) under the pretext that he lives in a flat, while his more affluent neighbours, who own individual chalet-style houses, are not required to make any contribution. As we might expect, the case is interesting not because it concerns refuse collection, which is quickly forgotten, but because it concerns the question whether the claimant does or does not have a right to initiate proceedings before an administrative tribunal to review a unilateral decision that is disguised as a classic contract.

President Luchon (playing the role of reviser): It is the only file which the president of the Litigation Section wants to pass to the Assembly quickly. There is another source of inadmissibility; (. . .) the co-owner has no mandate to act; he is a third party to the contract. There is after all a clause saying that the clauses are indivisible, that would be **less pretty** for the case. As for 'non-compliance with the statutory limitation period' I have looked at 'sufficient knowledge' ['connaissance acquise'],[62] but it is very **clear**, if I read Chapus properly yesterday evening, there is Chapus 25-3-1962 5th edition

---

[62] 'Theory of case-law according to which the non-compliance with the statutory limitation period of litigious claims is attributable to the party who brings the claim if this party had sufficient knowledge of the administrative decisions taken. The advantage lies in the fact that this knowledge is deemed to be absent when the administrative acts have not been officially publicized': Van Lang, Gondouin et al., *Dictionnaire de droit administratif* (1999). As the chronicles of *AJDA* will record later, after the settlement of this case, the new decision in discussion will oblige administrations to give more publicity to contracts which contain regulatory clauses: 'It was particularly opportune to impose the obligation on public institutions to ensure that contracts which create rights or obligations for third parties be publicized. This new rule must be welcomed because it will inevitably lead to a substantial movement towards the publication of contracts containing regulatory clauses' (p. 737).

p. 490, and 'connaissance acquise' is not recognized. That is **troubling because it would bring everything to a stop**; and if that
happened we could not **decently** go to the Assembly; yesterday
evening I said to myself 'this **cannot go** to the Assembly'. In any
case, the issue of 'sufficient knowledge' does not apply to regulatory
acts. Even so, we must **make an effort**; (turning towards the commissioner of the law) you can add this to your little basket.[63]

> *The president mixes in one fell swoop three value objects with
> which we are now very familiar: the movement of the claim (is it
> admissible or not?), the interest of a case (even if qualified as
> 'pretty') which justifies the participants in harbouring a passion for
> it today; lastly the importance of the formation of the judgment and
> the efficient management of files, for which, as we know, he is
> responsible. As it is about seizing the opportunity of this case to
> shake the case-law, we are ready to make an effort, but if the statu-
> tory limitation period has not been complied with, it will be impos-
> sible to accept the legal mean, which would immediately cause the
> interest of the members to plummet. The level of the formation of
> the judgment – sub-section, Section, Assembly – obviously depends
> on the importance of the stakes: 'it would bring everything to a
> stop'; as the question is thorny, we return to doctrine, here the
> famous Chapus's book, appearing like a lighthouse in the darkness.*

Deldago: I can no longer find the notes of president N,[64] but I
remember that we were **grasping at straws**; I drew up the draft
yesterday evening from memory.

President: I can only **escape** inadmissibility if this is a regulatory
act, but we must still make a **little effort** because if this is a regulatory contract, then there are still two months (of delay);[65] the second
argument*, that he is co-owner, is not raised by the consortium of
townships; the important point remains inadmissibility, I agree; the
Documentation Service has given me this, I have not read it yet; the

---

[63] Remember that during these sessions the commissioner of the law remains silent
and does nothing but write down the elements of the case of which he is taking note
in order to prepare his conclusions, which will be read during the session of judgment
proper.

[64] This is an example of the twists whose logic we saw in the last chapter: because
the case has dragged on, which is not uncommon, the president of the sub-section
is no longer the same person, so everything has to be recaptured 'from memory'.

[65] The claimant only set things in motion three years after the entry into force of the
contract, since he had to visit the Commission for access to administrative documents
in order that he might eventually get a copy of the contract entered into by the Mayor
and the refuse-collection company. This is why the question of non-compliance with
the statutory limitation period arises.

case-law 'has already gone far' on 'detachable contracts';[66] the decision *Croix-de-Seguey-Tivoli* has produced progeny here, there and everywhere;[67] the 'déféré préfectoral', that is entirely *ultra vires*; I looked to see whether it presented a **vibration**[68] towards **the path that we are following**; the commissioner of the law was very reluctant, the president of Litigation was even more so, in any case that is all in the past; I looked at the doctrine in the *Major Precedents*, and to my great surprise I found a justification which is **a little fragile** and when we leaf quickly through certain works **of doctrine**, Chapus does not mince his words and **even** the careful Dalloz opposes the Council of State, I am **inclined to make the final move**.

> To escape from inadmissibility and to prevent the claim from becoming as uninteresting as it is 'ugly', an 'effort' must be made; the president accumulates in one paragraph all the usual means that judges have at their disposal when they find themselves in a difficult situation ('grasping at straws' as the reporter puts it more crudely); the Documentation Service prepares, on request, a specific file of the corpus of texts and submits it in the form of a photocopied bundle to the member who requested it; the photocopies include the precedents and the cases that followed each precedent (hence the expression 'progeny'). These precedents and the cases that follow them together form a genealogical tree, as we will see further on. They form a fabric of traits and contradictory tensions which is more or less dense and from which the judges seek to extract a certain tendency in the case-law; the doctrine is added to this body of texts in order to understand the direction in which the totality is moving. It is a typical expression that the judges often only 'leaf through' the

[66] The theory of 'detachable acts' proves the creativity of the Council of State: we cannot bring a case against a contract, but we can act *as if* the preliminary decision to enter into the contract formed a 'detachable act' from the contract itself, a unilateral act which makes it fall into the category of administrative acts which are liable to a claim by a third party . . . For example if a Mayor enters into a contract with a company, a case against the contract cannot be brought but one can submit the decision of the municipal council to enter into the contract to the judgment of the administrative judge . . . The following question then is: if the 'detachable act' (the decision to enter into the contract) is rendered null and void, is the contract which followed it for that reason also null and void? No, precisely because the act can be 'severed' . . . The dictionary of administrative law with some irony defines it as a 'purely functional notion'.

[67] Council of State 21 déc. 1906, Synd. des propriétaires et contribuables du quartier Croix-de-Seguey-Tivoli, *Rec* 962, concl. Romieu. Extensively commented in Long, Weil et al., *Les grands arrêts* (1999).

[68] Remember that the French expression 'un frémissement' (shimmering) is a local term to signify that the case-law is in fact already in motion and that something important might happen.

doctrine. Since Chapus, in this case, does 'not mince his words' in asserting that the justifications are 'fragile', all this pushes the president 'to make the move', which he would not be able to do if Chapus had been clear and if there had been no 'vibration'. This is something like a barely noticeable gust of wind which lifts the veil of reasoning so that an effort can be made to make 'the case-law shake' if all other circumstances are pushing for it. . . .

But do we have a **firm rampart**? We dispute the regulatory act and not the rest; (how should we do that?) at this moment anything can be taken to court; that is what makes our lives **difficult**: this difference between the 'regulatory contract' and the 'individual act'; **it serves no purpose** to go to the Assembly in order to **uphold** the case-law (the reporter laughs; the commissioner of the law takes notes). The rental charge is intended to cover everything; there is another mean* which we cannot 'raise ourselves' since it is not of public interest. The decisions say that the regulatory clause is not important, that it is has no legal value, we cannot accept such a ground; there are indeed some precedents in this sense, **but** 36 decisions which recognize that 'a document inviting bids from private contractors' ['cahier des charges'] may have a regulatory aspect. The problem of the indivisible act remains, is the clause indivisible? That seems difficult; I **cannot make the effort** to say that it is divisible; I have searched in the 'déféré préfectoral'; the case-law is **very clear**; **even** Denoix de Saint-Marc has not succeeded in swaying the Section.[69] When it is indivisible it is indivisible, I am **not suggesting** that you should try to argue otherwise; that's all.

The president clearly links the level at which the formation of judgment takes place to the reversal of precedent: if a rule is merely applied to a case, then that is not interesting; we also see how concerned he is to construct 'firm ramparts' to avoid a situation in which 'everything can be taken to court'; finally, at the moment in which we are waiting to see if they will indeed shake the case-law, they take advantage of that time to measure, through a process of trial and error, what is weak and what is 'very strong' – The former in the form of precedents tending in one direction, which are contradicted by a mass of other precedents tending in another direction. The force of the latter is proved by the fact that even a prestigious commissioner – who subsequently became Vice-president of the Council – has not been able to 'sway the Section' in a case similar to this one.

---

[69] Section 20 janvier 1978, Syndicat national de l'enseignement technique agricole public, p. 22, conclusions M. Denoix de Saint-Marc.

Now that the reviser has finished summarizing the case for his colleagues, the discussion can begin. But whereas in the previous case the law had all the solidity of the Penal Code, and the 'scandal' arose from the fact that this law had never been applied, and anxiety was caused by trying to assess the political and financial consequences of the Council's decision, in this case the anxiety has quite different causes: this is a case in which the law itself becomes progressively unstable, the more it is explored. The judges tactfully ascertain the relevant case-law, in search of some 'shimmering', knowing that they will make no radical innovation but will simply 'make a move', the 'final move' after all the others that have been made in order to avoid formalism and artificiality. The strange thing is that, although the 'collective judge', *viva vox legis*, is supposed to bear the administrative law within him, in his body or brain, he always seems to be surprised by his own tendencies and contradictions, and he needs the summarizing packages of the Documentation Service to remind him of what he has decided in the course of so many decades. . . . Judges become hybrid beings for whom history stretches out over centuries, making them almost as immortal as Cagliostro, probing ceaselessly what they have truly wanted, judged, thought, in much the same way as a hypochondriac asking anxious questions about the functioning of his own organs, or as a Christian doing his examination of conscience, constantly measuring, balancing, probing what is solid and fragile, certain and weak, indisputable and modifiable.

But at the very moment when they hesitate about changing the law, an abyss opens before them, as if by modifying the delicate ecology of the administrative law they might provoke a catastrophe. Without a 'firm rampart' everything becomes open to argument, they realize with horror.

Dorval: Have you contacted him (the claimant)?

President Luchon: He disputes everything but he does not even have a lawyer; let's discuss the issues in their order: past the statutory limitation period or not? The question of the third party; divisibility or not? It is embarrassing to go to the Assembly with the statutory limitation period, for the rest of the questions: yes.

Dorval: We are **not going to the Assembly** to conclude the question of inadmissibility.

President: He wants to hold on to it, only a claimant without a lawyer can hold on to such a legal mean*; if we wriggle out of it, he will not be pleased.

Dorval: (reading the *Lebon* volume which he has picked out from the little library behind the reporter) I refer to *Bonnec* 25 3 1962, p. 349 (he reads).

Le Men: When does the statutory limitation period start? It's all linked; let's leave aside the date, that is the starting point of the limitation period for the decree; for the regulatory clause of a contract, it is the date of publication. If we reason on the basis of the 'regulatory contract', then the statutory limitation period does not begin until it is published. There are not fifty ways to consider this problem, it is either the publication, or the notification. We cannot say 'it has not been published so it is disputable at any moment' and 'we cannot notify each occupant'. If we were to **change** the system in that way, **everything** would be **disputable** at any moment, there is no obvious solution. **That is what makes it hard**, that **everything will be in flux**; what is the formality which makes the non-compliance with the statutory limitation period fall away; the principle of 'sufficient knowledge' does not apply in regulatory matters.

> *Two value objects manifest themselves here: the first, which is the reversal of precedent which they are carefully trying to experiment with; the second, which is very different and regards the practical consequences of the decision for judges and claimants. This gives rise to that truly magnificent sentence which at once explains the passion, the hesitation and the interest of the case: 'that is what makes it hard, that everything will be in flux'; far from being established, the whole administrative law has become unstable, slippery and shaken.*

De Servetière (who has experience because he was previously an elected representative): In small communities, they use bill-posters!

President: The file does not show that it hasn't been published; that argument has not been raised (Dorval passes the *Lebon* to Deldago).

De Servetière: The borough has to take responsibility, if it is a regulatory contract a notice has to be put up.

Le Men: If it is *ultra vires*, there must have been bill-posting on the matter.

Luchon: Very good, this is **very solid** ground.

Dorval: It's entirely **logical**; regulatory contracts affect third parties and we **recently decided** for the same reason (in a different case) that these acts had to be published; but why should it be included in the case-law now; we are not **at a point in time** at which we **want to open new possibilities** for litigation, the question is whether this is **opportune**.

President: Third parties can bring the case in a different way; but all those who have a lawyer dispute the 'detachable act'.

Dorval: If the case goes to the Assembly, that is the point of law that will be **weighed**.

Le Men (solemn): **We need to be hesitant** on this point, it is **important case-law**; two important developments persuade me to **make a move**; one legal, namely the 'prefectoral referral', and the other administrative, namely the multitude of actors. Concerning the first point, the Prefect can now initiate legal action (through a 'referral') while the addressee of the contract cannot, **that is artificial**. Besides, our law is constructed on the basis of certain concessions regarding bid documents and **now** we are multiplying contracts. It is inappropriate, because this causes certain clauses to be included in the contract which would otherwise be included in the bid documents. However, the **dams** proposed by Deldago are excellent, people should not be able to take any dispute to court.

> *This is a magnificent expression of the value object which we recognized above: hesitation, expressed as a duty which is linked to the importance of the issues – 'we need to be hesitant'; there is also a clear recognition of progression. The second assessor is persuaded to 'make a move' because the old solution is 'artificial'; he does not innovate, he does not change the law; he merely brings it into line with what it should be (since the Prefect can already contest certain contractual clauses, and because a recent law permits him to do so). This should be done while taking into account the effect of the practical context, namely that it is 'inappropriate'; but another value object subsequently appears to counter the risk that people might 'be able to take any dispute to court'. 'Ramparts' must be constructed immediately.*

President: Yes, the first **firm rampart** is that there must be legal standing; but if a case can be brought against the unilateral act of another civil servant, then what is the logic of such a barrier? The commissioner of the law will say 'you have to limit it to regulatory clauses', if we do that then we **open the door** to everything. I am playing the devil's advocate here, but all regulatory acts in general will be affected by this. If I allow it for contracts only, then I also **extend it to everything**; what is a 'regulatory rampart'?

Le Men: Every contract can be disputed by a third party who has legal standing, this is a completely different move.

President: They cannot dispute them for 60 years, **it would be a complete mess**!

Le Men: Quite, there must be **legal stability** (*sécurité juridique*), there must not be a constant threat of disputes, it would be a mess.

The essential phrase has been uttered: 'legal stability', which is immediately linked to a more popular but equally important expression – 'it would be a mess'. There would be no more time limits, no more limits on the number of third parties, and no limits on the divisibility of clauses. We would have left the realm of the law entirely. We are confronted here with two different new value objects, one that concerns the law, which judges will make more coherent and less formalistic by revising it or tidying it up without actually changing it, and another that concerns the organization of the litigious claims and the definition of the criteria for establishing legal standing before an administrative tribunal. The decision made in this case will make legal action easier or more efficient, and certainly more direct. More people will qualify as third parties with legal standing because any contract containing divisible regulatory clauses will be open to challenge: were the law to be extended, what the reporter describes as 'serious disorder' might ensue. The rest of the discussion is concerned with this risk and with the question of how to minimize it. What is at issue here is indeed a different value object, because, in extending the empire of the law, we also increase the workload of the judges, who are in danger of being overwhelmed by legal actions. The issue is how to draw a boundary between those claims that will be heard and those that will not, and the Council is very proud of the fact that it has only ever extended this boundary line since the original, somewhat narrow limits placed on it by Napoleon. It seems difficult to characterize the passage of the law without recognizing this extension of its conditions. How far does it extend? At what point does it begin?

Le Men: We say to someone 'bring a case against the regulatory clauses of a contract' **but subsequently** we say 'the contract is not divisible'; the task of managing this must be left to the judge who reviews the contract; on the definition of the regulatory clauses: by definition regulatory clauses are divisible; third parties do not have to go back to the contract.
President Huchon: **We touch on a very interesting point here**; this **changes everything**; all this **modifies** the notion of the 'detachable act'. But there is a serious obstacle: the case-law says something completely different about the 'detachable act'; all this must be taken into account, otherwise **it is not admissible**.

According to the present case-law, the claimant must have asked the judge to render null and void the decision of the town council in which it was decided to enter into the contract, but the claimant *does not request this at all, the argument* he has chosen to put forward must indeed be followed: it is one of the articles of the contract which he is disputing, and he is disputing it directly without using the complicated formula of the 'prefectoral deferral'; the question is whether or not the contracts are divisible or indivisible; we see that, as we go along and the discussion progresses, the sub-section becomes more passionate ('that is interesting' because that 'changes everything') and is better able to measure that which is 'changing' little by little.*

Le Men: We **could say** that he (the claimant) requests that the decision to enter into the contract be rendered null and void.

President: Ah no, no he explicitly mentions '2nd paragraph of article 7' of the contract, so we **cannot** interpret it in another way.

The sub-section can stretch the claim by 'interpreting' it in order to make it more interesting, and so that it provides an opportunity to overrule the present case-law. However, it cannot judge ultra petita in providing the claimant with a different legal mean* than that which he has raised, except if such an argument is 'raised by the judge himself' ('d'office') as described below.

Le Men: If we recognize the **difficulties** of the mechanism, we can understand the present case-law better.

De Servetière: Yes, but that would be too easy, public bodies could **disguise** unilateral decisions by turning them into contractual clauses and by subsequently saying that these clauses are indivisible.

President: That is perhaps exactly why **the present case-law will be maintained**; the Minister of State Reform must be warned, we must **anticipate** this point because it has practical consequences. And concerning the question of indivisibility, we have to **anticipate** social attitudes. The commissioner of the law (who is silently taking notes) must invoke a 'mean* of public interest' which must then be communicated to the claimant and to the company (he turns towards the reporter Deldago and then to his secretary):[70] can Miss N (the secretary of the sub-section) do that immediately? Can we agree on 29 January, we give them 15 days.

President: We now have to tackle the question of **substance**; we have not raised the principle of equality ourselves. Isn't it contrary

---

[70] Remember that 'communicate' is another intransitive verb to indicate the progression of the instruction meeting. A document arrives, a new argument is raised, the opposing party must be informed so that it can produce a reply in accordance with the principle that both parties are heard on each issue . . .

to the law of 10-7-1975 on 'refuse collection' included in tax and rent, from which we have **extracted** the mean* that we cannot ask private persons to pay the contribution to public services? There is indeed a flaw here. We ask them to use a bin liner and at the same time we do not say to them that there is a charge for refuse collection. Why don't they just pay for the van which collects the refuse, as Mr Crécelle says, and so on.

Dorval: I would love to ask De Servetière who has some **concrete experience** to tell us how to do it.

De Servetière: I myself would render the decision null and void, because the contribution is already financed by the rent; if it was about hygiene we could ask the user to make an additional payment, but only if it is for the convenience of the service. I render it null and void.

A trainee from the National School of Administration: From experience I can tell you that it is different in Nantes.

Le Men: All the same, I wouldn't be too hasty; the law allows for a contribution to be asked from the user of a service when it concerns 'health and hygiene', but not when it concerns the interest which a user clearly has in the service provided by the company collecting refuse?

De Servetière: Yes, that is the principle.

President: Yes, it is quite shocking, especially for the chalet-style houses whose owners could quite easily afford such a contribution; do we follow Le Men, does the law indeed say that?

Dorval: I prefer Le Men's approach because it goes into more depth in considering the problem and that is, after all, what characterizes the decisions of the Assembly.

Matthew: I am in favour of the more fundamental solution.

Trainee: I prefer the principle of equality; it is logical, it is obvious and it prevents us from having to immerse ourselves (in difficulties).

De Servetière: I prefer Le Men's solution.

Bruyère: I prefer the principle of equality.

Deldago: I want to stay with the reformed draft judgment; the principle of equality prevents clarification of the issue. It must be verified that reasons of health and hygiene are indeed waterproof and cannot be confused with something else.

Luchon (turning towards the author): What does the philosopher say?

BL: The philosopher is not sufficiently prepared to opine.

President: The commissioner of the law?

The commissioner of the law does not say anything.

President: Good, well that was **interesting**.

De Servetière: I have in fact encountered this claimant before, he attacks everything that moves.

President: Yes those are short but well-made claims.

We have let the discussion continue uninterrupted up to the point at which the observer experiences a brief moment of shame at being unable to make any other pronouncement on the case other than the learned word 'opine'! For the ethnographer, fortunately, everything becomes data from the field, including his own inability to formulate the expressions that would qualify him as a full member of the tribe. . . . No, he does not yet incarnate the *viva vox legis*! Once more, the question of admissibility having been resolved, we have reached the heart of the case, and everyone uses the concrete examples that are essential if there is to be any progress towards a solution, the partial and empirical evidence of common sense replacing the austere technicality of administrative law. Notice the concluding sentence of the president, in which we again see the form of quality control that allows him to say that this was an 'interesting case', that they did indeed hesitate, and that this regular claimant has done a good job.

Yes, they have judged well – or at least reviewed well. This obscure case will now be absorbed, turned into sediment and crushed in the edifice of administrative law. Of course, the claimant will never see the return of his contributions to refuse disposal, but his name at least will remain. The next edition of the *Major Precedents* will incorporate the case, and in so doing verify the feedback between the legal work of claimants and the legal work of those who either accept or decline to hear their legal arguments*. In a sense, in much the same way as limestone mountain ranges are just elementary life that has been turned into sediment, compressed, crushed, folded and then raised before being eroded, the law is made of no material other than the pleas of those claimants who are heard, which are collected, crushed, compiled and published, and finally incorporated in the *Lebon* volumes.

When we read the conclusions of the commissioner concerning this purchase of dustbins by a landlord, we again see the proliferation of sedimented claims, all of which have marked an era in administrative law and must be arranged, mobilized and edited in order to be able to effect this reversal of precedent. Trade unions, boroughs, chambers of commerce, or companies with more or less picturesque names are mingled with the conclusions of prestigious commissioners such as the famed Romieu, and with legal texts containing more or less evasive interpretations of doctrine. In the following table, we have made a list of all the references which the commissioner used to convince the judges in this case, and which composes the intertextuality of his conclusions. For each cited text, we have noted its date, a summary of its name, and in parentheses the argument which he uses as support, as well as its order of appearance in the reasoning.[71]

Example of intertextuality

(Table listing citations in support of the arguments brought forward in the conclusions)[72]

29-03-1901 Casanova (4: legal standing of third parties is already recognized)

04-08-1905 Martin conclusions Romieu + chronique *Major Precedents* (3: only for 'detachable act') (cited twice)

30-03-1906 Ballande (4: legal standing of third parties is already recognized)

21-12-1906 Croix-de-Seguey-Tivoli conclusions Romieu (3: only for 'detachable act') legal standing of third parties is already recognized (cited twice) (draw logical conclusions from this 'arrêt')

09-11-1917 Bosc et Vernazobre (right to dustbins)
21-02-1919 Caille (principle of equality)

---

[71] It would be very useful to do for legal references what scientometrics has so efficiently done for references in scientific articles (see Callon, Courtial et al., *La scientométrie* (1993)). Unfortunately, at present, the ARIANE database does not permit such cartographies, in particular because the decisions only cite texts of laws and regulations, so that the reasoning of the commissioners, the judges, the chroniclers and the commentators rely on preceding judgments, and nothing allows these two bases for judgment to be easily linked.

[72] In presenting his conclusion for the case we have just followed, the commissioner had to pass through the following stages: (1) he needs to prove that the Council has jurisdiction; (2) he needs to show that the claim is not admissible in light of the present case-law; (3) he needs to show that the claimant needed to dispute the 'detachable act'; (4) however, the legal standing of third parties is already recognized; (5) the reasoning of the Council has not been followed through; (6) since the Prefect is allowed to dispute the act by way of the 'déféré', why are third parties not allowed to do so?; (7) the distinction which is currently made between the two types of contract ('unilateral' and 'classic') is too subtle; (8) all things considered, the obstacle of 'sufficient knowledge' must still be overcome. Marc Sanson, affaire no. 135836, 10 July 1996.

19-12-1926 Decuty (4: legal standing of third parties is already recognized)

06-05-1931 Tondut (3: only for 'detachable act')

22-07-1933 Heimann (right to dustbins)

09-11-1934 Section Chambre de Commerce de Tamatave *a contrario* (2: Inadmissible in light of present case-law)

09-03-1938 Union de la propriété bâtie (weights of 'notifications' (circulaires))

01-03-1946 Section société l'énergie industrielle (5: reasoning 'is not followed through' ['inachevé'])

09-03-1951 Concerts du Conservatoire (principle of equality)

09-10-1954 Cassation Court (contract opposable to third parties)

26-11-1954 Section Syndicat de la raffinerie de soufre (4: legal standing of third parties is already recognized)

04-02-1955 Section Ville de Saverne (3: only for 'detachable act')

26-10-1956 Assembly (4: legal standing of third parties is already recognized)

11-01-1961 Barbaro

04-07-1962 Untersinger (principle of equality)

08-03-1963 Section Mailhol (4: legal standing of third parties is already recognized)

24-04-1964 Section, société de livraisons industrielles, conclusions Combarnous (3: only for 'detachable act')

29-04-1964 Missa (4: legal standing of third parties is already recognized)

31-10-1969 Asemblée syndicat des cannaux de la Durance (3: only for 'detachable act')

16-10-1970 Assembly Rueil Malmaison (1: jurisdiction of TA)

21-03-1972 Cassation Court (contract can be invoked against third parties)

15-07-1975 Law on the discarding of refuse (police in charge of refuse)

07-02-1977 Decree of application law on refuse (police in charge of refuse)

20-01-1978 Section Syndicat de l'enseignement technique, conclusions Denoix de Saint-Marx (3: only for 'detachable act')

20-02-1978 Section Enseignement technique agricole (4: legal standing of third parties is already recognized)

28-05-1979 Tribunal of conflicts, Cergy Pontoise (1: jurisdiction of TA)

06-06-1980 Darvennes (weight of notifications)
19-12-1979 Meyet (principle of equality)
1979 notes de RFDA (5: reasoning is not followed through)
02-03-1982 Law on the administrative 'déféré' of the Prefect (the Prefect has not disputed the act)
02-12-1983 Assembly Syndicats médicaux (4: legal standing of third parties is already recognized)
05-04-1984 Law on municipal hygiene
08-03-1985: Friends of the Earth (4: legal standing of third parties is already recognized)
26-04-1985 Ville de Tarbes (principle of equality)
27-12-1985 deliberation of SIVOM
01-10-1986 contract between SIVOM and company: article 7
06-01-1986 Law on decentralization
16-04-1986 Assembly compagnie luxembourgeoise (2: inadmissible in light of present case-law) (cited twice)
04-06-1986 Oléron (1: jurisdiction of TA)
01-10-1986 Chambres d'agriculture
(weight of notifications)
17-12-1986 Syndicat de l'Armagnac, conclusions Fornaccari (2: inadmissible in light of present case-law)
08-04-1987 Etudes et consommation CFDT
(principle of equality)
13-01-1988 Mutuelle générale conclusions Roux (3: only for 'detachable act')
29-07-1989 refusal of repayment for containers
by SIVOM
31-03-1989 département de la Moselle (7: the distinction civil judge / administrative judge is too subtle)
08-11-1989 Sourine (weight of notifications)
15-11-1990 Cassation Court
25-01-1991 Section, Brasseur, conclusions Stirn (6: if the Prefect can, why can a third party not?)
26-07-1991 Section Commune de St Marie (6: if the Prefect can, why can a third party not?)
01-08-1989 claim before the TA to render null and
void article 7
17-01-1992 rejection of the claim by the TA because
of inadmissibility
17-02-1992 Commune de Guidel (5: reasoning is not followed through)
10-04-1992 avis de Section + *AJDA* 1992. Gazette du palais (1: jurisdiction of TA)

> **22-06-1992 appeal to the Council of State**
>
> 13-05-1992 Commune d'Ivry sur Seine (7: the distinction civil judge / administrative judge is too subtle)
>
> 25-05-1992 Département de l'Ehrault (7: the distinction civil judge / administrative judge is too subtle)
>
> 13-07-1992 Law on refuse + parliamentary debates + explanation of motives (police in charge of refuse)
>
> 14-05-1993 Section radios locales privées (8: obstacle of 'connaissance acquise')
>
> 07-07-1993 Syndicat CGT de l'hopital Dupuytren (8: obstacle of 'connaissance acquise')
>
> 01-10-1993 Yacht Club Bormes les Mimosas (5: reasoning is not followed through) (cited twice)
>
> 28-02-1994 Desboit (*weight of notifications*)
>
> 07-10-1994 Section Lopez + *AJDA* chronicles (5: reasoning is not followed through)
>
> **10-07-1996 Assembly of the Litigation Section**
> **Various citations**
>
> 1990 Studies and document of the Council of State, no. 41 (5: reasoning is not followed through) article 1165 of the Civil Code, third parties are not affected by contractual clause
>
> Book of Pouyaud on the nullity of administrative contracts (7: the distinction civil judge / administrative judge is too subtle)

At first sight, what this table measures is the technicality of the procedure. The modification of precedents has to be done with as much care as altering the route of a railway track running through the centre of a town, or modernizing a telephone exchange. More than sixty documents of different types have to be rearranged to create scope for argument where none existed before. In bold, on the right, we find the elements of the claim, which stretch out over almost ten years, the Council itself allocating more than four years to judge the case. In italics, centred, we have noted all the references which the commissioner of the law uses to investigate the merits of the case. On the left, in roman letters, we find the sum total of citations that are essential if one is to make the claim admissible by linking it to all the judgments that the Council has already made. The corpus of texts stretches out over almost a century and the commissioner has to weigh the various tendencies in the case-law, mobilizing the uncertainties of doctrine, logic, understanding and opportunity. He wants the judges to 'make a significant move' while asking them to do nothing more than 'draw out the consequences' of 'their' decision of 1906!

> But if you have to **follow** your case-law, the claim of Mr Cayzeele would have no chance of **prospering**. According to present case-law, the direct claim of a third party to render a contract or a clause of a contract null and void is inadmissible (. . .) The third party can only ask for an administrative 'detachable act' to be rendered null and void because it was *ultra vires* if it took place prior to or posterior to the conclusion of the contract itself. p. 5 (. . .)
>
> We suggest that you **explore** a new path which would permit you to **deflect** your case-law and allow a third party, under certain conditions, to contest directly a contract to which he is not party. p. 7 (. . .)
>
> In such a way the impossibility for a third party to contest a contractual clause appears to be reduced (if not rendered **insubstantial**) and the case-law seems **formalist**. In the case at hand, the claim of Mr Cayzeele to contest the legality of the deliberation between the Mayor and the consortium of townships based upon the illegality described in article 7 of the contract is not admissible. However, his claim is only inadmissible if the legality of the clause is contested **directly**. The distinction indeed appears to be **subtle** to the eyes of the layperson. p. 9 (. . .)
>
> These drawbacks or in any case the subtlety of the present case-law could lead you to think about a **challenge directed to the heart** of the question of litigation concerning administrative contracts.
>
> However, this **is not** what we are suggesting to you. What we are concerned with is merely a deflection of your case-law, which stays entirely **in line** with its recent development and with the **will** of the legislator (as far as the 'prefectoral referral' is concerned). We especially want you to **draw out the consequences** of **your** decision of 1906 in *Croix-de-Seguely-Tivoli* regarding the admissibility of claims, **while avoiding** the multiplication of claims against contracts which have no connection, or only a remote one, to the claimant. p. 14

No, we should rest assured that it is not for the Council to 'challenge the heart' of what exists. As we shall see later, the law cannot permit itself the kind of audacities of which scientific researchers are so fond. There can be no legal revolution in the law, or else we would lose all predictability and we would lapse into 'a mess', and into expeditious justice, which is a contradiction in terms. The subtle art of the commissioner consists entirely in his reshaping, chewing over and digesting the sixty texts that he has cited, making them say nothing other than what they have always said, even if it was not clearly heard until today. Any innovation that counsellors make will not be 'too constructive' a solution, because any discussion about the heart of the problem is avoided, there is complete legal predictability, and the multiplication of cases is prevented.[73] The aim of the commissioner's conclusions is to express with even greater subtlety the

---

[73] Earlier, the commissioner rejected another solution as being 'very constructive'. The word 'constructive' is, as we know, a euphemism for unruly audacity.

will of the body of judges, which has remained unchanged since *Croix-de-Seguely-Tivoli* in 1906, and to follow the intention of the legislator who recently invented the 'prefectoral referral'.[74] Although he strips precedents of their clothing he does so only to reassure the judges that nothing truly new has happened, and his reasoning covers not only this very tiny minor claim concerning an obscure story of dustbins but also the major principles that underlie the distinction between bilateral contracts and unilateral regulations and that organize the whole State. It is entirely true of law that 'the more it changes, the more it stays the same'.[75]

It is at this point, when the deliberation comes to an end and the judgment conforms to the wishes of the commissioner, that we can ask whether or not anything has really happened. The published judgment tells us nothing other than that the claim has been judged admissible. Once the will of the legislator has been respected, once the 'logical consequences' of hundred-year-old decisions have been drawn out, once the evolution of changes in the case-law has been mapped coherently, the chroniclers we have met earlier must immediately turn to the task of interpreting the judgment so as to give it a meaning. Of itself, it remains incomprehensible. Let us follow some stages in the trial and error process by which they attempt, with great tact, to ascertain the intentions of the judges, who have partially accepted the words which the commissioner of the law placed in their mouths:

> In holding that regulatory clauses of contracts cannot be disputed by way of claims arguing that the act was *ultra vires*, the Council of State **remains attached** to the theory of the double nature of contracts such as has been sketched by the commissioner of the law Léon Blum (. . .) The Council in this way **opposes** the bulk of doctrine that is attached to the theory of 'l'acte mixte' (. . .)
>
> If the case-law previously was hardly convincing **in terms of pure logic**, it was even more **open to criticism** for the consequences it had for 'private individuals' ['administrés']. Although it accepted that contracts entered into by a public body and a private entrepreneur could give rise to obligations on private individuals, the Council of State **refused these individuals every possibility** to contest the contractual clauses in question by claiming that the act had to be attacked only through the procedure of *ultra vires*. (. . .) This situation was **shocking.** p. 735
>
> The Council of State **seized the opportunity** presented to it in the form of the appeal of Mr Cayzeele, to **overturn precedent.** Thus, regulatory clauses of contracts

[74] 'Claims formulated by the Prefect against the acts of local authorities which he deems to be illegal and which are brought before the administrative judge (. . .). From the law of 2 March 1982 onwards, this particular procedure of control has replaced the old system of "supervision" ['tutelle']': Van Lang, Gondouin et al., *Dictionnaire de droit administratif* (1999).

[75] What Bancaud, 'Une "constance mobile": la haute magistrature' (1989), regarding the Cassation Court, calls 'a mobile constancy'.

can **from now on** be the objects of claims based on the *ultra vires* doctrine. Of course, **the impact** of this overturning of precedent must not be **overstated** (. . .) At the same time, its impact must not be **underestimated.** p. 736

Following the *Cayzeele* case it is possible to obtain a judgment rendering regulatory clauses null and void without any procedural detour. **It is undeniable that some progress has been made.** p. 736

What is accomplished by the decision *Cayzeele* is therefore significant. It must, however, be emphasized that this new case-law **does not do away** with the distinction between litigation regarding a contract itself (between the parties to a contract) and litigation on the basis of *ultra vires.* **However, this decision must be regarded as following the logic of previous decisions.** p. 737

Nonetheless, in the decision *Cayzeele* it is difficult to see a first step towards the simplification of rules regarding litigious claims. On the contrary, the Litigation Assembly does not **seem** to have accepted the claim on the basis of *ultra vires* against regulatory clauses of a contract because it has **chosen to see regulatory acts included in the contract** as being 'separable' ['divisible'] from the contract. The decision *Cayzeele* therefore constitutes a **shift of perspective** rather than a **reversal of principle.** p. 738

Even though we may regret that the Council of State has not gone **even further,** it seems to us that the state of law after the decision of 10 July 1996 **is more satisfactory** than it was before. The possibility of claims of third parties against contracts which impose obligations on them is made at once **simpler and more efficient.** (2 October 1996, p. 738)

Might it not be said that the chroniclers themselves behave rather like haruspices interpreting the decisions of the Council? It is almost as though the administrative law were like some large, enigmatic and entirely mute animal, which is unable to justify its speech by means of clear explanations, so that it can only be understood by resorting to indirect signs. The Assembly, they say, 'seems to have accepted' a reversal that is at once of undeniable impact, limited, not to be 'underestimated', and which follows the 'logic of previous decisions', but which seems to be more a 'shift of perspective' than a 'reversal of principle'. But that is not at all clear. Everything depends on what, according to that wonderful expression, the Council has 'chosen to see' in the contract exposed to its scrutiny. Moreover, the large animal might have 'gone even further'; it is likely that by means of this calculated 'leak' the chroniclers are reflecting the controversies of the deliberation and preparing doctrine for a future reversal of precedent. In any event, what is clear is that the Council, while doing nothing more than remaining true to itself, has abandoned a 'shocking' solution which would have compelled it to 'remain attached' to an interpretation that was undeniably venerable, since it came from Léon Blum himself, but which also clashed with doctrine. At the end of the day, people express their satisfaction: the state of the law is more 'satisfactory', and the possibility for third parties to bring claims is 'simpler and more efficient'.

But in the end did anything happen or not? No, to the extent that they did no more than tidy up the law. Yes, because they now know more than they did before. It is really very strange that neither the uncertainty as to what the judges intended to say nor the strict continuity between past and present prevent the chroniclers from recognizing that the judgment effected a real change: '*Before* the decision of the "Assembly" of 10 July 1996', they write, 'the fate of the exception of illegality of regulatory clauses of a contract was at least uncertain' (p. 734). Today, it is no longer *uncertain*. The date of 10 July marks a turning point and puts an end to 'doctrinal controversies'. There is therefore indeed some historicity in this millimetre-by-millimetre progression, in which the only thing that is supposed to have happened is the clear affirmation of something that had already existed . . . This is a peculiar value object which has to conceal its modifications behind an appearance that is as immovable as marble, but which has to mark time by means of breaks that are clear enough to extinguish dangerous uncertainties or scandalous ambiguities. Has Mr Cayzeele therefore done some historical service to the law of contracts? He should not be too cocky about his role. With truly patrician arrogance, the chroniclers recall that the Council has merely 'seized the opportunity' that was presented by its being called upon to effect this reversal of precedent, which was compelled by the very logic of the case-law of the Council: everything has changed and yet nothing has changed at all; had there been no claim there would have been no scandal, but the claim was just a long-awaited opportunity to put the law in order. Such is the homeostasis of the law.

De minimis et maximis curat praetor

Were the Council ever truly to apply the celebrated maxim *de minimis non curat praetor*, it would have very little to do because, as the cases which we have followed so far suggest, it is asked to examine the most minor cases or microscopic claims: a pigeon here, a ski run or process of appointment there, a dustbin, an expulsion order – all of these being trifles which hardly seem to warrant the attention of the praetor. But in practice the praetor applies a somewhat different maxim: judges endeavour to link the tiniest concerns to the most important – *de minimis* et maximis *curat praetor*. As we saw in chapter 2, the judge tests his capacity to 'say the law' according to his capacity to bind the details of the claim, which might well seem derisory in the eyes of the law but which are obviously essential, and often vital, in the eyes of the claimant, in the mass of published texts. It is by means of this *principle of minimum and of maximum* that he is recognizable as a judge and that he himself defines that he has judged *well*. As we will see in the last chapter, it is not clear that any other function would be capable of carrying out this short-circuit. Perhaps this is what defines the specificity of legal enunciation as well as most of its bizarre characteristics.

Having waited until we reached this point, we can now conclude our prolonged immersion in the review meetings by recapitulating the movements which we were able to distinguish in the judges' reasoning. Our topic in this chapter was the dynamic, or passage, or translation of the law, which we addressed by drawing up a list of the value objects that are transferred in the course of action. Throughout, we emphasized the proliferation of terms, gestures, behaviours that give the impression that what happens or circulates does indeed have a density, an objectivity or a solidity that compels the modification of attitudes, the undoing of presuppositions and changes of opinion, or the reversal of precedent, as in the last of our cases. And this difficult movement, which creeps forward slowly, proceeds despite a number of oppositions and obstacles. The judges do not reason: they grapple with a file which acts upon them, which pushes and forces them, and which makes them do something. Nothing gives a greater impression of resistance, or of being a thing or a cause. Nothing seems more material or more real. But at the same time, this material has a very particular plasticity because each agent – claimant, lawyer, reporter, reviser, commissioner, formation of judgment, chronicler, academic – modifies the form taken by arguments, the salience of texts, and traces on this ectoplasm of the administrative law a set of divergent paths, mobilizing clans who confront each other with facts, precedents, understandings, opportunities or public morality, all of which are used to stoke the fire of the debate. And when this process comes to an end, it is never because pure law has triumphed, but because of the internal properties of these relations of force or these conflicts between heterogeneous multiplicities, and because the actors themselves consider that certain value objects have indeed been transferred and that conditions of felicity have indeed been fulfilled.

First, the *authority* of the actors undergoes a more or less complete metamorphosis throughout the ordeal of the process of review. And the positions of all of the participants, not just the judges, are modified: there are more or less respectable claimants, more or less talented lawyers, more or less sound commentators. Then there is the second value object, the claim itself, whose *ordeal* through the proceedings, which is expressed in the trial, lends itself very well to an analysis in

terms of conflict, progress, obstacles, turns, delays and victories.[76]
The third of the value objects that we identified, namely the *organization* of claims, files and judgments, which is a kind of logistics, enables the various stages of the proceedings to be made consistent with each other without doing too much demolishing or creating too many obstacles, and without making too many mistakes, or producing too much rubbish or wastage. Then, there is what we have called the *interest* of cases, without which the counsellors would long since have died of boredom, seated in their armchairs, their heads buried in their files. As we shall see, this is not so much a *libido sciendi*, but rather a *libido judicandi*, which is attached to the difficulty of the case, and which requires that one not judge too quickly; a kind of greedy anxiety that is both useful and paradoxical as a measure of the difficulty of the act of judgment: the more impossible it is to 'say the law', the more 'interesting' it is to do so.

We then identified a fifth value object, which was similar to the first except that it concerned the authority of the legal objects rather than human subjects. Each citation of a law in a 'dispositif', each reference to a precedent in a conclusion, each appeal to *Lebon* during a review session, each location of a judgment in 'Tables' by the chroniclers, modifies the *weight* of the text in question, giving it a consistency or solidity that will enable later texts to conflict with it, so the landscape of the law is modified as we go along, each day becoming either more contrasted or more salient, or alternatively becoming in places increasingly confused, uncertain or marshy. That is what enables precedents to serve as landmarks, turning points or boundary-posts in a history in which no event would otherwise be able to have a distinct existence. The sixth value object is the *quality control* that is continually exercised by all agents in a reflexive manner with respect to the progress of the process. 'Are we indeed in the process of making law? Have we judged well? Should we work in this way? Is the discussion closed?'; this is a kind of continuous anxiety which occupies consciences; it is a value object 'to the power of two', because it seeks to evaluate reflexively the valuation itself, to verify the felicity of conditions of felicity. Without these incessant scruples, how could they ever have the feeling of having judged well?

We believe that we have also identified a seventh value object, which is even more unusual, and which we have called *hesitation*. Those who enunciate the law seem almost to measure the realization

---

[76] Let us recall that most of the terms used in Greimassian semiotics to speak of fiction and its operations actually derive from legal proceedings, or in any case from a certain kind of 'staged' ordeal. Law might explain semiotics, more than semiotics explain law.

of their performances by their capacity to have hesitated well, extensively and sufficiently, to have crunched and crushed the content of their files by making them react with a sufficient number of texts. It is in fact only in this moment of abeyance, slowness or preliminary unlinking that they seem to find a proof of their freedom of manoeuvre, before then proceeding to the work of linking, knitting or deciding. Remember President Huchon's comment that 'we tend to consider ourselves too bound.' The scales of justice have first to tremble before they can faithfully record what is just. The eighth value object is still fresh in our memories: it is the *moyen*, the mean* or *means* of action, a means of transport, a lever, a reason, a hook or a trap (what metaphor would be adequate to describe this particular UFO?) which enables the transportation of obligation from one end of the procedure to the other, and from a text to the case at hand. As we have just seen, the ninth consists of the coherence of the law as it is modified, of shifting it from a state in which it was formal, artificial, inefficient or indirect to a more satisfactory condition in which it becomes a little more efficient, direct, legible or comprehensible. The final value object, the tenth, is a kind of prerequisite for the whole process itself and defines the internal and external *limits* of that which either does or does not activate the law, and which delimits two equally terrifying extremes: at one extreme there is a tide of claims, a loss of legal predictability or a paralysing of the administration: anyone can take legal action about anything; at the other extreme, the opportunity to appear in court is so closely restricted that no case could ever get under way, and the law is reduced to a rump, or to the good will of the sovereign.

Value objects modified during the ordeal

1   the *authority* of the agents participating in the judgment
2   the *progress* of the claim as it moves through obstacles
3   the *organization* of cases, which enables the logistics of claims to be respected
4   the *interest* of cases, which is a measure of their difficulty
5   the *weight* of texts, which makes for an increasingly contrasted landscape and history
6   the process of *quality control* by means of which the conditions of felicity of the process as a whole are verified reflexively

> 7 *hesitation*, which produces freedom of judgment by unlinking things before they are linked up again
> 8 the *means** or *arguments** which compel the linking of texts to cases
> 9 the *coherence* of law itself as it modifies its internal structure and quality
> 10 the *limits* of law, which are defined by regulating the right to launch or suspend a legal action

The ethnographer is all too conscious of the fact that this list of value objects might look like something of a ragbag to professional jurists, because it makes no distinction between what for them is essential and what is peripheral. Doubtless, lawyers would immediately be able to identify which of these conditions of felicity characterize pure law and would relegate the others to the role of mere intermediaries, additives, servants or baggage. However, our concern is not to decide who is right here, the specialist or the observer. Not so long ago, scientific researchers would first have put forward the ideas, theories or results of their discipline, while completely omitting any mention of their laboratories, instruments, colleagues, budgets or articles, or any mention of the process of trial and error that characterizes experiments, or the strange ways in which objects mix themselves with the words that are used to describe them – all of these things being considered too trivial to mention. Had the ethnographer pointed out at that time the multiplicity of the elements that are peculiar to science 'in action' rather than science 'in theory', these researchers would doubtless have taken umbrage, and described this whole menagerie, bric-a-brac or hotchpotch as simple and insignificant intermediaries. It has taken some time for both anthropologists of science and scientists themselves to draw up carefully a jointly compiled list of *mediations* that are necessary for the world to be articulated in scientific practice. Even now, these difficulties have not yet been entirely overcome.[77] And if it has taken so much effort to include the practice of science in the description of its virtues, why would it take any less effort to make the description of the law compatible with the practice of judges? In presenting their domain to

---

[77] On these questions, see Latour, *Pandora's Hope* (1999b). A technical sense is given to the difference between intermediaries – which transmit their causes faithfully and without deformation – and mediations – which simultaneously redefine their causes and their consequences.

others, is it possible that lawyers leave out most of the elements that would make it comprehensible, not to experts of course but precisely to those outsiders to whom they address themselves?

In any case, the composition of modernism is such that the most reliable analyses of the truth factories that are so important to its success do not necessarily come from those who work in them.[78] Moreover, and as we shall see in the last chapter, this is what justifies an ethnographic description of modes of enunciating truth. The position of the ethnographer is quite different, depending on whether he studies things that are nearer his culture or further away. In the case of things that are further away, what is initially striking is the hustle and bustle of a complex and contradictory practice, and the ethnographer does not rest until he has found its hidden structure by means of powerful intellectual constructions. With things that are nearer, on the other hand, the power of the intellectual structures that are already used by the actors themselves to define their own activity – Science, Law, Religion, Politics, Economy, each in its own domain – serves as a veil to the understanding of multiple, heterogeneous and frequently contradictory practices. If, over there, the ethnographer has to make such an effort to understand what people are doing, here on the contrary, he must do a great deal to forget the all-too reasonable reasons that agents give for their behaviour; he should not hesitate to go as far as possible following their stammering, their hesitations, their delays, and to find in their meandering pathways the reason for the sustained links that are created by the intermingling of all these activities, which are not in any way explained by separating them into pure and distinct spheres. The ethnographer, remaining quite unashamed of his ignorance, will have to persist in describing the law 'in action' for some time to come.

Having reached this point, the readers might sympathize with those counsellors who would have preferred the ethnographer to delete all verbatim remarks from this book, much as some scientific researchers would rather not have seen the daily life of their laboratories exposed to the gaze of the public. Doubtless, both feel that the process by which humble practices of interaction metamorphose into objective truth should remain a trade secret known only by initiates. They are presumably worried that respect for the solidity of the law and the truth of science will be lost if the public sets about discerning the humble immanence of the laboratory or the court that lies behind these two forms of transcendence. Exactly the opposite is true. It is

---

[78] On the anthropology of modernism, see Latour, *We Have Never Been Modern* (1993).

by turning fabrications into closely guarded secrets that the public is prevented from understanding the capacity of humans to utter truths that exceed and escape them on all sides. In believing that they are protecting the public from revelations that it would find disturbing, scientists and jurists ultimately prevent the public from having any confidence in the extraordinary capacity that we have to charge small words and texts with realities that are more solid and more enduring than themselves. What is the origin of the kind of defeatism that compels us to believe that if a human speaks he inevitably and quite pitifully lapses into error and illusion, and a thundering voice must always emerge from nowhere – the voice of nature or the voice of Law – to dictate his behaviour and his convictions? Are we poor earthlings really so impoverished? The way in which unquestionable truths are gradually constructed through human interactions has always seemed to me to be more interesting, more enduring and more dignified.

5

Scientific objects and legal objectivity*

In which the readers are led, in spite of themselves, to shift their attention
to scientific practice – where they are compelled to compare a
neuroscience laboratory with the Council of State – where the readers
learn to their surprise that objectivity and detachment defines law rather
than science – in which it becomes clear that scientific information
differs totally from legal qualification – which allows the readers to
redistribute more fairly the respective virtues expected from scientists
and from judges

Portrait of the Council of State as a laboratory

'Like it or not, those are the facts'; 'whether it pleases you or not, we
have reached our decision': the solidity of facts and the rigour of the
law are two kinds of solidity to which one can only submit. What
makes a comparison between the world of science and that of law all
the more interesting is that both domains emphasize the virtues of
a disinterested and unprejudiced approach, based on distance and

*A version of this chapter translated by Alain Pottage has appeared in Martha
Mundy and Alain Pottage, *Law, Anthropology and the Constitution of the Social:
Making Persons and Things* (Cambridge Studies in Law & Society). Cambridge:
Cambridge University Press, 2004.

precision; in both domains participants speak esoteric languages and they reason in carefully cultivated modes; both scientists and judges seem to attract a kind of respect that is unknown in other human activities. In this chapter, we shall attempt to establish a relation, not between 'science' and 'law', but between two laboratories, that of my friend Jean Rossier at the Ecole de Physique-Chimie, and that of the Council of State.

Rather than base our comparison on what scientists and lawyers say about themselves, the ethnographer will rely on the results of field work, which pay close attention to places, forms of life, conditions of speech and all those minor details which together, little by little, by minor brushstrokes, allow one to redefine science and law. In developing this approach, we shall see that epistemology has adopted a number of the features of its elder sister, justice, and that the law often clothes itself in powers that only science can provide. Far from confirming established clichés, a systematic comparison of those two sets of practices allows us to make a more differentiated portrait by distinguishing scientific objects from legal objects. Perhaps the anthropologist of science, having spent so much time hanging around in laboratories, will finally find in the Council of State those celebrated virtues of objectivity that he sought in vain in the laboratory.

Let's abandon for an instant our dear Palais-Royal, let's cross the river Seine and penetrate one of those many laboratories which cover the Latin Quarter, making it a secular equivalent of those many convents whose ceaseless prayers used to ascend to Heaven. Although the Council of State is not a public place, while the court is in session the public is admitted to certain areas at certain times. Ushers and receptionists police the otherwise invisible distinction between those places which are open to the public and those (rather more numerous) places which are reserved for the work of the counsellors, for their offices and for the absolutely secret process of deliberation. Here, at the Paris School of Physics and Chemistry, no area is really a public place, but, once one has been granted admission by one of the neuroscientists, no area is out of bounds.[1] In each building, there is an entirely different distribution of space: anyone can attend the hearings of the Council, but only at certain times, in certain seats and restricted areas; beyond that, no outsider has access to the work of the law – only trainees, government commissioners with the appropriate

---

[1] Ophir and Shapin, 'The Place of Knowledge' (1990). On the disposition of those complex spaces, see Galison and Thompson, *The Architecture of Science* (1999), to be compared with the study of legal iconography, for instance Jacob, *Images de la justice* (1994).

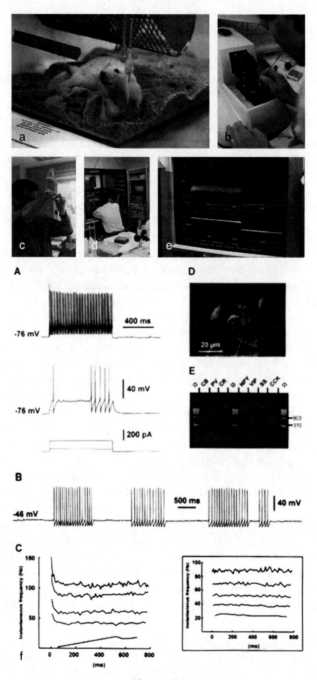

Figure 5.1

credentials or a somewhat nosey ethnographer. The laboratories of my friend Rossier are open only to scientific personnel, but no area is barred to the authorized visitor. Whereas the presence of a stranger in judicial deliberations would corrupt the nature of the activity and vitiate the judgment on grounds of procedural impropriety, the presence of a visitor in the laboratory might get in the way of the researchers' work, but it would have no influence on the nature of their work on the brains of white mice, into which they have inserted fine glass tubes. The two laboratories therefore have a very different relation between public and private: although 'ignorance of the law is no excuse', the last stages of its flowering remain completely secret; by contrast, although laboratories are closed to anyone who is not an employee, in principle anyone could understand what goes on inside, which is in no way mysterious: 'we have nothing to hide', they would say.

After many months at the Council, the ethology of our friends in the laboratory seems quite astonishing. Here, no one is formally dressed, there are no serious tones of voice, no solemn gait, no refined and smoothly intoned turns of phrase, no elegant conversation; instead, one finds raised voices, incongruous laughter, casual dress in the 'American' style, the occasional outburst, or tirades launched against oscilloscopes which do not describe their phosphorescent curves as they should, against guillotines which are too blunt to lop off the heads of laboratory rats, against micro-pipettes whose incisions do not allow the researcher to probe a neuron held under the microscope, or against some especially obtuse referee who rejected one excellent paper. Whereas in the Council speech flowed effortlessly from silver-tongued counsellors, here it is interrupted, hesitant, embarrassed – sometimes to the point of becoming gibberish. That is not to say that visitors are unable to understand what is being said, but rather that *gestures* can take the place of words, and that, at numerous points in their discourse, researchers *replace speech* with a finger pointed at the phenomenon produced by an instrument, a phenomenon that reveals itself only hesitantly because it is dependent on the visibility of an individually isolated neuron, and hence on a technical and scientific prowess that often misfires, and which constantly has to overcome obstacles such as blocked pipettes, inaccessible neurons or unintelligible results. Whereas the counsellors sound like books because they move from the text of *Lebon* volumes to the text of their decisions, and thence to the text of the productions and memoirs in defence that compose the stratified layer of the file, always remaining within the world of texts, laboratory researchers are forever crossing the deep chasm that separates a rat's neuron, pulsating under a micro-pipette, from the human phrases that are spoken in relation to that neuron. It is hardly surprising that they should so often hesitate, begin again or remain in suspense, dumb for several minutes, or that the homogeneity of their speech acts should be disrupted by exclamations such as: 'I've got it!', 'that's it!', 'I've lost it!' or 'silly bugger!'

The question of homogeneity or heterogeneity between texts and things marks a contrast which would strike even the most inattentive visitor. One can climb from the cellars of the Palais-Royal, in which linear kilometres of archives lie in hibernation, to the attics which house the offices of the commissioner of the law and the Documentation Service, without finding any real difference between the various objects that are essential to each branch of the work of the Council: files, more files, nothing but files, to which one should add cupboards, tables and chairs – which differ in price, depending on the rank of the employees and the place in the roster – varying numbers of books and, last but not least, as we saw in chapter 2, a profusion of elastic bands, paper clips, folders and rubber stamps. Besides the telephones and staplers, all of these tools have an intimate connection with textual matter, and the computer database, which allows the decisions of administrative law to be viewed online, cannot be considered as a scientific instrument – that is, as what allows the phenomena of nature to be written down and made compatible with texts.[2] But in the laboratory, no room looks like any other, because the differentiation of space is effected by the distribution of the machines which allow the competences of the physiologist, the neurophysiologist, the molecular biologist, the peptide chemist, the radiographer and the bio-informatics expert to be co-ordinated in the context of a single experiment. When the counsellors meet in debate, they all look like one another, the differences between them being found only in terms of how much experience each has of administrative law: no one voice carries more weight than another (if one overlooks the fine gradations of prestige). When experimenters get together, they might well have no understanding of the instruments, competences or difficulties of a neighbour with whom they have worked for years, but they know precisely when he or she can take over from their own know-how, and to what extent they can trust this expertise implicitly. Whereas, by definition, counsellors only judge cases of which they have no knowledge, and to which they are being introduced for the first time, using no instruments other than their memory and a few notes, each researcher only deals with that part of a rat's 'file' with which they

[2] On what is an instrument, see Latour, *Science In Action* (1987).

are perfectly acquainted, thanks to the narrow window opened by an instrument, discipline or speciality that it will have taken them years to master.

Therefore, the nature of the Council does not depend on its equipment, but on the homogeneity of the world of files that are kept, ordered, archived and processed, and upon the homogeneity of a staff that is renewed, maintained and disciplined. The Council can deal with a high turn-over of cases precisely because its counsellors are largely interchangeable, and because there is only a limited division of labour.[3] The nature of the laboratory is crucially dependent upon the heterogeneity of its equipment, on its rapid renewal and on the diversity of competences grouped together in one place. Whereas an inventory of the Council's furniture and files would yield no explanation of what it actually does, an inventory of the laboratory and its tools, noting their age and cost, their distribution in space, their sensitivity and the academic qualifications of their operators, would tell you almost everything you wished to know about the nature of the place: 'Tell me what your instruments and specialities are, and I'll tell you who you are and where you are placed in the hierarchy of the sciences.' The same comparison can be summarized in the observation that the Council costs a lot in terms of brain-power, but almost nothing in terms of equipment other than paper; a laboratory costs a lot in terms of wetware, but even more in terms of equipment and software. If some new Commune were once again to raze their palace to the ground, but leave the counsellors a complete collection of the *Lebon* volumes, the following day they could render judgment almost exactly as they had done before; if the mob were to chase Rossier from his laboratory and pillage his equipment, he would be unable to say anything at all precise about rats' brains before having regained the totality of his paraphernalia.

Let us pay closer attention to the shared bodily attitudes of the inhabitants of these two places. More often than not, laboratory researchers are found gathered in a concentric circle around an experiment, at the centre of which lies the particular phenomenon which is being submitted to a kind of proof or ordeal (in the present case, the electrical stimulation of a particular neuron, which enables the chemical neurotransmitters expressed by the neuron to be collected at the other end of the axon).[4] They are constantly talking, somewhat

[3] Remember that one of the many peculiarities of the French judges in administrative law is that they go back and forth between business, active administration, elective function and their job at the Council. Thus, at any given moment, about half of the members are actually out of the Council. See chapter 3.

[4] Lynch, 'Sacrifice and the Transformation of the Animal Body into a Scientific Object' (1988).

enigmatically, about the stammering being which they have coaxed into a kind of hiccupping speech, or at least which they have coaxed into indicating, by means of oscillations and chemical outputs, what it thinks of the proof to which it has been submitted. They resemble a group of gamblers huddled around a cockfight on which each has staked his fortune; they may not be shouting or screaming like madmen, but there can be no question but that they are passionately interested in the fate of their neuron, and in what it might have to say for itself. . . . On the other hand, passion is the least appropriate term to describe the attitude of judges in the course of a hearing. There is no *libido sciendi* there. No word is pronounced more loudly than another. Leaning back in their chairs, attentive or asleep, interested or indifferent, the judges always keep themselves *at a distance*. Only the claimant suffers to any degree. Although he is often (but not always) present, he understands no more of what is being said about his case than the rat understands of the clamoured observations made about the structure of its brain. In any event, the passion of the claimant is what is of least interest in the procedure of the case: it does not count; or rather, it no longer counts or does not yet count. Whereas in court judges are entirely unmoved by a case in which only the claimant is passionately engaged, the objects studied in a laboratory do not understand how their judges can be so passionately interested in matters to which they themselves are utterly indifferent. One thing is sure: the *libido judicandi* is very specific.

This marked difference is even found in the writing activities to which scientists also devote themselves, although they spend less time writing than the counsellors. As we know very well, instruments, equipment, chemical reagents or animals are not the end products of laboratory activity. A research team which was content to conduct research of the highest quality, but which never produced a scientific article, would soon lose its reputation, unless it gave up basic research in order to develop industrial applications. In terms of the production of writing, a scientific institution resembles the Council of State, and in both cases one could compile a statistical inventory of the number of pages produced by each of the members of the institution, and even of the number of citations of their respective works. However, this resemblance is dispelled as soon as one looks at the nature of scientific articles, which are quite unlike a legal decision, which the French, remember, call 'arrêts', that is, 'stops'. Rather than 'stops', researchers write, if we may say, 'please-go-ons'; in fact, it is they, to borrow a legal term, who produce *claims* in which the scientific author figures more as a claimant than as a judge. That is, each scientific article functions as a judgment passed on claims made by colleagues, or as a 'plaint' made to those same colleagues on behalf of a phenomenon whose existence is claimed by the article. In other words, the objectors to whom a scientific article is addressed are not true judges because: (a) they are of the same professional category as their author; (b) they cannot bring discussion to an end; (c) they themselves are judged (sometimes very harshly) by the claimant, with whom (d) they share the rights to extend, re-open or close the discussion. Whatever the mechanisms which bring a scientific controversy to an end, they are necessarily very different from those which were invented by the Council to close cases.[5]

However surprising it might seem, scientific articles are much more passionate than administrative law texts. That is because they push a claim as far as possible, by throwing everything into the pot in order to meet all possible objections, by ignoring some objections, or by highlighting those objections which allow them to emphasize a particular experiment or result. All of this passion, energy, all of these rhetorical flourishes, which make even the most theoretical or esoteric of scientific articles more beautiful than any opera, are absent from the decisions of the Council, which have to reference all of the relevant texts (imagine a scientist being obliged to cite each of the sources she used), to answer each of the arguments invoked (imagine a researcher being forced to avoid none of her referee's objections) and *only* those arguments (imagine how horrified a scientist would be if she were asked to address only those questions asked of her by others rather than the hundreds she has asked of herself), to add as few innovations as possible to the knowledge established by their predecessors (all scientific authors dream of triggering a scientific revolution) and to do all of this in such a way as to close the discussion once and for all (whereas researchers dream only of re-opening the discussion, or, if they are the ones who bring it to an end, of doing so in their own terms and to their own advantage).[6] The point is that researchers write for other researchers whose invisible but constraining presence informs everything they write, whereas judges, above all if they are judges in a court of last instance, write only for the claimant's lawyer, and, secondarily, for their colleagues and the writers of legal doctrine. They have different addressees.

There are of course situations in which science assumes the air of the courtroom. One example is given by the celebrated Commissions

[5] Jasanoff, 'What Judges Should Know about the Sociology of Science' (1992); Michael Lynch, Cole et al., *Truth Machine* (2009).
[6] Myers, *Writing Biology. Texts and the Social Construction of Scientific Knowledge* (1990).

of the Academy of Sciences which were set up in the nineteenth century to settle (on behalf of scientists) disputes arising between those particularly irascible researchers who were impervious to any of the normal means of resolution (short of a duel!). Today, we have juries, public forums or televised debates in which one researcher in the field of gene therapy is set against another, in the presence of an audience which is supposed to decide between them.[7] There are also large areas in which scientists cast as experts appear before judges in order to give evidence about matters within their area of expertise (the insanity of the defendant, the source of DNA taken from the scene of the crime, the validity of a patent application, the risks of a particular product and so on). But each of these situations bears the imprint of law rather than that of science. In the nineteenth century, the Academy of Sciences was able to issue quasi-decisions to put an end to scientific controversies only because its authority was almost like that of the law, and because, even then, its decisions were only *quasi*-decisions which were not binding upon anyone, and which could not prevent disputes from resurfacing elsewhere, in other forums or in other laboratories.[8] In science, there is no such thing as 'the authority of the adjudicated case (*res judicata*)'. On the other hand, when an expert gives evidence in court, the judge and the law take all precautions to ensure that what the expert says should be neither a judgment nor a warrant for judgment, but that it should serve only as a form of testimony which does not usurp the role of the judge.[9] These hybrid situations show quite clearly that these activities, these forms of writing, are as different as oil and water, remaining separate even when they have been mixed quite violently.

What should one call the very distinctive grouping of white coats gathered passionately around the ordeal to which some new entity (in this case an isolated neuron that has been made visible as a distinct individual) has been subjected, and which allows the scientists, by means of a chaos of hesitant observations and in a flourishing of partial (in both senses) texts which are published as quickly as possible, to generate claims that are fiercely defended, and which at the same time judge that claims previously published by themselves or by

---

[7] Jasanoff, *Science at the Bar* (1995).
[8] On the famous case of Louis Pasteur, see Geison, *The Private Science of Louis Pasteur* (1995).
[9] See Alder, *The Lie Detectors* (2007), for a very amusing case of incommensurability. On the long history of the distinction, see Shapiro, '*Beyond Reasonable Doubt*' (1991), and, of course Jasanoff, 'What Judges Should Know about the Sociology of Science' (1992) and *Science at the Bar* (1995). For direct reference to the famous Daubert case (1993), see http://laws.findlaw.com/us/509/579.html.

their colleagues are invalid, obscure, false, unfounded or quite simply banal and uninteresting – all of this determined within a domain (laboratory, discipline, literature) that is both jealously guarded and yet open to all, and whose boundaries might be challenged by any outsider? Are they judges deciding claims made by other judges? That would be unthinkable. Might they then be some kind of gang or mafia? Scientific activity sometimes looks suspiciously like these associations, especially in its blend of extreme rigour and complete lawlessness. And yet the answer again has to be 'no', because there is a third party in all disputes, a judge who is mute but who nevertheless determines the issue, to whom all parties agree to defer without discussion (while discussing incessantly!) and of whose role one finds traces in the archaic legal practices of the ordeal and divine judgment: namely, the very objects of experiments that are subjected to the ordeal of proof in order that they might say something about that which is said of them – something at once inaudible and conclusive, the celebrated *aitia, res, causa*, thing or *chose* that the history of science in European languages borrowed from the world of law.[10] In order to understand the very special mode of enunciation that one finds in the core of the laboratory, one has to look to torture, to the history of interrogation or the subtle arts of the Inquisition; that is, to the very practices that modern law now regards as shameful and archaic and from which it is at once proud and ashamed to have escaped.[11]

'We have ways of making you talk' might say the physiologist, betraying the slight trace of sadism which is present in even the most innocent experiments. But the word argument*, as we have seen, doesn't have the meaning it has in law, because the neuron that is subjected to questioning makes no complaint, formulates no claim, and the process to which it is subjected is not regarded as an offence.[12] The non-human which is submitted to the ordeal – the rat, neuron, DNA or neuropeptide – occupies both the position of a judge of last instance – in the sense that it passes judgment on what is said about it – and that of the plaintiff, because it is represented by an intermediary, the impassioned scientist who has taken on its case, and who

---

[10] Thomas, 'Res, chose et patrimoine' (1980).

[11] The bloody ritual of scientific experiment resembles more the ancient justice narrated by Foucault, *Discipline and Punish* (1975). For a more recent case study, see Lynch, 'Sacrifice and the Transformation of the Animal Body into a Scientific Object' (1988).

[12] Except by animal rights activists, who regard laboratory experiments as just as cruel as the ancient ordeals, and therefore worthy of vigorous prosecution before the courts.

contributes article after article to the scientific literature arguing for the recognition of its own right of existence and that of its *thing*, its *cause* and its own particular causality, before a tribunal of judges composed of her own colleagues, who are never in a position to pass final judgment, unless they defer to the incontestable (but always contested) evidence of matters of fact, which themselves speak clearly only if scientists have unfolded their properties in a more or less public display that they have collectively agreed to treat as final.

One can see that it is impossible, in depicting the way in which even the most banal experiments stage the scientific ordeal of truth, to base ourselves on the prevailing idea that the sciences are pure, objective, disinterested, distant, cold and self-assured. It is also impossible to make a direct comparison between science and law, without first describing those aspects in which each bears features that seem to have come from its counterpart. In both practices one finds speech, facts, judgments, authorities, writing, inscriptions, all manner of recordings and archives, reference works, colleagues and disputes, but their distribution is at once too similar to warrant a distinction between the facts of science and the fact of law, and too different for them to be seen as a single function. In order to make sense of this overlap we shall, as ever, proceed cautiously, feeling our way forward.

For now, the essential point is that the facts, contrary to the old adage, obviously do not 'speak for themselves': to claim that they do would be to overlook scientists, their controversies, their laboratories, their instruments, their articles and their hesitant speech, interrupted occasionally by deictic gestures, which only make things audible and visible. On the other hand, nothing of what goes on in the laboratories of the School of Physics and Chemistry would be comprehensible without noticing that what the people in white coats say is constantly being observed, validated, understood and interrupted, both by the omnipresent speech of even the most distant colleagues, and by those matters of fact whose centrality is acknowledged by all, and to whom all scientists defer as their sole appellate court.[13] To say that scientists simply reach an agreement between themselves as to what the things they're talking about are saying, would be to understand nothing of the peculiar force of their activity, and even less of their motivating passion. Also, the speech that circulates in the laboratory between scientists, their colleagues and their objects – and in respect of which

---

[13] On the legal history of facts, see Shapin and Schaffer, *Leviathan and the Air-Pump* (1985). On the delicate system of phonation necessary to 'make facts speak by themselves', see Latour, *Politics of Nature* (2004).

each is at once judge and party, speaking and mute, audible and inaudible, beginning and end – doesn't only have the form of a legal action or case; it also has an intimate connection with the question of what things are, or rather what they do to claims that have already been lodged.

Scientific propositions are transformed into a 'case' that can be judged by the peculiar interaction of disciplines: 'if the experiment is properly constructed', says researcher A, 'we should be able to get object B to transform the published claim C into medium D, yielding either a better-established certainty or a magnified doubt, at least from the point of view of colleagues from discipline E (as defined by us), to whom we have addressed our latest article F'. Finally, we should notice that this intervention will further enlarge a corpus of documents and claims whose future development will supply the criteria by which this whole procedure will be either validated or invalidated. Impassioned scientists, having promoted their object as much as possible in their articles, leave it to history, to the court of history, and thus to future scientists, to judge whether they were right or wrong in making a particular assumption. Strangely, as we shall see, judges – real judges – cannot place their faith in this Last Judgment of History. However slow or tardy they might be, they simply don't have the time to let others decide for them.

How to produce detachment

Let us now return to the Right Bank, cross the courtyard of the Louvre, and return to the Palais-Royal, with its ornamental gold and marble, its grand staircase, its historical paintings and its republican frescoes. After his encounter with the laboratory, the ethnographer finds himself both more at ease and much more awkward. Amidst the men in white coats, he stood, arms dangling helplessly, not knowing quite what to do with himself, finding himself obliged to take notes in all sorts of uncomfortable postures, just as distanced from the researchers he was studying as the latter were from their headless rats. Nevertheless, he could at least talk to his scientific colleagues, with whom he shared a wish to know; now and then he could ask for explanations, even suggest hypotheses, and his own stammers hardly seemed out of place in the concert of hesitations, reprises, exclamations and surprises which accompanied the spectacle of proof and demonstration. He too could point to the phenomena in question, cloaking them in the fragile web of his metaphors, allusions and approximations. He was, of course, clumsy and incompetent. But having agreed to stand aside a little to let him see the performance they had staged and which they were describing, his colleagues the researchers could easily allow him to share their passion and even, on occasion, grasped his own false, naive, or badly formulated ideas, because even a child could speak aptly in the face of the phenomena undergoing interrogation. Back in the Council, the observer takes his invisible place without ruining the uniformity of the courtroom; he is seated writing at a table amidst people who have seated themselves at the same table to write. Yet he is no more their colleague than he is their companion at dinner. Not only do they not share his *libido sciendi*, but even the interested observer has to remain as dumb as a carp, incapable of uttering any well-turned phrases, valid judgments or plausible hypotheses. He could of course stammer something or other, but the whole point is that the judges don't stammer: the moment he opened his mouth it would become obvious that he was not a member of this group.

We have left behind the amiable confusion of the laboratory, with its scattered journals, boxes of samples, its dripping pipes, purring centrifuges, overflowing dustbins, its raised voices and the general agitation that precedes, accompanies and follows the tension and emotion of an important experiment. There are indeed some signs of disorder in the Council, but they are strictly confined to the tables over-laden with files, behind which one can barely make out the heads of the formally but elegantly dressed counsellors. In any case, this disorder is only temporary, because inside each file one finds a very precise order, prescribed by the schedule of review which requires that each item be ordered, named, stamped, in accordance with a procedure which would be rendered invalid by any kind of modification. The impression of disorder is due only to the accumulation of pending cases; or, once a file has regurgitated its contents, to the abundance of legislative texts which have to be addressed, to the number of technical annexes or to the weight of documentation and the intensity of the exchange which generated so many formal replies. Once the file has been replaced in its box file, once the case has been dealt with, order is immediately restored, and that is precisely how counsellors and lawyers deal with things. Once the file has been closed, they give it no more thought; they move on to another case, another file. A case is something that is opened and closed like a box file.

It might be said that, even in the laboratory, disorder is more apparent than real, because each object, instrument, or experiment depends on an ordered document called 'the protocol book', which is more rigorous than any schedule of review. It is a sort of general audit of scientific activity in the laboratory, in which researchers note down what they propose to do, the raw results they obtain and provisional hypotheses suggested by those results. Indeed, this great book has recently been given a quasi-legal status as a result of the spread of cases of fraud and of patents. Nevertheless, there is a world of difference between these two kinds of accounting, because the protocol book doesn't contain the activity of the laboratory in the way that a file quite literally or physically *contains* cases referred to the Council. The laboratory could never be described by a unity that is as precise, as defined, as calibrated and as homogenous as the number, nature and placement of the Council's files. No claim has the closed, round and polished form of a grey cardboard folder, which is easily transportable, in which everything is held and which forms the small world to which the judge has to restrict himself, on pain of a penalty. The work of the laboratory spills over at all points, depending as it does upon the future action of colleagues, the progress of technology, the complex play of inter-citation, industrial production, public reaction. Only the box of tricks of scientometrics has managed to describe laboratory work in more or less coherent and standardized terms.[14] By contrast, there must be something in the file itself, in its closure, that supplies an essential reason for law's difference from the sciences.

To understand this difference, the file has to be seen in the context of the attitude of the counsellors who analyse, supplement or discuss it. Coming from the laboratory, the ethnographer is immediately struck by the *indifference* with which members of the Council treat the documents which they have in front of them. In Rossier's laboratory, the act of writing was always an intensely passionate moment, and the rewriting of articles prior to publication involved heated discussions about what could or could not be said, about how far one could go without going too far, or about what had to be concealed for tactical or political reasons.[15] They seemed more like lawyers preparing a case on behalf of their client than judges drafting their decisions. Rather, counsellors are as a rule indifferent to their file, and this indifference is punctuated by pulled faces, sighs, lapses of memory, a whole *hexis* of disinterest which contrasts very sharply with the obligation that laboratory researchers should be deeply, bodily and passionately engaged in their observations about a matter

---

[14] Callon, Courtial et al., *La scientométrie* (1993).
[15] On the writing skills of scientists at work, see, among many other sources, Latour, *Science in Action* (1987); Licoppe, *La formation de la pratique scientifique* (1996); Knorr-Cetina, *Epistemic Cultures* (1999).

of fact.[16] In science, as in Christian religion, it is necessary to display an attitude that declares a profound and sincere adherence to whatever one is saying, an adherence that will only be renounced when one is forced to do so by one's colleagues or (which amounts to more or less the same thing) by the facts. At the Council, on the other hand, it is essential to show, by means of a subtle body language, that one is quite indifferent to the argument one is making: 'If you don't accept my argument, you will accept the claim', a judge might say with Olympian calm, before embarking only a few minutes later on a line of reasoning that is diametrically opposed to the first. An observation made by a counsellor about a colleague who used to be a physicist reveals this difference quite nicely: 'Like a true scientist, he adheres *too closely* to his solution, contrary to myself.' For this particular counsellor, the *libido sciendi* displayed by his colleague, a former particle physicist, was quite incompatible with the work of a judge.

In the procedures of the Council of State, especially when they are contrasted with the scientific mode of attachment, one finds an accumulation of micro-procedures which manage to produce detachment and to constantly reactivate doubt.

The reporter

When, in the course of a review meeting, the reporter is asked to re-read his notes, he will have no recollection of them, several months having gone by since his examination of the file.[17] Imagine how embarrassed a scientist would be if she were asked to present a research report which she had written six months or a year earlier, which she had not read again since then, and whose contents she had entirely forgotten. What is even more astonishing is that, at the time of his initial examination of the file, the reporter would have prepared two contradictory drafts of decisions (the drafts of judgment), one

---

[16] Unfortunately, we don't have for judges as precise a history of attitudes as we have for science (thanks to Shapin, *A Social History of Truth* (1994), and, more recently, *The Scientific Life* (2008). When reading Maltzman et al., *Crafting Law on the Supreme Court* (2000) or Smolla, *A Year in the Life of the Supreme Court* (1995), one can easily see that there exist huge differences across cultures in which all different sorts of bodily attitudes are authorized or not. American pragmatism has allowed much more passion to be expressed than in France where legal positivism is more influential. Holmes, 'The Path of Law' (1897), would be as exotic in France as John Dewey's view on scientific practice.

[17] Remember that the review meeting precedes the deliberation properly speaking, it is a way to rehearse the arguments before submitting the case to colleagues.

arguing for a rejection of the request, the other for declaring the decision null and void, should his colleagues not adopt his reasoning. So, not only does he have no recollection of the case, but he arrives at the hearing prepared for one course . . . and its opposite. For a scientist, this would be quite scandalous; it would be like deciding at the last moment, in the light of his colleagues' reactions, whether the phenomenon she was talking about existed or not, which would mean preparing two articles, two posters, two slideshows: one for and one against its existence. Worse still, once the discussion has come to an end, the president of the assembly may ask the reporter to draft a third project. And, far from taking umbrage at this expression of bad faith, the reporter politely gets on with the job, immediately setting about writing another 'draft' – which might even be contrary to that which he will vote for later.[18] A scientific researcher would be made mincemeat of if she was required to write an article that went against her own beliefs on the pretext that the colleagues in her research team had formed a consensus opinion that contradicted those beliefs; she would insist that her minority view was represented in the final report, and would slam the door behind her if it wasn't.[19] In any case, for her it would be a matter of conscience. It is not that judges don't have consciences, but that they place their scruples elsewhere.[20]

We should not assume at this point that the counsellors are disinterested in the sense of being indifferent, blasé or bored by the cases that they deal with, or that they are detached in the manner of an automaton. Quite the contrary, they have plenty of interests, otherwise no one would stay at the Council for more than a couple of weeks. As we have seen, there is the legal complexity of the case itself the structure of administrative law; the social, political, economic or governmental implications of cases; the peculiarity of certain claimants; the scale of the injustices that are sometimes committed; the prestige of the State; the intellectual pleasure taken in extracting simple arguments* from an obscure case; the pleasure of standing out

---

[18] 'We are evaluated on the quality of our reasoning, but not on our solution: everyone agrees that *we could have decided otherwise*, this is not a surprise for anyone, but on the quality of the conclusions, yes, there is a strong peer pressure toward excellence', says a commissioner of the law.

[19] Except, of course, if she is in one of those many new hybrids of science and law where she has to participate, for instance, in a consensus conference: see Hermitte, 'L'expertise scientifique à finalité de décision politique' (1997).

[20] A commissioner reading the manuscript disagreed somewhat with this contrast: 'My perception is rather different. A judge, if he decides not to follow his colleagues, can do it for ever. To the bitter end, he can stick to his opinion and sink with it at the end.'

amidst colleagues of one's own intellectual level; to say nothing of
the gentleman's club-like environment in which future careers are
plotted and past failures repaired. There are many sources of interest,
but every effort is made to ensure that they are not attached to
the file, to the bodies of opinion-givers or to solutions adopted –
in much the same way as they are in everyday life – because they
are held apart from the matter at hand, the object itself, by a
distance that progressively becomes almost infinite. It is at this point
that one can best gauge the abyss that separates law from science:
whereas in the laboratory every effort is made to make a connection
between the particularities of the object in question and what is being
said about it, in the Council, by contrast, everything is done to ensure
that the final determination is distanced from the particularities of
the case.

The reviser

Nowhere is this contrast clearer than in the procedural phase where
the *reviser* re-presents the reporter's note of the case. From the perspective of the scientist, this procedure is quite absurd. Having just
spent half an hour listening to someone reading in a monotone voice
a text which explains the whole case, the reviser, who is more highly
placed in the hierarchy of the Council, takes up the story again from
the beginning, this time in oral form. The process of revision is nevertheless an essential moment in the process of judgment because the
reviser is the only person to have re-read the file the previous day, or
the day before that, and to have retained all of the details of the case
in his mind. Remember that none of the others is familiar with the
case and none of them will read the file again, with the exception of
the commissioner who will later become familiar with the case yet
another time. This is another procedure that would seem out of place
in science: the more the case progresses, lingers or makes its way up
the hierarchy of judgment, the more it is dealt with by people who
are distanced from the file and who have no knowledge of it. In
science, this would be like asking people who had fewer and fewer
competences in the specific aspects of the subject to allocate claims
about controversial discoveries; or as though, in relation to a difficult
question concerning invisible galaxies, one were to ask certain people,
chosen precisely because they knew nothing whatsoever about galaxies, to determine the question, on the basis of no information other
than an account of the case given by people more competent than
themselves.

But of course the procedure of revision is neither bizarre nor especially incongruous. As we shall see, what is at issue is not *information*; judges do not exactly determine the particularities of the case; there is more to the reviser's reprise than a simple process of repetition. In the guise of a simple process of repetition, the reviser effectively *transforms* the case by altering the respective proportions of fact and law, placing more emphasis than did the note on strictly legal questions. The particular case becomes less important than the point of law into which it is subsumed, or than the particular reform of administrative law prompted by the case. Therefore, the reviser has less to say about the facts (less, that is, than the reporter, who in turn had less to say about them than the lawyer, who had less to say than the claimant, who, of course, talks *mainly* about the facts!) and more to say about the law. When the judgment is delivered, nothing will remain other than the 'green slips' we have encountered above,[21] which summarize the whole case in a single sentence – such as, for example: 'Where a Prefectural authority refuses to take cognizance of the peremption of a licence to work a quarry, made pursuant to article 106 of the Code of mines, can that order be reviewed on the grounds that it is *ultra vires*?' Nothing remains of the particular case, whose detailed facts can be discovered only by looking up the case on the computer database. There is no path relaying the 'green slip' to the precise nature of the case, and yet, for the judges to whom this lapidary sentence is addressed, the essentials of the experience are indeed summarized in a single sentence.

The word 'fact', which is used in both science and law, might well have led us astray in our comparison, because the same word is used so differently in each domain that it seems almost to be a homonym, or a 'false-friend'. The 'facts' in a legal file constitute a closed set, which is soon made unquestionable by the sheer accumulation of items, and to which it soon becomes *unnecessary* to return. Facts are things that one tries to get rid of as quickly as possible, in order to move on to other things, namely the particular point of law that is of interest, and to which the judges will be entirely devoted from that point on.[22] In the laboratory, on the other hand, a fact occupies two somewhat contradictory positions: it is simultaneously that which is spoken of, and that which will determine the truth of what is being said about it. Therefore, one can never really dispose of the facts in order to move on to something more important. Unless, that is, one confuses laboratory facts, as I have described them, with the 'sense

---

[21] See p. 102 for an example and a definition.
[22] See Cayla, 'La qualification ou la vérité en droit' (1993).

data' of the empiricist tradition which was invented by Locke and Hume for reasons that were more political than epistemological – 'sense data' being the incontrovertible basis of our sensations, which the human mind is supposed to combine in such a way as to develop more general ideas. But, as we shall see, the way in which this kind of fact distinguishes that which is debatable from that which is not has nothing to do with the mode of speech of researchers. It owes more to law than to science.[23] Rather than confuse the two, we should sharpen the contrast: when it is said that the facts are there, or that they're stubborn, that phrase doesn't have the same meaning in science as it does in law, where, however stubborn the facts are, they will never have any real hold on the case as such, whose solidity depends on the rules of law that are applicable to the case.[24]

Nevertheless, it should not be assumed that there is a crisp distinction between the scientist's 'respect for the facts' and the lawyer's emphasis on form or indifference to the claimant's demands. In the laboratory, the particular facts don't count either: the rat which gave its brain to the experiment thereby donates its body to science, and the body will be summarily incinerated; a particular neuron, having ceased to live, will be abandoned in much the same way; also, raw data will be very quickly forgotten. The phenomena put to the proof of an experiment are interesting only because they are the instantiation of a problem, the exemplification of a theory, the point of an argument or the proof of a hypothesis.[25] But how does this differ from the movement of law, since both regimes drop the substance they talk about in order to address that which it exemplifies? The difference consists entirely in the possibility that a theory, if it is a good one, has to be able to generate the fact by a process of

---

[23] Poovey, *History of the Modern Fact* (1999).

[24] In one instance Dorval, regarding a case of water mills 'fondés en titre', shifts abruptly to the facts of the matter by saying: 'It's funny, I know the region quite well, and I don't see where this mill is . . .', but then he abandons immediately this parenthesis to go back to what the expression 'fondés en titre' could imply: 'it's supposed to be lost after a "deep transformation", do we *know* what a "deep transformation" consists of?' The common-sense empirical fact has been touched, and left aside to concentrate on what the case-law has to say about 'deep transformations'.

[25] It is Kant in his *Critique* who has used the mixed metaphor of the scientist as a judge, thus introducing a catastrophic confusion between the two roles: 'Reason holding in one hand its principles, according to which alone concordant appearances can be admitted as equivalent to laws, and in the other hand the experiment which it has devised in conformity with these principles, must approach nature in order to be taught by it. It must not, however, do so in the character of a pupil who listens to everything that the teacher chooses to say, but of an appointed judge who compels the witnesses to answer questions which he has himself formulated' (1950, p. 20).

retroaction: the theory includes all the important details of the fact, otherwise it would not be the theory *of* that particular fact and would be no more than an unfounded hypothesis, pure speculation or a simple proposition which had never been put to an empirical test. This retrodictive path doesn't exist in law, where, in any case, it would be quite meaningless: the whole power of administrative law could not allow anyone to predict anything about the pigeons encountered in chapter 1, or to anticipate in any way the death of the young man at the ski station that we studied in chapter 2. Once the possibility for a third party to attack the clauses of a contract is allowed by the Council, as we just saw in chapter 4, no powerful mind is helped in any way to learn anything about Mr Cayzeele's dustbins. Whereas what makes our friend Rossier such a good neuroscientist is that his theory of the expression of neurons is able to retrace the precise path of each of the neurons he has sacrificed throughout the experimental process, or of any other neuron included in his experimental protocol. In law, so long as you have grasped the point of law, you don't have in your grasp a fact which is liable to emerge unpredictably to surprise you at any moment; in science, if you have grasped the theory you should be able to return to the facts from which you began, and even anticipate new facts.

The commissioner of the law

Let us continue to follow the other minor procedures which compel even the most interested, passionate or expeditious of counsellors to become indifferent, objective, fair and dispassionate. Could one imagine anything in science resembling the commissioner of the law, who remains silent throughout the whole review meeting, taking notes? Is this person the secretary to the meeting? Hardly, since his notes are made for his own use only, in that they help to prepare him for his reading of the file, which he will go over from beginning to end. Might he then be the ultimate expert to whom less skilled counsellors have entrusted the task of finding the right solution? No, because he is often younger than the president of the assembly, who will subsequently pass judgment on his commentary. Now, he keeps quiet, and they do the talking; in a few days' or weeks' time, he will speak, and they will keep quiet.[26] In that case, why not get it over

---

[26] Remember that one feature of French administrative law is that the whole procedure is written without any oral argument except the presentation read by the commissioner of the law, out loud and standing, which is called his 'conclusions' for the reason that it does *not* conclude the judgment . . . law is really queer.

with, and ask him to give his opinion there and then? Because the object is to get things over with, but to do so *within all the appropriate forms*, having once again explored the relationship between this particular case and the law, the case in its entirety and the law in its entirety. One might say that the commissioner of the law has been entrusted with a particular task of quality control, in that he is asked to retrace the course taken by the claimant, the lawyers, the judges of first instance, the reporter and the reviser, before going on to review the vast accumulation of two centuries of administrative law, in order to ensure that the whole thing is properly and securely bound together. Thanks to him the law is made to stand against the law. He is the person who tests connections and ensures coherence, and who reassures his colleagues that the daily process of stitching things together has not corrupted administrative law in any way. The silence of the commissioner throughout the review meeting, the formal reading of his conclusions during the session, his return to silence throughout the stage of the deliberation (in which, it should be remembered, the judges have no obligation to adopt his reasoning), then the separate publication of his conclusions – which might or might not differ from those of the judgment, which is itself published – function as a set of mechanisms invented entirely within the Council of State so as to produce a mode of detachment which in science would seem incongruous, not to say comic.

In science, the role of the commissioner could be replicated only by entrusting a scientist with the overwhelming task of reviewing his entire discipline from the beginning, in order to test its coherence and to ensure its relation to the facts, before proposing the existence or non-existence of a given phenomenon in a formal deposition, although the final decision would not be his, and although he would have to work alone, guided only by his own knowledge and his own conscience, being content to publish his conclusions quite independently. Although something like this role can be found in the form of scientific review articles,[27] which are commissioned from experienced scientists in mid-career, who are expected to summarize the state of the art for their peers, review articles don't have this peculiar mixture of authority and absence of authority. Either the commissioner is like a scientific expert, in which case his greater authority should relieve his peers of their obligation to doubt – he knows more about the issue than they do – or he is simply not playing the role of the expert, in which case why place on his shoulders the crushing burden of having to review the whole case in order to enlighten the process of

[27] Bastide, Callon et al., 'The Use of Review Articles in the Analysis of a Research Area' (1989).

judgment? The role of the commissioner resembles that of a scientist only to the extent that he speaks and publishes in his own name; similarly, there is something of the commissioner in all scientists, who see themselves as liberty enlightening the world. The commissioner is, then, a strange and complex hybrid, which has something of the sovereignty of *lex animata*, law embodied in a human, but whose pronouncements bind no one but himself, whereas in the old world sovereigns always had the last word. In that case, what does he do? What is his function? He gives the whole section the occasion to doubt properly, thereby avoiding any precipitously reached solution, or any cheaply bought consensus. He is, in a sense, an airtight chamber for the avoidance of certainty, a kind of injunction to avoid agreement, an obstacle deliberately placed along the entire length of the path of judgment, a grain of sand, occasionally a scandal, but in all cases an irritant, or a resistance; the commissioner is the most peculiar example of a producer of objections, or, let's risk the word, of *objectivity*.

The importance and the ambiguity of his role are clearest in those cases in which he argues for the overruling of existing precedents, this being the legal equivalent of the process (which so excites researchers) by which scientific paradigms are overthrown. Because he, unlike his colleagues, is not bound to reach final judgment, he can allow himself – with one eye on the case itself, and another on the whole corpus of law – to suggest substantial alterations to this vast structure, whose coherence is produced by a kind of ongoing balancing act, like a cyclist in the saddle. Precisely because he is not obliged to do anything but prompt the law in the moment, without himself having to pass judgment, he can allow himself to indulge in the sort of audacious developments or deepening which would terrify the counsellors, who are always kept in harness, bearing on their shoulders the weight of administrative realities and the obligation to close the case. There is always a certain freshness to commissioners of the law, and they are in any case worn out after a few years.[28] But unlike scientists, who dream of overturning a paradigm, of putting their names to a radical change, a scientific revolution or a major discovery, commissioners of the law invariably present their innovations as the expression of a principle that was already in existence, so that even when it deeply transforms the corpus of administrative law it is 'even more' the same than it was before. This prowess is required by the essential notion of legal stability (*sécurité juridique*), which would

[28] On the function and careers of the 20 commissioners (for 200 counsellors) at work in the Counsel, see chapter 3.

seem quite out of place to a researcher. Just imagine the effect of a notion of 'scientific stability' on research: what was discovered would have to be expressed as a simpler and more coherent reformulation of an established principle, so that no one could ever be surprised by the emergence of a new fact or a new theory . . .

The *'formation de jugement'*

Let's get it over with! We've had enough! We know enough to pass judgment! It is as plain as day that claimant A is in bad faith, drug dealer B a toad and claimant C a fussy nit-picker, that Minister D is plain incompetent, decree E a tissue of absurdities, and police Prefect F a public menace, so why prolong the discussion? The facts are blindingly obvious. We have already read the open-ended note of the reporter, heard the reviser, spent two hours in the review meeting discussing the case, the president has consulted on the matter with the president of the Litigation Section, we have heard the conclusions of the commissioner of the law, and still you haven't finished? No sooner has the commissioner sat down than deliberations are resumed again, this time with a new set of discussants, that is, a fresh set of people who are ignorant about the case, who have heard neither the reporter nor the reviser, who have heard nothing of the discussion, and ask the same old naive questions. Isn't that all extremely disheartening? Why not give the file to the commissioner and close the case for good. Let's say no more about it. Enough procrastination. Yet, it is essential to hesitate and doubt, precisely so as not to rush towards blindingly obvious truths. The tedious succession of reviews and revisions, the meticulous verifications of bureaucratic stamps and the repetition of preambles ensures that blind, stumbling justice can walk in a straight line and say exactly the right thing. All these procedures of detachment allow the law to ensure that it has doubted properly, whereas almost all the elements of a laboratory tend to the speediest possible acquisition of certainty. If Justice holds a balance in hand, it is not because she weighs exactly, but because the balance has not yet shaken for long enough.

Common sense finds the slowness of both law and science incomprehensible: 'why take so much trouble to judge?', it demands. 'Why go to so much hassle to know?', it asks, astonished. Do we really need all these distancing procedures in order to deal with a case about dustbins, pigeons, planning permissions or appointment procedures? Is it really necessary to spend so much money, to mobilize the best and the brightest students of the National School of Administration and to spend years on claims which could easily be resolved with a bit of common sense and a measure of good faith? Conversely, is it really necessary to sacrifice hundreds of rats, to mobilize an elite of men in white coats or to invest in extremely expensive instruments in order to learn how our brains work or how many stars there are in the sky? What a waste of time! How slow! If the production of doubt in law and of knowledge in science were criticized in these terms by ordinary common sense, judges and scientists would immediately join forces to celebrate the necessity of time, slowness, care, expense, elitism, quality and respect for procedure. Both scientists and judges would exclaim that common sense, with its crude methods, could produce neither this effect of slowness of judgment nor confidence in certainty: it would reach a conclusion too quickly, too hastily and on the basis of superficial first impressions; all of us depend vitally on these costly and ponderous institutions, which require the complex elaboration of an esoteric vocabulary and the application of procedures that are exasperatingly meticulous, because these are the only means we have to avoid arbitrariness and superficiality.

And yet common sense is right: things *have to be brought to an end.* And here, once again, science and law, which seemed for a moment to be united in their defence of their processes, rather than their privileges, are shown to be quite different. At the Council of State, every effort is made to sustain doubt for as long as possible, but when a decision is reached it is made once and for all. In the laboratory, every effort is made to reach certainty, but in the end it is left to others, to colleagues, to a point in the future, to the dynamic of the scientific field, to decide on the truth value of what is said. An attitude completely opposed to what one finds in law: suddenly, after months or years of waiting, the case has to be concluded. And this is not just a possibility but an obligation, which is inscribed in the law: a judge has to decide, otherwise he would abuse his authority. Although he has gone to all this trouble to slow things down, to observe formality, to collectivize, to become detached and indifferent, to distance himself, judgment must now be issued. That is the object of the process of deliberation. The only available escape route lies in deciding that the decision cannot be taken alone, that the case is too serious, so that one has to remove the case to a stage further up the hierarchy.[29] But this change of direction only puts off the inevitable.

[29] Remember that there are five different levels inside the same Council of State, from the president of the sub-section judging by decree, sub-sections judging by themselves, sub-sections judging together, the whole Litigation Section, and finally the Assembly of the Council, in order to judge cases from the least to the most important.

The Council of State will have to make the decision. It is the ultimate tribunal. The only way to get judgment over with is to pass judgment.

A laboratory works in quite the opposite way: it has gone to considerable trouble to cover its back, to multiply its data, to verify its hypotheses, to anticipate objections, to choose the best equipment, to recruit the best specialists; it has drafted the most combative article, chosen the best journal, organized the most skilful leaks to the press, and then suddenly, at the last moment . . . except that there is no *last* moment! Quite unconcernedly, the researchers, having passionately pursued the truth, and now being unable to control the fate of their claims, leave it to others to take care of verifying them. 'We'll soon see what they have to say; the future will tell whether we were right or not.' The tribunal of history is a strange sort of court because it lacks the most essential quality of a court: the absolute obligation to pass judgment now, without putting it off until later, and without delegating the task to someone in the future, who might be better qualified or superior in rank to oneself. Having accumulated their proofs of modesty and distance, the judges abruptly, and with the greatest arrogance, take on the wrath of sovereignty: they decide the issue. Scientists, having exercised all the passions of knowledge and every pretension to certainty, suddenly become modest and humbly defer to posterity.

Chains of references and chains of obligations

But to distinguish passion on one side and detachment on the other, scientists' interest and lawyers' disinterest, modesty and authority, or closure and openness, is to make what is still only a surface comparison, lying in the indeterminate zone between psychology and ethology, between procedure and content. In order to deepen the analysis, which aims to distinguish scientific and legal activity, which are so often confused, we should now, at the risk of tiring the reader, trace out the workings of these two modes of enunciation even more closely, by distinguishing the chains of reference which anthropologies of science have studied very closely, from legal chains, which are so very difficult to describe.[30] However, the task is not impossible, because the fabrication and processing of files reveal the traces of these two ways of establishing relations, which in one case are made of information, and, in the other, of what can only be called 'obligation'. But

[30] On chains of reference, see Hacking, *Representing and Intervening* (1983), and Latour, *Pandora's Hope* (1999b).

what does that mean? We shall try to describe what is transported from one layer of inscription to another in the course of an experiment, and what happens to a file when it undergoes the process through which legal grounds* are extracted from it. Our hypothesis is that most of the superficial features that we have set out so far are explained by the differences between these two orders of circulation.

A common origin: exegesis

Before exploring these differences, we should recall the common origin of both legal and scientific practices, the ancestral learning that still constitutes the basic apprenticeship of scientists and lawyers, namely, the manipulation of texts, or of inscriptions in general, which are accumulated in a closed space before being subjected to a subtle exegesis which seeks to classify them, to criticize them and to establish their weight and hierarchy, and which for both kinds of practitioner replace the external world, which is in itself unintelligible. For both lawyers and scientists, it is possible to speak confidently about the world only once it has been transformed – whether by the word of God, a mathematical code, a play of instruments, a host of predecessors or a natural or positive law – into a Great Book, which might equally well be of nature or culture, whose pages been ripped out and rearranged by some diabolical agency, so that they have now to be compiled, interpreted, edited and rebound. With scientists, as with judges, we find ourselves already in a textual universe which has the double peculiarity of being so closely linked to reality that it can take its place, and yet unintelligible without an ongoing work of interpretation.[31] And for both scientists and jurists this incessant activity generates new texts, whose quality, order and coherence will, paradoxically, increase the complexity, disorder and incoherence of the corpus they leave to their successors, who will themselves have to take on this labour of Sisyphus or Penelope. Stitching, weaving, reviewing and revising of Exegesis, mother of both science and law.

The common exegetical role of the good researcher and the good lawyer can be seen in the way that they both evaluate stacks of heterogeneous documents by attributing a different value of trust to

---

[31] This is the main thrust of Pierre Legendre from *L'empire de la vérité* (1983) to *Sur la question dogmatique en Occident* (1999). The main work on the differential practices of writing and the influence of print remains Eisenstein, *The Printing Press as an Agent of Change* (1979).

each. Just as the expression 'This decision will be published in the *Lebon*' carries more weight than 'aux tables' in the description of a precedent, so an article published in *Nature* or *Science* will elicit a greater degree of attachment than a preprint posted on a website. Both scientists and lawyers have great respect for existing publications – which in both disciplines can be tracked down by a coded scheme of citation and references – and yet both have a certain distance from, or defiance or even disrespect for too close a linkage of references. Just as a commissioner will say, quite politely, that 'This decision seems to me to be quite isolated, and, in truth, quite unrepresentative of the case-law', so a researcher will have no hesitation in writing that 'Although there are a number of experiments which assume the existence of this phenomenon, no conclusive proof has ever been provided.' Both differentiate very subtly between those documents which are assured and those which leave enough gaps and contradictions on which to hang the argument, or to suggest alternative formulations. Both kinds of practitioner work collectively, and without the close collaboration of their colleagues they would be quite unable to say anything at all. In both domains, everything may already have been written, but still nothing has yet been written, so that it is necessary to begin again, collectively, with a new effort of interpretation.

However, whereas in the Council of State the act of writing is always explicit, in a laboratory such as that of Rossier it always seems to be a mere appendage of scientific work, or perhaps even a kind of chore. For example, on arrival at the Council, each new member receives two documents: the *Memento du reporter devant les formations administratives du Conseil d'Etat*, and the *Guide du reporter de la Section du Contentieux*. These substantial volumes, which explain in detail how to draft notes and decisions, are essentially style manuals paying as much attention to the form of bureaucratic stamps and endorsements as they do to the proper layout of paragraphs or correct punctuation. Although there are (especially in the United States) courses which provide future scientists with a training in writing skills, most laboratory workers would be surprised to find their activity described as a work of exegesis. Until this character was revealed by the anthropology of science, scientific texts were assumed to be nothing more than supports for information, whose only virtue was transparency, and whose only defect obscurity. In order to reconnect the sciences with their ancient roots, these texts had to be seen in the light of the output of laboratory instruments and the important role of intertextuality. Only then could scientific authors once again appear as hermeneutists, as writers or scholars, except that the texts

Scientific objects and legal objectivity

they compare incorporate textual proofs extracted from phenomena put to an experimental trial. Counsellors, on the other hand, are always talking about their writing activities, and quite often speak in formulaic phrases made up of citations. For them a text is never just a support for information, and is never evaluated on the basis of its clarity alone; indeed, that much becomes obvious if one reads any of their writings!

If we remind ourselves of their common roots, it becomes impossible (whatever might be said in the vast body of writing on the subject) to distinguish scientific texts, which are supposed to be factual and impersonal, from legal texts, which are supposed to have the special property of doing what they say, or, depending on the circumstances, of saying what should be done. There are of course a number of differences, but we should hesitate to understand these in terms of the conventional distinction between fact and value, or between declarative and performative statements.[32] Scientific texts, as we have already suggested, resemble neither the mythical statements of rhetoricians or philosophers of language ('water boils at 100 degrees') nor affirmations ('the decision made on 17 April 1992 by the administrative court of Grenoble is hereby overturned'). The reason is that, unlike the manuals or encyclopaedias with which they are so often confused, the scientific or research text that emerges straight from the laboratory deals not so much with a fact that has to be described, as with a profound *transformation*, which the word 'information' does not really describe. Unless, that is, the term is understood etymologically, to mean placing within a *form*, the latter being understood quite literally or materially, as consisting in a graph, equation or table. No *in*-formation can be produced without a cascade of these sorts of *trans*-formations.[33] Moreover, no scientific article would make do with one single such transport, with just one representation in the form of a graph, but has instead to orchestrate dozens, each linked to the other so as to compose a drama or a chain of reasoning, each one being precarious in the sense that it seeks to carry over all of the relevant elements of the preceding layer while at the same time thoroughly modifying them so as to give added force to the particular theory, formula or interpretation.[34] Finally, as we

---

[32] This is the weakness of the otherwise magnificent book on speech acts by Austin, *How to Do Things with Words* (1962): the real differences cannot be seen by grammar alone, nor by short interactions, but by following the whole regime of enunciation.

[33] Lynch and Woolgar (eds.), *Representation in Scientific Practice* (1990).

[34] See, especially, Galison, *Image and Logic* (1997).

have just observed, this whole process of transformation takes the form of a claim or petition, which is characterized by uncertainty and risk, and which the authors release into the mass of existing publications.[35] The truth value of the statement will be attributed retroactively, from the treatment that the claim or petition receives at the hands of other authors, supporters as well as detractors. This sort of textual trail, or complex alchemy, has no more to do with the common-sense notions of a factual statement than it does with legal texts.

To be sure, it is possible to retrieve numerous traces of this very particular kind of activity that one finds in laboratories in judicial files, but far from defining the nature of judicial activity, it merely organizes *a few of its segments*, the remainder being characterized by activities that are more properly legal. For example when the Council has judged (see p. 101) that a map for a building authorization is 'said to be' annexed to the Declaration of Public Utility file even though it is not physically present in the annex, provided it can be consulted somewhere at the Mayor's office, the question whether a map was annexed to a file could have been answered by a referential gesture of pointing to the file; and yet, as we have seen, this was not the question, since they eventually decided that the maps could be adjudged to have been annexed 'by connectivity', namely without any possible referential gesture. In this manoeuvre, the furrow of one referential chain is abandoned in favour of another, which we have still to define. The differences between law and science are clearly revealed in the clash or interruption of these two furrows. For example, if the question whether an acknowledgement of receipt was actually sent is raised in the course of a hearing, and the file contains the appropriate post office form, signed and dated by the claimant, the quality of the reference is unquestionable; similarly, when the assembly is convinced, having taken a common-sense approach in reading tracts annexed to a file, that a candidate defamed his opponent to some degree on the eve of the election; or, again, where an aerial photograph attached to a file allows the judges to establish whether or not a park is fully enclosed by a wall, this being the point at issue, the judges retrace a short referential chain by doing what geographers, geologists or surveyors might do, that is, by superimposing layer upon layer of documents and tracings, which are very different in terms of their materiality (photographs, graphs, documents and plans) but which, by their nature, keep information intact across a play of transformations. But the judges' confidence would soon

---

[35] See Fleck, *Genesis and Development of a Scientific Fact* (1935) for a classic analysis of this alchemy.

Figure 5.2 a = a neuroscientist's deck; b = a counsellor's table.

evaporate if, instead of having to make the few referential steps which they take when they track a map, graph, signature or opinion through their files, they had to cross the dozens of transformations that are necessary for scientists to establish a reasonably solid proof in a somewhat specialized field. Would a judge agree to entrust his

judgment to an electronic microscope which requires 100 or so adjustments, each of which completely transforms the initial sample?[36]
A judge would exclaim indignantly that he needed a more 'direct
contact' with reality.

On the other hand, would a researcher agree to make a decision
on the basis of a frame that was as narrowly defined as what is contained 'within the limit of the file'? The short referential chains which
are contained in the folder would soon be disrupted by slippages,
dislocations and changes of register which would be horrifying to
scientific researchers. When a judge says that there is nothing in the
file to the effect that a foreigner expelled from France had children
born in France, he satisfies himself with the limits defined by the
adversarial logic of the case, and settles for an inquiry as to whether
any defence submission had disputed the fact, using the phrase, 'and
that point was not contested'. A procedure of this sort, which requires
that one keep to the traces accumulated in the file, would freeze the
blood of a scientist. He too, like his judicial critic, would demand a
more direct, richer and more living contact with reality! 'Let's put
the file to one side and go and see what's happening for ourselves,
let's do some field work, question the witnesses, forget the pathetic
arguments of the lawyers and escape from the straitjacket of this
paper world, which is unable to capture reality.'[37] But at this point,
the researcher would have confused the complex mechanism of
exchange of memoirs among the parties with her own (equally
complex but radically different) way of gaining fresh information.
Her objective is always to know more, and she would expect there to
be established a two-way path between the offices of the Council and
the facts, which would allow the transportation of (appropriately
transformed) information to be continually improved. But, as a result,
she would accumulate more and more data without yet being able to
pass judgment. The process of review would be inflated to quite fear-
some proportions, and no decision would ever be reached. She would,
in fact, be engaging *in research, not judgment.*

Lawyers and scientists are each scandalized by the other's forms of
enunciation. They both speak truth, but each according to a quite
different criterion of truth. Judges consider that scientists have access
to what is only a pale version of reality, because they write articles

---

[36] Galison, *Image and Logic* (1997).
[37] In the classical opposition between the inquisitorial and adversarial system of law,
it is worth noting that 'inquisitorial' does not refer to anything as horrible as the
Inquisition but rather portrays the judge as a scientist exploring, with all means at
his disposal, what is a given state of affairs by opposition to the adversarial principle
where the judge sits and waits (see Stirn et al., *Droits et libertés* (2006), p. 36).

which have a relation to the facts they describe that is so indirect that there are dozens of steps in their reasoning, and as many leaps from each graphic representation to the next. Scientists, on the other hand, don't understand how judges can be content with what is wrapped in their files, or how they can apply the term 'incontrovertible fact' to a submission that has not been contradicted by a counter-submission. Scientists, by contrast, measure the quality of their referential grip in terms of the mediated character of their instruments and their theories. Without making this long detour, they would have nothing to say other than whatever fell immediately before the senses, which would be of no interest, and would have no value as information. Judges, for their part, hold that the quality of their judgments is closely dependent on their ability to avoid the two hazards of *ultra petita* and *infra petita*: that is, issuing a judgment that either goes beyond or falls short of that which the parties have asked for. What seems to judges to be a major failing is considered by scientists to be their greatest strength; yes, they can only attain precision by progressively distancing themselves from direct contact with common sense and the senses. And that which scientists regard as the greatest defect of law is taken as a compliment by the counsellors: they do indeed stick to what can be elicited from the file, without addition or subtraction. Here, we have two distinct conceptions of exactitude and talent, of faithfulness and professionalism, of scruple and objectivity.

Two different ways of transmitting something to someone

It might be argued that these differences are quite minor by comparison with what both have in common, namely the reduction of the world to paper. From this overly general perspective, the way to put the world into science or the world into law resembles trying to stuff a quilt into an envelope. But these are two very different modes of reduction, and the whole aim of this section is to distinguish them. The important thing is to understand how the relation between the legal file and the particular case is unlike the relation between a map and the territory, if maps are taken as both a symbol and an example of chains of reference.

Legal reduction seeks to constitute a domain of unquestionable fact as quickly as possible (which means only that there should be no submission from the defence contesting those facts), so that it can then subsume the facts into a rule of law (which is in practice a text) in order to produce a judgment (which is, in reality, a decree, a text).

Scientific reduction effects the same astonishing economy because it
too replaces the richness and complexity of the world in all its dimension with paper and texts. But the approach it establishes is utterly
different because, once one is in possession of a piece of paper, a
document or a map, it is always possible to retrace one's steps, returning to the territory to pick up the trail, once one has found the sign-
posts, the surveyor's stakes or the right perspectives and calculations
of angles. At each point, the reasoning process takes hold on the
superposition of instruments, graphs, theodolites, markers, gradua-
tions and measurements which enable reasoning to act as though it
was always moving from like to like above the abyss of the transformation of matter. But in law, even when resemblance or precedent is
invoked, what is involved is never a precise superposition.[38] When the
reporter says:

> **Marchand**: One of the arguments alleges a procedural impropri-
> ety, on the basis that the plan was neither initialled nor numbered
> by the *commissaire enquêteur*; this allegation is not supported by
> the facts because although the register was initialled only on every
> other page, this is not serious because the defines case-law a leaf
> as a folded sheet.

the minuscule portion of reference that enables him to verify the
signature is immediately diverted, or, more precisely, relayed, by the
legal definition of what 'a leaf' is. This does indeed involve tracing a
path, but in this case it binds a factual element to what lawyers call
a 'qualification': 'Is this a leaf in the sense that the term is used in
article 13–25 of the Procedural Code of the Declaration of Public
Utility?'[39] Someone who holds a map in their hands also holds the
territory, or at least a two-way path that would allow her *to learn
more* on the occasion of the next iteration, or on the occasion of her
next visit to the territory; someone who holds a file has established a
connection that means that he will *no longer* have to learn anything
more from the fact, and which, on his return, will allow him to
transport an unquestionable decision, an 'arrêt', a *stop*.

The difference between reference and qualification is clearly exem-
plified in a case in which a sub-section had to decide whether the
illustrator of a gardening magazine, who had been refused a highly
coveted press card on the grounds that she did not deal with current

[38] Except when it is really a copy-and-paste question, as on p. 136.
[39] This is the proof that it is difficult to qualify the meaning of the word 'qualification' in law (or that of 'distinguishing' in Common Law). See Cayla, 'La qualification'
(1993).

affairs, could have the decision of the journalists' professional body overturned. As one might expect, there was some discussion of the distinction between current affairs and seasonal affairs: are this year's peonies, peach trees or kiwi fruit 'current affairs'? Is the person who illustrates them 'a journalist'? But this question of substance would lead nowhere, because the question is not whether an illustrator of current affairs is really, truly, fundamentally or referentially a journalist, but whether, as against the professional body of journalists, she is able to establish that quality 'within the meaning of article L 761–2 of the Labour Law Code'. There is simply no relation between this and a definition of essence, nature, truth or exactitude. Or rather there is, but the relation is one of simple connectivity: it is not necessarily the case that progress in one dimension advances things in the other dimension, or vice versa.

It being the case that Mrs Eyraud claims the status of a professional journalist as an illustrator-reporter; and pursuant to the provisions of the third subsection of article L.761–2 of the Labour Law Code, which states that 'The following participants in the editorial process shall be treated as professional journalists: translator-editors, stenographer-editors, sub-editors, illustrator-reporters, photographic reporters, except advertising agents, and those who participate in the editorial process only occasionally'; given that according to the facts of the case the duties of Mrs Eyraud, who is employed by the magazine *Rustica* as an illustrator, consist in the illustration of sheets which are designed to describe methods and techniques of gardening; and given that in this case these illustrations are sufficiently linked to current affairs as to characterize their illustrator as a reporter in the meaning of the foregoing provisions; Mrs Eyraud is therefore able to claim the benefit of article L.761–2 of the Labour Law Code.

Even in this very simple case, the two forms of discourse, that of the dispute itself and that of law, remain absolutely heterogeneous. What does it mean to say that 'in this case these illustrations are sufficiently linked to current affairs'? However much you play with the meaning of article L 761–2, it will not provide you with the answer to that question. The text says nothing other than that, in this particular case, the judges considered Mrs Eyraud to be a reporter *within the meaning of the article*. Full stop. 'Yes, but is she really a journalist?', one might ask. What does the notion of a 'sufficient link' mean? That question would carry us all the way along a referential chain, distancing us from another chain, that which ensures the fragile and provisional linkage between a text and a particular case through the mediation of a legal qualification.

Ah, you might say, but this is a very familiar kind of operation: this is just a process of classification. In much the same way as a postman uses the postcodes written on envelopes to sort letters into boxes ordered by the codes, so a legal file allows one to order the facts of the particular case according to the relevant categories, such as, for example, legal error, *ultra vires* or public works.[40] But the word 'classification', like the words 'reduction', 'fact', 'reasoning', 'judgment' or 'qualification', changes its meaning depending on the kind of enunciation that we're trying to characterize. A process of scientific classification would allow one to subsume each particular instance within the category in such a way that, having established that A is an instance of B, anyone who had B in their possession could obtain A, or at least all of the relevant features of A. If A is an instance of an acetylcholine receptor, given a knowledge of acetylcholine receptors, I would know all that there is to be known about A. But this is *not* how particular facts are qualified by legal rules: nothing in article L 761- 2 tells one whether the facts of the next case will or will not disclose a sufficiently close connection to current affairs. The rule contains no knowledge or information about the particular facts, except in the most superficial sense; one might say, for example, that such and such a case is one of *ultra vires*, which would mean that the *Service des analyses* should steer it towards a particular assembly specialized in those topics. But, as we have seen in chapter 2, this kind of ordering is of assistance in logistics rather than in judgment. Minor referential chains (A is an instance of B) are subordinated to what, from the point of view of the law, is the only true kind of chain: A is an instance of B *as it is defined by* article C or precedent D. Whereas in science the relation between the instance and category is taxonomic, in law this is only superficially true. In both cases one finds linkages and pathways establishing numerous relations between texts and events, but in each case the grids differ as much as a grid of fibre optic cables differs from an urban gas supply network. Viewed from the point of view of science, what is transported by law can only disappoint.

To enter a referential chain is to approach things quite differently from a legal file. The cascade of transformations which produces information is such as to oblige the protagonists to produce that rarest of commodities: new information about newly forged beings, which have come into contact with science and which have to be recognized, taken into account, ordered and qualified in such a way that, once these requirements have been satisfied, one might return to them in

---

[40] As we have seen in chapter 2, these simple cases of classifications without any judgment are made precisely *before* the beginning of the extraction of means and by secretaries who are not judges (see p. 77) which is proof enough that judging is not simply referring a token to a type.

order to gather supplementary information or fresh knowledge, until eventually they have been so thoroughly disciplined, understood, trained, domesticated and mastered that they can be put in a 'black box', at which point they can be considered as known, and used as the premises of new processes of argumentation or experimentation.[41] This dynamic of knowledge patterns the world with two-way paths which eventually saturate the territory that is being mapped, thoroughly confusing the two registers in a single truth-telling discourse.

Those who are recognized by their colleagues as the fortunate producers of new and reliable information will be rewarded with eponymy; their name will forever be associated with a particular discovery, such as Newton's laws or Boyle's law. Strangely, eponymy exists in law but it rewards not the judge but the claimant, whose name will forever be associated with an important decision which, as they say, is a 'landmark decision'. Although the name of the commissioner is sometimes attached to a decision through the pages of the *Lebon*, above all if his conclusions are published, no one remembers the name of the author of a landmark decision, which is necessarily anonymous; and, as we know, every effort is made to ensure that change is presented in terms of legal stability.[42] Whereas in science everything is done to ensure that the impact of new information upon a body of established knowledge is as devastating as possible, in law things are arranged in such a way as to ensure that the particular facts are just the *external* occasion for a change which alters only the law itself, and not the particular facts, about which one can learn nothing further, beyond the name of the claimant. In law too, paths are traced across the world, weaving numerous relations between claimants, legislative acts, decrees and Codes, but these links do not produce any information or novelty: they are traversed by 'les moyens de droit' (legal arguments*), vehicles that are every bit as original as information, but which are quite different, and which we have to

---

[41] For two recent marvellous examples see Rheinberger, *Toward a History of Epistemic Things* (1997), and Knorr-Cetina, *Epistemic Cultures* (1999).

[42] What is called in history of science 'Whiggish history' (a term coming itself from the history of English politics) has become a sin – the sin of anachronism – but it is the highest virtue in law, as we can see in this interaction: 'Here an *effort of interpretation* is necessary. We have to follow President Audent's dictum that a text should be interpreted not as it was written but as the authors *would have reacted* had they had before them the same facts as today. So by the words "head of the territory" we *should understand* "representant according to the law of 1984".' This virtue of Whiggishness is well understood in the endless discussions about the American Constitution; see, for instance, Dworkin, *Freedom's Law* (1997).

study further if we are to describe them properly. In following the paths of scientific information – cascades of perilous transformations – researchers are going to bump into powerful centres of calculation which will offer, in a reduced scale, precise descriptions of the world. She who holds the laboratory holds the world. Nothing of the sort with the fragile chains of obligations: he who holds the law, holds only the law – and yet you can cross the whole world with it without being surprised at any point and without ever trying to build an accurate description of what it is.

The difference is clearest in the situation where a counsellor, addressing a difficult point, exclaims that 'Since last week, we *know* that . . .' The knowledge in question does not rest on a newly established connection between a fact and a theory, across the hazardous passage of a referential chain; rather, it means that 'We have decided the question, and there is therefore nothing more to be discussed.'[43] If the same phrase, 'since last week we know that', may be used to celebrate the certainty that 'since 15 January 1999 the existence of eight planets outside of the solar system have been proven', as well as to say that 'since our Cayzeele decision of 10–7–1996 we know that regulatory clauses of contracts can be disputed by way of claims arguing that the act was *ultra vires*', this proves that the verb 'to know' is too ambiguous. In both cases, some undisputable statement has been generated; in both cases, there is a difference between today and yesterday; in both cases, history has taken a turn, but in the first case it is possible to move *back and forth* from the statement published in *Nature* and the tiny signals interpreted by powerful computers, whereas in the second case, even though the law might be richer, not a bit of new knowledge has been acquired on Mr Cayzeele and his dustbins . . . Where the development of astronomy tells a story which is common to those who know and to what is known, the law develops as if it had remained in a perfect homeostasis and teaches nothing new about the case at hand but simply maintains the predictability of law. Science is a two-way ticket; law a one-way only. Which is another way of saying that law produces no new knowledge, and yet it extends 'everywhere', as we shall see, its strange fibrous protective mantle. It has better things to do than to know: it maintains the fabric of imputations and obligations.

---

[43] The Professor of Administrative Law at Sciences Po, to a question about the retroactivity of administrative acts, answers: 'I don't know, because I don't know what the Constitutional Council would have decided; in the absence of a case-law, I don't know.'

Comparative table of the two enunciation regimes

Reference chains	Chain of obligations
The work of writing is implicit	The work of writing is explicit
The sources of inscriptions are heteregenous (from matter to form)	The sources of inscriptions are homogeneous (from paper forms to paper forms)
Inscriptions by non-humans	Inscriptions by humans
Information = transformations	Information = following forms
Cascades of transformations that allow the reference to access far-away phenomena	Short segments of information, just to check the factual part of the file
Common sense is abandoned for grasping facts and their theories	Common sense is maintained all along to hold to the factual claims
In case of doubt, leave the laboratory and go back to the field	In case of doubt, ask for more documents but stay in the limit of the file
Review has no limit	Process of review should be limited
Facts and theories evolve in common	Once facts are stabilized, the real legal work begins
The link between map and territory is made through the discovery of a constant	The link between a law and a case is made by 'x is a y *in the sense* of the article z'
Taxonomy by the inclusion of an example in a type	Taxonomy by connection between a token and a type without definition of the essence
Two-way movements from data to form	One-way only
Iteration and development of the corpus of knowledge	Homeostasis of the corpus of law
Production of new information	Stability of established connections
Eponymy of the researcher	Eponymy of the claimant
Networks traced by the movement of information	Networks traced by the movement of 'moyens*'
Centres of calculation and scale models	Archives are incorporated by the judges' memories

Res judicata pro veritate habetur

Is there any attachment that is stronger than legal obligations or the certainty of facts? No, and this is what made us launch this (occasionally daring) comparison between two activities which are entirely different, but whose precise and intricate fabric remains largely unknown to the broader public. But, as we have seen, popular representations of law and science confuse the features of the two activities so much that they are of no assistance in elaborating this comparison. However striking the differences, and however much those differences are accentuated at each stage of the comparison, they are difficult to pin down because, on the one hand, judges have appropriated the scientist's white coat in order to represent their role, while, on the other, scientists have borrowed the judge's robes of purple and ermine in order to establish their authority. At the risk of momentarily abandoning ethnography to engage in philosophy, we shall conclude by drawing up an inventory of these unfortunate swaps, so as to render unto Caesar that which is Caesar's, and to render unto Galilee that which is Galilee's.

Most of the qualities that are commonly attributed to scientists are drawn from the micro-procedures invented by lawyers to produce their fragile ethos of disinterest.[44] Indifference to the outcome of a case, the distance established between the mind and the object that is being spoken about, the coldness and rigour of judgment – in short, everything that we associate with objectivity – belongs not to the world of the laboratory or of calculation, but to the judicial bench. Or rather, we should distinguish 'objectivity' as the basis of a mood of indifference and serenity as to the solution, from what might be termed 'objectity': the ordeal by means of which a scientist binds her own fate and that of her speech to the trials undergone by the phenomenon in the course of an experiment. Whereas objectivity, paradoxically, pertains to the *subject* and his *interior state*, objectity pertains to the *object* and its peculiarly *judicial* role. The same adjective – 'he has an *objective* mind' – can therefore point to two quite different virtues, one of which is essentially just a particular form of subjectivity (distance, indifference, disinterest) and the other a very specific form of subjectification in which the researcher subjects herself to an experimental object. Doesn't this common-sense admiration for the objectivity of scientists imply that they should sit as judges? And when, on the other hand, common sense complains about the fragility of its jurists, doesn't this imply that they should display the same kinds of objects as laboratory researchers?

The strange thing about legal objectivity is that it quite literally is *object-less*, and is sustained entirely by the production of a mental state, a bodily *hexis*, and quite unable to resign its faculty of judgment by appealing to incontrovertible facts. It therefore depends entirely on a quality of speech, deportment, dress, and on a form of enunciation, and therefore on all of those external appearances that have

---

[44] For reasons which have been studied in Shapin and Schaffer, *Leviathan and the Air-Pump* (1985).

been derided since Pascal, without recognizing that this respect for appearances is a form of objectivity that is unattainable for scientists. Scientists speak inarticulately about precise objects, lawyers speak in precise terms about vague objects. That is because judges have no superiors to whom they might refer the task of judgment (unless, of course, they are judges of first instance). Scientific objectity, on the other hand, is distinguished by the fact that it is *subject-less* because it accommodates all sorts of mental states, and all forms of vice, passion, enthusiasm, speech deficiencies, stammers or cognitive limitations. However unfair, excessive, expeditious or partial researchers might be, they will never lack an object. Above each of them, like the sword of Damocles, hang the facts – or rather the strange hybrid produced by the encounter between incontrovertible facts and controversial colleagues – and this threat is sufficient to call even their most extreme enthusiasms or injustices to order. Suspended above researchers, there is always a third object that is appointed judge and charged with deciding on their behalf, to which scientists delegate the task of judging, without worrying whether they themselves, in their own consciences, are 'objective'.[45] As for judges, they have no one else to judge on their behalf, and they can become 'objective' only by constructing an intricate and complex institution which detaches and isolates their consciences from the ultimate solution.[46]

Having rendered unto judges an objectivity that is a form of subjectivity, and unto scientists an objectity predicated upon the guaranteed presence of the object, we can now locate the second feature that common sense surreptitiously displaces from the realm of law to the realm of science, namely, the ability to have *the last word*. The invention of the role of the expert has allowed two quite opposing functions to be confused, because it requires that scientists, having been diverted from their roles, occupy the throne of supreme court judges, cloaking their testimony in the incontrovertible authority of the facts as judged (*res judicata*). But there is a huge difference between expert and researcher.[47] For the latter, there is no such thing as the authority

---

[45] In the formulation given by Stengers, 'an experiment is the invention of a power to grant things the power to grant the experimenter the power to speak in their names': *The Invention of Modern Science* (2000), p. 102.

[46] A commissioner adds in commenting on the present passage: 'In brief, the scientist believes he discovers (and has to make a strong effort at self-analysis to remind himself that, in part at least, he has been constructing his facts). The judge believes that he is constructing his solution (and has to make the same effort at self-analysis to realize that in effect he has been discovering the solution).'

[47] For a recent presentation of the difference, see Callon et al., *Acting in an Uncertain World* (2009); see also Jasanoff, *The Fifth Branch* (1990).

of science 'as judged', and if she were to come across a set of propositions that the current, fragile, state of scientific controversy had made
unquestionable, what would she do? Why, of course, she would
immediately question them! She would return to her laboratory, carry
out new experiments, re-open the black box that her colleagues had
just sealed closed, change the protocols or, if she herself shared their
conviction, she would use this guaranteed output to construct a new
experiment and to engender new facts. In science, incontrovertibility
is always the high point of a movement by which the work of
information/transformation is continually renewed. When discussion
comes to an end, it does so only so as to inaugurate a new phase of
intense discussion about entities which have only recently come into
existence. When the expert scientist is given the power to decide or
not decide, to 'bind or to unbind', she is lent the regalia of a mode of
sovereignty that belongs exclusively to law.[48]

This confusion would be especially harmful because what the
judges call 'having the last word' resembles neither the authority of
the expert nor the scientists' endless renewal of discussion.[49] Indeed,
however forceful the authority of *res judicata* in law, what is involved
is always, as lawyers say, the 'exhaustion' of the available channels
of appeal. The end of a case never reaches a limit that is any more
grandiose than this particular kind of exhaustion: 'it's reported in the
Lebon volume', 'the issue has been decided', 'as the law now stands',
'unless the European Court of Human Rights rules to the contrary'.
Nothing said in the Council of State is more juicy, or more sublime,
than these sorts of expression. When they reach the 'end' of a hearing,
judges take care to ensure that this ending is not clothed in the grandiose forms of Incontrovertibility. When Roman lawyers intoned the
celebrated adage *res judicata pro veritate habetur*, they were declaring
that what had been decided should be taken *as* the truth, which
means, precisely, that it should in no way be confused *with* the truth.
The esteemed role of the expert corresponds neither to the model of
scientific research, which re-opens a discussion that had been closed

---

[48] This is all the more dangerous in a country like France where justice and truth
have been confused too much, as Garapon, *Bien juger. Essai sur le rituel judiciaire*
(1997), shows very well: 'In contrast with Common Law, justice, in France, has
something do to with the interiority and not only with outside behaviour. This difference explains the confidence in France and the diffidence elsewhere in the power
of full confession. In one case, justice protects against the intrusion into the interiority, in the other justice is taken as a prolongation of the benevolent action of the
sovereign' (p. 174).
[49] For a marvellous example, see Lynch and McNally, 'Science, Common Sense and
Common Law' (1999).

too quickly, nor to that of the judge, because the latter demands of closure nothing more transcendent than a simple end to the discussion. This kind of immanence is a modest, constructive or even constructivist solution: given that there is no one above us, and that the case is simply stopped by the decision which is precisely called 'a decision' or an 'arrêt', that which we know without engaging in further discussion, we know because, quite simply, we have exhausted the discussion. There is no further appeal. Full stop.

It might be said that in this respect judges offer to scientists what epistemologists have described as Science's nightmare: the example of a mode of unfettered arbitrariness in which a closed assembly decides, without reference to any external arbiter, with no tools other than words and by simple consensus, what should be held as the truth. On that basis, they would be entirely free to call a cat 'a dog', to consider a slave a free man, to say that a contractual clause was a separate agreement or to extract from silent texts a set of 'general principles of law' whose writing no one had ever witnessed;[50] in short, to exercise all the prerogatives of the technique of *fictio legis* which, by means of 'praetorian glosses', ensured that the citizenry mistook bladders for lanterns.[51] Clearly, nothing could be more disturbing from the viewpoint of scientists, who are concerned to build as much reality as possible into their statements, than this capacity to invent everything anew. One could detect in this model the horrendous notion of 'social construction', a spectre summoned up by sociologists so as to scare epistemologists by threatening that all quests for the truth end up in a locked room where a secret ballot is held to decide what will henceforth *count as* the truth. But, in the same way as an expert has nothing in common with real scientific work, so social construction manufactured behind closed doors has nothing in common with real legal elaboration.

Once again, the advantages of not confusing the distinct features of these quite specific forms of enunciation become clear. Just as scientists can indulge in all kinds of moods, being as passionate or partial as they like, because the laboratory object occupies the same

[50] See Braibant, *Le Droit administratif français* (1992): 'the judge does not create those principles, but discovers and formulates them. He extrapolates them sometimes from precedents applied to specific cases. Sometimes he creates them slowly, by successive moves, before giving them a solemn form' (p. 213); and Ewald, 'Une expérience foucaldienne' (1986).

[51] But *fictio* has in law a very precise meaning – see Thomas, '*Fictio Legis*' (1995) – which is always difficult to focus without giving it either too little or too much solidity. See the dispute around the 'arrêt Perruche' in Cayla and Thomas, *Du droit de ne pas naître* (2002).

place as a legal text or a binding precedent, so, by contrast, lawyers can indulge a power to invent fictions, and to introduce what they call 'constructive solutions', because, precisely, in making their decisions they have no object, or no objectity, to deal with. What is so shocking about the fantastic image of 'social construction' is that it applies a model of legal decision-making to scientific objects: in which case, of course the special prowess of adjudication does indeed turn into a cynical nightmare of arbitrariness. But the point is precisely to avoid confusing the two things. Indeed, our attempt at clarification seeks to remove from science the power to have the last word which was entrusted to it in error or through cowardice, and to encourage it to resume the construction of those referential chains whose continual movement loads them with information that is more and more reliable, more and more precise, and more and more capable of sustaining discussion. On the other hand, if legal enunciation is relieved of the impossible task of transporting information and uttering the truth, it is left free to circulate through the fine channels of that very particular kind of vehicle, which is the only one capable of freighting and transporting those priceless commodities that are known as 'means*', 'qualifications', 'obligations' and 'decisions'.

It would, thus, be quite wrong to draw a contrast between science, set against an intangible reality that resists all attempts to manipulate it, and which cannot be twisted in accordance with our desires, and law, which, because it consists only in words and consensus interpretations reached in a closed hearing, can say whatever it likes so long as it is authorized to have the last word.[52] Law has its own resistance, its own solidity, rigidity or positivity, and even its own objectivity, which, despite the admission that it is constructed, has no need to be envious of scientific realism. We know that scientists speak the truth about phenomena precisely because they can manipulate, transform and test them in thousands of ways, and because they can use experimental techniques to insinuate themselves into the most intimate details of their material existence. It is precisely because reality is not intangible, and because it bears no relation to the 'matters of fact' imagined by epistemology, that science can speak quite faithfully about reality. It is therefore pointless to distinguish science and law in terms of the differences between objects and signs, hard and soft, unquestionable and arbitrary. If *res judicata* are not to be (mis)taken for the truth, the point is not that this justifies some form of cynicism, but that it has *better things to do* than mimic or approximate to the

---

[52] This is the weakness of the term 'legitimate', overused by sociologists to misunderstand both law and society: see Favereau, 'L'économie du sociologue' (2001).

scientific truth: it has to produce justice, and declare the law, in accordance with the existing state of the texts, taking into account the precedent, with no arbiter other than the judges, who have no one to judge for them.

It might be said that this simply revives the old distinction between judgments of fact and judgments of value. We would be more inclined to see this distinction itself as the echo of something invented by the great seventeenth-century English philosophers, who, for reasons which were largely political, inappropriately crossed law with the emerging laboratory sciences.[53] Indeed, it is strange to note that the scenography of empiricism borrows the definition of a fact from judges so as to apply it to science, whereas, as we have seen, it in no way defines the articulation between researchers and their objects. In the empiricists' imagination, raw facts, the essential 'data' or 'sense data', have the peculiar virtue of being both insignificant and incontrovertible.[54] They constitute the raw material of judgment, which gets under way by ordering them, associating and combining them in the human mind. But isn't this precisely the relationship that jurists have to the facts, which have to be defined as quickly as possible so as to move on to what really matters, namely, processes of qualification or scholarly explanation? But in what laboratory would one find a researcher dealing with simple 'sense data'? Only an empiricist could imagine that the articulation between a scientific article and what it describes could be anything like this extravagant division between that which is questionable and that which is unquestionable. Once it is recognized that the very definition of 'raw facts' is a strange hybrid of law and science, it becomes easier to understand how the virtues of distance, indifference, detachment or disinterestedness, which characterize the work of judges, came to migrate to the scientist, or to the quite improbable and highly politicized historical figure of the expert, who has the capacity to bring discussion to an end by arrogating to himself the power to bind or unbind by delegating the issue to 'matters of fact'.[55] This is a deviation from the careful work of scientific research, but it is an even greater derailing of law, which only allowed itself to bring discussion to an end precisely because it could *not* delegate the task of ending a dispute to any authority other than its own fragile immanence. By means of this spectacular manoeu-

---

[53] See the role of Boyle in this cross-over, as narrated in Shapin and Schaffer, *Leviathan and the Air-Pump* (1985).

[54] Poovey, *History of Modern Fact* (1999). In spite of what Kant believed in his *Critique*, judgment and knowledge are quite incompatible.

[55] For a full treatment of the argument, see Latour, *Politics of Nature* (2004).

vre, empiricism led us to confound the virtues of politics, science and law in a Gordian knot, thereby turning those virtues into vices.

The seventeenth-century representation of matters of fact was based on the suppression of something which is now being brought to our attention more and more insistently, namely the common etymology that links things and cases, causes to causes, thing and *Ding*. By a strange inversion, and as a result of being bombarded by states of affairs coming from the social world, scientific objects have once again become cases that are subject to common discussion in a Parliament or a courtroom.[56] Having emerged from the courtroom, or at least from those extraordinary forums which preceded courts, the two etymological genealogies had gradually become separated by the supposed distinction between the arbitrary discussions of judges and the supreme tribunal of experts speaking in the name of incontrovertible facts, beyond any human affair, trial or plea. But, having extended laboratory life to all of our collective existence, it seems that, as the project of modernism gradually exhausts itself, there is now no fact that is not also a cause or a claim: all matters of fact have become *matters of concern*. That is why it is all the more important, now that former matters of fact have been restored to their common origins, not to confuse the characters of science and law. Clearly, in order to deal with matters of concern that are so intermeshed, it is hopeless to characterize the work of scientists in terms of what was nothing more than the usurpation of legal or political authority, just as it is impossible to demand that lawyers replace scientific enunciation. What modernism had distinguished by the *nature* of the two domains – incontrovertible facts on the one hand and, on the other, negotiable values – without paying proper attention to the different tasks of the scientists and lawyers, should now be redistributed by the nature of the two jobs of jurists and scientists who have to tackle conjointly the same matters of concern. It is precisely because there are no longer two distinct domains of reality, that we should be all the more careful in distinguishing the complementary functions of lawyers and of researchers. It is now essential that science should not be asked to *judge*, and that law should not be asked to pronounce *truth*.

That would be to confuse the last of the features which distinguishes these two modes of attachment: whereas scientific research can engage with the turbulent or violent history of innovation and controversy, a history that is continually being renewed, law has a

---

[56] See the important work of clarification carried out by Hermitte, *Le sang et le droit* (1996).

homeostatic quality which is produced by the obligation to keep the fragile tissue of rules and texts intact, and to ensure that one is understood by everyone at all times. A premium is put on legal stability but there is no such thing as scientific stability. Scientists, once they have added their own particular pebble to the edifice of a discipline, might well see themselves in the role of Samson shaking the columns of the temple, overturning paradigms, overthrowing common sense and bankrupting old theories. Legists, even when they make an especially daring argument for overturning established precedents, have to secure the integrity of the legal edifice, continuity in the exercise of power and smoothness in the application of the law.[57] Science can tolerate gaps, but the law has to be seamless.[58] Science can draw on lively controversy, but the law has to restore an equilibrium. Although one might speak admiringly of 'revolutionary science', 'revolutionary laws' have always been as terrifying as courts with emergency powers. As one interviewee suggested, 'Our first concern is for stability; we have to plough a furrow that is as straight and as deep as possible, because litigants expect coherence and transparency.' All those aspects of law that common sense finds so irritating – its tardiness, its taste for tradition, its occasionally reactionary attitudes – are essential to law's functioning. Like the Fates, the law holds in its hand the fine thread of the whole set of judgments, texts and precedents, which cannot be broken without lapsing into a denial of justice. Whereas the scientist can satisfy herself with partial information because she knows that the power of her instruments will enable other scientists, at some point in the future, to refine the science and extend the chains of reference, a judge has to ensure that holes are repaired immediately, that tears are darned without delay, gaps filled and cases resolved. Whereas the fabric of science extends everywhere but leaves a lot of voids, rather like a lace cloth, the fabric of law has to cover everything completely and seamlessly. Two entirely different ways to cover the whole world.

[57] There is a huge difference between a paradigm shift as described by Kuhn, *The Structure of Scientific Revolutions* (1962), and a change in case-law as described, for instance, by L Berre, *Les revirements de jurisprudence en droit administratif* (1999).

[58] The Code Civil in its article 4 states that the judge cannot use the obscurity of the law as a pretext for abstaining from deciding a case.

6

Talking of law?

In which we submit to the prevailing figures of explanation and theorization – where the author thinks he has to explain the limits of his approach and the eminently particular nature of his field – In which he tries to prove why one cannot avoid talking of law in general terms – In which the author, forgetting all moderation, undertakes a definition of law

The dangers of exoticism

'A Huron in the Palais-Royal' is the title of a well-known article by Jean Rivero, in which the institution submits itself to the 'anthropological gaze' of one of its members, laughing at its own shortcomings, its odd ways, and entertaining itself with the show of its own strangeness.[1] It's true that the Council lends itself rather well to this slight distance that the ethnologist could adopt as well to do his job of describing and analysing. Montesquieu's *Lettres persanes* genre always has its little effect, especially since administrative law is not something with which the general public is familiar; in the average French person's eyes it seems as distant as the rules of Bantu marriage or Earth of Fire initiation ceremonies. As for the Council of State, the ethnographer did not meet a single outside person, throughout his entire study, who knew it well enough to say more than a few words on its missions – apart from professional jurists, of course.

[1] Rivero, 'Le Huron au Palais-Royal' (1962).

Thus, everything seems to facilitate the work of the researcher, who may believe himself to be authorized to speak of tribes, rituals, sacrifices, symbols and mysteries regarding the State counsellors and their esoteric practices. Does ethnology not bear in its very etymology this *ethnos*, this people, this culture whose study is supposed to be the actual subject of the discipline? Is the ethnographer not the one who compares cultures by identifying their distinctive features?

Yet once the jokes are over and the derisive smiles have been wiped off people's faces, this type of attitude may lead to nothing but the despicable form of exoticism that is called Occidentalism. By combining his inquiry with a distancing, the ethnographer of contemporary societies simply reproduces the sins of former anthropology which studied other peoples only because of their distance. Even if the Palais-Royal seems strange to us, we must refuse this cheap foreignness, like the mirages of Orientalism and the intricacies of unfathomable Asia. To do his work, the ethnographer cannot be content to treat his contemporaries, his closest neighbours, *as badly* as distant peoples have been treated until now; that is, by studying them in the mode of culture and trying to find myths, rituals, symbolic behaviours and other sub-conscious structures for them. By turning his hitherto distant gaze to the present, the researcher will realize that, as an ethnographer, he has nothing to say about contemporary societies; nothing in his toolbox withstands proximity; any semblance of explanatory power that he had over foreigners depended entirely on the infinite distance at which he maintained them so over-accommodatingly. If it wants to study its own world, anthropology will have to agree to re-equip itself entirely, like an explorer who goes off on an expedition to the tropics and who, by a stroke of fate, is forced to discover the North Cape fjords.

The reason for this weakness of ethnography withdrawn into itself is no longer all that difficult to grasp. To compare different, equally distant, interesting and curious cultures, it was necessary for their particularities to be set against an unquestionable background, like masks from diverse origins on the white wall of a primitive art museum. As we know, the white wall is nature – or rather, *it was* nature: the universal source of agreement that constituted the common base of physical anthropology and against which the singular features of a particular culture could stand out starkly.[2] If it seemed that

---

[2] On all these points of symmetrical anthropology, see Latour, *We Have Never Been Modern* (1993). For a reconstruction of the anthropology of natures, see Descola and Palsson (eds.), *Nature and Society* (1996), and Descola, *Par delà nature et culture* (2005).

modern societies would never be able to be studied by anthropologists (except on their fringes, where eccentric peoples exist), it was because they generated nature in the three forms of scientific objectiveness, technical effectiveness and economic profitability. The whole world was composed of cultures, *except* those ones. Fortunately, nature has started to become scarce in the past few years. The white wall of museums has darkened, chipped, cracked; it has become as complicated, heterogeneous and entangled, as rich, sometimes as beautiful, as the objects that were supposed to be hung on it. Let's say that nature no longer provides the unquestionable basis on which cultures can be made comparable, by way of contrast. Neither objectiveness nor effectiveness nor profitability have withstood the investigations of the anthropology of science, techniques and markets. There is no longer a nature but many natures or, in other words, elaborations of the pluriverse. It therefore becomes possible to study contemporary societies, but from an entirely different viewpoint from that of exoticism: and *nor* do they appear as cultures submitted to the ethnographer's gaze.

A new question is then raised, which has nothing to do with distance or proximity: how can constructions of the world be made *comparable*, now that the nature–cultures relationship no longer allows for appropriate relations to be established? My reason for investigating law was to answer this question, and not to turn the body of the Palais-Royal into a micro-culture comparable to others, for example to that of the National Assembly[3] or the laboratories of the CERN.[4] If Western societies no longer define themselves in terms of a privileged relationship with nature, which sets them aside from other peoples left in their state of cultures 'among others', and if it is impossible to treat the West as a particular culture without exoticizing it, then it is necessary to find an alternative capable of showing up the new contrasts that no longer evoke cultures to be compared against a unified background. It is this project, started with the anthropology of science, techniques and markets, that is continued here with the anthropology of law: contemporary societies have to reanalyse their own differences without referring to either the over-rapid unity of nature or the over-easy diversity of cultures. Let them

[3] We can usefully compare the results of the present study with Marc Abelès's attempt to 'ethnologize' French Members of Parliament by means of the usual tools used to study 'savages' – Abelès, *Un ethnologue à l'Assemblée* (2000) – tools that are reduced to notions of myths, rites and symbols.
[4] The difference is clear between a classical cultural anthropology and that which takes 'multinaturalism' seriously – Galison, *Image and Logic* (1997), and Knorr-Cetina, *Epistemic Cultures* (1999).

express their contrasts in their own terms and according to their own categories. If they became capable of describing again what they had that was theirs, they could resume more egalitarian and interesting relations with the 'others'. But those others would have become, dare I say, *otherwise* others; they would no longer have to choose between remaining cultures or moving closer to nature, that is, universal objectivity, efficiency, profitability. Anthropology would then become the master of ceremonies, the 'chargé de protocole' of a worldwide diplomacy under the aegis of which contracts, started so disastrously in the era of conquests and empires, could be resumed.[5]

I therefore use the term 'anthropology' here not in the sense of a vaguely ironical return to an attitude of distancing; instead, it refers to a study started all over again, in our own societies, of what it is that defines modernization now that nature is no longer enough to do so, and that might enable us to discover the contrasts which really interest us and without which we would no longer – in our opinion – be human. If we have never been modern, what has happened to us? Anthropology cannot be a human *science* without again running the risk of defining the human, the *anthropos*. Once these contrasts have been revived, we will be able to return to the negotiating table with other peace proposals: 'Here, in our opinion, is what constitutes *our* humanity; what about yours?' That is why exoticism is a bad research method as well as a political mistake; it causes one to be wrong about oneself as well as about others. Far from turning our gaze to peripheral, amusing, archaic or quaint aspects of these modern societies, far from forcing them to remain in the narrow frame of rituals and symbols, we should search for what lies at their core: science, techniques, the market and, of course, law.[6] The comparison is no longer between cultures, or between cultures and nature, but between contrasts: 'If you force us to lose the difference between this and that form of existence, life is no longer worth living.' This is a matter not of calm comparison, but of risky *negotiation*. How, for example, do we answer the question of the universality of law, if we don't know, in our own terms, in what form law exists *at home*? How can we claim to impose the reign of law, the rule of law, 'everywhere', if we have no idea of the veritable mode of existence of our own rule of law?

---

[5] On this key concept of diplomacy as an ideal of the social sciences, see Stengers, *Cosmopolitiques*, vol. VII (1997); Latour, 'War of the Worlds' (2002c).

[6] This is obviously the weakness of this 'anthropology of contemporary worlds' that anthropology claims to do while studying only the fringes: Augé, *Pour une anthropologie des mondes contemporains* (1994).

We see that, thus defined, the ethnography of law resembles the ethnography of science. When, in the absence of anthropology of scientific and technical practices, the concept of a universal scientific objectivity and industrial efficiency reigned without being questioned, it was totally impossible to start something like a negotiation. From the outset, the 'others' were reduced to nothing before they even opened their mouths – unless they became 'the same' through education, Westernization or modernization. In the meantime, until this integration had taken place, they could only have more or less 'symbolic representations' of 'nature' as known by 'Science' – representations that could be respected with hypocritical condescension, especially since we knew just how unrelated to things themselves they actually were. Tolerating those whom we have deprived of access to ontology requires little effort. Yet there would have been no point in exoticizing science by considering scientists as savages and experiments as rituals. We cannot, without mistaking our target, do *cultural* anthropology of *nature*! It was better to completely revise our thinking, on the basis of new research, about what sort of strange beast lived in the West under the name of objective science.[7] And we soon realized that there was not much connection between universal Science – notwithstanding the fact that it had always served as a yardstick in encounters with other peoples who were thus deprived, by opposition, of objective knowledge – and the otherwise fascinating anthropological reality of Western science. Faced with Science, cultures had no option but to abdicate; faced with the new image that the West gives of its multiple interlinking sciences as it painfully withdraws from the modernist parenthesis, negotiations can be resumed. Their outcome has in any case become *uncertain* once again.

We can imagine that the same might be true for law.[8] To be sure, the question is less difficult than in the case of science, for whereas

---

[7] The same applies to studies – unfortunately less developed – of that other monster, the market, which bears no more resemblance to economic theory than science does to epistemology. See Callon (ed.), *The Laws of the Market* (1998).

[8] In a book filled with ideas, Denys de Béchillon, thinking that he was founding the anthropology of law on an obvious fact, attests to the extent to which jurists' ethnocentrism precludes even the beginning of negotiations on the nature of law. *'The only general certainty:* norms, all norms, are constructions *of the mind*, objects of a *purely* mental nature, products of the *human* psyche. The production of rules is an *act of* thought, and therefore has to be analysed *first* by means of tools suited to activities of the mind' (Béchillon, *Qu'est-ce qu'une règle de droit?* (1997), p. 109) (my italics). The 'only certainty' is, in my opinion, exactly the reverse; if we want to do a little anthropology of law, we first have to accept that no culture has ever reduced the rule, the law, punishment and justice to something cognitive, to a mere

we can't talk of 'local science' without declaring war, everyone can recognize in others a legal order, albeit entirely different. When the term 'anthropology of law' is pronounced no one draws their gun, whereas they shoot even before the words 'anthropology of science' have been uttered. Although there has been talk about 'wars of science',[9] the idea of a 'war of law' would seem meaningless, for dreams of judicial universality have never been as great as projects for scientific, industrial or economic unification. It is from law that, since Montaigne and Pascal, we have taken the canonical terms of an honest relativism that weights both differences and similarities: 'true this side of the Alps and false beyond'. It is, moreover, from comparative law that the first anthropologists learned to respect differences. In other words, legal pluralism is part of law whereas until recently there was no such thing as scientific pluralism.[10] In laws there is something that lends itself to comparison without immediately arousing horror. One can always say: 'You proceed like that in your country, oh, that's so interesting; in our country we proceed like this.' What is true in the rules of inheritance or penal law would not apply to gravity. Whereas it would be difficult for biologists to recognize the same physiology as their own in traditional cures, simply practised with different rules, nothing prevents the English Lords Justice, responsible for cases against the Crown,[11] to recognize in the Council of State a practice that certainly warrants the name of law, even if nothing can cross the Channel without hours of laborious translation. Everyone agrees that, for law, a *translation* can cover the difference – something which in science would seem not only impossible but even scandalous. The ethnologist can therefore hope to highlight the contrasts of law without triggering the same shock as when he is dealing with science; he can hope to weave between relativism and universalism without verging on exoticism. In other words, law has

---

human contrivance. Objectivity, the outside presence of the rule, even in 'our societies', even in positivism: these are the decisive elements to take into account. Starting the negotiation by demanding that all peoples agree to see law as something mental is a renewal, in the form of an unquestionable obviousness, of the imperialism that we claim to be leaving behind us.

[9] Jurdant, *Impostures intellectuelles* (1998).

[10] That is the usefulness of the principles of analysis and tolerance developed by Rouland, *Aux confins du Droit* (1991).

[11] Only recently, which is a good argument for the Council of State. It took 150 years for English law to guarantee citizens the same freedom to prosecute the state as in French law (Freedman, *The Conseil d'Etat in Modern France* (1961)). See the work of Carol Harlow at the London School of Economics, in comparative administrative law (Harlow, '"La huronne au Palais-Royal" or a Naive Perspective on Administrative Law' (2000)).

suffered less from the ravages of modernism; it has kept to itself, in its habits, its slowness, even its techniques and its vocabulary, something that is more easily made the stuff of anthropology.[12] If legists are so often made fun of, it is because they have never really been modern . . .

There is nevertheless some exoticism left, against which the observer has found himself cornered by reactions in his field, despite his efforts and good intentions. Contrary to all the new rules on relations between researchers and respondents, which always require a more or less stable form of equality,[13] he has found himself in the archaic position of the invisible fly, forced to watch from afar as human beings move about before it. Never, in his long career, had he done research among people with so little interest in his study, its consequences and possible feedback – with the exception of course of his tutors and guarantors. Never, in fact, had he participated in an institution with so little concern about being studied, so indifferent to outside scrutiny. Whereas the Trobriandais read Malinowski from their primary school years, the Torres Strait islanders celebrate the anniversary of the missionaries' arrival as the 'Day of Light', the Achuars guide green tourists through their forests chanting passages from Descola's 'The Spears of Twilight', the Council of State seems to consider any study in the human sciences, the anthropology of law, administrative science and even legal doctrine with the same aloof indifference as Jane Goodall's chimpanzees considered articles on primatology! There is something so extreme in this that it had to be turned into a field datum, a feature of the landscape to describe: how can a contemporary institution, at the heart of the State, remain so unreflexive when everything is shaking around it? 'What is the point of serving something that no longer serves any purpose?' wondered Régis Debray when he haughtily resigned from the Council.[14]

Yet there should be no lack of worries for this prestigious institution: we know that half of the Council's work consists in processing cases that many say the judiciary could do just as well and even better. The slowness of procedures, the absence until recently of an effective emergency appeal,[15] and the notorious absence of application of

---

[12] See the excellent example of Strathern, *Property, Substance and Effect* (1999).
[13] This is what Michel Callon calls 'reflexive institutions', which enter into a totally different relationship with the social sciences, compared to the former observer–observed relationship (Callon, 'Ni intellectuel engagé, ni intellectuel dégagé' (1999)).
[14] Debray, *Loués soient nos seigneurs* (1996), p. 590.
[15] Colcombet, 'Rapport . . . relatif au référé devant les juridictions administratives' (1999).

decisions could all leave prevailing doubt as to the effectiveness of administrative law. The other half of its mission, in the Counsel Sections, consists in polishing texts that hardly seem to resemble counsel and, as Kessler pointed out over thirty years ago: 'they waver between questions of general opportunity and judicial amendments'[16] – since the government could always ignore the Council's corrections. In these two main functions the Council is only reactive, waiting for the government to submit texts to it or for plaintiffs to trigger proceedings. In the Supreme Court market, competition is also stiff: the Constitutional Council, guardian of the law, reduces the Council of State's role to little more than verifying the legality of decrees; the Cassation, for the judiciary branch, in many instances, seems more open, more generous and liberal than it; and the European courts more and more often get the better of it, as supreme decisions have to a large extent been shifted from Paris to Luxembourg, Strasbourg and The Hague. Even when everything works well, when cases don't drag on for too long, there is always a nagging doubt on the effectiveness of its rulings, for once it has been sentenced the administration often remains as passive as stone. More seriously, the State that the Council of State advises resembles that of Napoleon, Clemenceau or de Gaulle no more closely than it resembles that of Constantin. The European 'machine' which has moved to Brussels has retained none of the features of the French-style administration: neither the textual habits, nor the sense of the public good, nor the relationship with law are the same; yet its decisions take precedence. As Debray also said: 'the Council of State is a place of excellence, but there needs to be a State to counsel . . .'.[17] And now the lower administrative courts and especially their appeal courts have started to deal with most of the interesting cases, thus reducing the Council's work to mere *cassation* with far less variety than before.

It may be said that they are still in the business of giving opinions, which the Council can issue at the government's request, some of which are noteworthy, like the one on the Islamic headscarf. But how can these opinions be properly made if the Council is cut off from all social science, with hardly any link to the universities, even those specialized in administrative law, without any contact with political scientists, anthropologists or philosophers of law, or even with the doctrine elaborated by academic jurists? Is it possible that French

---

[16] Kessler, *Le Conseil d'Etat* (1968), p. 292.

[17] Debray, *Loués soient nos seigneurs* (1996), p. 590. His former colleagues responded to his remark by pointing out, somewhat cruelly, that the former revolutionary lacked all the qualities of patience that it takes to make a good administrative judge.

intellectual life is so weak that nothing can be lost in by-passing it? In short, in the eyes of the fly, compelled by its informers' indifference to remain on the wall, the Council is in a period of crisis, or at least it should be. The State is busy disappearing, swallowed up by Europe, liberalism, regulation and globalization. Incapable of reforming itself, it produces evidence of its inefficiency daily. It needs to be overhauled, yet its adviser, its guardian, its mentor, its Cato insists on pretending that nothing is wrong! To deal with such a major crisis, the institution should be buzzing with clubs, think-tanks and commissions, all drawing on everything that, in politics, in administrative science, in doctrine, in management, in the media and at the National National School of Administration should make it possible to reinvent the State along with its behaviour, principles, structure and missions. Whereas it should be devouring the research proposals that it receives from political scientists, all that can be heard in the corridors of the Palais-Royal are the wheels of hand-trucks carrying heavy files, pushed from room to room by the bailiffs. Whereas the judiciary has undergone immense change, administrative law seems unconcerned about its future.[18] Not the slightest think-tank, even merely informal, on the crisis of the Council of State – the very word 'crisis' seems to shock: crisis? what crisis? – instead, a magnificent bicentenary, an unqualified celebration of the self, a flawless confidence.[19] In the final analysis, the symbol with which we started the first chapter (see p. 2) was well chosen: a magnificent piece of architrave, floating in the sky, proudly linked to nothing.

Yet it seems obvious that, like dancing the tango, it takes two to diagnose a crisis. There was little point in the ethnographer – unless he resorted to a unilateral critical discourse – studying the Council of State with a tone of decline as if the State were sinking before his eyes, even if that may have produced some handsome effects of exoticism, like a sort of *Tristes tropiques* in the heart of Paris. In the absence of partners *inside*, interested in a reflexive use of the social sciences, it was better for the eye of the fly to move on to

---

[18] See, for example, a useful clarification in Karpik, 'L'avancée politique de la justice' (1997).

[19] For example, in an interview with someone who came through 'the outside way' in mid-career: 'One way of showing that one is worthy is to show that one understands the rules without the rules ever being spoken. The institution functions like that; it would lose something if it clarified things about itself; and this is not a question of hypocrisy, it's not that there are skeletons in the cupboard; no, *it's better if things aren't said*; the clarification of rules of functioning would lead to a paradox.' It is difficult to embark on the adventure of reflexive institutions with such principles.

something else, to drop the institution of the Council of State as such and to concentrate on its legal work, by assuming somewhat daringly that even an organ in a state of latent crisis could afford ideal access to the legal way of telling truth. That is why the readers will have found no administrative or political comment in these pages, no evaluation of the actual role and function of the Council, no measurement of its real place in the State. Unable to enter into a relationship of connivance, I have extracted the legal work from the institution like a physiologist might have extracted bone marrow from a dog, knowing full well that it was not the entire animal. To study the Council of State, I have disregarded the State – and willingly acknowledge the paradox. This was the only way of resisting the exoticism imposed on the ethnographer by those indifferent to his study.

For my project I have found only advantages in this situation – even if it seems absurd for a political scientist or evaluator of public policies. At the Council the law is presented in a particularly purified form: the procedures all exist in writing; in the different Administrative Sections all the branches of law can be found; the work is collective and collegial and can therefore be studied without too much difficulty by the observer who, once introduced, disturbs no one and is spared from making careless assumptions on internal debates or on the judges' innermost beliefs, for everything is said in front of him; the blood and guts of penal law are not distractive; no barrister waving his arms about dramatically disrupts the amendment of texts. If an opportunity exists to study 'pure' law, it is clearly the one offered by the Council. I therefore limited myself strictly to taking advantage of the review meetings to see how empirical methods could serve to further the broader project of an anthropology of Western forms of veracity applied to the particular case of law.[20]

---

[20] To my great surprise, I found very few precise empirical descriptions on the making of the law. What we could antiphrase as 'descriptive legal epistemology' – Atias, *Science des légistes, savoir des juristes* (1993) – is as undescriptive as it is epistemological. Even semiotics usually remains programmatic, apart from Greimas who, like Landowski, 'Vérité et vérédiction en droit' (1988), limits himself to published texts without any focus on interlocution. Not surprisingly, it is in ethnomethodology that the most detailed attention to the formatting of law is found (Travers and Manzo, *Law in Action* (1977), Lynch and Bogen, *The Spectacle of History* (1996)), but it concerns the application of the law to facts, rather than the birth of law itself. A little higher upstream, in Parliament and the Ministries, one finds useful studies on law-making, for instance Lascoumes, *Au nom de l'ordre* (1989).

A strange form of autonomy

Assuming that he avoided talking about the State, would the ethnographer know enough to talk about 'the Law'?[21] Is the Council under investigation not so particular, its forms of litigation so original, administrative law so different from the other branches of law, the position of the litigants so strange,[22] the judges so different from the others, that it would be impossible to draw any conclusions whatsoever on the nature or the essence of legal activity? Is the anthropologist not in danger of judging *ultra petita*, the theoretician's favourite sin? Yet the members whose hesitations I studied in detail relentlessly refer to something that is supposed to be Law, 'le Droit', and constantly question the quality of their relationship with that object of value. Even if they are not reflexive in the somewhat facile sense expected by the observer, one cannot deny that the counsellors are reflexive on the limits, the quality and the force of their function as judges. We have followed many examples of this.[23] It therefore seems that in order to finish this work, questions on the nature of Law in general cannot be avoided, under the pretext that they are too broad, since these considerations serve as resources for the actors themselves to explore everything, even the very quality of their judgments. This does not mean that they are going to question themselves seriously and in every respect on the nature of the Law – on the contrary, on several occasions we have noticed that underlying problems are considered as trivial as they are philosophical – but rather that invoking the Law *as a totality* is part of the subject that I have decided to report on. As semioticians would put it, the Law with a capital 'L' is the unquestionable *addresser* of all their speech acts.[24] While the question of scientific method only rarely arises in researchers' talk (where it has a decorative, polemical, educational role), doing law, speaking law and remaining within the limits of the law appear to

[21] Remember that Law with a capital 'L' is a way to translate in English the French word 'le droit' that is clearly distinct from 'la loi'. For once French has more words than English.

[22] All the commentators of this text who were from the judiciary were surprised by this feature of administrative law – 'it seems that the applicant is an intruder, that he is there simply to afford an opportunity to change the administration', 'it is a judge who makes the power tolerable for the citizens' – which a counsellor eagerly confirms: 'Yes, the judge is an administrator (of human passions). He does not produce the new rule of law out of industrious fervour or intellectual fever; he does so because he is surrounded by litigants *and he can't get rid of them*' (my emphasis).

[23] For example, in episodes on pp. 49, 59, 26.

[24] Greimas, 'Analyse sémiotique d'un discours juridique' (1976) – by opposition to the addressee to which the discourse is sent.

be among the characteristics of the legal beast itself. In other words: what is the *vinculum juris*? – this is what we need to understand.[25]

It is as if there were no degrees in law: either one is fully into it, or one is not in it at all and begins to talk about other things. Its conditions of felicity and infelicity have particularly abrupt limits. The ethnographer noticed this many times, by becoming aware for example of his own stuttering, of the extent to which it was impossible for him, even after several years of familiarization, to get gradually closer to the legal utterance. To speak the law he lacked not only words and concepts, but everything, absolutely everything. To legally state something, he would have had to become a State counsellor.[26] There are undefined degrees of scientificity but the law is entirely present or entirely absent. One can babble about science without being a researcher, but one cannot talk about law without being a lawyer. This is evidenced in the somewhat desperate efforts of commentators – of whom there are many – to define Law:[27] any attempted definition, as rough or sophisticated as it may be, always ends up resorting to the adjective 'legal' to qualify it. Whether one is trying to establish it in terms of bills, rules, sanctions, authority, the common good, the monopoly on violence, or the State, it is necessary every time to specify 'provided that they are legally valid'. To describe Law convincingly, one has to have already leapt into it. In other words, an inevitable *tautology* is part and parcel of the definition of Law.[28]

[25] This is the expression of Tarde in *Les transformations du droit* (1893 [1994]).

[26] Conversely, it was so difficult to talk of the thing itself without belonging to the judges' profession, that it was very difficult for him not to say 'we have judged' when he was talking of a case in 'his' sub-section. He had never even thought of saying, when studying scientists performing experiments, that 'we have proved the existence of this phenomenon'. The strength of belonging to a profession does not have the same effect on the speech acts.

[27] As in negative theology, there is even a sort of *apophatic* legal theory: 'The law', explains Atias, 'is neither constitutive, nor creative, nor declarative. It neither recognizes, nor consecrates, nor attributes, nor sanctions. These are only apparent effects of the implementation of the law [. . .] The question is whether law has something specific': Atias, *Philosophie du droit* (1999), p. 293.

[28] An example among many can be found in Carbonnier, *Flexible droit* (1998): 'One simply has to recall the classical definition of the *legal* act: a manifestation of will that is intended to produce *legal* effects, alterations in the *legal* organization; in other words, that is intended to introduce a human relationship into the sphere of *law*' (p. 35, my emphasis). Another example is found in Hart, *The Concept of Law* (1997): 'In the case of rules *of law*, this foreseeable consequence [the sanction] is clearly determined and officially organized, whereas in the case of *non judicial* rules, even if the same hostile reaction to deviation is probable, it is not organized and its nature is not defined' (p. 23); and 'Such rules *of law* do not imply duties or obligations. Instead, they provide individuals with the *means* to fulfil their intentions, by endowing them with the *legal power* to create, through *determined procedures* and

This tautological feature seems so constituent of the thing itself that one finds it in the two main schools of thought, jusnaturalism and positivism which, as we know, provide polar-opposite definitions of the foundations of Law. Each in its own way – despite the great divides that seem to oppose them – simply repeats firmly that Law is 'always already present'. Either, like the jusnaturalists, we take as a base the existence of a law that *precedes* all positive law or, on the contrary, we decide, like the positivists, to recognize as law only that which has *already* been defined by a legally constituted authority. In neither case can one go beyond law and establish it on some hetero-geneous foundation. For the first school, a nature exists over and above laws, but this nature is already judicial to the extent that it could in principle be used to rectify positive law;[29] for the others, there is nothing above the rule of law, other than a pyramid of posi-tive laws, the famous hierarchy of norms of which the extremity must, by construction, still be Law.[30] One could say that for these two schools, which differ in every other respect, there is no possible and progressive genesis of the Law. For a reason that seems essential to its nature, the commentators, jurists and philosophers of law have a particular form of *autochthony* that precludes a mundane genealogy being found for it. Law always has to be already born.

The ethnographer is, of course, not equipped to treat such sublime questions; he can address them only indirectly, with the methods, limits and data of his field work. But there is a feature, easy to identify in the cases that we have encountered, which could explain this neces-sity for tautology, so present among legists: in each of these examples the Law is found in its entirety. Law is fractal. In other words, it seems that there is law when it is possible to mobilize a certain form of totality with regard to an individual case, irrespective of how tiny

---

in certain conditions, structures *of rights* and duties within the *limits* of the coercive apparatus *of the law*' (p. 45, my emphasis). One can hardly be more tautological! Luhmann would go so far as to claim that this tautology is a sociological necessity (see below).

[29] Although the jusnaturalists have never really been able to define the exact resem-blance between the founding natural law and the established positive law, which is hardly surprising considering that it would amount to confusing the reference chains of the sciences with legal sequences. On this point, see the preceding chapter on the notion of superimposition. If it does exist, natural law is as mute as the unfounded foundations of positive law.

[30] Even with the notion of *Grundnorm* in Kelsen, clearly explained by Béchillon, *Qu'est-ce qu'une règle de droit?* (1997): 'Kelsen does not assume that a fundamental norm "exists" in the positive judicial order; he simply states that we absolutely need to use the fiction of a fundamental norm if we want to consider the Constitution [the peak of the pyramid] as a legal norm' (p. 234).

it may be – and this is precisely why we call some reasoning 'legal'.[31] When, in the preceding chapters, we discussed the transit of law, when we defined it as a movement of interconnection of a specific case with a corpus of texts, when we stressed the hesitation of the judges who may lose interest due to all the micro-procedures of the Council, when we examined how the corpus of precedents ended up absorbing individual cases, we covered some of the mechanisms through which a particular conflict ended up *involving* the totality. The literal and not metaphorical totality: in a few steps, via several translations, an obscure affair of expulsion of foreigners, of dustbins, of municipalities, ended up being linked, connected, to all administrative law, the Constitution, the General Principles of Law, the Human Rights Convention, as well as the decrees of François I or the letters patent of Louis XIV. Henceforth, if you touch Mr Cayzeele's dustbin, this date of opening of the hunting season, this building permit, these water rights '*fondés en titre*', you will, by means of the administrative courts and the Council of State, via a string of lawyers and judges, end up by also stirring the immense seamless web of relations, of all relations, already established and validated, codified and enforced. It may even occur that, due to some reversal of jurisprudence, this obscure case might end up being embedded in wider general principles that will for years to come define our common existence and serve others, later, in defending their weak personal claims.

Is this not moreover what common sense understands as 'legal protection': that everyone helps everyone else; that the torments of some alter the condition of the lives of all? What do we actually mean when force is contrasted with law, if not that the former cannot establish this interweaving of the local and the global that only the latter can achieve? If we take the proverbial contrast between thugs threatening you with a baseball bat and a police officer threatening you with his truncheon, we can morph from one situation to the other without any solution of continuity, through all the (regrettably all-too-frequent) cases in between, by gradually increasing the quality of

---

[31] The fact that the Law is, so to speak, without history, as if it had always been there, is found in the stunning chapter by Boureau on the legal action of English monks: 'The judicial obstinacy of Thomas [the hero of the *jus commune* chapter] should not cause us to lose sight of the fact that recourse to the courts or legal arbitration remained one of the many possibilities in cases of conflicts. But this mode of solving conflict instituted a new configuration of social relations, more than a place, in a world where competition for land and power had become denser. By opening up new procedures and subjects of conflict, the law made it possible to *exit the local*, the face-to-face situation': Boureau, *La loi du royaume* (2001), p. 194 (my emphasis).

the relationship between the specific case and the totality.[32] If the thugs threatening you have written proof that they are authorized by a text which defines with precision the punishment to which you are liable if you refuse to hand them your wallet; and if this punishment is not decided on the spot but later, elsewhere, on the basis of a file, by other people who stall for a long time, by means of a regular procedure, before stating their decisions, which you receive in the form of a letter delivered by a postman, well then, you have been mistaken, these thugs were actually respectable police officers under the rule of law – and you can safely hand over your wallet. But if, by a morphing the other way round, the police officers who arrested you started insulting and beating you, have no signed warrant of arrest, and even their insignia have been removed – in short, if you exclude each of these forms of life that make it possible to attach the local situation to all the links mobilizing the totality – then you have again been mistaken: these honest cops in uniform were simply thugs who were all the more dangerous because they were wearing a pointed hat. How can the ones be distinguished from the others, if not by examining whether it is possible or not, in local interaction and successive stages, to *steer* all the other interactions that flawlessly, uninterruptedly, constitute everything connecting the ones to the others? It is hardly surprising that by talking about Law we always talk about *the entire corpus of law*: it is because we try through a near-obsessive act of writing to tie up and continuously to link all the successive acts that constitute all times, places and people, by means of an unbroken path that can theoretically lead – with a series of signatures, acts and decrees – from any specific point to all the others. It seems difficult to deny that Law is related to a particular form of mobilization of the totality in the individual.

But what mode of mobilization and what type of totality? There is already a totality that critics of the autonomy of law mobilize without too much precaution, and which they see as 'society'. We know that a fierce struggle opposes those interpretations of law that could be called internalist, which stress the autonomy constituting the legal thing and, on the other hand, those that are externalist, which refuse any autonomy of law and make it emerge from a series of power struggles in which it served at worst as a décor and a lure and, at best, as a tool to facilitate the aims of social engineering. As with Bourdieu, the supposed autonomy serves to conceal even more

---

[32] Since antiquity, this fictive example has been used in reflection on law, as for example in Hart, *The Concept of Law* (1997). See also Schütz, 'Saint Augustin, l'Etat et la "bande de brigands"' (1992).

profoundly the 'symbolic violence' that it may exercise. The law simply 'legitimizes' force – a legal term whose meaning has been altered by critical sociology.[33] The situation very closely resembles the well-known struggle in the history of science, between the advocates of an internal history and those of an external history, where the former lays claim to concepts and the latter to context.[34] In both cases it is an agreed definition of the social that makes the discovery of the particular type of autonomy of the legal thing or the scientific thing impossible. As always, the social blinds.[35] To explain the swift transit of rules and of facts, analysts appeal to society to provide them with forms of causality without even being able to explain how these causal forces may have a bearing on the case at hand. Consequently the externalists, both in law and in science, always give their opponents points: there is *less* in the cause than in the effect, for the social is always weaker and especially less mobile than that which it is supposed to explain. When all's said and done, when faced with the sociology of law or of science, the best is to adopt the internalists' approach.[36] In the interweaving of legal concepts and scientific facts, there are *more associations*; we discover a *more complete* construction of society than in all the explanatory factors mobilized by the externalists. This I have often shown: how can the sciences be explained in terms of their social context, when they totally disrupt *that which constitutes* the context?[37] What is true of the sciences is even more so of law: how can law be explained in terms of the influ-

[33] On the inversion of the word 'legitimate' in Bourdieu's sociology, see the devastating critique by Favereau, 'L'économie du sociologue' (2001): 'Law clearly has no chance faced with the two main theoretical languages in contemporary social science [. . .] law is either misleading, if we place it in a logic of pure reproduction, or else useless, if we place it in a logic of pure coordination' (p. 295 and citation, p. 142).

[34] The history of this debate was recounted for the sciences in Shapin, 'Discipline and Bounding' (1992).

[35] On the necessity to undo society progressively in order to explain the sciences and their numerous links with the collective, see in particular Latour, *Reassembling the Social* (2005).

[36] This Béchillon clearly recognized in a vigorous programmatic text on the goals and methods of the anthropology of law. Béchillon, 'La valeur anthropologique du Droit' (1995). It is also the basis of Thomas's argument on Roman law: there is more Roman *society* in the *concepts* of Roman law than in the society that surrounds them and claims to explain them. Thomas, 'La langue du droit romain' (1974). Thomas sees the reason for this in the fact that law manages to break and delay the continuity of the social which would otherwise be too great. This is also the meaning of Tarde's sociology; see Tarde, *Les transformations du droit* (1893 [1994]).

[37] Here we recognize the principle of what is known as the sociology of translation: the social is to be explained, not be used as an explanation. See, for example, Tarde, *Monadologie et sociologie* (1999).

ence of the social context, when law itself secretes an original form of contextual networking of people, acts and texts, so that it would be very difficult to define the notion of social context without resorting to legal concepts?[38] There is no stronger metalanguage to explain law than the language of law itself. Or, more precisely, law is *itself its own metalanguage.*

While in the history of science there is always reason to waver between the construction of the social by scientists and the explanation of their discoveries by an appeal to the social,[39] one can hardly not be struck by the disproportion between the richness of the construction of society by law and the poverty of explanations of law in terms of society. Explicitly, continuously, obsessively, law seeks to pave the way for the effective mobilization of the totality in the specific case. Procedure, hierarchy of norms, judgment, file and even the wonderful word 'moyens*' to which we have devoted so many pages: all the terms speak of this movement of totalization and mobilization, of controlling and reinforcing, of steering and connecting. All express the putting into movement, into context. But to explain these movements the advocates of the social are often unequipped. They affirm that in the notion of society they always possess an undefined pool of explanatory forces, but here they lack precisely the *means* to mobilize these forces so that they can feed into the collective and *impact* on the proceedings. They find themselves in the same situation as generals who have a powerful, well-trained army but who, lacking transport for their troops, are unable to take them into battle. How can the balance of power be shifted in law? Where are the vehicles? Where are the roads? People talk of force, power, structure, habits, traditions, mentalities: sure, but how can they be put into action here, there and now? On the other hand, if you ask how the European Convention of Human Rights can be transported to the expulsion case of the foreigner Mr Farouk, the answer is simple: it is there, in

[38] We clearly see this in the definition of collective persons in the work of Greimas, 'Analyse sémiotique d'un discours juridique' (1976); in the foundations of civil society in Thomas, 'L'institution civile de la cité' (1993); in the splendid definition of the public agent reconstructed in Cayla, 'L'inexprimable nature de l'agent public' (1998a); and in the above-mentioned example of Bourreau's English monks (citation, p. 257). In all cases, the law alters the very definition of context, local and global, and also of which connections are possible and impossible.

[39] The esoterism of the solutions might discourage the most audacious: in what way is the theory of relativity stronger than the conception of the social context that tries to contextualize Einstein? (Galison, 'Einstein's Clocks: the Place of Time' (2000). In what way is Lord Kelvin's physics more precise than the British Empire in defining the empire and its spatio-temporal extension? (Smith and Wise, *Energy and Empire* (1989))?

foreigners' rights, since the decision was taken on such-and-such a date, authorizing Article 6 to be invoked against the Prefects' decisions. Making the connection, linking up these elements, weaving the social: all this is law itself. To be sure, it is a very peculiar type of link, a particular mode of totalization, among others.[40] It does not encompass the entire collective, but it does define a vehicle, a movement of aggregation, the *vinculum juris* that can still be assigned from one end to the other, whereas the social explanation, since the beginning of the sociology of the social, is still waiting to be given the appropriate wiring finally to enable the individual case to benefit from this tremendous lift that it constantly promises but never delivers.

While the study of science and techniques compelled us to abandon the sociology of the social for that of *association*, the analysis of law encourages us in that direction even more. The situation is particularly disadvantageous for explanations based on society, for in none of the cases observed in this book do we find a clear-cut distinction between that which classically might resemble the social and that which could be called law. On the contrary, law is mixed with everything – and it says so itself.[41] We have seen in the preceding chapter how, in a few minutes of reasoning, we were able to move through political considerations, economic interests, confessions free of prejudices, concerns about opportunity, justice, good administration, all of which impacted on, disturbed and suspended the making of law. Yet the presence of all these elements was never enough: in short, the message was that it was time to 'start being legal'.[42] Hence, even in

---

[40] See the *technical* type of link in Latour, *Aramis* (1996a), the *religious* type in *Jubiler* (2002d) and the *political* type in 'What If We Talked Politics a Little?' (2002b). Each form totalizes but under a different type of regime or connection. The social is therefore not what explains but what needs to be explained: Tarde, *Monadologie et sociologie* (1999).

[41] And saying so shocks no-one, as I noticed when I gave the first versions of this chapter to the actors themselves, whereas the sciences' bond with their context has always triggered perilous negotiations with the researchers who read me. When one hands them the mirror of ethnography, researchers react very differently from jurists who are shocked only by the exhibition of the Counsellors' interlocution and not by the words of the impalpable Body.

[42] As a counsellor wrote in an evaluation of the present chapter: 'Contrary to science, law, at least as it is experienced by the judge, is a perfectly self-conscious construction. We know full well, when we do law, that we do not discover it; we build it, kneading it with assumptions, convictions, perfectly random choices. We deliberately give it the appearance of rigour; the show of objectiveness comes afterwards, as proof of the coherence of what we have built.' But he immediately adds: 'To be sure, there too there is naivety: the multiple conditions cause a judge to be under an illusion if he believes that he is really a free builder. Far more than he thinks, he is busy "discovering" the rules written by other social forces, other historical determinants.'

the case where the actors, without waiting for the critics to denounce the presence of the social behind the form of law, openly deploy the panorama of their interests, from the legal point of view *nothing follows*. All the social interests, all the power struggles can push the wheel, but the judicial vehicle will not budge an inch if it is not hitched onto law. One of the main research programmes of the sociology of law, according to which a relationship has to be established between the corpus of rules on the one hand and society on the other, does not withstand examination: law is already of the social, of association; alone it processes more of the social than the notion of society from which it is in no way distinct since it works on it, kneads it, arranges it, designates it, imputes it, makes it responsible, envelops it.[43] Law judiciarizes all of society, which it grasps *as a whole* in its own *peculiar* fashion.[44] To be sure, the sciences do nothing else, but through a very different form of mobilization, agitation, transformation, totalization and translation. In both cases the project that consists of plunging their autonomies into a bath of the social, hoping that they gradually dissolve, can but result in their complete disappearance – and in the consequent loss of these two elements so indispensable to the existence of the social. What would a society be without law, facts, techniques? How would it survive? Of what would it consist? How could it be unified, totalized? By what route would it be led to grant the support of all its members to one of them? In law, as in science, techniques, economics and politics, the sociologists of the social take the consequence for the cause: instead of studying the practical means that form and shape society, they talk about a society that is already present, both mysterious and inexplicable, to try to explain the only thing that has the power to engender it.[45]

[43] A recent presentation of the sociology of law annihilates its project from the third sentence, by proudly announcing that its programme aims to: 'study relations between law and society, that is, the way in which *law*, designed as a more or less structured set of rules, principles and decisions, enters into a relationship with the *social body*, understood as arrangements of individuals, groups and institutions situated in the ambit of law' (italics in the text): Serverin, *Sociologie du droit* (2000), p. 3. Law reduced to a body of rules, the social to an arrangement of individuals, and everything mysteriously plunged into 'the ambit of law': here we find all the features of the sociology of the social that have already rendered science, religion, techniques, politics and economics incomprehensible. How strange, really, this sociology of the social always fighting to blind itself.

[44] It is in this sense that it can be described as the oldest social science: Murphy, *The Oldest Social Science* (1997).

[45] It is not purely by chance that another great founder of sociology, Gabriel Tarde, was also a jurist. When he accused Durkheim, with his notion of society, of taking the consequence of human actions for their explanatory cause, he was thinking of

We easily understand that the fact of the social explanation of law being inoperative does not prove that in society law forms a homogeneous and self-regulated whole. To escape the difficulty, it would be pointless to think of law as entirely autonomous, a sphere apart and self-maintained within society, itself consisting of a set of subsystems in which one could even – why not? – comfortably house Science! The readers will have recognized Niklas Luhmann's view of the social; in fact it amounts to abandoning any effort at defining varieties of autonomy, to obtain only purified forms severed from any relationship with their empirical existence.[46] This, moreover, amounts to taking for each domain the most simplistic definition and often the most ethereal one that it gives itself. We can see why jurists like to believe themselves safe in a sub-system *à la* Luhmann, just as scientists take great pleasure in fortifying the walls of their scholarly autonomy . . .[47] They all see themselves as King Midas and believe that everything they touch becomes scientific or legal. The effort to make Science a sub-system on its own verges on the ludicrous, but in the case of Law the imposture appears even quicker since, to believe in its distinction, one does not even have the excuse of a clear cut operated by the walls of laboratories and the lab assistants' white jackets. Law plunges into everything without having its own domain. We have witnessed this amply: the Council of State is not made 'of

---

the course of law – and never found a better example than the history of science. 'This conception, [mine] in short, is almost the opposite of that of the *unilinear evolutionists* [Spencer] and also of Mr Durkheim. Instead of explaining everything by the supposed imposition of a *law of evolution* that constrains overall phenomena to be reproduced, to repeat themselves identically in a certain order, instead of explaining the *small* by the *big*, the *detail* by the *general*, I explain the similarities of the whole by the accumulation of small elementary actions, the big by the small, the general by the detail': Tarde, *Monadologie et sociologie* (1999), p. 63 (his emphasis).

[46] Luhmann, *A Sociological Theory of Law* (1985), where law is defined as 'a cognitively open and normatively closed system' (p. 282), the tautological definition of law being put forward as a quality of description which, precisely, brings it closer to the definition of autopoiesis in biology (p. 288).

[47] The project of the theory of systems is of course honourable: to avoid the vacuity of the social, we acknowledge the autonomy of the various ingredients constituting it: Luhmann, *A Sociological Theory of Law* (1985). The mistake is to believe that there is only one form of autonomy, that of sub-systems. Nothing proves that science and law can be autonomous *in the same way*. Nothing proves, moreover, that one can borrow from biology a clear definition of the totality; as if we knew what type of society fomented an organism! See, for example, Lewontin, *The Triple Helix* (2000), and Kupiec and Sonigo, *Ni Dieu ni gène* (2000). The problem is similar with Bourdieu's notion of 'field', which affords all domains with the same type of autonomy: Favereau, 'L'économie du sociologue' (2001).

law' but consists of walls, corridors, frescoes, files, a body of members, texts, careers, publications, controversies. If there is law in it, if it is capable of saying the law, it is surely not because it belongs to a system distinct from the rest of the social world, but because it stirs it in its entirety *in a certain mode*. It is this mode that the theory of systems forgets to characterize, thus transforming society into a series of inter-related fields which are in the end all made of the same stuff. Law is not made 'of law' any more than a gas pipe is made *of* gas or science *of* science. On the contrary, it is by means of steel, pipes, regulators, meters, inspectors and control rooms that gas ends up flowing unin-terruptedly across Europe; and yet it is well and truly gas that circu-lates, and not the land, nor steel. Yes, law is indeed autonomous compared to the social, for it is one of the means for producing the social defined as association, for arranging and contextualizing it. No, there is no domain, no territory that belongs to law. Notwithstanding the claims of jurists served by the sociologists of systems, it does not form a sphere; without the rest holding it, law would be nothing. Yet it holds everything, in its own way.[48]

If we have so much difficulty focusing precisely on the form of autonomy peculiar to Law, if it requires so much care to deploy its fabric without damaging it, this may be due to another feature which can but strike the observer: its superficiality. If it holds everything, if it makes it possible to link all people and all acts, if by way of a continuous route it authorizes the Constitution to be linked to a tiny case, it is also because it extracts only a tiny part of their essence from all situations.[49] Its fabric resembles that of a delicately knitted lace. This is what common sense retains of its movement when it qualifies it as cold, formal, meticulous, abstract, empty. Indeed, empty it should be! It is wary of fullness, of any ballast that would slow it down, make it heavy, prevent it from linking up what it retains of the world, via its own course. It can go everywhere and make everything coherent provided that it drops almost everything. As we have seen in the preceding chapter, it does not try to tilt the territory over into the map through the solid grasp of a reference path. Unlike science, it never embarks on the impossible trial of constructing, in powerful

[48] Admirable '*but*' of Atias – 'The rule of law is merely superimposed on a reality that it does not fundamentally alter *but* on which it acts': Atias, *Philosophie du droit* (1999), p. 298.
[49] Legendre always talks of the 'imbecility' of the jurist. Legendre, *L'empire de la vérité* (1983). On the voids of law, see Carbonnier, *Flexible droit* (1998), p. 38. As Béchillon says, 'law is cold'; that is where one has to start or, to express the same distance from common sense, 'law is another world': Hermitte, 'Le droit est un autre monde' (1998).

calculation centres, the scale models that resemble the world and make it visible at a glance. What is a notary's act in relation to the dwelling in which we live? How can this fragile sheet of paper be compared to the thickness of walls and memories? No resemblance, no mimicry, no reference, no plan. Yet, in case of conflict, inheritance or dispute, it is clearly through the striking link between this derisory sheet and the body of texts, via lawyers and judges, that I could prove, authenticate, my property – and keep my house. The link is tiny yet total; the grip is infinitely small yet capable of linking up with all the rest.

There is no point in studying law in depth! The relationship between appearances and reality, which is so important in science, politics, religion and even art, is meaningless here: appearances are everything, the content is nothing.[50] This is what makes law so difficult to comment on for the other professions intoxicated by their desire for depth. It can be seen very clearly in a few public disputes in which the Council was involved during the summer of 2000: as soon as it had banned the morning-after pill, the newspapers, over-interpreting their motives, immediately accused the counsellors of having bad intentions; they were criticized for taking civil society's place by censuring morals. The legal truth is so light, so flat, that it cannot be grasped by minds that want to get to the bottom of things.[51] In fact, with a perfectly healthy sense of superficiality, the judges recalled the impossibility of giving nurses the right to prescribe contraceptives – a right reserved for doctors in terms of Article 11 of the law of 19 May 1982.[52] In another case, where the judges had banned a film that had

---

[50] See Legendre's fine argument on emblems: 'Because the form is the limit and the limit is the State'.

[51] It is, moreover, the same incomprehension that causes a multiplication of penal cases in order to relieve the hunger for justice, replace rituals of expiation that old religions no longer allow and, in general, cater for all the world's miseries: Boltanski, *Distant Suffering* (1999). This is why the bonds of law are as inappropriate as metro seats for the pains of the homeless. 'Modern justice therefore seems to be more concerned with relieving the traumatism of the judicial ritual – even though it is controlled by the rights of the defence and the public gaze – than with the social normalization into which it plunges the person to be tried. The judicial ritual, its forms, its game, its exteriority, has something more respectable for the accused than the apostolic world of social work. Is it not better to ask an accused to simulate than to invade his "secret garden"? Is it not an aggression to understand someone in spite of themselves?' (Garapon, *Bien juger* (1997), p. 263).

[52] 16 June 2000, 1st sub-section: 'Considering that in terms of the third paragraph of Article 3 of the same law, stemming from Article 11 of the law of 19 May 1982, "hormonal and intra-uterine contraceptives cannot be delivered without a medical prescription" [. . .] Considering that, in terms of the disputed measures, the Minister of Education has authorized school nurses to prescribe and deliver [this product] to

caused a scandal, the press immediately loosed its fury against a shameful act of censorship in a free country! But the judges had simply reaffirmed that one could not simultaneously say that a film consisted of a continuous sequence of shockingly violent scenes, and ban it only for people under the age of sixteen, without the Ministry having extended its powers *ultra vires*.[53] Nothing else; nothing strong; nothing true; nothing sensational; nothing sentimental; nothing even fundamentally right: a reminder of a simple principle of non-contradiction, fragile and soft, always to be taken up again and reinterpreted, which prohibits, 'in terms of the current laws', too much incoherence in the scattered actions of human beings – Ministries included. Nothing but surface, nothing but filaments, nothing but laces; just the links that move fast and move straight and tangle us up, hold us and protect us – provided that they remain at the surface, that they engage us lightly, that we ourselves remain at the surface, hardly engaged, so as to be able to monitor and interpret them. Here the ethnographer feels despondent: will he ever be *superficial enough* to grasp the strength of the law?

Cornu bos capitur, voce ligatur homo

'The ox is held by the horns, but humans are tied up by voice.' The anthropology that I practise, that has given itself the task of studying contemporary forms of truth-telling, cannot ignore any of those who

---

adolescents [. . .] this product, which constitutes a hormonal contraceptive in terms of the law of 28 December 1967 [. . .] can, in the application of the above-cited measures of Article 3 of the law of 28 December 1967, be prescribed only by a doctor and dispensed only in a pharmacy [. . .]; hence, the Ministry [. . .] has misjudged these legislative measures by entrusting school nurses with the role of prescription and dispensing.'

[53] 30 June 2000, 2nd sub-section: Here again the reasoning is crystal clear. Since the Ministry had required that the film be accompanied by the warning 'This film, an uninterrupted sequence of intensely crude sex scenes and particularly violent images, can profoundly disturb certain viewers', we can conclude that this results from the ruling 'that it thus constitutes a pornographic message and incentive to violence likely to be seen or perceived by minors, and which could fall under the measures provided for in Article 227–24 of the Penal Code; that, therefore, since the measures of Article 3 of the aforementioned 23 February 1990 decree do not stipulate that a cinematographic work can be banned for minors of under the age of 18 in any way other than its inclusion on the list of pornographic films or incentives to violence, subject to the measures of Articles 11 and 12 of the 30 December 1975 law, the film was included on this list', and consequently 'the Minister of Culture and Communication's decree of the 22 June 2000 decision is *ultra vires*'.

speak the truth. Just as it was necessary to renew the description of science, techniques, religion and economy, so too it has to alter the ways of expressing the strength of legal bonds. As I have said, this is the only way for Westerners, once they have finally dragged themselves out of modernism for once and for all, to reopen negotiations with the other collectives, which the diktats of universality could not initiate. Whereas, when imperialism prevailed, Westerners presented themselves to the rest of the world as the vehicles of objectivity, efficiency and profitability, of the true faith and the true law, it would not be inappropriate for them to agree to speak again, and to present themselves more modestly, as those who cannot survive without maintaining a number of contrasts that are particularly dear to them. Behind the exaggerations, the turgidity and the terrors that precluded the establishment of contact and the extension of empires, it would be good to discover which contrasts to treasure again. Then, and only then, will those who are no longer modern be able to set out again on the conquest of a world that is no longer afraid of them.

To start the study of law, this new more diplomatic anthropology first has to deflate the excessive claims that jurists were entrusted with, just as the anthropology of sciences has had to modify somewhat its epistemological claims by making science valuable for reasons very different from unquestionable objectivity. But the difficulty of law stems from its superficiality, from the 'little transcendence' that binds humans as tightly as a yoke, without for all that mobilizing any power from on high. Just as, in the name of Science with a capital 'S', the care of replacing politics, religion, morality and everything else right up to the State was entrusted to the few rare and fragile referential chains, so too the boat has been heavily laden by endowing Law, with a capital 'L', with the impossible virtues of sovereignty, law, morals, the social link, justice, politics and even religion. This inflation rendered the sciences – in the plural and with a small 's' – invisible and inoperative; it probably renders law – with a small 'l' – impossible to represent and cherish. By demanding too much from it, we prevent it from transporting the only good that it is capable of carrying. To misuse the neat expression that Garapon borrowed from La Fontaine: it is time to disburden the ass of all the relics that prevent it from treading lightly.[54]

As we saw in the preceding chapter, it is impossible to expect law to transport any *information* whatsoever. To be sure, there exists,

[54] Garapon's book, *Bien juger. Essai sur le rituel judiciaire* (1997), was first called *L'âne chargé de reliques* (The ass carrying relics) from a well-known La Fontaine fable.

embedded in files, small referential chains – plans, maps, testimonies, fingerprints, various experts' reports – but they are always too short and are interrupted too quickly to offer the very specific type of certainty that belongs to the sciences. From the point of view of information, law is always lacking and can but disappoint those who expect it to satisfy their *libido sciendi*. Learning that she is a journalist 'in the sense of Article R-126' hardly reassures the claimant we met in chapter 5 as to her *essence* as a journalist; it is only the fact of being able to stand up to those who, *in case of dispute*, refuse to issue her a press card that will enable her to plead for this privilege when some gate-keeper asks her to *prove* it. Unlike scientific information, the law constructs no model of the world that, via a series of transformations, would make it possible to revert to the original situation by foreseeing their nature from far away. Learn the entire *Lebon* by heart and you will know nothing more about France. You will have learned only law, occasionally punctuated by the more or less moving complaint of a few actors with colourful names. Wanting to transport knowledge via the routes of law would be like trying to fax a pizza – and there would be no point in trying to increase the power of the model, it is simply not the right medium. Law, like religion, like politics, deceives those who want to transport information.[55]

Yet *all* of France, through its hollow paths, its quarries opened unlawfully, its civil servants, its ski slopes and its dustbins, may find itself present in the *Lebon* volumes, in a certain form of totality that is both highly disappointing and soundly tied up. Even if it offers no information, law does not amount to this formal game closed in on itself, a reference unto itself, to which its critics want to limit it. It does more than inform: it formats. As we learned, this formatting is also rare and fragile. In the immense mass of actions accomplished daily by the French in their relations with the administration, as tentacular as the State may be, very few constitute a grievance, and of those grievances, only a tiny proportion are turned into a formal plea. The procession of petitions through administrative laws accounts for nothing more than minute paths in the body of practices, barely more than those marked by the footpaths left by animals in the mountains. Seen from afar, related to all interactions, law hardly exists; it remains invisible, it hardly counts: a transparent network, a minute tattoo, an infinitesimal sign. To respect it better, one first has to rarefy its presence, to empty it out, to lighten it, to treat it as a

---

[55] On the disappointment constituting religion and politics, see Latour, *Jubiler* (2002d).

reticule: law lets the world go by; light, it exists only as a trace, emptier than lace; 99.99 per cent of the network traced by the movement of law consists of holes.

But what does the remaining 0.01 per cent do that is so crucial, so capital, that we end up talking of Law as if it were the only, ultimate barrier separating us from primitive chaos, animality, barbarism? (Expressions that prove a sound ignorance of the physics of chaos, of biology and of 'barbarians'). Law is said to be related to the notion of rules and sanctions. What an exaggeration, once again! A social life that depended on the *Lebon*, the *Journal Officiel* and the Civil Code to elaborate, teach, apply, maintain and sanction its rules of functioning would be pretty miserable. As we saw in the cases that we examined, there has to be a world already strongly structured, richly furnished, populated with actors in full possession of their faculties, subjected to regulated habits, for a petition to be able to be compiled, for a counsellor to extract the arguments*, for a sub-section to draw out a decision, for a sentenced civil servant to be compelled to apply the Council's decision. Without an abundance of ordinary rules, law won't budge. It moves along its tortuous path only when everything else is in place. Wanting to define law by means of rules is like reducing science to concepts.[56] More generally, nothing proves that the notion of a rule is applicable to humans. Wittgenstein showed this a long time ago: one can never say of a human action that it 'obeys', that it 'follows' or 'applies' a rule; one can only say that it *refers to it*.[57] In the field work we have found many examples of connections being made between documents and legal texts, archives, citations, authorizations and invocations, but not the slightest case of a mere application of a rule of law. Judges archive, plead, cut and paste, recount, mount, elaborate, hesitate, cite and connect the *texts* of rules – but obey them?

If the importance of the rule for the definition of the judicial has been inflated so much, it is because law has been too often confused with politics. The philosophers of law often talk about the rule sanctioned by public authority as they would about a rampart, the only one against violence and arbitrariness. But this means that against the Barbarians they have erected a Maginot Line that is even more fragile than the first, and more easily circumvented since, as they themselves admit, it is made of nothing but paper. If public life had

[56] See the very useful clarification in the last part of Béchillon, *Qu'est-ce qu'une règle de droit?* (1997), but the solution that he gives in terms of a model would amount to confusing the law and the organization; see below.

[57] See Collins and Kusch, *The Shape of Actions* (1998). As the authors show, only computers 'follow' rules, and, here again, they do not 'apply' them.

only law to defend itself from violence, it would have sunk into noth-
ingness long ago. For law to be a force, to have teeth, the entire circle
of representation and obedience constantly has to be covered; this is
statesmen's job. If there is one thing that law does not know how to
replace, it is the gradual composition of sovereignty that is achieved
by politics – a very specific form of enunciation, with its own particular vehicles and labours.[58] Confusing the autonomy of politics with
the heteronomy necessary to law is more than a crime, it is a major
political mistake. Law alone can never create totalities that have not
already been spawned and maintained by the never-ending circle of
sovereignty.[59] Here again, one chooses the wrong medium if one
thinks that the vehicle of law transports authority; on the contrary,
authority has to be pre-established for the real work of law to begin.

At one stage Mrs Thatcher decided to take the philosophers of
science literally by trimming down all the funding of British laboratories, to see whether Science – consisting, according to the rational-
ists, of nothing but immaterial concepts – would resist. We tremble
at the thought of situations in which jurists might be taken literally
and no basis given to the common good other than the obligations
of law. The Council of State knows this well; it has survived every
regime, including that of Vichy, owing only to its indifference to the
nature of the sovereign.[60] The finest body of State counsellors cannot
speak more than the law. Conversely, given its heterogeneous composition, the Council is in a better position than any other court to
recognize the shifting boundaries between opportunity 'in the interests of good administration' and the law per se.[61] The fact that the
State counsellors carefully measure the frailty of the bonds of law is

---

[58] This is probably what Hart recognized in the difference, so important in his view,
between primary rules and secondary rules; Hart, *The Concept of Law* (1997). On
the work of what Plato called 'autophuos', see chapters 7 and 8 of Latour, *Pandora's
Hope* (1999b). Unfortunately, the vehicle of politics is described as little as that of
science and law, notwithstanding, or rather because of, political science, which has
transformed the circle of representation into a movement of forces and interests
drowning everything in the bath of the social.

[59] A problem that has become classical since Hobbes – which limits the meaning of
'totality', discussed above, to that which is 'authorized' by the sovereign. See also
the case of international law. The fact that law is also different from morality is
amply contained in the maxim *Summum jus summa injuria*.

[60] On Vichy, see Collectif, *Deuxième centenaire du Conseil d'Etat* (2001). In 1943
the honourable *Semaine juridique* published an article by E. Bertrand entitled 'Du
contrôle judiciaire du dessaisissement des juifs et de la liquidation de leurs biens.
Etude critique de jurisprudence': Rouland, *Aux confins du Droit.* (1991), p. 58.

[61] This is what the president of Litigation says: 'Sometimes we revise when opportune,
if the text is not incompatible with anything; we amend it by administrative opportunity, in the interests of good administration.'

a result of their constant coming and going between politics, the administration, business and the function of judge. Even less than all other judges can they share the illusion that civilized life hangs on a thread, that of law.

While law cannot replace the hard work of composing the political collective, it cannot serve as a substitute for religion either. If it has been inflated out of all proportion by being turned into the thing that can protect us from civil war, what can be said about those who see the rule of law as the only thing wrenching us from animality by way of a 'symbolic break' that supposedly elevates us to speech? We are thus said to be the children of men thanks to Law! Quite a strange mixture of Lacanian psychoanalysis, Roman law, Cesaro-papism and the cult of the State, of which Pierre Legendre constructed an emblem that is equally as fascinating as it is dogmatic.[62] It is asking too much of law, not enough of religion, too much of psychoanalysis, not enough of politics. Law does not save; nor does it humanize, administer or spare us any problems. *Law replaces nothing else.* We do not define it any better when we make a ritual out of the trial, a symbolic place out of the court, a therapy out of the legal stage.[63] But the tribunal does not heal any more than it saves. It is too pale, too formal; if offers no satisfaction to honour, no reparation to suffering. No more than it allows humanity to be born, does it allow a dignified mourning of death. A society has to be really sick to no longer treat itself with anything but the obsessive shifting and stubborn sequence of petitions, decisions and compilations of jurisprudence. No, decidedly, it is necessary to lighten the burden of the ass, to unload all the treasures carelessly entrusted to jurists, so that they can save at least what they have of their own.

But, one might say, if it neither saves nor heals, nor protects nor sanctions, if it neither shelters nor informs, what does law actually

---

[62] All Legendre's books form a single book in which one finds a mixture of what we are trying to distinguish carefully here. From Legendre, *Trésor historique* (1992) to Legendre, *Sur la question dogmatique en Occident* (1999), without any noteworthy progression, we find the same argument. Its reasons are, moreover, sound, as he wants to fight against his pet hates: communication, management, science and sociologism; in short, against a reduction of law to something else. But his defensive solution ends up inflating law out of all proportion by mixing it with other forms of virtue without it being possible to specify clearly its own contribution. Legendre is carried away. In the final analysis, law is respected as little in his own mediation as in that of the sociologists of the social and of the 'legitimization' which confuses it with a simple technique of domination.

[63] Although this is what Garapon tries with talent to do when he borrows ethnologists' little rite-myth-symbol toolkit to redefine legal practice; see Garapon, *Bien juger* (1997).

do? Is it a light mist that rapidly lifts, a play of the mind, an illusion just good enough to legitimize power struggles by covering them with its cloak; or else simply a technique in the service of a social engineering that one needs to consider as coldly as a butcher's knife? It is true, the temptation is huge to consider it as simply a technique, and jurists as the engineers of social engineering, where the corps of counsellors resembles that of the 'Ponts et Chaussées' and the 'Corps des Mines'. It is true that the now 'technique' can have several meanings applicable to law: it is esoteric knowledge reserved for the specialist; compared to the normal course of action, it is often in a subordinate position, that occupied by technicians who take care of means and not ends; finally, it skilfully makes it possible to subvert the usual order, by way of subtle innovations, not to say clever tricks, which enable the engineers to make themselves indispensable.[64] But none of these meanings have anything specific, for law is not a technique in the fourth sense, the most important one: it never manages to *fold* space-time, to replace its injunctions by another matter. The humblest technique – this lamp, this ashtray, this paper-clip – mixes periods, places and totally heterogeneous materials; it folds them into the same black box, causing those who use them to act, by diverting the course of their action. Law is incapable of that. It is *the least technical* of all forms of enunciation: never can it replace orality, textuality, the laborious embodiment of meaning, just as one cannot calculate law by summing it up by the mediation of some mechanical device – like a calculator replacing mental calculation – nor delegate one's relations in another matter to sum it up or express it otherwise. A glance at the Palais-Royal is enough to convince us: Cicero in a toga would blend into the scenery without any difficulty. Apart from the database that makes archiving easier than with wax tablets, there is not the slightest tool that makes it possible to accelerate the efficiency of law in 2001 compared to Caesar's day. It has been said that Napoleon's armies marched at the same speed as those of Alexander until the invention of the railway, which radically changed the art of warfare. Well, no radical innovation has altered the art of enunciating the law: at the Palais-Royal petitions progress at the same speed, and function with the same tools, as at Augustus' *curia*. We can of course talk of 'legal techniques', but the meaning remains metaphorical: no operating report is expected from the Council, no button to press so that the Vice-president can more directly and efficiently control the production of law today than he did yesterday. No! – speech is still

---

[64] On all of these definitions, see chapter 6 of Latour, *Pandora's Hope* (1999b). On technical mediation, see in particular, Latour, *Aramis* (1996a) and 'The Ends of Means' (2002a).

slow and tortuous, there is still the obligation to swallow administrative law ruling after ruling, with no short-cuts, no cribs. No acceleration, no delegation, no stunning innovation. Once again, nothing replaces law, if not the renewed expression of law itself. For an essential reason that we shall soon discover, law, unlike techniques, is neither folded nor delegated. It has meaning only if it is unfolded, deployed, spread out.

So then, is it a fiction? The term certainly exists: *fictio legis*, invested with all the prestige of Roman law. Yet, here again, to grasp the meaning of the word 'fiction', like that of 'technique', the regimes of enunciation and not only the contradictory uses of ordinary language must be compared. If fiction is defined as the capacity to *shift* any particular actant in another time, another space, another actor and another material – a quadruple shift which has been studied countless times by semioticians[65] – then law can almost be understood as the opposite of fiction: it *repairs* the damage that fiction has done. We can therefore understand that the *fictio legis* – see, for example, the episode on p. 54 – follows exactly the opposite path to fiction: whereas we might expect the narrative invention to transport us into another time and place, lulling us with a 'once upon a time', legal fiction allows for the forced attachment of an enunciator to his or her statement, contrary to all appearances (it is only here that the two meanings meet). A slave will be considered as a free man, the dead as living, a son the father of his own father, an airfield legal[66] and so on, *only just so as to allow the law to pass by* and statements to be attached without encountering the abyss of the legal void, that is, the cessation of the passage of law.[67] Whereas fiction chases the reader far away, legal fiction fixes and binds back to its paperwork. Whereas fiction moves and blinds, legal fiction calms and reassures. We could of course aesthetize law, treat the legal text as a literary work – it would not prevent the two regimes of enunciation from leading in opposite directions.[68] The law would have it that statements cannot be detached from enunciators without leaving a clearly visible trace

---

[65] On shifting out see Greimas, 'Analyse sémiotique d'un discours juridique' (1976). On fiction, the best presentation is still Pavel, *Fictional Worlds* (1986). On the enunciation inscribed in the text, see the piece of bravura by Eco, *The Role of the Reader* (1979). On the very particular meaning of the word in administrative law, see Costa, *Les fictions juridiques en droit administratif* (2000).

[66] Witness the episode on p. 55.

[67] On all these examples, see the article by Thomas, 'Fictio legis' (1995).

[68] The fact that the counsellors find the files 'pretty' or 'interesting', proves not that they aesthetize them, but that they prepare themselves to hesitate and thus to judge, and thus to do a truly legal job, as we saw in chapter 4. Considering the difficulties that I had in writing and translating this book, I will risk the hypothesis that law is the only regime of enunciation that cannot be easily aesthetized . . .

behind them. Fiction, on the other hand, benefits precisely from effacing the paths that should remain impossible to retrace.

Everything happens as if law were interested exclusively in the possibility of *re-engaging* the figures of enunciation by *attributing* to a speaker what he or she said. Linking an individual to a text through the process of qualification; attaching a statement to its enunciator by following the sequences of signatures; authenticating an act of writing; imputing a crime to the name of a human being; linking up texts and documents; tracing the course of statements: all law can be grasped as an obsessive effort to make enunciation *assignable*. What you have said engages you; your identity can be proved by a particular civil document; are you authorized by a text to occupy this position or to speak these words?; the meaning of these words depends on this other text; this action is imputable to you; these others hold your act of writing against you; the receipt slip of this acknowledgement of receipt has indeed been signed by you. It is essential that enunciation plans not be disconnected – an impossible and endless task since, by definition, the act of enunciation multiplies the plans.

We have perhaps got to the point of equilibrium that this chapter was supposed to reach: to give sufficiently to law for its existence to come from the outside with its own force and efficiency; not to charge it with transporting any functions other than its own. Talking of symbols with respect to law could only weaken it, this is easy to understand. When the human sciences resign themselves to symbols, it is because they have abandoned the task of understanding the particular mode of existence, with which humans enter into relationships. Saying of the human psyche that it is symbolic is a way of no longer recognizing the invisible beings with which the conscience has to grapple.[69] Saying that religion is symbolic means voluntarily giving up the idea of endowing the divinities with any form of ontology, making them the vague consequences of a storm within the brain.[70] Saying of scientific facts that they are symbolic means shrinking from before the enormous difficulty of finding their very particular mode of existence, which is precisely the fact of not being natural.[71] Likewise, saying of law that it is symbolic, something mental, a product of the human brain, a random social construction, would amount to capitulating from the outset by giving up the idea of discovering the

---

[69] See the distinction between anxiety and fear in Nathan, *L'influence qui guérit* (1994), whose cure consists, on the contrary, of abandoning the symbol for risky negotiations with the divinities themselves.
[70] Claverie, *Voir apparaître, regarder voir* (1991); Piette, *La religion de près* (1999), whose methods have renewed the sociology of religion considerably.
[71] Latour, 'For Bloor and Beyond' (1999a).

ontology that suits it uniquely. The social sciences will never get out of the dead-end into which their epistemology has dragged them, unless they give up symbols in order to grapple with ontology. The risks are huge; the gains also. They would talk about reality, finally, instead of that which forever veils it. Imagine that: social sciences which would be realistic rather than critical or sceptical; social sciences which would be constructive and no longer prisoners of social constructivism, that debilitation of the soul?

If it seems so difficult to endow law with its particular form of ontology, with its somehow objective existence, outside of any social construction, independent of the mind, it is because the place is already occupied by an *exaggerated* version of its presence: that which attributes the theory, or rather theories, of natural law to it. One would need the wings of a dove, the antennae of an ant or the pincers of a shrimp to touch on these matters delicately enough. One would need to be able to maintain the intuition upon which natural law is based simply by ridding it of its astounding claim of being the foundation of all law. Yes, Law is indeed outside of humans; no, it says nothing that enables us to read nature's inalterable message under the altered text of humans.

To perform this operation, one has to distinguish law from yet another form of enunciation, that which could be called 'organization'.[72] Considered in their *content*, legal texts distribute roles and functions, attribute capacities, assign authority, create entities, provide for appeal procedures, and so on. By means of as many *scripts* they cover countless human interactions – which are always, in a sense, situated *above* the scripts that give them their action programme, their roadmap. This function is crucial, and one could consider all law as organization. Yet that would mean losing sight of the particular vehicle of law. The organizational content forms a much vaster set than the rules of law.[73] Every institution, firm, family and even individual produces an indefinite number of scripts that serve as behavioural models. But these scripts, models, distributors, organization charts and *dispatchers* do not necessarily have legal consequences. Only a small proportion of them will constitute a grievance leading

---

[72] The best formulations of forms of enunciation peculiar to the organization are found in Taylor and Van Every, *The Emergent Organization* (2000), and Cooren, *The Organizing Property of Communication* (2001).

[73] This is what makes Béchillon's solution of the rule as a model of distribution of competencies insufficient, albeit tempting: Béchillon, *Qu'est-ce qu'une règle de droit?* (1997), p. 173. Moreover, to find the definition of law again, the author has to add the adjective 'legal' in the course of a sentence, once again finding the tautology that he wanted to avoid but that I believe is a constituent part of law.

to 'law' – and only in the event of dispute if their possibility of lodging a complaint is recognized.[74] Thus, law refers to scripts like everything else, in its own way, without for all that being reduced to them.

Is this referral, this particular movement, this obsession with attribution enough to recognize the objectivity of law, the profound conviction shared by all jurists, even the most hostile to natural law, that they are dealing with something which is beyond them and to which they are accountable, without adding anything that transcends humble practice? Is it enough to recognize that there is law in the world just as there are cows and prions, clouds and divinities? One should be able to say of law that it is there at birth. It precedes us and survives us. We live in its house. Yet it says nothing, informs us of nothing; we have to do all the work. On the one hand, natural law corresponds to a deep-seated intuition; on the other, it is totally wrong about the ontology of the thing that it wants to respect. But if we follow the hypothesis introduced into the contrast with fiction, we may have a solution that brings out the contrast – law cannot be a substitute for anything – without, for all that, loading it like the fabled ass bearing the relics. The solution would be to recognize that law is indeed a mode of exploration of being, a particular mode of existence, and that it has its own ontology, that it engenders humans without being made by them, that it does belong to a prestigious category of 'factishes'.[75] It does what no other regime of enunciation does: it keeps track of all disengagements, to tirelessly reconnect statements to their enunciators, via the perilous routes of signatures, archives, texts and files.

Better than any other act, the humble signature reveals the very particular form of assignation of law.[76] Its very nature resides in its shakiness, its deformed, twisted, wobbling design because it puts back together two sides of enunciation that are incompatible in all the other regimes: the enunciator inscribed in the text (who cannot be seen) and the enunciator who is postulated by the inscription (who is also invisible). When one appends one's signature, one produces an irremediably deformed mark which seals the threshold that no other enunciation opens, the abyss that no other words can fill, the rift that

---

[74] This is the very clear difference, in administrative law, between the measures of internal order, at the bottom, and government acts, at the top, which cannot be attacked even though they have the *same organizational content* as the rest of the law. This is evidence that one cannot consider the rule of law as a model of behaviour.

[75] Latour, *Pandora's Hope* (1999b), last chapter.

[76] Analysed so well by Fraenkel, *La signature. Genèse d'un signe* (1992); see also de Sutter and Gutwirth (2006) 'Droit et cosmopolitique'.

no other text can mend. In this small mystery of assignment and imputation, there is reattachment of the figures of enunciation by the spider's web of law, enough to nourish the strongest admiration for jurists' work, without adding the charge of solving the greatest mysteries, without demanding that law be more true, just, legitimate, moral or human.

In this book I have tried to provide evidence of that by capturing law in the ceaseless movement of documents that, in case of dispute, serve to constitute a sound case, provided that other texts have offered a procedure of resolution which, if attacked, makes it possible to go right through to the end by following the process step by step, from court to court and text to text, including all the links established prior to that, which other agents, our dear counsellors, endeavour to make coherent through a continuous process of reparation, updating, forgetting, rectification, codification, comments and interpretations, so that nothing is lost and nothing is created, everything that inexorably passes by – time, humans, places, goods, decisions – remains attached by a continuous thread, so that legal stability serves as a net for all potential applicants, and humans may live in the house of law. . . . The sentence is long, and cannot be shortened, but does it not contain the essential features of what should be entrusted to the particular vehicle of law? Yes, law is formal, but its reality is indeed to *precede* any enunciator, any speaking human, for whom it accompanies all the overwhelming disengagements, all the fabulous fictions, all the audacious organizations, with work that, as far as possible, is not overwhelming, fabulous or audacious, and that reconnects, preserves, links up, assigns, retraces. To celebrate it, there is no point in playing the great organs of nature, religion, the State. Law already has enough totality attached to it for us not to add all these dead weights that, in any case, make an awful noise. No, Law's music is more discreet. Without it, we wouldn't be human; without it, *we would have lost the trace of what we had said.* Statements would float around without ever being able to find their enunciators. Nothing would bind the space-time entity in a continuum. We would be unable to find the trace of our actions. There would be no accountability. Is this not enough to present ourselves with some self-respect before other peoples? To ask them to have a closer look at what we call the 'rule of law' and rightly see as a treasure to be cherished?

Glossary of technical terms

This two-entry glossary summarizes the translations that have been chosen for the main technical words of French administrative law in this book. We have not tried to find for each French term what would have been a technical term with roughly the same meaning for an English-speaking specialist of administrative law. We have simply tried to find terms just as uncommon in English as they are in French for most readers ignorant of the law, which will not distract attention from the main focus of the book – the passage of law, while still retaining, when possible, some of the flavour of the French etymologies.

French – English glossary

Actes de gouvernement: acts of State

Annulment: to render a decision null and void (in opposition to rejection of the claim)

Arrêts: decisions, judgment

Assemblée du Contentieux: Litigation Assembly

Assemblée Générale: General Assembly

Assesseur: assessor

Commissaire du gouvernement: either 'commissioner of the law' to designate those who speak in the name of the law, or 'government envoy'

Conclusions du commissaire du gouvernement: conclusions
Conseil Constitutionnel: the Constitutional Council
Conseil d'Etat: Council of State
Conseiller d'Etat: Counsellor of State
Contentieux: Litigation
Contentieux administratif: administrative litigation
Contradictoire, le contradictoire: adversarial process; procedural propriety; due process
Contrôle: review
d'Assemblée: *see* Assemblée Générale and Assemblée du Contentieux
de Section: *see* Section, Sous-section, Sous-sections réunies
Droit: the Law with a capital 'L'
Droit administratif: administrative law
ENA (Ecole Nationale d'Administration): National School of Administration
Erreur de droit: legal error
Evoquer, évocation: de novo review; substantive review
Faire grief: constitute a grievance
Faute simple: fault, negligence
Faute lourde: gross negligence
Grands arrêts: *Major Precedents*
Instruction: review process
Intérêt à agir: legal standing
Lebon: *Lebon* volumes
Légalité externe, moyens de légalité externe: external legality, means of external legality
Mesures d'ordre interne: internal regulation
Moyen, moyen de droit: mean, legal mean, ground*, argument*, reason*
Moyen d'ordre public: mean of public interest
Plan d'instruction: instruction schedule
Président de sous-section: sub-section president
Projet: draft
Rapporteur: reporter
Recours pour excès de pouvoir: *ultra vires*
Référé: emergency appeal; interlocutory appeal
Renversement de jurisprudence: reversal of precedent
Requérant: litigant, plaintiff, claimant
Réviseur: reviser
Séance d'instruction: review meeting
Section, *see* Section du Contentieux, Sections administratives, Sous-section
Section administrative: Counsel Section

Section du Contentieux: Litigation Section
Sections administratives [du Conseil d'Etat]: Counsel Sections
Sous-section: sub-section
Sous-section jugeant seule: sub-section judging by itself
Sous-sections réunies: sub-sections working together
Tardiveté: non-compliance with the statutory limitation period
Tour extérieur: outside way
Vice de forme: mistake in the drafting
Visa: citation, what is taken into consideration

English–French glossary

Acts of State: 'actes de gouvernement' covers major politically sensitive decisions of High Policy which are not appropriate for the courts to review (Bell et al., *Principles of French Law* (2008), p. 180)
Adversarial process: le contradictoire
Administrative Law: droit administratif
Administrative Litigation: contentieux administratif
Assessor: Assesseur
Commissioner of the law: Commissaire du gouvernement
Conclusions: conclusions du commissaire du gouvernement
Constitutional Council: le Conseil Constitutionnel
Council of State: Conseil d'Etat
Counsel Section: Section administrative
Counsellor, Counsellor of State: conseiller, conseiller d'Etat
Decisions: arrêts
De novo review: évoquer, évocation
Draft: projet
Emergency appeal: référé
External legality, means of external legality: légalité externe, moyens de légalité externe; the external legality covers not only authority to make a decision, but also the formalities as to how a decision is taken before the decision can be validly made (Bell et al., *Principles of French Law* (2008), p. 181)
Fault: faute simple
General Assembly: Assemblée Générale du Conseil d'Etat
Government envoy: commissaire du gouvernement
Gross negligence: faute lourde
Instruction schedule: plan d'instruction
Internal regulation: mesures d'ordre interne; the internal affairs of an administrative organization which should not be the subject of

judicial intervention, but rather should be left to internal hierarchical procedures (Bell et al., *Principles of French Law* (2008), p. 180)

Law, with a capital 'L': le Droit

Lebon volumes: le *Lebon*

Legal error: erreur de droit

Legal mean: moyen, moyen de droit

Legal standing: intérêt à agir

Litigant: requérant, plaignant

Litigation, Litigation Section: la Section du Contentieux du Conseil d'Etat

Litigation Assembly: Assemblée du Contentieux

Major Precedents: *Grands arrêts*

Mean: moyen, moyen de droit

Mean of public interest: moyen d'ordre public

Mistake in the drafting: vice de forme

National School of Administration: ENA (Ecole Nationale d'Administration)

Non-compliance with the statutory limitation period: tardiveté

Null and void [to render a decision]: annulation (in opposition to rejection of a claim)

Outside way: tour extérieur

Plaintiff: requérant

Reporter: rapporteur

Reversal of precedent: renversement de jurisprudence

Review: contrôle (Maximum control is exercised over decisions which affect civil liberties or other rights of the individual; normal control involves the court ensuring that the facts are sufficient to justify the decision and that the legal powers had been correctly interpreted; minimum control is exercised over decisions which contain a significant element of policy judgment or technical evaluation or form part of the internal discipline of the public service (Bell et al., *Principles of French Law* (2008), p. 186)

Review meeting: séance d'instruction

Review process: instruction; examine a case: instruire un dossier

Reviser: réviseur

Sub-section: sous-section de la Section du Contentieux

Sub-section judging by itself: sous-section jugeant seule

Sub-section president: sous-section président

Ultra vires: recours pour excès de pouvoir

Visa: visa

Bibliography

Abelès, Marc (2000). *Un ethnologue à l'Assemblée*. Paris: Odile Jacob.

Alder, Ken (2007). *The Lie Detectors: The History of an American Obsession*. New York: Free Press.

Anonyme [Association française pour l'histoire de la justice, ed.] (1992). *La justice en ses temples. Regards sur l'architecture judiciaire en France*. Poitiers: Brissaud.

Atias, C. (1993). *Science des légistes, savoir des juristes*. Aix en Provence: Presses de l'université Aix-Marseille.

Atias, Christian (1999). *Philosophie du droit*. Paris: Presses universitaires de France.

Augé, Marc (1994). *Pour une anthropologie des mondes contemporains*. Paris: Aubier.

Austin, J. L. (1962). *How to Do Things with Words*. Oxford: Clarendon Press.

Baker, Keith (1987). 'Politique et opinion publique sous l'Ancien régime'. *Annales ESC* 1: 47–71.

Bancaud, Alain (1989). 'Une "constance mobile": la haute magistrature'. *Actes de la Recherche en Sciences Sociales* 76/77: 30–48.

Bastide, F., M. Callon et al. (1989). 'The Use of Review Articles in the Analysis of a Research Area'. *Scientometrics* 15-5–6: 535–62.

Bechillon, Denys de (1995). 'La valeur anthropologique du Droit'. *Revue Trimestrielle de Droit Civil* 4: 835–59.

Béchillon, Denys de (1994). 'Sur la conception française de la hiérarchie des normes. Anatomie d'une représentation'. *Revue Interdisciplinaire d'Études Juridiques* 32: 81–125.

Béchillon, Denys de (1997). *Qu'est-ce qu'une règle de droit?* Paris: Odile Jacob.

Bell, John, Sophie Boyron and Simon Whittaker (2008). *Principles of French Law – second edition*. Oxford: Oxford University Press.

Berre, Hughes Le (1999). *Les revirements de jurisprudence en droit administratif de l'an VII à 1998*. Paris: LGDJ.

Boltanski, Luc (1984). 'La dénonciation'. *Actes de la Recherche en Sciences Sociales* 51: 1–39.

Boltanski (1999). *Distant Suffering: Morality, Media and Politics* (trans. Graham D. Burchell). Cambridge: Cambridge University Press.

Bourcier, D., and P. Mackay, eds. (1992). *Lire le droit; langue, texte, cognition*. Paris: LGDJ.

Bourcier, Danièle, and Claude Thomasset, eds. (1996). *L'Ecriture du droit. Législation et technologie de l'information*. Paris: Diderot Multimédia.

Bourdieu, Pierre (1986). 'La Force du droit'. *Actes de la Recherche en Sciences Sociales* 64: 3–19.

Bourdieu, Pierre (2005). 'From the King's House to the Reason of State: A Model of the Genesis of the Bureaucratic Field', pp. 29–54, in *Pierre Bourdieu and Democratic Politics*, ed. Loïc Wacquant. Cambridge: Polity.

Boureau, Alain (2001). *La loi du royaume. Les moines, le droit et la construction de la nation anglaise, XI°–XIII° siècles*. Paris: Les Belles Lettres.

Braibant, Guy (1992). *Le Droit administratif français*. Paris: Presses de la Fondation nationale des sciences politiques et Dalloz.

Bui-Xuan, Olivia (2000). *Les femmes au Conseil d'Etat*. Paris: L'Harmattan.

Burdeau, François (1995). *Histoire du droit administratif. De la révolution au début des années 1970*. Paris: Presses universitaires de France.

Callon, Michel, ed. (1998). *The Laws of the Market*. Oxford: Blackwell.

Callon, Michel (1999). 'Ni intellectuel engagé, ni intellectuel dégagé: la double stratégie de l'attachement et du détachement'. *Sociologie du Travail* 1: 1–13.

Callon, Michel, Jean-Pierre Courtial et al. (1993). *La scientométrie*. Paris: Presses universitaires de France.

Callon, Michel, Pierre Lascoumes and Barthe Yannick (2009). *Acting in an Uncertain World. An Essay on Technical Democracy* (trans. Graham Burchell). Cambridge, Mass.: MIT Press.

Cambrosio, Alberto, Camille Limoges et al. (1990). 'Representing Biotechnology: An Ethnography of Quebec Science Policy'. *Social Studies of Science* 20: 195–227.

Carbonnier, Jean (1998). *Flexible droit. Pour une sociologie du droit sans rigueur*. 9th edn. Paris: Librairie générale de droit et de jurisprudence.

Cassin, Barbara (1995). *L'effet sophistique*. Paris: Gallimard.

Cayla, Olivier (1993). 'La qualification ou la vérité du droit'. *Droits* 18: 4–17.

Cayla, Olivier (1998a). 'L'inexprimable nature de l'agent public'. *Enquête* 7: 75–97.

Cayla, Olivier (1998b). 'Le coup d'état en droit?' *Le Débat* 100: 108–32.

Cayla, Olivier, and Yan Thomas (2002). *Du droit de ne pas naître. A propos de l'affaire Perruche*. Paris: Gallimard.

Charvolin, Florian (1993). *L'invention de l'environnement en France (1960–1971). Les pratiques documentaires d'agrégation à l'origine du Ministère de la protection de la nature et de l'environnement.* Paris: Ecole nationale supérieure des mines de Paris.

Chevalier, J. (1994). *Science administrative.* Vol. I. Paris: Presses universitaires de France.

Claverie, Elizabeth (1991). 'Voir apparaître, regarder voir'. *Raisons Pratiques* 2: 1–19.

Claverie, Elizabeth (1992). 'Sainte indignation contre indignation éclairée, l'affaire du Chevalier de La Barre'. *Ethnologie Française* 22(3): 271–89.

Colcombet, François (1999). 'Rapport fait au nom de la commission des lois sur le projet de loi, adopté par le Sénat, relatif au référé devant les juridictions administratives'. *Assemblée Nationale* (2002).

Collectif (2001). *Deuxième centenaire du Conseil d'Etat. Deux volumes spéciaux de la Revue administrative.* Paris: Presses universitaires de France.

Collins, Harry, and Martin Kusch (1998). *The Shape of Actions. What Humans and Machines Can Do.* Cambridge, Mass.: MIT Press.

Cooren, François (2001). *The Organizing Property of Communication.* New York: John Benjamins.

Costa, Delphine (2000). *Les fictions juridiques en droit administratif.* Paris: LGDJ.

Costa, Jean-Paul (1993). *Le Conseil d'Etat dans la société contemporaine.* Paris: Economica.

Dagognet, François (1974). *Ecriture et iconographie.* Paris: Vrin.

de Geouffre de la Pradelle, Géraud (1995). 'La réforme du droit de la nationalité ou la mise en forme juridique d'un virage politique'. *Politix* 32: 154–71.

Debray, Régis (1996). *Loués soient nos seigneurs. Une éducation politique.* Paris: Gallimard.

Deguergue, Maryse (1994). 'Les commissaires du gouvernement et la doctrine'. *Droits* 20: 125–32.

Descola, Philippe (1997). *The Spears of Twilight. Life and Death in the Amazon Jungle* (trans. Janet Lloyd). London: Flamingo.

Descola, Philippe (2005). *Par delà nature et culture.* Paris: Gallimard.

Descola, Philippe, and Gisli Palsson, eds. (1996). *Nature and Society. Anthropological Perspectives.* London: Routledge.

de Sutter, Laurent, and Serge Gutwirth (2006). 'Droit et cosmopolitique. Notes sur la contribution de Bruno Latour à la pensée du droit'. *Droit et Société*, 259–89.

Dupret, Baudoin (2001). 'Le droit en action en contexte. Ethnométhodologie et analyse de conversation dans la recherche juridique. Dossier coordonné par B. Dupret'. *Droit et Société* 48.

Dworkin, Ronald (1997). *Freedom's Law: The Moral Reading of the American Constitution.* Cambridge, Mass.: Harvard University Press.

Eco, Umberto (1979). *The Role of the Reader. Explorations in the Semiotics of Texts.* London: Hutchinson.

Eisenstein, Elizabeth (1979). *The Printing Press as an Agent of Change.* Cambridge: Cambridge University Press.

Ewald, François (1986). 'Une expérience foucaldienne: les principes généraux du droit'. *Critique* 471–2: 788–93.

Favereau, Olivier (2001). 'L'économie du sociologue ou penser (l'orthodoxie) à partir de Pierre Bourdieu', pp. 255–314, in *Le travail sociologique de Pierre Bourdieu. Dettes et critiques. Edition revue et augmentée,* ed. Bernard Lahire. Paris: La Découverte.

Fleck, Ludwik (1935 [1981]). *Genesis and Development of a Scientific Fact.* Chicago: University of Chicago Press.

Foucault, Michel (1975). *Discipline and Punish. The Birth of Prison.* New York: Pantheon.

Fraenkel, Béatrice (1992). *La signature. Genèse d'un signe.* Paris: Gallimard.

Freedman, Charles E. (1961). *The Conseil d'Etat in Modern France.* New York: Columbia University Press.

Galison, Peter (1997). *Image and Logic. A Material Culture of Microphysics.* Chicago: University of Chicago Press.

Galison, Peter (2000). 'Einstein's Clocks: the Place of Time'. *Critical Enquiry* Winter: 355–89.

Galison, Peter, and Emily Thompson, eds. (1999). *The Architecture of Science.* Cambridge, Mass.: MIT Press.

Garapon, Antoine (1997). *Bien juger. Essai sur le rituel judiciaire.* Paris: Odile Jacob.

Geison, Gerald G. (1995). *The Private Science of Louis Pasteur.* Princeton: Princeton University Press.

Goody, Jack (1986). *La logique de l'écriture.* Paris: Armand Colin.

Gramaglia, Christelle (2005). 'La mise en cause environnementale comme principe d'association. Casuistique des affaires de pollution des eaux: l'exemple des actions en justice intentées par l'Association Nationale de Protection des Eaux et Rivières'. Paris: Thèse Ecole des mines.

Greimas, A. J. (1976). 'Analyse sémiotique d'un discours juridique', pp. 79–128, in *Sémiotique et Sciences Sociales,* ed. A. J. Greimas. Paris: Le Seuil.

Greimas, A. J., and J. Courtès, eds. (1982). *Semiotics and Language: an Analytical Dictionary.* Bloomington: Indiana University Press.

Hacking, Ian (1983). *Representing and Intervening: Introductory Topics in the Philosophy of Natural Sciences.* Cambridge: Cambridge University Press.

Harlow, Carol (1977–8). 'Légalité, illégalité et responsabilité de la puissance publique en Angleterre', *Etudes et Documents* 29: 335–54.

Harlow, Carol (2000). ' "La huronne au Palais-Royal" or a Naive Perspective on Administrative Law'. *Journal of Law and Society* 27(2): 322–7.

Hart, H. L. A. (1997) *The Concept of Law.* 2nd edn, with a postscript edited by Penelope A. Bulloch and Joseph Raz. New York: Oxford University Press.

Heinich, Nathalie (1995). 'Les colonnes de Buren au Palais-Royal. Ethnographie d'une affaire'. *Ethnologie Française* 25(4): 525–40.

Hermitte, Marie-Angèle (1996). *Le sang et le droit. Essai sur la transfusion sanguine.* Paris: Le Seuil.

Hermitte, Marie-Angèle (1997). 'L'expertise scientifique à finalité de décision politique'. *Justices* 4: 12–20.

Hermitte, Marie Angèle (1998). 'Le droit est un autre monde'. *Enquête – Anthropologie, Histoire, Sociologie* 7: 17–38.

Holmes, Oliver (1897). 'The Path of Law'. *The Harvard Law Review*: 457–78.

Hutchins, Edward (1980). *Culture and Inference. A Trobriand Case Study.* Cambridge, Mass.: Harvard University Press.

Hutchins, Edwin (1995). *Cognition in the Wild.* Cambridge, Mass.: MIT Press.

Jacob, Christian (1992). *L'empire des cartes. Approche théorique de la cartographie à travers l'histoire.* Paris: Albin Michel.

Jacob, R. (1994). *Images de la justice. Essai sur l'iconographie judiciaire du Moyen-Age à l'Age classique.* Paris: Le Léopard d'Or.

James, William (1907 [1975]). *Pragmatism. A New Name for Some Old Ways of Thinking Followed by The Meaning of Truth.* Cambridge, Mass.: Harvard University Press.

Jasanoff, Sheila (1990). *The Fifth Branch: Science Advisers as Policymakers.* Cambridge, Mass.: Harvard University Press.

Jasanoff, Sheila (1992). 'What Judges Should Know about the Sociology of Science'. *Jurimetrics Journal* 32: 345–59.

Jasanoff, Sheila (1995). *Science at the Bar. Law, Science and Technology in America.* Cambridge, Mass.: Harvard University Press.

Jeanneau, B. (1962). 'La nature des principes généraux du droit en droit français'. *Travaux de l'Institut de Droit Comparé* 23: 203.

Jones, Carrie, and Peter Galison, eds. (1998). *Picturing Science, Producing Art.* London: Routledge.

Jurdant, Baudoin, ed. (1998). *Impostures intellectuelles. Les malentendus de l'affaire Sokal.* Paris: La Découverte.

Kant, Emmanuel (1950). *Critique of Pure Reason* (trans. Norman Kemp Smith). London: Macmillan.

Karpik, Lucien (1997). 'L'avancée politique de la justice'. *Le Débat* 97: 90–107.

Kessler, Marie Christine (1968). *Le Conseil d'Etat.* Paris: Armand Colin.

Knorr-Cetina, Karin (1999). *Epistemic Cultures. How the Sciences Make Knowledge.* Cambridge, Mass.: Harvard University Press.

Kuhn, Thomas (1962). *The Structure of Scientific Revolutions.* Chicago: University of Chicago Press.

Kupiec, Jean-Jacques, and Pierre Sonigo (2000). *Ni Dieu ni gène.* Paris: Le Seuil – Collection Science ouverte.

Landowski, Eric (1988). 'Vérité et vérédiction en droit'. *Droit et Société* 8: 45–59.

Lascoumes, Pierre (1989). *Au nom de l'ordre. Histoire politique du Code Pénal.* Paris: Hachette.

Latour, Bruno (1987). *Science In Action. How to Follow Scientists and Engineers through Society*. Cambridge, Mass.: Harvard University Press.

Latour, Bruno (1988). *The Pasteurization of France* (trans. A. Sheridan and J. Law). Cambridge, Mass.: Harvard University Press.

Latour, Bruno (1993). *We Have Never Been Modern* (trans. Cathy Porter). Cambridge, Mass.: Harvard University Press).

Latour, Bruno (1996a). *Aramis or the Love of Technology* (trans. Cathy Porter). Cambridge, Mass.: Harvard University Press.

Latour, Bruno (1996b). *Petite réflexion sur le culte moderne des dieux Faitiches*. Paris: Les Empêcheurs de penser en rond.

Latour, Bruno (1999a). 'For Bloor and Beyond – a Response to David Bloor's "Anti-Latour"'. *Studies in History and Philosophy of Science* 30(1): 113–29.

Latour, Bruno (1999b). *Pandora's Hope. Essays on the Reality of Science Studies*. Cambridge, Mass.: Harvard University Press.

Latour, Bruno (2002a) 'The Ends of Means'. *Theory, Culture and Society* 19(5/6): 247–60.

Latour, Bruno (2002b). 'What If We Talked Politics a Little?' *Contemporary Political Theory* 2(2): 143–64.

Latour, Bruno (2002c). 'War of the Worlds, What about Peace?' Chicago: Prickly Paradigm Press.

Latour, Bruno (2002d). *Jubiler ou les tourments de la parole religieuse*. Paris: Les Empêcheurs de penser en rond.

Latour, Bruno (2004). *Politics of Nature – How to Bring the Sciences into Democracy* (trans. Cathy Porter). Cambridge, Mass.: Harvard University Press.

Latour, Bruno (2005). *Reassembling the Social. An Introduction to Actor-network Theory*. Oxford: Oxford University Press.

Latour, Bruno, and Jocelyn De Noblet, eds. (1985). *'Les «vues» de l'esprit: visualisation et connaissance scientifique*. Paris: Culture Technique.

Latour, Bruno, and Steve Woolgar (1979). *Laboratory Life, the Construction of Scientific Facts*. Princeton: Princeton University Press.

Lebon, Jean (1990). *Meurtre au Conseil d'Etat*. Paris: Calmann-Lévy.

Legendre, Pierre (1975). 'Prestance du Conseil d'Etat (à propos d'un livre récent)'. *Revue Historique du Droit Français et Etranger* octobre-décembre: 630–4.

Legendre, Pierre (1983). *L'empire de la vérité. Introduction aux espaces dogmatiques industriels (Leçons II)*. Paris: Fayard.

Legendre, Pierre (1992). *Trésor historique de l'Etat en France. L'administration classique*. Paris: Fayard.

Legendre, Pierre (1998). *Leçons I. La 901ème conclusion. Etude sur le théâtre de la Raison*. Paris: Fayard.

Legendre, Pierre (1999). *Sur la question dogmatique en Occident*. Paris: Fayard.

Lewontin, Richard (2000). *The Triple Helix. Gene, Organism and Environment*. Cambridge, Mass.: Harvard University Press.

Licoppe, Christian (1996). *La formation de la pratique scientifique. Le discours de l'expérience en France et en Angleterre (1630–1820)*. Paris: La Découverte.

Long, Marceau, Prosper Weil et al. (1999). *Les grands arrêts de la jurisprudence administrative*. Paris: Dalloz.

Luhmann, Niklas (1985). *A Sociological Theory of Law*. London: Routledge.

Lynch, Michael (1988). 'Sacrifice and the Transformation of the Animal Body into a Scientific Object: Laboratory Culture and Ritual Practice in Neuroscience'. *Social Studies of Science* 18: 265–89.

Lynch, Michael, and David Bogen (1996). *The Spectacle of History: Speech, Text and Memory at the Iran Contra Hearings*. Durham, NC: Duke University Press.

Lynch, Michael, Simon A. Cole, Ruth McNally and Kathleen Jordan (2009). *Truth Machine: The Contentious History of DNA Fingerprinting*. Chicago: University of Chicago Press.

Lynch, Michael, and Ruth McNally (1999). 'Science, Common Sense and Common Law: Courtroom Inquiries and the Public Understanding of Science'. *Social Epistemology* 13(2): 183–96.

Lynch, Mike, and Steve Woolgar, eds. (1990). *Representation in Scientific Practice*. Cambridge, Mass.: MIT Press.

Mallard, Alexandre (1998). 'Compare, Standardize and Settle Agreement: On Some Usual Metrological Problems'. *Social Studies of Science* 28: 571–601.

Maltzman, Forrest, James F. Spriggs et al. (2000). *Crafting Law on the Supreme Court. The Collegial Game*. Cambridge: Cambridge University Press.

Massot, Jean (1999). *Le Conseil d'Etat. De l'An VIII à nos jours. Livre jubilaire du deuxième centenaire. (Catatogue de l'exposition)*. Paris: Société nouvelle Adam Biro.

Massot, Jean, and Thierry Girardot (1999). *Le Conseil d'Etat*. Paris: La documentation française.

McEvoy, Sebastian (1995). *L'invention défensive*. Paris: Métailié.

Mercier, Michel (1991). 'Les images de microscopie électronique; construire un réel invisible'. *Culture Technique* 22: 25–34.

Mogoutov, Andrei (1998) 'Données relationnelles en sciences sociales: essai de minimalisme méthodologique', Pratiques de formation, Université de Paris VIII (www.aguidel.com).

Mundy, Martha, and Alain Pottage (2004). *Law, Anthropology and the Constitution of the Social: Making Persons and Things* (Cambridge Studies in Law & Society). Cambridge: Cambridge University Press.

Murphy, Tim (1997). *The Oldest Social Science*. Oxford: Clarendon Press.

Myers, Greg (1990). *Writing Biology. Texts and the Social Construction of Scientific Knowledge*. Madison: University of Wisconsin Press.

Nathan, Tobie (1994). *L'influence qui guérit*. Paris: Odile Jacob.

Ophir, Adi, and Steven Shapin (1990). 'The Place of Knowledge: A Methodological Survey'. *Science in Context* 4(1): 3–21.

Pavel, Thomas (1986). *Fictional Worlds.* Cambridge, Mass.: Harvard University Press.

Perelman, Chaim (1982). *The Realm of Rhetoric.* Notre Dame: University of Notre Dame Press.

Piette, Albert (1999). *La religion de près. L'activité religieuse en train de se faire.* Paris: Métailié.

Poovey, Mary (1999). *History of the Modern Fact. Problems of Knowledge in the Sciences of Wealth and Society.* Chicago: Chicago University Press.

Rainaud, Nicolas (1996). *Le commissaire du gouvernement près le Conseil d'Etat.* Paris: LGDJ.

Rheinberger, Hans-Jorg (1997). *Toward a History of Epistemic Things. Synthesizing Proteins in the Test Tube.* Stanford: Stanford University Press.

Richards, Thomas (1993). *The Imperial Archive.* London: Routledge.

Rivero, Jean (1962). 'Le Huron au Palais-Royal, ou réflexions naïves sur le recours pour excès de pouvoir'. *Recueil Dalloz*: 37–57.

Roquemaurel, Josselin de (1997). *Les membres du Conseil d'Etat et les entreprises (1945–1994). Maîtrise d'histoire contemporaine.* Paris: Université de Paris IV.

Roqueplo, Philippe (1990). 'Regards sur la complexité du pouvoir: enquête dans les cabinets ministériels'. *Annales des Mines* juin: 4–30.

Rosental, Claude (2008). *Weaving Self-Evidence. A Sociology of Logic* (trans. Cathy Porter). Princeton: Princeton University Press.

Rouland, N. (1991). *Aux confins du Droit. Anthropologie juridique de la modernité.* Paris: Odile Jacob.

Schütz, Anton (1992). 'Saint Augustin, l'Etat et la «bande de brigands»'. *Droits* 16: 71–82.

Serres, Michel (1987). *Statues.* Paris: François Bourin.

Serverin, Evelyn (2000). *Sociologie du droit.* Paris: La Découverte.

Shapin, Steven (1992). 'Discipline and Bounding: The History and Sociology of Science as Seen Through the Externalism Debate'. *History of Science* 30: 334–69.

Shapin, Steven (1994). *A Social History of Truth: Gentility, Civility and Science in XVIIth Century England.* Chicago: Chicago University Press.

Shapin, Steven (2008). *The Scientific Life. A Moral History of a Late Modern Vocation.* Chicago: University of Chicago Press.

Shapin, Steven, and Simon Schaffer (1985). *Leviathan and the Air-Pump. Hobbes, Boyle and the Experimental Life.* Princeton: Princeton University Press.

Shapiro, Barbara (1991). *'Beyond Reasonable Doubt' and 'Probable Cause': Historical Perspectives on the Anglo-American Law of Evidence.* Berkeley: University of California Press.

Smith, Crosbie, and Norton Wise (1989). *Energy and Empire. A Biographical Study of Lord Kelvin.* Cambridge: Cambridge University Press.

Smolla, Rodney A. (1995). *A Year in the Life of the Supreme Court.* Durham, NC: Duke University Press.

Stengers, Isabelle (1997). *Cosmopolitiques*, vol. VII: *Pour en finir avec la tolérance*. Paris: La Découverte – Les Empêcheurs de penser en rond.

Stengers, Isabelle (2000). *The Invention of Modern Science*. Minneapolis: The University of Minnesota Press.

Stirn, Bernard (1991). *Le Conseil d'Etat. Son rôle, sa jurisprudence*. Paris: Hachette.

Stirn, Bernard, Duncan Fairgrieve and Mattias Guyomar (2006). *Droits et libertés en France et au Royaume-Uni*. Paris: Odile Jacob.

Strathern, Marylin (1999). *Property, Substance and Effect: Anthropological Essays in Persons and Things*. London: Athlone Press.

Suchman, Lucy (1987). *Plans and Situated Actions. The Problem of Human Machine*. Cambridge: Cambridge University Press.

Tarde, Gabriel (1893 [1994]). *Les transformations du droit. Etude sociologique*. Geneva: Berg International.

Tarde, Gabriel (1999). *Monadologie et sociologie*. New edn. Paris: Les Empêcheurs de penser en rond.

Taylor, James R., and Elizabeth J. Van Every (2000). *The Emergent Organization. Communication as Its Site and Surface*. London: Lawrence Erlbaum Associates.

Thévenot, Laurent (1993). 'Essai sur les objets usuels. Propriétés, fonctions, usages'. *Raison Pratique – Les Objets dans l'Action* 4: 85–114.

Thomas, Yan (1974). 'La langue du droit romain. Problèmes et méthodes'. *Archives de Philosophie du Droit* 19: 104–25.

Thomas, Yan (1980). 'Res, chose et patrimoine (note sur le rapport sujet–objet en droit romain)'. *Archives de Philosophie du Droit* 25: 413–26.

Thomas, Yan (1993). 'L'institution civile de la cité'. *Le Débat* 74: 23–44.

Thomas, Yan (1995). '*Fictio Legis*: L'empire de la fiction romaine et ses limites médiévales'. *Droits* 21: 17–63.

Tocqueville, Alexis de (2003). *Democracy in America: And Two Essays on America* (trans. Gerald E. Bevan with an Introduction and Notes by Isaac Kramnick). London: Penguin Classics.

Travers, Max, and John Manzo (1997). *Law in Action: Ethnomethodological and Conversation Analytic Approaches to Law*. Sudbury: Dartmouth Publishing Co., Ltd.

Van Lang, Agathe, Geneviève Gondouin et al. (1999). *Dictionnaire de droit administratif*. Paris: Armand Colin.

Weller, Jean-Marc (1999). *L'Etat au guichet*. Paris: Desclée de Brouwer.

Wise, Norton, ed. (1995). *The Values of Precision and Exactitude*. Princeton: Princeton University Press.

Index